LEADERS OF THE PACK

TEACHING TEXTS IN LAW AND POLITICS

David A. Schultz
General Editor

Vol. 35

PETER LANG
New York • Washington, D.C./Baltimore • Bern
Frankfurt am Main • Berlin • Brussels • Vienna • Oxford

LEADERS OF THE PACK

Polls & Case Studies
of Great Supreme Court Justices

EDITED BY
William D. Pederson
and Norman W. Provizer

PETER LANG
New York • Washington, D.C./Baltimore • Bern
Frankfurt am Main • Berlin • Brussels • Vienna • Oxford

Library of Congress Cataloging-in-Publication Data

Leaders of the pack: polls and case studies of great Supreme Court
justices / William D. Pederson, Norman W. Provizer, editors.
p. cm. — (Teaching texts in law and politics; v. 35)
Includes bibliographical references and index.
1. United States. Supreme Court—History. 2. Constitutional
history—United States. 3. Judges—Rating of—United States.
I. Pederson, William D. II. Provizer, Norman W. III. Series.
KF8742 .L43   347.73'26'09—dc21   2002014654
ISBN 0-8204-6306-X
ISSN 1083-3447

Bibliographic information published by **Die Deutsche Bibliothek**.
Die Deutsche Bibliothek lists this publication in the "Deutsche
Nationalbibliografie"; detailed bibliographic data is available
on the Internet at http://dnb.ddb.de/.

Cover design by Joni Holst

The paper in this book meets the guidelines for permanence and durability
of the Committee on Production Guidelines for Book Longevity
of the Council of Library Resources.

© 2003 Peter Lang Publishing, Inc., New York
275 Seventh Avenue, 28th Floor, New York, NY 10001
www.peterlangusa.com

Printed in the United States of America

For

Peggy and Norman Kinsey

and

Rosalyn and Jennifer Provizer

TABLE OF CONTENTS

Prelude ix
    Sherman G. Finesilver and *Norman W. Provizer*

1. Selecting and Ranking Great Justices: Poll Results 1
    Robert C. Bradley
2. John Marshall: The Supreme Court's Louis Armstrong 23
    Norman W. Provizer
3. Joseph Story and a National System of Law 35
    Danny M. Adkison
4. Roger B. Taney: A Jacksonian Chief Justice Who Favored "Dixie"
    on the Bench 51
    William D. Pederson and *Frank J. Williams*
5. John Marshall Harlan the Elder: Color-Blind Justice 61
    Linda Przybyszewski
6. Oliver Wendell Holmes: The Evolution of a Great Justice 74
    James Chowning Davies
7. Louis D. Brandeis: The Justice as Prophet and Teacher 90
    Stephen K. Shaw
8. Benjamin Nathan Cardozo: Striking a Balance Between Stability
    and Progress 99
    James B. Staab
9. Hugo L. Black: Constitutional Literalist and Absolutist 132
    Henry J. Abraham
10. Felix Frankfurter: Constitutionalist Progressive 142
    Dennis J. Coyle
11. William O. Douglas: A Judge for the 21st Century 158
    James Chowning Davies
12. Charles Evans Hughes: An Eighteenth Century Statesman
    Redivivus 177
    John R. Vile
13. Harlan Fiske Stone: New Deal Prudence 190
    Theodore M. Vestal
14. Earl Warren: Justice as Fairness 200
    Norman W. Provizer and *Joseph D. Vigil*

15. William J. Brennan, Jr. and Human Dignity 215
      Rodney A. Grunes
16. William H. Rehnquist and the Conservative Counterrevolution 232
      Barbara A. Perry
17. Justice Sandra Day O'Connor: Tall in the Saddle 246
      Neil T. Erwin
18. Why No More Giants on the Supreme Court: The Personalities
    and the Times 262
      David Schultz

List of Contributors 275

Index 277

PRELUDE

Sherman G. Finesilver
Norman W. Provizer

Greatness and leadership are two ideas that often intersect. And, in many ways, the two concepts come together in the imagery of leading the pack. At one level, leading the pack implies the kind of separation that connotes greatness. After all, when we say that John Marshall is a leading justice, it is another way of noting that he is a great one as well. In one form or another, greatness is what separates the leader from the rest. As Howard Gardner reminds us, "to call Einstein a leader seems a stretch, unless one adds a descriptor such as a 'leading physicist.'"[1]

At the same time, however, leading the pack also implies a sense of connection, not one of separation. This sense of connection refers to the leadership dimension of the relationship, or, if you will, the ability to exert a significant and disproportionate influence on the cognitive, emotional, and/or behavioral patterns of others relative to the articulation, acceptance, and achievement of collective goals.

On the greatness front, Alan Dershowitz writes that the Supreme Court "can be no greater than the justices who serve on it" and that greatness "requires an ability and willingness to transcend partisan politics and result-oriented decision-making."[2] In the wake of the Supreme Court's involvement in Election 2000, Dershowitz argues that "the public is ready to insist on greatness as the criterion for service on the Supreme Court," and he recommends the establishment of a nonpartisan commission to review candidates "under the broadest criterion of greatness."[3]

Of course, despite his use of the singular idea of a criterion to describe it, Dershowitz understands that greatness is far from a one-dimensional concept. And, like so many things, it is something that is often easier to see in someone "unremarkable" than to define in the abstract.

In his effort to explore the multidimensions of greatness, Henry Abraham lists a number of qualities that, taken together, may indicate the criteria for greatness. Of Abraham's ten qualities, several are more generic than Court-specific (absolute personal moral and professional integrity; an able, agile, lucid mind; and diligence and industry). Additional qualities occupy a middle ground (professional expertise and competence, including analytical powers; appropriate professional educational background or training; the ability to communicate clearly, both orally and in writing, most especially the latter—in other words, craftsmanship and technique; and resolute fair-mindedness and impartiality). And several are Court-specific (demonstrated judicial temperament; a solid understanding of the proper judicial role of judges under our written Constitution; and on-Court leadership ability).[4]

Relative to leadership and the characteristics that help define its qualities from a Court perspective, one might list the following six ideas:

(1) clarity of writing, not only in style, but also in terms of establishing reasoned guidelines for lower courts;
(2) consistency of principles, while still exhibiting a willingness to reevaluate past decisions;
(3) initiative in shaping and leading public opinion in terms of both the legal community and the broader society;
(4) the ability to build consensus on the Court;
(5) specific assistance to the legal profession through interaction with the bar;
(6) the lasting impact of the principles espoused.[5]

Obviously, whatever lists are used for guidance, differences in interpretation remain. That fact should surprise no student of the Court. Yet, despite such differences, there are points of "remarkable agreement" concerning the names of the "remarkable people" who have been the leaders of the pack. And that, too, should come as no real surprise.

NOTES

1. Howard Gardner, *Leading Minds: An Anatomy of Leadership* (New York: Basic Books, 1995): 5. See page 6 for Gardner's definition of leadership.
2. Alan Dershowitz, *Supreme Injustice: How the High Court Hijacked Election 2000* (New York: Oxford University Press, 2000, 200–206.
3. Dershowitz, *Supreme Injustice*, 203–204.
4. Henry Abraham, "Preface" in William D. Pederson and Norman Provizer, eds., Great Justices of the U.S. Supreme Court (New York: Peter Lang, 1993), xii-xiii. Also see Abraham's *Justices, Presidents and Senators* (Lanham, MD: Rowman and Littlefield, 1999), 1–7. As part of that discussion, Abraham notes Sheldon Goldman's eight items "associated with the ideal type judge" in 1982. Those are: Neutrality as to the parties in litigation; fair-mindedness; great familiarity with the law; ability to think and write logically and lucidly; personal integrity; good physical and mental health; judicial temperament; and the ability to handle judicial power sensibly.
5. Sherman Finesilver, "Leadership on the United States Supreme Court," in Pederson and Provizer, eds., *Great Justices*, 355–365.

CHAPTER ONE

Selecting and Ranking Great Justices: Poll Results

Robert C. Bradley

Ultimately, legal historians, judicial scholars, interested court observers, and the general public determine which Supreme Court justices deserve the accolade "great," thus assigning them to a preeminent group of jurists who have served on the nation's highest bench. To conclude that a justice is "great," it is necessary to establish a frame of reference for what constitutes "great." Examination of the several lists of great justices of the United States Supreme Court issued in the twentieth century is instructive in developing that framework. A list drafted in 1983 synthesized four lists made in the 1960s and 1970s, and its author claimed it was "the definitive list." [1] However, numerous changes in the composition of the justices as well as public concern about the selection process following the Robert Bork and Clarence Thomas nominations and their aftermaths make it worthwhile to determine if the 1983 list remains valid.

This chapter presents a more recent list of great Supreme Court justices, based upon responses to surveys administered to several groups, including judicial scholars, state judges, attorneys, and pre–law students. In addition to being asked to identify great justices, respondents were asked also to establish a rank order among those they listed as "great" and to discuss the criteria they used to identify and rank order each justice on their lists.

Not only do results of this survey yield a more current list of Supreme Court greats, but this work also reports the first systematic effort to survey various groups interested in or directly involved with the legal system and to discern any similarities or differences in their assessments of the justices listed. Further, this list is the first to use a set of ranking criteria rather than list the justices chronologically.

Problems inherent in trying to list the great justices of the Supreme Court, reasons why these difficulties should not dissuade others from attempting to compile rank-ordered lists of the justices, and prior lists will be discussed in some detail. Also reviewed will be the administration of the surveys used to develop the list reported in this work. Finally, there will be some reflections on the survey findings, along with general observations about the selection process for Supreme Court justices.

Difficulties of Compiling a List of Court "Greats"

A significant obstacle to making a list of Supreme Court "greats" is the lack of objective standards against which the justices may be compared. As Justice Felix Frankfurter (1957, 784) pointed out, "Greatness in the law is not a standardized quality, nor are the elements that combine to attain it." The quality of greatness on the Supreme Court seems to fall into that category of phenomena, such as obscenity or art, where a consensus definition is virtually impossible to achieve but where one recognizes it after seeing or experiencing it.

While a list of traits or abilities desirable in a justice can be constructed, it is extraordinarily difficult to apply those characteristics to specific individuals. Objective indicators with precise measurements for most of the items constituting such a list would be quite hard to formulate.[2] Or, as David O'Brien (1996, 57) contends, "Any definition of judicial merit is artificial." As a result, subjective evaluation rather than measuring against agreed-upon standards serves as the basis for distinguishing the "greats" from their Supreme Court brethren. Both public and scholarly discourse on the subject of Supreme Court greats becomes difficult because individuals use different subjective criteria to evaluate past and present members of the Court.

In compiling a list of Supreme Court greats, consideration has to be given as to whether current members of the Court should also be evaluated. Even if current and recently retired justices are excluded, the composition of such a list means examining at least a century and a half of Supreme Court history. This poses another substantial difficulty in devising lists of Supreme Court greats. The business, functions, and status of the Supreme Court have changed dramatically since its inception.[3] As Chief Justice Rehnquist (1987, 311) observed, "Despite its lack of the power of the purse or the sword, and despite its occasional retreat in the face of antagonistic popularly elected branches of government, the Court has grown steadily in prestige and authority throughout the two centuries of its existence."

While this observation should come as no surprise to interested court observers, it reflects that the duties of the Supreme Court justices have also changed profoundly since the Court's opening session on February 1, 1790. It is quite difficult to draw meaningful comparisons among Joseph Story, Benjamin Cardozo, and Hugo Black, as each served on the Supreme Court at different times and addressed dissimilar legal controversies under different caseload constraints.

Is it a fruitless endeavor, then, to attempt to identify the "great" Supreme Court justices? Do the difficulties of devising a list of great justices outweigh the value of formulating it? The answer to both is "no." First, the Supreme Court is a powerful force in our nation with the proven capacity to influence the welfare and behavior of the American public through decisions that influence the nation's future direction. The most recent example, of course, is the Court's role in determining the outcome of the 2000 presidential election. The Court can also have an impact on American society's fundamental values, as reflected in its decisions on abortion, various religious practices and displays, obscenity, the death penalty, and redistribution of political power through reapportionment rulings. [4]

Often the opinions and perspectives of a particular justice set the foundation for some of the Court's most important rulings, such as John Marshall's pronouncement in *United States v. Burr* (1806) that a president could be subject to a court order, Holmes's expression of the "stream of commerce" concept in *Swift & Co. v. United States* (1905), or his "clear and present danger" standard that was refined so eloquently in his *Abrams v. United States* (1919) dissent. Such standards, concepts, and tests impact subsequent Court rulings for decades and are devised by justices who often later are considered as "greats," partly because of their immense contributions to the development of constitutional law and authority of the Supreme Court. More generally, in regard to the Court's policymaking process, noted Court scholar Lawrence Baum (1992, 27) comments, "the single most important factor shaping the Court's policies at any given time may be the identity of its members." The policymaking decisions of the Court are partly the product of the interaction among its members. Much as occurs in other small-group decisional situations, justices have opportunities to persuade their colleagues. The justices differ in their desire to wield influence and vary in possession of certain qualities and personality traits that determine interpersonal influence on the court.

Being able to identify great justices could contribute to the understanding of why certain issues were addressed by the Court in particular terms. In addition, an identification of Supreme Court greats could offer insight as to why the Court rendered certain decisions or policies. As Baum observes, "a highly skilled justice has relatively great influence on the Court" (1992, 40).

Identifying the attributes associated with being a "great" on the Supreme Court should be meaningful also to the private and public power brokers involved in the selection of justices. If those who possess power in the nomination and confirmation of justices were interested in merit, then it would be prudent for them to discern the attributes perceived to be commonly held by Supreme Court greats.[5] Specifically, presidents appear to have strong incentives to select individuals of high competence for Supreme Court service. A candidate lacking that characteristic is likely to embarrass the president and is at risk of not being confirmed by the Senate.[6] Also, if a candidate is highly skilled, shares the president's policy goals, and is confirmed as a member of the Supreme Court, then the president's impact on the Court is enhanced.[7] In fact, membership change has been identified as being probably the most important source of policy change on the Supreme Court. [8]

Another reason for undertaking the task of identifying Supreme Court greats and their attributes is reflected in the prior efforts to list great justices. While the concept of greatness on the Court may not be subject to empirical standards, an examination of the previous rosters of great justices demonstrates that the concept not only has meaning for interested court observers, but also that there is some consensus possible about who the "greats" are and what constitutes greatness. As John Frank, a Court scholar and former law clerk for Justice Hugo Black, says in *Marble Palace:* "Choosing great justices is a little like choosing pretty girls: there is considerable room for personal taste in the selection. Nonetheless, there are certain commonly accepted estimates" (Frank 1958, 43). These "estimates" will not be addressed. In discussing the prior lists of Supreme Court greats, similarities and differences of the justices will be examined as well as why constructing another list is justified.

Prior Lists of Supreme Court Greats

Various individuals, including Supreme Court justices, law professors, and students of the court, have developed lists of great American judges. Some lists have extended to lower courts.[9] Presumably the lists were developed after examination of all facets of the judges' behavior, but there were a few that concentrated on a singular aspect of a judicial career, such as the issuance of dissents.[10]

The number of judges on the lists varies. For those not focused exclusively on dissents, Justice Hughes compiled the shortest list, which included eight Supreme Court justices. Frank (1958) compiled the longest list, twenty-three justices.[11] The average number contained on the lists of "greats" is thirteen. Lists restricted to the Supreme Court most often contained nine greats, a number which several listmakers acknowledged was influenced by lists of great baseball players.

More significant than the number of justices are the different motives of the authors of these lists. Most have indicated their reasons for developing their list, but others do not appear to have a clear motive.[12] One motive apparently common to several listmakers is to question the value of prior judicial experience as a prerequisite for Supreme Court service. In a celebrated address at the University of Pennsylvania Law School, Justice Frankfurter argued that the skills and abilities developed while serving either as a state or lower federal court judge are not applicable to the functions and responsibilities performed by Supreme Court justices. Frankfurter concluded, "The correlation between prior judicial experience and fitness for the functions of the Supreme Court is zero" (1957, 795). To buttress his argument, Frankfurter developed a list of sixteen Supreme Court justices whom he considered preeminent. Of that number, only six came to the Court with any prior judicial experience. Frankfurter asserted that "it would demand complete indifference to the elusive and intractable factors in tracking down causes, in short, it would be capricious, to attribute acknowledged greatness in the Court's history either to the fact that a Justice had had judicial experience or that he had been without it" (1957, 784-785).

In *Marble Palace*, Frank countered the notion that prior judicial experience is an essential qualification for Supreme Court service. Attacking President Dwight Eisenhower's preference for Court appointees with previous judicial experience, Frank argued that "history proves that the best Supreme Court Justices are likely to be those who have not been judges before" (1958, 43). Frank, much like Frankfurter, supported his contention by developing a list of great Supreme Court justices. In examining his list of "greats," Frank found that the majority had no prior judicial experience at either the state or federal level. Frank went further, citing many Court justices who had considerable judicial experience as failures on the high court. As additional evidence in support of his argument, Frank noted that a list of eight outstanding justices previously developed by Charles Evans Hughes included only two with prior judicial experience. Frank concluded, however, that previous judicial experience is not necessarily an insurmountable barrier to greatness on the Supreme Court. The careers of Justices Oliver Wendell Holmes and Benjamin Cardozo provide ample proof that outstanding justices can come from lower courts (1958, 43–45).

A more recent analysis by two judicial scholars examined how the first ninety-six Supreme Court justices compared on the basis of their prior judicial experience. The results of that analysis clearly confirmed the notion that holding a prior judgeship had no bearing on the performance of a justice on the Court. In fact, the justices who had the highest performance scores were those who had no previous judicial experience.[13] In light of Walker and Hulbary's results, it is not unreasonable to suggest that previous judicial experience may have an adverse impact on a justice's Court performance.

A possible negative relationship between prior judicial experience and performance on the Supreme Court was explored in a 1970 study published in the *American Bar Association Journal*.[14] The findings of that study showed a much higher percentage of great justices had no prior judicial experience as compared to those who did. A conclusion drawn from these findings stated that if great justices are desired for the Supreme Court, appointees should not be required to have prior judicial experience.[15]

It may come as quite a surprise to recent presidents and their advisers that prior service as a state or federal judge is no guarantee of distinguished service on the Supreme Court. In considering future Court appointees, presidents should heed the finding that prior judicial experience is not related to superior Court performance and is possibly an adverse influence. Given the heavy reliance currently placed on track records established during prior judgeships, the import of this message seems to have been lost during the selection of recent justices. From the perspective of Frankfurter, Frank, and others, this bias toward nominees with prior judicial experience is an unfortunate barrier which may prevent service on the Supreme Court by some with potential to become great justices.

Apart from questioning the link between prior judicial service and Court greatness, lists of great justices have been compiled for various reasons. Some appear to have been motivated by this country's tradition of listmaking,[16] while loftier motives compelled others. Hughes (1928, 57–58) developed a list of "greats" to support his argument that influence can be exercised by any of the "brethren," not just the chief justice. Bernard Schwartz (1979) argued that the changes in American law warranted a revision of the list of great American judges produced by Roscoe Pound (1938, 407).

Another noteworthy difference between the various lists of great justices is the criteria used to identify particular justices as outstanding. While most authors indicated the criteria upon which the inclusion of justices on their lists was based, some did not (Pound 1938; Blaustein and Mersky 1972; Asch 1971). When used, criteria have ranged from the specific, such as frequency of dissent (Nagel 1970), to the abstract, including prophetic vision (Currie 1964) and affirmative approach to the judicial role (Schwartz 1979). Generally, the criteria have emphasized the ability of great justices to distinguish themselves by their opinion writing, creativity, leadership, impact on the law, and intellectual capacities.

Despite numerous differences in the lists, there are some shared qualities. All have been compiled according to the perceptions and feelings of the list author. Two exceptions are James Hambleton (1983) and Blaustein and Mersky (1972). To a large extent, Hambleton relied on the efforts of previous listmakers to develop his list. He developed a roster of all-time "greats" by choosing those justices who were most frequently included on four prior lists of great judges (464). Unfortunately, however, Hambleton did not provide a rationale for his choice of these four lists, nor did he account for the fact that two of these lists included state supreme court justices, thus reducing the number of United States Supreme Court justices on the lists.

Blaustein and Mersky (1972, 37) used responses from their 1970 poll of sixty-five law school deans and professors of law, history, and political science to compile a list of twelve "great" justices. Poll participants were selected because they were presumed to be experts on the Supreme Court and its decisions. The participants were asked to grade each of the first ninety-six justices as (a) great, (b) near great, (c) average, (d) below average, (f) failure. Other than the grading instructions and a chronological list of justices, the participants were given no guidance as to what criteria to use in grading the justices.

While the Blaustein and Mersky study is noteworthy for its use of a survey instrument to poll experts, it is clearly dated. More than three decades have passed since it was conducted. In addition, Blaustein and Mersky provided no specific indication as to how the poll results were used to compile the list of "great" justices. The study cited John Marshall as being the only justice rated "great" on all the ballots, that Brandeis and Holmes received sixty-two and sixty-one votes, respectively, in the "great" category, and that Black was in fourth place with forty-two votes as "great"(1972, 40). There was no discussion for the basis of inclusion of the other eight justices on the list of twelve "greats."

Another feature common to different lists is the chronological listing of justices. Presumably, even among an elite group of justices, substantive differences can be noted. Yet, when the commentary by the listmaker directly indicated that certain justices exhibited more "greatness" than others, the order in which the great justices were listed was not altered.

One objective of this study was to devise a list of great justices that would reflect a rank order according to some criteria of greatness and not be just another chronological roster. Another was to specify the method by which justices were included on this list so that others, if so inclined, could replicate the study in the future. Efforts to achieve both objectives are detailed.

Data Collection and Analysis

Adopting an approach similar to that used by Blaustein and Mersky, results from surveys administered to several groups were used to compile the great justices list. To avoid author perceptions or feelings from introducing bias into development of the list, the survey was constructed to give no indication of the criteria to be used, a technique that Blaustein and Mersky employed. As evident from examination of the survey instrument in appendix B, the survey instructions told participants to use any criteria they wished to both identify and rank great justices.

The survey was designed to be short and easy to complete in an attempt to maximize the response rate. Participants were asked to respond to two questions: first, to list and rank-order a maximum of ten great justices; second, to discuss briefly the criteria they used to accomplish their response to the first question. Ten was selected as the maximum number partly because that number had been used in prior lists and partly because of the surveyors' determination that a classification of greatness should be reserved for the top ten percent of a group. Only two respondents expressed any reservation about being restricted to ten choices. Interestingly, a number of respondents in each survey group listed fewer than ten "greats," some as few as five.

Instead of administering the survey only to those involved in academic pursuits concerning the Supreme Court, it was decided to survey members of

several groups that could be collectively classified as interested Court observers. In addition to judicial scholars, the survey also polled state judges, attorneys, and university undergraduate and graduate students enrolled in law-
related courses. Not only was the survey designed to determine which justices
were selected, how they were ranked, and why, but also, if it were possible, to
determine whether a consensus existed among various groups about who were
the "greats," as well as what criteria were used to make that designation.

Students in law-related courses were included primarily as a test group for
the initial administration of the survey. To gauge the validity of the survey,
polls were done of students in three courses: an undergraduate honors course
that focused on the First Amendment, an undergraduate constitutional law
course, and a graduate seminar on judicial politics. The survey was administered to a student audience attending a mock trial jointly sponsored by a law
fraternity and university law club. One hundred and seventeen undergraduate
and graduate students were surveyed in the four settings. In addition to other
questions already discussed, the instrument used in the student surveys included several questions related to the students' academic backgrounds.

Satisfied with the face validity of the survey, there were two changes made
before the instruments were mailed to other participants. First, the questions
about academic background were deleted as being irrelevant to judges, attorneys, and scholars. Second, a chronological list of Supreme Court justices was
attached to the survey. David Souter and Clarence Thomas were not on the list,
as they had not been nominated for a seat on the Court by the date of this project.

A total of 493 surveys were mailed to scholars, judges, and lawyers. Surveys were mailed to 221 scholars listed in the 1989 *Membership Directory* of
the Law, Courts, and Judicial Section of the American Political Science Association. An additional 36 surveys were mailed to scholars listed in the 1988
Membership Directory of the Law & Society Association. Since neither the
state nor county bar associations would divulge their membership lists, names
and addresses of the 115 local attorneys to whom surveys were mailed were
obtained from the listing of attorneys in the telephone directory. Finally, a 1988
list by the Bureau of National Affairs of Illinois judges and the addresses of
their courthouses was used to send surveys to 121 state and local judges. The
judges were selected to give representation to the different court levels and
geographic distributions in the state.

Findings

Responses were excluded from the following tables when respondents indicated
that either they objected to the survey or were otherwise unwilling to rank the
justices listed on their surveys. For example, one respondent observed, "I don't
really view any justices as 'great.' Hence, I am unable to provide a list for your

study....I do consider some individuals as "great," e. g., Einstein, Beethoven, Bach, Picasso, Freud, etc."

There were a few returned surveys where the respondents claimed a lack of sufficient knowledge of the Court and its history to reply to survey questions adequately.

To rank the justices, a simple scoring system was devised. Each justice was awarded points based on his/her listed position on the survey. For instance, if a justice were listed first, then s/he was given ten points. If a justice were listed second, then s/he was given nine points. This scoring system gave points in descending order throughout the remaining positions on the list. A justice not listed among ten positions on a survey received no points for that survey. The rankings reflected on the tables that follow are based upon the cumulative number of points that a justice received among all the surveys analyzed.

Table 1 reports the results of responses from the ninety-six scholars. When compared to the list of twelve "greats" on the Blaustein and Mersky study, there are some differences. Justices Joseph Story, Roger Taney, Charles Evans Hughes, and Harlan Fiske Stone were included in the Blaustein and Mersky roster of "greats"; they were not on the list compiled from this survey. Justices William Brennan and William O. Douglas, absent from the Blaustein and Mersky list, appear on the list of great justices from this survey. There were similar findings, too. John Marshall emerged in the top spot on both lists, the clear first choice of a great justice in both surveys. Almost 80 percent of the scholar respondents in the present survey ranked Marshall first on their lists. Justices Holmes and Brandeis did quite well on both surveys. Justice Holmes was the most frequent choice for both second and third and Brandeis appeared most often at both fourth and sixth positions. Possibly due to the passage of time since the Blaustein and Mersky poll, Chief Justice Earl Warren, as well as Justice Brennan, did quite well in this survey.

While the survey response rate among scholars was good at slightly more than 40 percent, the response rate from judges was considerably lower. Only fourteen surveys from judges were included in the analysis. More returned surveys, but because they did not rank the justices, those surveys were not included. In fact, more than any other group of respondents, judges were less willing to rank-order justices on the survey.

As in table 1, Marshall and Oliver Wendell Holmes finished first and second in a rank order of great justices, according to Illinois state and local judges. After the first two positions, the rank order in table 2 differs considerably from the Current List in table 1. Justice Benjamin Cardozo, who emerged in the tenth position as a great justice according to scholars, was ranked in third position by the judges. Comparing the two tables, other differences of less magnitude can be seen in the listed positions of the justices. For example, Earl Warren is ranked lower by judges than by scholars. In addition, Chief Justice William

Howard Taft was included in the great justices roster by judges, but not by scholars, while judges left out Justice Harlan I, whom the scholars listed.

Table 1	Great Justices Per the Scholars	
Rank	**Current List**	**Blaustein & Mersky's 12 "Greats"**
1.	John Marshall	John Marshall
2.	Oliver Wendell Holmes	Joseph Story
3.	Earl Warren	Roger B. Taney
4.	Louis Brandeis	John Harlan I
5.	William Brennan	Oliver Wendell Holmes
6.	Hugo Black	Charles E. Hughes
7.	John Harlan I	Louis D. Brandeis
8.	William Douglas	Harlan F. Stone
9.	Felix Frankfurter	Benjamin N. Cardozo
10.	Benjamin Cardozo	Hugo Black
11.		Felix Frankfurter
12.		Earl Warren

Table 2	Great Justices Per the Judges
Rank	**Justice**
1.	John Marshall
2.	Oliver Wendell Holmes
3.	Benjamin Cardozo
4.	Louis Brandeis
5.	Earl Warren
6.	Hugo Black
7.	Felix Frankfurter
8.	William Brennan
9.	William Douglas
10.	William Taft

Examining table 3 reveals that local attorneys have their own roster of great justices, different from those compiled by either scholars or judges. The response rate for local attorneys was about double that of the judges. There were twenty-seven surveys returned by attorneys used to compile the list in table 3. As in tables 1 and 2, Marshall and Holmes top the list. However, in contrast to the lists devised by scholars and judges, Chief Justice Marshall is not the clear favorite for first position among local attorneys. Marshall and Holmes tie for the top position in table 3. Also, local attorneys included a number of justices on their lists of "greats" who did not appear on the lists in tables 1 and 2, such as Taney, Story, Harlan II, and Rehnquist. The inclusion of Chief Justice Rehnquist marks the debut of a current Supreme Court member on a list of great justices in this study. Interestingly, Justice Brennan, who made it on the lists in tables 1 and 2, did not make it among the ten great justices compiled from local attorney responses.

Table 3   Great Justices Per the Attorneys

Rank	Justice
1. (tie)	John Marshall
	Oliver Wendell Holmes
3.	Louis Brandeis
4.	Benjamin Cardozo
5.	Felix Frankfurter
6.	Earl Warren
7.	William Douglas
8.	Hugo Black
9.	Roger Taney
10. (tie)	Joseph Story
	John Harlan II
	William Rehnquist

Table 4   Great Justices Per the Students

Rank	Justice
1.	John Marshall
2.	William Rehnquist
3.	Sandra Day O'Connor
4.	Warren Burger
5.	Earl Warren
6.	William Brennan
7.	Oliver Wendell Holmes
8.	Harry Blackmun
9.	Thurgood Marshall
10.	Hugo Black

Students were more likely to include current justices on their rosters of "greats" than members of the other groups surveyed.

The list in table 4 reflects the results from eighty-nine student surveys. For students, like the other groups of respondents, John Marshall was the top choice among "greats." After Marshall, the list of "greats" for students as reflected in table 4 is quite different from the lists in prior tables. For instance, three members of the Court at the time of the survey—William Rehnquist, Sandra Day O'Connor, and Harry Blackmun—are listed as great justices. With the inclusion of retirees Warren Burger, Brennan, and Thurgood Marshall, recent jus-

tices dominate the list in table 4. Also, Justices Brandeis, Cardozo, and Frankfurter, included by scholars, judges, and attorneys, do not appear on the student
composite list of "greats" Justice Holmes, who is listed in either first or second
position in the other tables, is ranked seventh on the student list. The list compiled from student survey responses perhaps reflects name recognition of sitting and recent justices more than a measure of greatness.

Table 5 is a composite list of great justices based upon the combined survey results of the four participating groups.

Table 5   Great Justices Per Overall Results

Rank	Justice
1.	John Marshall
2.	Oliver Wendell Holmes
3.	Earl Warren
4.	Louis Brandeis
5.	Hugo Black
6.	William Brennan
7.	Benjamin Cardozo
8.	Felix Frankfurter
9.	William Douglas
10.	William Rehnquist

Comparison of the various lists reveals that table 5 most closely resem-
bles the list of great justices in table 1, which was based upon results from
scholars' surveys. Since scholars constituted the second most numerous group
of respondents, this finding is not completely surprising. The impact of the
most numerous group, students, is diluted to some extent because their rankings
are much more evenly distributed among the justices than were the rankings by
scholars. Students included names from a much larger group of justices on
their surveys than other respondents and listed justices other than Marshall and
Holmes in the top two positions on their surveys with greater frequency.

The justices listed in the top four positions in table 1 and 5 are identical.
After the first four, some differences appear in the two tables. The most obvious differences are that John Harlan I, listed in table 1, does not appear in table
5, and Chief Justice Rehnquist, not in the scholars' top ten "greats," is in table
5. More subtle differences appear in some shifting of the rankings of the justices from table 1 to table 5. For instance, Justices Black and Brennan switch
positions, and Cardozo is ranked higher.

The wide range of criteria used by survey respondents to identify a justice
as "great" appears in table 6.

Table 6   Respondent Criteria Cited

Leadership on Court	Impact on Law
Writing Ability	Impact on Society
Judicial Restraint	Intellectual/Legal Ability
Judicial Activism	Protection of Societal Rights
Enhance Court's Power	Dissent Behavior
Length of Service	Personal Attributes
Protection of Individual Rights	

As reflected in table 6, the criteria used to establish a justice as "great" varied. Many of these criteria listed are the products of combining specific comments on the surveys. For instance, when respondents discussed specific opinions to illustrate the writing style of a justice, those were incorporated into the criteria listed as "Writing Ability." When specific comments about a justice, such as "first female on the Court" or "exhibited perseverance,"were made, these were incorporated into the criteria listed in table 6 as "Personal Attributes."

The various groups of respondents used different criteria to identify the outstanding justices. Table 7 shows the most frequently cited first criterion for each group of respondents.

Table 7   Most Frequent First Criterion by Group

Respondent Group	First Criterion
Attorneys	Leadership; Impact on Law
Students	Writing Ability
Judges	Writing Ability; Intellectual Ability
Scholars	Writing Ability

Table 7 reveals at a glance that writing ability was the most important criterion in selection of great justices; three of the four groups listed it most frequently as their first criterion. Scholars, by comparison, designated writing ability as their first criterion only infrequently and, based upon their first criterion notations, were more concerned with leadership and impact on the law.

Dissimilarities in criteria for selection of great justices among the respondent groups are evident in table 8.

Examination of table 8 reveals differences as to how frequently certain criteria were mentioned on the surveys by the various respondent groups and whether certain criteria were mentioned at all by some groups. While both judges and scholars mentioned intellectual ability more often than any other criterion, intellectual ability was ranked fourth in regard to frequency of mentioned frequently by both attorneys and students, such as personal attributes and protection of individual rights, were not mentioned frequently by either judges or scholars. Conversely, the criterion of leadership was listed frequently by both judges and scholars but not by attorneys or students. Judges were the only respondents who used length of service very frequently as a criterion of greatness.

Table 8   Top Five Respondent Criteria by Frequency

Attorneys	Judges	Scholars	Students
Writing Ability	Intellectual Ability	Intellectual Ability	Writing Ability
Personal Attributes	Leadership	Writing Ability	Personal Attributes
Protection of Individual Rights	Impact on Law	Leadership	Protection of Individual Rights
Intellectual Ability	Writing Ability	Enhance Court's Power	Intellectual Ability
Impact on Law	Length of Service	Impact on Law	Enhance Court's Power

Conclusion

This study represents the first scholarly attempt to assess whether different groups of Supreme Court observers use the same criteria as the basis for their lists of great justices. In addition, it is the first to undertake a rank ordering of the "greats" who have served on the Court. To achieve its ends, the study used the results from mail surveys to construct rosters of great justices and to compile lists of the criteria most often used by respondents to identify certain judges as "great."

While there seems to be almost universal agreement that greatness has been exhibited by justices of the Supreme Court, there has been a lack of consensus as to who are the great justices as well as to what criteria should be used as the basis for that determination. Based upon examination of the preceding tables, greatness on the Supreme Court is subjective. There are certain commonalities among the different lists of great justices as well as the criteria cited in making the determination of the "greats." But there are differences, too. John Marshall, for example, is obviously regarded as a "great" among the great justices. So is Oliver Wendell Holmes and, to a lesser degree, Louis Brandeis and Earl Warren. But what about Benjamin Cardozo, who ranks near the top of the lists for judges and attorneys, but barely makes the scholars' list and doesn't appear on the students' list? Apparently, the identity of the group evaluating the justices influences the outcome of the "greats" list.

Much the same can be said for the most frequently used criteria applied to justices to determine if they are "great." Writing and intellectual ability seem to be a common criteria used among different groups, but protection of individual rights is a criterion used frequently by only two groups, attorneys and students. And leadership appears to be an element necessary for greatness for judges and scholars to rank a justice as "great," but attorneys or students apparently do not consider it an essential.

Based upon this project's survey results, what can be concluded about the 1983 definitive list of all-time, all-star, all-era Supreme Court "greats" that depended primarily on lists from the 1960s and 1970s? First, the lineup seems to have changed. Story, Hughes, and Taney have been replaced by Brennan, Frankfurter, and Douglas, while Holmes, Marshall, Cardozo, Black, Warren, and Brandeis remain. John Harlan I and William Rehnquist follow closely.

Finally, what are the future prospects of having great justices serve on the Supreme Court of the United States? The immediate future, unfortunately, seems dismal. The last impact of the Bork affair appears to be on presidents who are considering nominees to the Supreme Court. If the nominee is to achieve Senate confirmation, then picking an individual who has written to create, refine, or support any concept or theory outside mainstream legal thought is problematic. In addition, presidents would be well advised not to select anyone who has expressed in writing an opinion on a controversial issue such as abortion. Articles and opinions, especially innovative or controversial ones, provide ample fodder for the opposition political party, interest groups, and the media to derail a nominee's confirmation to the Court.

Given the prevalent combative atmosphere surrounding the selection process for Supreme Court justices, the norm for nominees may be to select "stealth" candidates about whom little is known or likely to be discovered due to the relative absence of a paper trail. Then how can the president or the Senate discern the writing and intellectual abilities of such "stealth" nominees? The very paucity of works they have authored may raise the chances for the confirmation of such candidates considerably.

One wonders how some of the great justices in our nation's history would fare today either in getting nominated or confirmed to the Supreme Court. How would a Holmes do, given his numerous forthright opinions issued on the Massachusetts Supreme Court? How would a Cardozo do with his numerous opinions issued on the New York Court of Appeals and his many written commentaries on the nature of the legal system? How would a Brandeis do with his record as an attorney using innovative tactics to support oftentimes-controversial positions on pressing social issues? The sad fact is that it would be unlikely that any of these preeminent jurists would even be nominated to the Court given their voluminous paper trails.

If the above scenario is valid, then what will happen to the idea that the Supreme Court is not only the highest court in the land but also constitutes a collection of the best legal minds in the country? Perhaps some substantial changes would be appropriate to increase the focus of attention on the Supreme Court nominee's skills and capacities rather than their abilities to pass whatever prevailing "litmus test" is being applied at the time of their nominations. If such changes were made, they would enhance prospects for additions to the future roster of Supreme Court justices. If no changes are implemented, the relevancy of discussing greatness in the context of the Supreme Court may be questioned in the future.

APPENDIX A

Prior Lists of Great Judges

Author and Date: Charles Evans Hughes (1928)
John Marshall
Joseph Story
Benjamin R. Curtis
Samuel F. Miller
Stephen J. Field
Joseph P. Bradley
Horace Gray
David J. Brewer

Author and Date: Roscoe Pound (1938)
John Marshall
James Kent
Joseph Story
John Bannister Gibson
Lemuel Shaw
Thomas Ruffin
Thomas McIntyre Cooley
Charles Doe
Oliver Wendell Holmes
Benjamin Nathan Cardozo

Author and Date: Felix Frankfurter (1957)
John Marshall
William Johnson
Joseph Story
Roger Taney
Benjamin Curtis
John Campbell
Samuel Miller
Stephen Field
Joseph P. Bradley
Stanley Matthews
Edward White
Oliver Wendell Holmes
William Moody
Charles Evans Hughes
Louis Brandeis
Benjamin Nathan Cardozo

Author and Date: John Frank (1958)

John Marshall	William H. Taft
William Johnson	George Sutherland
Joseph Story	Pierce Butler
John McLean	Harlan Stone
Roger Taney	Benjamin Nathan Cardozo
Benjamin Curtis	Roger B. Taney
John Campbell	Samuel Miller
Samuel Miller	John Harlan I
David Davis	Oliver Wendell Holmes, Jr.
Stephen Field	Louis Brandeis
Joseph P. Bradley	Charles Evans Hughes
Morrison Waite	Harlan Fiske Stone
John Harlan I	Benjamin Nathan Cardozo
David Brewer	Felix Frankfurter
Oliver Wendell Holmes	Robert H. Jackson
William Moody	Hugo L. Black
Charles Evans Hughes	William O. Douglas
Louis Brandeis	Earl Warren

Author and Date: Albert Blaustein and Roy Mersky (1972)
John Marshall
Joseph Story
Roger B. Taney
John Harlan I
Oliver Wendell Holmes, Jr.
Charles E. Hughes
Louis D. Brandeis
Harlan F. Stone
Benjamin Cardozo
Hugo Black
Felix Frankfurter
Earl Warren

Author and Date: Bernard Schwartz (1979)
John Marshall
James Kent
Joseph Story
Lemuel Shaw
Oliver Wendell Holmes
Benjamin Nathan Cardozo
Hugo Lafayette Black
Arthur T. Vanderbilt
Earl Warren
Roger John Traynor

Author and Date: James E. Hambleton (1983)
John Marshall
Joseph Story
Roger B. Taney

Oliver Wendell Holmes, Jr.
Benjamin Nathan Cardozo
Louis Dembitz Brandeis
Charles Evans Hughes
Hugo Black
Earl Warren

Prior Lists of Great Dissenters

Author and Date: Karl Zobell (1959)
William Johnson
Benjamin R. Curtis
John Harlan I
Oliver Wendell Holmes

Author and Date: Congressional Quarterly (1990)
William Johnson
Benjamin R. Curtis
John Harlan I
Oliver Wendell Holmes
Louis D. Brandeis
Benjamin Cardozo
Harlan Stone
Felix Frankfurter
William Brennan
Thurgood Marshall

APPENDIX B

Survey for Great Justices Project

Please take a few minutes of complete the survey. Thank you for your time and effort.

1.   Using any criteria that you wish to employ and considering all the justices who have sat on the Supreme Court, list and rank order ten Supreme Court justices who you consider as great. You can refer to the attached *Chronological List of Supreme Court Justices.* You do not have to list ten justices but the maximum number of justices that can be listed is ten.

1. _____	6. _____
2. _____	7. _____
3. _____	8. _____
4. _____	9. _____
5. _____	10. _____

2.   Please indicate briefly the criteria that you used to consider certain Supreme Court justices as "Great Justices." Also, please indicate the criteria that you used to rank the justices in the order that appears on your lists.

NOTES

Preparation of this chapter was supported in part by the College of Arts and Sciences at Illinois State University. I gratefully acknowledge the assistance of Brian Hamilton, a graduate student at Illinois State University, in the data collection.

1.   James E. Hambleton, "The All-Time All-Star All-Era Supreme Court" *American Bar Association Journal*, 69, 464.
2.   Sheldon Goldman, "Federal Judicial Recruitment," in *American Courts: A Critical Assessment* (Washington, DC, 1991), 201–202.
3.   "The Supreme Court at Work," *Congressional Quarterly* (Washington, DC, 1990), 3–59.
4.   William C. Louthan, *The United States Supreme Court* (Englewood Cliffs, 1991), 43.
5.   Henry J. Abraham, *Justices and Presidents* (New York, 1985), 11.
6.   Baum, *The Supreme Court*, 4th ed. (Washington, DC, *Congressional Quarterly*, 1992), 40.
7.   Ibid., 155.
8.   Abraham, 11. See note 5.
9.   Roscoe Pound, *The Formative Era of American Law* (Boston, Little Brown, 1938); Bernard Schwartz, "The Judicial Ten: America's Greatest Judges," *Southern Illinois Law Journal* (1979): 405–407.
10. Karl A. Zobell, "Division of Opinion in the Supreme Court: A History of Judicial Disintegration," *Cornell Law Quarterly* 44 (1959); *Congressional Quarterly* (Washington, DC, 1990).
11. Charles Evans Hughes, *The Supreme Court of the United States* (New York, 1928).
12. Pound, *The Formative Era of American Law*; Sidney H. Asch, *The Supreme Court and its Great Justices* (New York, 1971).
13. Thomas G. Walker & William E. Hulbary, "Selection of Capable Justices" in *The First One Hundred Justices* (Hamden, CT: Archon, 1978), 66.
14. Stuart S. Nagel, "Characteristics of Supreme Court Greatness" in *American Bar Association Journal*, (1970): 957–959.
15. Ibid., 958–959.
16. George R. Currie, "A Judicial All-Star Nine," in *Wisconsin Law Review* (1964: 3–31); Hambleton, (See note 1).

FOR FURTHER READING

Abraham, Henry J. *Justices and Presidents.* New York: Oxford, 1985.
Asch, Sidney H. *The Supreme Court and its Great Justices.* New York: Arco, 1971.
Atkinson, David N. "Minor Supreme Court Justices: Their Characteristics and Importance," *Florida State University Law Review* 3 (1975): 348–359.
Baum, Lawrence. *The Supreme Court,* 4th ed., Washington, DC: *Congressional Quarterly,* 1992.
Blaustein, Albert P. and Roy M. Mersky. "Rating Supreme Court Justices," *American Bar Association Journal* 58 (1972), 1183–1189.
———. *The First One Hundred Justices.* Hamden, Connecticut: Archon, 1978.
The Supreme Court at Work. Washington, DC: Congressional Quarterly, 1990.
Currie, George R. "A Judicial All-Star Nine" *Wisconsin Law Review* (1964): 3–31.
Frank, John P. *Marble Palace: The Supreme Court in American Life.* New York: Alfred A. Knopf, 1958.

Frankfurter, Felix. "The Supreme Court in the Mirror of Justices," *University of Pennsylvania Law Review*, 105, 1957: 781–796.

Goldman, Sheldon. "Federal Judicial Recruitment." *In The American Courts: A Critical Assessment*, eds. John B. Gates and Charles A. Johnson, Washington, DC: Congressional Quarterly Press, 1991.

Hambleton, James E. "The All-Time All-Star All-Era Supreme Court," *American Bar Association Journal* 69 (1983): 462–464.

Hughes, Charles Evans. *The Supreme Court of the United States.* New York: Columbia University Press, 1928.

Louthan, William C. *The United States Supreme Court.* Englewood Cliffs, NJ: Prentice-Hall, 1991.

Nagel, Stuart S. "Characteristics of Supreme Court Greatness." *American Bar Association Journal* 56 (1970): 957–959.

O'Brien, David M., *Storm Center. The Supreme Court in American Politics.* 4th ed. New York: Norton, 1996.

Pound, Roscoe. *The Formative Era of American Law.* Boston: Little, Brown, 1938.

Rehnquist, William H. *The Supreme Court.* New York: William Morrow, 1987.

Schwartz, Bernard. "The Judicial Ten: America's Greatest Judges." *Southern Illinois University Law Journal,* (1979): 405–447.

Walker, Thomas G. & William E. Hulbary. "Selection of Capable Justices." In *The First One Hundred Justices,* edited by Albert P. Blaustein and Roy M. Mersky. Hamden, Ct: Archon, (1978).

Zobell, Karl A. "Division of Opinion in the Supreme Court: A History of Judicial Disintegration." *Cornell Law Quarterly* 44 (1959):186–214.

CHAPTER TWO

John Marshall: The Supreme Court's Louis Armstrong

Norman W. Provizer

Singer Bing Crosby described Louis Armstrong as "the beginning—and the end—of music in America." After all, the New Orleans-born trumpeter virtually defined the art of the coherent jazz solo, as he blended the blues with the American popular song in highly innovative style. The United States Supreme Court, as well, has its own Armstrong-like figure whose power and imagination continue to resonate with vital clarity to this very day. That figure, of course, is Chief Justice John Marshall. What Armstrong is to American music and the jazz tradition, Marshall is to the American system of constitutional law and judicial authority.

It is often said that the chief justice of the United States plays the role of *primus inter pares* on the nation's highest court. But while the chief justice may be "first among equals," one chief justice stands out as truly first among the small band of men who, through the twentieth century, have occupied the only judicial position directly mandated by the Constitution. Though Marshall died in Philadelphia more than a century and a half ago, he remains "the great chief justice," his stature undiminished by the passage of time.

Marshall was neither the first chief justice of the United States (that honor rests with John Jay), nor a man generally considered to be one of the nation's Founding Fathers. Yet he was one of the critical architects of the American political system as we know it today. "More than any other man, more than Washington or Jefferson or Lincoln," Fred Rodell wrote in 1955, [Marshall] put flesh on the skeletal structure, the bare bones of the Founding Fathers' Constitution—and put it there to stay. Most of what he did to steer for his own times and chart for the future the main course of the country's development, economically, socially, politically, is with us yet... and in this fact lies the real mark and monument of Marshall's greatness" (76). To borrow the subtitle of Jean Edward Smith's biography of Marshall (1996), the chief justice was the "definer of a nation."

The circumstances of Marshall's appointment give some indication of the scope of his achievement as chief justice. Following the election of 1800, lame-duck President John Adams found himself with a vacancy at the head of the Supreme Court. Oliver Ellsworth had retired, and Adams responded by selecting John Jay again to take up the reins of the Court. Jay, however, declined the appointment, noting that in him the Court could not possibly "obtain the energy, weight, and dignity which were essential to its affording due support to the national government, nor acquire the public confidence and respect which, as the last resort of the justice of the nation, it should possess."[1]

The office was then offered Marshall, the forty-five-year-old secretary of state in the outgoing administration. Previously, Marshall had turned down an associate justice position on the Court. This time, however, he accepted the nomination and he officially took office on February 4, 1801, exactly one month before the transfer of presidential power to Thomas Jefferson.

Once on the Court, Marshall stayed for more than thirty-four years until his death on July 6, 1835 (just months before his eightieth birthday). During those years, Marshall set a course for the Court that moved it from its unsteady and uncertain role in American life to a position of power and prestige. Never again would anyone be able to turn down a seat on the Court by arguing that it was an insufficient and insignificant institution on which to serve.

While Marshall succeeded in securing an independent and autonomous national appellate judiciary that could act as a force for the rule of law, he never confused that power and prestige with Court hegemony. He well understood that to be independent and autonomous, the Court had to function within limits, avoiding a direct connection to politics. Moderate and statesmanlike, the chief justice understood the need to blend restraint into the formula of activist sentiments. According to G. Edward White's assessment, Marshall's efforts in this regard produced "the distinctive blend of independence, sensitivity to political currents, and appearance of impartiality that has since constituted the challenge of excellence in appellate judging in America" (1976, 10). He provided, in short, for the very genesis of the nation's judicial tradition.

Before the Court

Marshall was born on September 24, 1755, in what would soon become Fauquier County, Virginia. He was the first of fifteen children born to Thomas and Mary Marshall (all of whom survived to adulthood). Thomas had grown up in Westmoreland County, where he was both a friend and neighbor to George Washington. The Marshall family moved to the western Virginia frontier, where Thomas served in a variety of positions, including an agent for Lord Fairfax, a surveyor, county sheriff, a justice of the peace, and a representative to the Virginia House of Burgesses.

The environment in which John Marshall grew up was one influenced by the church (he was an Episcopalian who developed opinions close to Unitarianism) and by the law. Though John did not receive an extensive formal education, his father (and the teachers he provided) gave the young Marshall a firm base of knowledge in history, literature, and the classics. At the same time, his physical surroundings among the mountains of the Virginia frontier gave him, in the words of Justice Joseph Story, a "robust and vigorous constitution which carried him almost to the close of his life...."[2]

John, like his father, was caught up in the winds of revolutionary war. After fighting against the British as a member of the Virginia militia, the young Marshall became a lieutenant in the Continental army. He served in New Jersey, New York, and Pennsylvania, as well as in Virginia. And during the trials of Valley Forge, he was referred to as the "best-tempered man" in the camp.

Marshall soon joined George Washington's command group and emerged as the deputy judge advocate and a captain. In late 1779, Marshall's enlistment expired and he visited Yorktown as an eligible bachelor. He caught the eye of young Polly Ambler. They were married in 1783 when Marshall was twenty-seven and his bride almost seventeen. Over the years, the Marshalls would have ten children and John would remain devoted to Polly until her death in 1831. Before his marriage, Marshall had spent six weeks in 1780 attending William and Mary College, where he studied law under George Wythe. While his notebooks contain a lot of doodlings concerning Polly, his performance during the term was sufficient to gain him entrance into the Phi Beta Kappa Society.

In the summer of 1780, he was admitted to the bar of Fauquier county with a license signed by Governor Thomas Jefferson—a distant relative who would become Marshall's major political and philosophical rival. John and Polly settled in Richmond and he began his development as a successful member of the bar. In 1782, Marshall was elected to the House of Delegates in the Virginia General Assembly and served on the judicially oriented Executive Council of that body. The year after he married Polly, he was reelected to the House of Delegates. Marshall was also elected to the Richmond city government and chosen as city recorder in 1785, as well as serving on the Hustings Court. He returned to the state legislature in 1787.

Despite his periodic service in legislatures, including Congress, Marshall was never captivated by the legislative branch of government. If anything, he tended to be disenchanted with the legislative process to which he was exposed. Still, his legislative activity reinforced his stature as an able and influential member of Virginia's elite.

Though Marshall was clearly a member of that elite (and a Mason), his paternalistic orientations remained untinged by aristocratic pretensions. He clothed his six-foot frame quite casually and never lost his amiable and informal personality. This casual attitude sometimes carried over to Marshall's work—much to the dismay of certain clients. If Marshall had tendencies toward disorganization (as well as a hint of laziness, according to the French observer La Rochefoucald-Liancourt), he nevertheless had vast talents that were widely recognized.

The true depth of those talents would soon be apparent as the United States prepared to replace the Articles of Confederation with a Constitution providing for greater national unity.

In the Virginia Legislature, Marshall was involved with the structuring of the ratifying convention that would decide the fate of the 1787 Constitution in that state. He was elected as a delegate to the convention from Henrico County, which contained Richmond. At that convention, the thirty-three-year-old Marshall exhibited both the power of his thought and some of the ideas that would mark his tenure as chief justice. No matter how casual he might have appeared, Marshall's piercing eyes transmitted his seriousness of purpose. After Patrick Henry spoke against ratification. Marshall, an advocate of the Constitution, responded. He answered those who saw danger in the proposed national government by referring to the role of the judiciary in the new constitutional system. If the government "were to make a law not warranted by any of the powers enumerated, it would be considered by the judges as an infringement of the Constitution which they are to guard. They would declare it void."[3]

In getting the best of the exchanges with the anti-Federalists at the convention, Marshall showed the effectiveness of his analytical approach. Later Thomas Jefferson reportedly remarked, "You must never give (Marshall) an affirmative answer, or you will be forced to grant his conclusion."[4] This backhanded compliment shows how well Marshall used logic and syllogistic reasoning, skills that would come to characterize so many of his court opinions.

After the ratification of the Constitution, there was talk of Marshall running for Congress. But he rejected this idea, just as he would reject appointments to be the U.S. attorney for Virginia, the attorney general of the United States, and the minister to France, all offered to him by the new administration of George Washington. Marshall seemed more interested in building his practice (and speculating in land) to provide security for his family than he was in official positions. He did, however, return to the Virginia Legislature and in 1795 became acting attorney general for the state (though he had lost an earlier electoral bid for that office). Unlike other positions, these did not unduly interfere with Marshall's private pursuits.

As the leading Federalist in Virginia, Marshall's ongoing involvement in politics continued to build the tension between himself and Jefferson, the dominant anti-Federalist. In fact, Jefferson expressed his desire to be rid of Marshall by saying, "I think nothing better could be done than to make him a judge."[5] That was exactly what would occur before too long, with results quite contrary to Jefferson's view that as a judge, Marshall would be effectively silenced.

Before he was to don judicial robes, however, Marshall entered the vortex of international affairs. His stand on the controversial, pro-British Jay Treaty had been to avoid knee-jerk reactions and to call for an in-depth examination of all of the treaty's implications. A similar attitude would mark his brief tenure as one of a trio of commissioners sent to France by President John Adams. Marshall had earlier refused to be appointed the American minister to France, though he later had second thoughts about that decision. This time the mission would be a temporary one, and it would afford him the chance to be exposed to Paris.

He was forty–two years old when he (along with a fellow Federalist, Charles Pinckney, and a Republican, Elbridge Gerry) became directly embroiled in the French connection to American partisan politics. The French (like the Jeffersonian Republicans) were angry over the Jay Treaty, and the purpose of the commission was to normalize relations between the United States and revolutionary France. The negotiations, however, never got very far. The commission soon became embroiled in the XYZ affair. Three agents of Talleyrand, the French foreign minister, had suggested that amity between the United States and France could be purchased by a loan and bribes. The Americans refused, and only Gerry remained in Paris.

At home, the XYZ affair produced outrage among Americans who believed the nation's honor had been offended. The outrage turned into war fever among the extreme Federalists, who saw an opportunity to tar their Republican opponents with the brush of anti-French sentiment. Marshall, who had been involved in the affair, maintained a moderate stance and counseled against an avoidable war. Reason, not passion or extreme partisanship, was Marshall's guiding light.

A similar approach was also evident when Marshall finally consented, at the urging of George Washington, to run for Congress in 1799. He was elected to the Sixth Congress by a narrow margin and during the campaign he had to square his Federalist affiliation with the unpopular Alien and Sedition Acts that had been passed by the Federalists to control the criticisms made by their Republican opponents. He did this by expressing his opposition to the acts, while, at the same time, downplaying their significance. In reality, Marshall, playing a leadership role in the House, distanced himself from extremist Federalist thought without abandoning a fundamentally Federalist perspective.

In Congress, Marshall voted against his "party" on changes in the Sedition Act. He also rose to defend Adams when the president was under attack from extreme elements within the Federalist camp. In 1800, the president appointed Marshall the secretary of war. He was confirmed for that post, but never served in that capacity, for three days after the confirmation, Marshall was nominated to be secretary of state. Since Marshall had asked Adams to withdraw his nomination as secretary of war, he accepted the appointment as secretary of state.

He served in that position for less than a year until the end of the Adams administration. During that brief period, he was also nominated and confirmed as chief justice. Thus, for several weeks, Marshall was both a cabinet official and chief justice (though he did not draw his cabinet salary during that time). During his first forty–five years, Marshall had established himself as an actor of some significance on the still–young American political scene. If his career had ended with the Republican victory over the Federalists in the election of 1800, Marshall would have been, at least, a footnote in American political history. That, however, did not happen. He went on for more than thirty–four years as chief justice, establishing the independent judicial power of the Supreme Court and thereby shaping the course of American politics and securing a prominent position in the nation's history.

On the Bench

As chief justice, Marshall quickly capitalized on the potential of his position. Recognizing, for example, that the Court's place in the American system of government would be enhanced if it spoke as an institution, he ended the practice of issuing opinions *seriatim*. In other words, instead of the justices individually offering their views on a case, there would now be an opinion of the Court written by one of its members. Institutional identity was needed if the Court as an institution was to capture its rightful, proper, and independent role in the still new system of constitutional government.

Though in no way an advocate of unlimited centralization, Marshall was convinced of the need for federal supremacy in order to have an effective state and an orderly society based on the rule of law. As a soldier at Valley Forge, he had witnessed firsthand the costs that accompanied the absence of central authority. As a Federalist, he saw in the Constitution a solid foundation for the establishment of such authority, but that foundation would have to be protected from erosion and reinforced to withstand attacks. A guardian was required to insure the survival of the Constitution and the rule of law. And logically, that guardian should be the federal judiciary.

The challenge facing Marshall was to translate this vision into a concrete reality. For this task, he was uncommonly well suited. Marshall combined an attractive, convivial, and engaging persona—reflecting modesty as well as self-confidence—with an incisive mind and astute political judgment. This combination enabled him to become the dominant voice on a Court that was not without other prominent members. Of the 1,006 individually written opinions produced by the Court during Marshall's tenure, the chief justice authored 519, and he was in the position of a dissenter in a constitutional matter only once, in 1827. There would be dissents from Marshall's holdings (notably by Justice William Johnson). Still, the chief justice's ability to transform his vision of the Court into a standard to be followed by all of its members was remarkable. While Marshall was not alone on the Court, he was then as he still is today, in the words of James Bradley Thayer's 1901 essay on Marshall, quoted in Kurland (1967), "first with no one second."

The list of Marshall decisions that occupy a critical place in the development of America's constitutional system is extensive, including the classic quartet of *Marbury v. Madison* (clearly establishing the principle of judicial review, in 1803); *McCulloch v. Maryland* (emphasizing national supremacy and a broad perspective on congressional power, in 1819); *Dartmouth College v. Woodward* (protecting property rights against state actions through the Constitution's contract clause, in 1819); and *Gibbons v. Ogden* (providing a comprehensive view of interstate commerce and the primary role of the national government as the regulator of that activity, in 1824).

In his portrait of Marshall, Herbert Johnson refers to *McCulloch* as the chief justice's most significant decision (a perspective that is widely shared), while *Marbury* appropriately is labeled his "most artful in terms of political acumen" and *Gibbons* as his most "encyclopedic statement of the law" (1980, 290–297). In addition to the classic quartet, there was also B*arron v. Baltimore* (which limited the application of the Bill of Rights to the federal government, in 1833); *Cohens v. Virginia* (reaffirming the Supreme Court's power to review judgments by state courts, in 1821); *Fletcher v. Peck* (combining the contract clause with the theme of natural rights, in 1810); and a host of lesser–known but nevertheless important decisions.

This is not to say that Marshall or his judicial opinions are beyond criticism. The surface logic of *Marbury,* for example, covers a leap of faith regarding the role of the judiciary in governing, and its specific conclusion relative to the facts of the case (dicta aside) is unnecessary. Yet the power of Marshall's often repeated words—"It is emphatically the province and duty of the judicial department to say what the law is"—defines a core value in a system operating under rules, rather than whim. In *McCulloch,* the chief justice reminds us that "courts are the mere instrument of the law, and can will nothing" and then proceeds to will an expansive view of national power ("Let the end be legitimate, let it be within the scope of the Constitution, and all means which are appropriate, which are plainly adapted to that end, which are not prohibited, but consistent with the letter and spirit of the Constitution, are constitutional.") The seeming contradiction is reconciled, quite properly, by Marshall's insistence that "we must never forget it is a Constitution we are expounding. To expound is to interpret, and to perform that function the

Court, by necessity, must occupy that grey area which is less than pure will, but more than a mechanical instrumentality of the law."

Only by understanding both the imperatives of judicial activism and the requirements of judicial restraint could Marshall firmly establish the foundations of judicial power. In this sense, Marshall was a master blender, mixing together often conflicting principles with practical considerations and presenting the results with compelling, if not always impeccable, logic.

In *Marbury,* he hit Jefferson's weak flank while avoiding a no-win and therefore potentially disastrous confrontation. Marshall not only picked his battles carefully, he also comprehended the importance of distinguishing law from politics if the rule of law were to survive. Right after *Marbury,* Marshall's Court would allow the Jeffersonians to eliminate the separate court of appeals judgeships created by the 1801 Judiciary Act. In 1805, Marshall himself was a very restrained defense witness during the Senate trial of impeached Justice Samuel Chase. The ardent Federalist Chase was not removed from the Court, and another cautious step toward a truly independent judiciary was taken. Two years later, Marshall (as part of his circuit duties) presided over the treason trial of Aaron Burr in Richmond. Again, the chief justice exhibited skills that were crucial in developing the supremacy of law doctrine. While exercising care in dealing with presidential claims of executive privilege, Marshall did not shy away from issuing rulings and excluding evidence that moved the jury toward its not-guilty verdict. Jefferson's response, not surprisingly, was anger aimed at Marshall. Yet, in looking at the Burr trial, it is Marshall's standards linked to the rule of law—and not Jefferson's passion and pursuit of Burr—that are most compelling.

As George Haskins points out "One reason for the success of the early Marshall Court in proclaiming a rule of law free from the intrusion of politics...was that by attending to its business in a lawyer–like fashion the Court began to win the respect of important people in the Republican camp."[6] Even the very pro–Republican newspaper, the *Aurora,* would refer to the chief justice as "a star of the first magnitude."[7] Marshall was thus the critical architect of the constitutional system not only because of his proclamation of principles, but also due to his abilities in putting those principles into practice. The result of his vision and his talents has been aptly summarized by the concluding comment of Charles Curtis: "What we owe to Marshall is the opportunity he gave us of combining a reign of conscience with a republic"(1971, 198).

This is not to deify Marshall. By contemporary standards, the fact that he sat on the *Marbury* case would raise more than a few eyebrows since it was the failure of Secretary of State John Marshall to insure the delivery of Marbury's commission that set the scene for the historic opinion. Even more questionable, according to Gerald Gunther (1969), was Marshall's secretive publication, under pseudonyms, of a third–person defense of his *McCulloch* decision.

Later in his career, Marshall's holding in the Cherokee Nation case *Worcester v. Georgia* (1832) produced the remark attributed to President Andrew Jackson by Horace Greeley: "John Marshall has made his decision. Let him enforce it."[8] Whatever the ethical merits of the decision, this was the kind of direct confrontation Marshall had traditionally tried to avoid. Here he failed. In fact, during his last years in the Court (1831–1835), Marshall's influence in general declined. He began anticipating retirement in 1828, but stayed on, convinced that President Jackson (who represented more popular democratic, rather than Republican principles) would undermine the grand edifice of the Court and the supremacy of law with Marshall's replacement. In 1831, Marshall underwent surgery in Philadelphia to remove kidney stones. While he apparently recovered from that problem, within three years he developed an enlarged liver that led to his death in 1835. And it was during his funeral cortege in Philadelphia on July 8, the often repeated story goes, that the Liberty Bell rang for the last time before cracking.

Marshall's fear that his vision of the rule of law would not survive was unfounded. For just as the Court had captured its Republican members (rather than the other way around) even after they had become the majority in 1811, so too would the firm foundation Marshall established continue to support the ongoing development of an independent judiciary after his passing. What he had created, through his commitment and his Hume–like skepticism, would not die with him.

Coda

Though Marshall was a man who enjoyed his leisure time and his annual vacations in the mountains of Virginia, he did manage a few added activities beyond his duties as chief justice. From 1805 to 1807, he published a five–volume biography of George Washington that enjoyed some commercial success. This aided Marshall in meeting payments on his Fairfax land speculation. Overall he was unhappy with his effort at biography and the practical problems encountered. Later, Marshall served as a member of the Committee of Vigilance to defend Richmond. In 1823, he became president of the Richmond auxiliary of the American Colonization Society (an organization that dealt with the slavery problem by encouraging a black return to and colonization of Africa). Like his opposition to reforms for increased religious freedom and church–state separation in Virginia and his disinterest in broad universal suffrage, Marshall's ability to live with slavery is a fact that does not add to his reputation for greatness. In the context of the times, however, his were understandable sins. And to Marshall's credit, he did, at least, see the dangers contained within the practice of slavery for the South and the nation.

In 1829, he was elected to serve in the convention convened to revise the Virginia Constitution. A fellow delegate writing on that convention noted Marshall's talent for distilling "an argument down to its essence." Throughout his career, on and off the bench, this talent characterized Marshall's analysis of issues and helped create the cogent and compelling statements for which he was (and still is) recognized. In the words of Marshall's contemporary Rufus King, "His head is the best organized of anyone I have ever known."

The scope of Marshall's abilities led Justice Oliver Wendell Holmes to say that "if American law were to be represented by a single figure, skeptic and worshipper alike would agree without dispute that the figure could only be but one alone, and that one John Marshall." In his extensive, four–volume biography of Marshall published during the second decade of the twentieth century, Albert Beveridge found Marshall "so surpassingly great and good" that he almost seemed divorced from mankind. Yet, as Holmes pointed out, admiration for Marshall is not limited to his worshippers, for even the most skeptical of his critics have tended to concede that Marshall during his tenure (one of the longest in Court history) earned the title of "the great Chief Justice."[9]

Marshall may have lost the only case he argued before the Supreme Court as a lawyer *(Ware v. Hylton* in 1796), but he won a world after he joined that Court. He was a Federalist with an interest in the protection of private–property rights. Yet to concentrate on such labels is to simplify Marshall's contribution, and by so doing distort it beyond recognition. Marshall's vision would never have taken hold if such simple labels truly captured its essence. John Randolph, who admired Marshall's mind much more than he did the chief justice's opinions, once said in frustration over Marshall's reasoning, "wrong, all wrong, but no man in the United States can tell why or wherein."[10] Such was the towering presence of this man who, through principles and practice, carved out a tradition that has endured for the ages. No wonder John Adams would express such pride in his selection of Marshall to lead the Court.[11]

Of course, neither Marshall nor Armstrong represented the "end" of things in their respective fields. Music and constitutional law would continue to find new paths to follow, but not without the lasting influence exerted by both men. Armstrong has been described as an engaging, down–to–earth person who was a cautious revolutionary, but a revolutionary nonetheless. That description, as well, fits the great chief justice whose life helped shape a nation and the modern concept of liberal democracy.

NOTES

1. Quoted in Henry Abraham, *Justices, Presidents and Senators* (Lanham, MD: Rowland and Littlefield, 1990), 62.
2. On Marshall's life, see: Smith (1992); Baker (1974); Adams (1937); and Herbert Johnson, "John Marshall," in Leonard Friedman and Fred Israel (eds.), *The Justices of the United States Supreme Court 1789–1978,* Volume 1 (New York: Chelsea House, 1980), 290–297.
3. Quoted in Jean Edward Smith, *John Marshall* (New York: Holt, 1996), 137.
4. Leonard Baker, *John Marshall* (New York, 1974), 153–154.
5. Leonard Baker, *John Marshall* (New York, 1974), 189.
6. George Haskins, "Law versus Politics in the Early Years of the Marshall Court," *University of Pennsylvania Law Review* 130 (1981): 23. Also, see the Haskins and Herbert Johnson volume in the Holmes *History of the Supreme Court* series, *Foundations of Power: John Marshall, 1801–1815* (New York: Macmillan, 1981); G. Edward White, *The Marshall Court and Cultural Change, 1815–1835* (New York: Oxford University Press, 1991); and Charles Hobson, *The Great Chief Justice: John Marshall and the Rule of Law* (Lawrence: University Press of Kansas, 1996). Hobson is also the editor of several volumes of the John Marshall papers published by the University of North Carolina Press.
7. Cited in Smith, *John Marshall,* 325.
8. Cited in Smith, *John Marshall,* 518.
9. Charles Curtis, "Review and Majority Rule," in Edmond Cahn (ed.), *Supreme Court and Supreme Law* (New York: Simon and Schuster, 1971), 198.
10. Cited in Smith, *John Marshall,* 518.
   While there are references to Adams labeling his appointment of the "plain, sensible, cautious and learned," Marshall as the proudest act of his life, David McCullough points out in *John Adams* (New York: Simon and Schuster, 2001) that the nation's second president was most proud of achieving peace with France in 1800, and that the appointment of which he was proudest was that of Marshall (p. 567).

FOR FURTHER READING

Adams, John (ed.). An Autobiographical Sketch by John Marshall. Ann Arbor: University of Michigan Press, 1937.

Baker, Leonard. *John Marshall: A Life in Law,* New York: Macmillan, 1974.

Beveridge, Albert. *The Life of John Marshall,* 4 volumes. Boston: Houghton Mifflin, 1916–1919.

Corwin, Edward. *John Marshall and the Constitution.* New Haven: Yale University Press, 1921.

Faulkner, Robert. *The Jurisprudence of John Marshall.* Princeton University Press, 1969.

Gunther, Gerald (ed.). *John Marshall's Defense of McCulloch v. Maryland.* Stanford: Stanford University Press, 1969.

Haskins, George and Herbert Johnson. *Foundations of Power: John Marshall. 1801–1815.* New York: Macmillan, 1981.

Hobson, Charles. *The Great Chief Justice: John Marshall and the Rule of Law.* Lawrence: University Press of Kansas, 1996.

Kurland, Philip (series ed.). *James Bradley Thayer, Oliver Wendell Holmes, and Felix Frankfurter on John Marshall.* Chicago: University of Chicago Press, 1967.

McCullough, David. *John Adams.* New York: Simon Schuster, 2001.

Mason, Francis (ed.). *My Dearest Polly: :Letters of Chief Justice John Marshall to His Wife.* Richmond: Garret and Massie, 1961.

Rodell, Fred. *Nine Men.* New York: Random House, 1950.

Servies, James. *A Bibliography of John Marshall.* Washington: U.S. Commission for the Celebration of the 200th Anniversary of the Birth of John Marshall, 1956.

Smith, Jean Edward. *John Marshall: Definer of a Nation.* New York: Henry Holt, 1996.

Stites, Francis. *John Marshall: Defender of the Constitution.* New York: Harper Collins, 1981.

White, G. Edward. *The Marshall Court and Cultural Change, 1815–1835.* New York: Oxford University Press, 1991.

CHAPTER THREE

Joseph Story and a National System of Law

Danny M. Adkison

Joseph Story, born in Marblehead, Massachusetts, in 1779, was just thirty-two years old when President James Madison nominated him to be an associate justice of the United States Supreme Court. Despite being the youngest person ever to serve that august institution, Supreme Court historians and experts are nearly universal in their praise of his intellect, scholarly contributions, and development of important constitutional law.

There are more ironies in Justice Story's experience on the Supreme Court than just the unlikely combination of his youthfulness and scholarly pursuits. For example, Justice Story became a defender of the "old law." Furthermore, his father was a revolutionary who participated in the Boston Tea Party, but Justice Story, after the death of his mentor and friend, Chief Justice John Marshall, became a defender of the status quo. Although Story was a member of the Jeffersonian Republican Party, Thomas Jefferson himself urged party cofounder James Madison not to appoint Story to the Court.

Beginnings

Joseph Story's father, Elisha Story, was a physician and an active member of the Republican Party, first in Boston, then Marblehead. Story's mother, Mehitable Pedrick Story, instilled in her son a love of literature and a desire for greatness. Every biographer of Story recounts his early affinity for writing poetry. One asserted that "literature, next to jurisprudence, was his greatest love."[1]

The Power of Solitude, a collection of Story's poems, was first published in 1802, and a second, longer edition was published two years later in 1804, the same year Story married Mary Lynde Fitch. Six months later, his young twenty-three-year-old bride suddenly died. Story, in apparent grief, burned all copies of *The Power of Solitude* in his possession.[2] Two months later, Story's father died. Story threw himself into his work.

Story was, as it turned out, well suited to the study of law. Critics had declared him inept as a poet. But along with his love of literature, Story seemed to possess an innate ability to study and master scholarly subjects. This had been obvious following his sudden departure from Marblehead Academy. Determined to enter Harvard, Story studied on his own in preparation for admittance. It was after seeking admittance that he learned of Harvard's requirements to gain entrance to the term already begun. His reaction to this challenge revealed an approach to learning that would serve him well in his later professional development.

Given only six weeks to learn the material, Story returned home and, without benefit of tutor, mastered grammar, rhetoric, logic, and the works of Sallust, the *Odes of Horace,* three books of Livy and Homer, and Xenophon's *Anabasis.* Returning to Harvard, he was again offered for examination and obtained his matriculation.[3]

Story was graduated second in honors from Harvard in 1798. Chosen to deliver the poem at commencement, he subsequently burned copies of this poem. Having abandoned any dreams of gaining respectability as a poet, Story decided to study law, apparently "for the lack of anything better to do."[4] Unlike his poetry, his legal endeavors (as lecturer, author, and justice) would capture the attention of the world.

Joining the Marshall Court

Story applied his ability to teach himself to his legal career. It took him a while to build his client base, but over time his reliability and honesty won him a faithful following. Reared in a family in which politics played a significant role, Story was drawn to politics, too. His first legal treatise, *A Selection of Pleadings in Civil Actions,* was published in 1805, the same year that the voters elected him to a seat in the state legislature.

Three years later he won a seat in the U.S. House of Representatives in a special election. Whether, as some believe, he refused to run for a full term, or whether the party denied him the nomination because of his opposition to Jefferson's embargo, his tenure in Congress was short. The next time he returned to Washington, DC, in an official capacity it was as Justice Story.

He is a "pseudo-republican" and "too young," Jefferson told President Madison in his argument against Joseph Story as a potential appointee to the U.S. Supreme Court. At first, Madison seemed to follow Jefferson's advice. When a vacancy occurred on the Court in 1810, President Madison nominated Levi Lincoln, formerly Jefferson's attorney general, even though Lincoln had told Madison that his failing eyesight would not permit him to fulfill the duties of a justice. Without delay, the Senate consented to Lincoln's appointment. After the Senate vote, Lincoln officially refused to serve. Next, Madison nominated an old friend, Alexander Wolcott. The Senate overwhelmingly rejected his appointment. Time was running out for Madison, and, in fact, did expire before an appointment was made. The result was a cancellation of the Court's 1811 term. On his third attempt to fill the vacancy, Madison turned to John Quincy Adams. Despite the Senate's unanimous consent, Adams, too, refused to accept the appointment.

It finally became Story's turn. Against all of Jefferson's warnings, Madison nominated Story to the Court. Why? Given Jefferson's advice and Madison's initial actions, no simple answer can explain Story's appointment. One factor was that during this time yet another seat on the Court became vacant. Madison needed a nominee whom the Senate would approve and who would accept the appointment. Madison was also determined to nominate a New Englander since the justice would be riding circuit in that region. Finally, Madison was aware of Story's excellent legal mind. By this time, Story had made a name for himself, serving as winning counsel in the famous Yazoo land deal case, *Fletcher v. Peck.*[5]

The Senate unanimously approved Story's appointment. Shortly afterward, Madison nominated, and the Senate approved, his second and final appointment to the Supreme Court. The membership of the Court would remain fixed for the next eleven years. Justice Story remained on the Court until his death in 1845, becoming an active jurist, a friend of Chief Justice Marshall, and, as evidenced by his written opinions, a supporter of the Union and the Constitution.

Judicial Authority and the Union

It is not mere coincidence that Article I of the U.S. Constitution pertains to Congress. Clearly, the Framers deemed the legislative branch the most important of the three they created. In *Federalist* 51 Madison, under the pen name of Publius, wrote, "In republican government the legislative authority, necessarily, predominates." Congress was not only the first branch of government to be described in the Constitution, but the legislative article was the longest of the seven articles. Article II, pertaining to the executive branch, was shorter. Shortest of all, however, was Article III, dealing with the judicial branch. Whether from time constraints, or from less experience in designing a judiciary, or from attempts to avoid the inevitable conflicts that would arise in discussions of the courts, or some other reason, the Framers said little about federal courts. Perhaps they viewed the judiciary as the branch needing the least specificity due to the lack of threat posed by the courts relative to the other branches. Publius's description of the federal judiciary is widely quoted: "Whoever attentively considers the different departments of power must perceive, that in a government in which they are separated from each other, the judiciary, from the nature of its functions, will always be the least dangerous to the political rights of the constitution; because it will be least in a capacity to annoy or injure them" (*Federalist* 78).

Thus, the only court specifically mentioned in Article III was the Supreme Court. Sensing that the creation of lower federal courts would raise serious issues about their relationship to existing state courts, the delegates at the Convention sidestepped the issue. The opening sentence of Article III stipulates, "The judicial power of the United States, shall be vested in one Supreme Court, and in such inferior courts as the Congress may from time to time ordain and establish." Many of the states later would construe the word "inferior" literally.

The first Congress created lower federal courts in the Judiciary Act of 1789. The jurisdiction of the Supreme Court and the courts created by Congress was stipulated in Section 2 of Article III. Left unanswered, however, was the exact relationship between state courts and federal courts. Justice Story, immediately upon arriving at the Supreme Court, would be involved in addressing the thorny question of federal-state legal interaction. His involvement, however, actually began in an important case prior to his appointment to the Court.

Fletcher v. Peck (1810)

In *Marbury v. Madison (1803)*, the Supreme Court ruled that the federal courts had authority to judge the constitutionality of acts of Congress. If a federal court deemed a law passed by Congress unconstitutional, the court could declare the law "null and void." Chief Justice Marshall's logic in the *Marbury* case was unimpeachable. Any law repugnant to the Constitution was null and void; Section 13 of the Judiciary Act of 1789 was repugnant to the Constitution, therefore, Section 13 was null and void. Unimpeachable, that is, to those accepting Marshall's premises. Some states did not. This became clear when the Supreme Court had the opportunity to rule, for the first time, on the constitutionality of state laws.

At issue was action taken by the Georgia legislature. The Georgia legislature had sold land to a group known as the Yazoo Land Companies. When the public learned that bribery was involved in the sales, there was an outpouring of sentiment to rescind them. In the meantime, some of the land had been resold by the Yazoo Companies to parties uninvolved in the scandal. When the Legislature did rescind the sales, one buyer—Robert Fletcher—sued John Peck in federal court to have his purchase nullified and his money returned.

Since the parties involved lived in different states, the federal courts assumed jurisdiction in the case based not on subject matter but diversity of citizenship. Peck won in the early stages of the case, and Fletcher appealed to the U.S. Supreme Court. Story was substituted as the lawyer for Peck for oral arguments before the Supreme Court in 1810.

For Peck to prevail, the Supreme Court would have to declare the Georgia legislature's act that rescinded the land grants unconstitutional. The Court already had endured criticism for declaring an act of Congress unconstitutional. Now, it was being asked to rule that an act of a state legislature was unconstitutional..

Chief Justice Marshall did, indeed, rule that the act of the Georgia legislature in rescinding the sale of the land was unconstitutional. In doing so, the Court established the precedent that state government actions were subject to review by the Supreme Court, a ruling significant at several levels. The decision itself has been described as "one of the most important decisions in the history of the Court."[6] Marshall's nationalistic leanings are clearly evident in his opinion. Relying on his interpretation of the Constitution's "contract clause" and also "general principles" (an oblique reference to natural law), Marshall, writing for a unanimous Court, set the stage for more significant cases that would follow. And where did Marshall get the ideas for his written opinion? From Peck's lawyer, Story, during oral argument before the Court.[7]

The ruling is taken for granted today. But on the heels of the *Marbury* decision and Justice Chase's impeachment, it was a rather bold decision. Story's participation in the Yazoo Land case no doubt won him the attention of then-President Madison. Madison, too, had nationalistic leanings and would have agreed with the position taken by Story. Furthermore, by relying on the "contract clause," the Court established a means for challenging substantive acts of state governments and protecting something dear to Story's heart—the notion of "vested" property rights. Story would have a chance to rule on the question of vested property rights and the relationship of federal and state courts in his first year on the Marshall Court.

Story's Nationalism

Few doubt the importance and significance of the *Fletcher* decision and Story's role in it, but Story's first full opinion while serving on the Supreme Court is considered one of the three most important decisions issued by the Court in the first fifty years of the nation's existence.[8] It has been described as the "keystone of the whole arch of Federal judicial power,"[9] and attributed with having provided the basis for constitutional issues of the entire Marshall era. The case was *Martin v. Hunter's Lessee,* and the issue presented "equaled, perhaps even surpassed, that in *Marbury*."[10]

Martin v. Hunter's Lessee (1816)

This case began as *Fairfax's Devise v. Hunter's Lessee* (1813). Involved in the case were the Jay Treaty, the highest court in Virginia, and the land rights of British subjects. Because Chief Justice Marshall had a personal involvement in the case, he recused himself. Justice Story wrote the decision.[11]

Former British national, Lord Fairfax of Virginia, willed his land in northern Virginia to his nephew in England, Denny Martin. Subsequently, the Virginia legislature passed a law confiscating the land of British loyalists. Relying on this law, Virginia authorities granted a portion of Lord Fairfax's land to David Hunter. Martin sued Hunter in Virginia courts. His claim to the land was based on his uncle's will and anticonfiscation clauses found in the Jay Treaty. Hunter's claims to the land were predicated on the assertion that the land was the property of Virginia prior to the formulation of the treaty and, therefore, the treaty was not pertinent to Virginia's control of the land.

Not surprisingly, Virginia's highest court ruled for Hunter. Martin appealed to the U.S. Supreme Court, which reversed on the grounds that the treaty, which is described in Article VI as the "supreme law of the land," was controlling. Having so ruled, the Supreme Court instructed the Virginia Court to change its ruling. The Virginia Court refused to do so. Its reason for refusing was that the U.S. Supreme Court lacked the authority to judge a decision of a state's highest court.

At this point, the case became *Martin v. Hunter's Lessee*. The case raised constitutional issues of incredible proportions whose resolution would have tremendous ramifications for the development of the national government in general and the national judiciary in particular. Stripped to its essence, the fundamental question raised by *Martin* was whether or not the Framers had created a genuine national government. The Virginia court's argument was strong and straightforward:

> The court is unanimously of opinion that the appellate power of the Supreme Court of the United States does not extend to this court, under a sound construction of the constitution of the United States; that so much of the 25th section of the act of Congress to establish the judicial courts of the United States, as extends the appellate jurisdiction of the Supreme Court to this court, is not in pursuance of the constitution of the United States; that the writ of error, in this cause, was improvidently allowed under the authority of that act; that the proceedings thereon in the Supreme Court were, *coram non judice*, in relation to this court, and that obedience to its mandate be declined by the court.[12]

Justice Story was acutely aware of the magnitude of the fundamental issues raised by the Virginia court's position. He addressed the issue directly, and in a unique way. One of the issues at the framing of the U.S. government in 1787 was the relationship between the national government and the states.

The United States was operating as a confederation at the time of the drafting of the Constitution. The Articles of Confederation created a federation of sovereign states. The other method of arranging the relationship between the central government and the states was called "consolidation" or " national." The issue was important because of implications for the type of system the Framers had approved. Madison stated the issue of national-state relations from the Anti-Federalist point of view: "But it was not sufficient," say the adversaries of the proposed Constitution, "for the convention to adhere to the republican form. They ought with equal care to have preserved the *federal* form, which regards the Union as a *Confederacy* of sovereign states; instead of which they have framed a *national* government, which regards the Union as a *consolidation* of the States."[13] It was not that easy from reading the Constitution of 1787 to make a determination. The Constitution did not have an article devoted to the issue. Furthermore, the words "confederation," "confederal," "federal," "national," and "consolidation" did not appear anywhere in the document. Writing as Publius, Madison had attempted to answer the question in *Federalist* 39. In that essay, Madison turned to the Constitution itself for evidence of the Framers' intentions. He examined five topics using the Constitution to answer the question: Had the Framers retained the confederation form of government or scrapped it for a national system? One of Madison's examples even touched on the judicial branch. In discussing the "extent of the central government's powers" Madison made this observation: "It is true that in controversies relating to the boundary between the two jurisdictions, the tribunal which is ultimately to decide is to be established under the general government. But this does not change the principle of the case. The decision is to be impartially made, according to the rules of the Constitution; and all the usual and most effectual precautions are taken to secure this impartiality."[14]

Madison concluded his examination of the question with this sentence: "The proposed Constitution, therefore, even when examined by the rules laid down by its antagonists, is, in strictness, neither a national nor a federal constitution; but a composition of both."[15] No doubt, Justice Story felt that he was in a situation similar to Madison's when Madison had authored this essay.

Just as the Anti-Federalists must have been hanging on Madison's every word, so, too, the states' rights advocates at the time were anxious to learn how the Court would rule in this case. Could a national court, the Supreme Court, not only rule on a civil case that a state's highest court had ruled on, but, if it reached a different conclusion, also force the state to abide by the federal court's decision?

Justice Story answered in the affirmative. As partial support for his argument, Story relied on a portion of the Constitution that has since seldom been mentioned by the Court—the Preamble: "The Constitution of the

United States was ordained and established, not by the states in their sovereign capacities, but emphatically, as the preamble of the constitution declares, by the people of the United States. There can be no doubt that it was competent to the people to invest the general government with all the powers which they might deem proper and necessary; to extend or restrain these powers according to their own good pleasure, and to give them a paramount and supreme authority." Concerning state sovereignty, Story left no room for doubt: "The Constitution was not, therefore, necessarily carved out of existing state sovereignties; nor a surrender of powers already existing in state institutions...."[17] While some confusion may have existed during the ratification of the proposed Constitution of 1787, Story was not confused about the foundation of that document. Unlike the Articles of Confederation, a compact among the states, the U.S. Constitution was an act of the people of the nation.

Since the facts of *Martin* raised issues about the appellate jurisdiction of the U.S. Supreme Court, Story quoted from Article III extensively. After having doing so, he made it clear on what authority the national courts were acting: "Such is the language of the article creating and defining the judicial power of the United States. It is the voice of the whole American people solemnly declared, in establishing one great department of that government which was, in many respects, national, and in all, supreme."[18]

Virginia's position in the case was similar to the position Maryland would take later in the *McCulloch* case: nowhere did the Constitution specifically give the Supreme Court power to reverse a final decision of a state's highest court. Story's decision anticipated, and may have supplied, the same arguments Marshall would use in *McCulloch*, but Story once again injected a reference to the Constitution which, as he had already pointed out, drew legitimacy from the American people rather than from the states: "The constitution unavoidably deals in general language. It did not suit the purposes of the people, in framing this great charter of our liberties, to provide for minute specifications of its powers, or to declare the means by which those powers should be carried into execution.... The instrument was not intended to provide merely for the exigencies of a few years, but was to endure through a long lapse of ages... Hence its powers are expressed in general terms, leaving to the legislature... to adopt its own means to effectuate legitimate objects...."[19]

All that was left was for Story to address Virginia's remaining defense, that its courts, having taken jurisdiction of a case, made its decision final. If the Supreme Court wished to express its opinion on the dispute, it had the right to do so, but was not vested with authority to supersede a decision made by Virginia's highest court. So went Virginia's final argument. Story relied on the "plain and obvious import" of the Constitution to counter the state's argument. If a state court exercised jurisdiction in a dispute, were federal courts preempted from enforcing a different decision in the same dispute? Story's answer was that no such limitation existed in Article III: "The appellate power is not limited by the terms of the third article to any particular courts. The words are the judicial power (which includes appellate power) shall extend to all cases, etc., and in all other cases before mentioned the Supreme Court shall have appellate jurisdiction. It is the case, then, and not the court, that gives the jurisdiction."[20]

In fact, Story found that the Framers had anticipated this relationship between federal and state courts. What else could explain the language of Article VI that stipulates that the Constitution and laws of the United States made in pursuance thereof, and all treaties made, shall be the supreme law of the land, and that judges in every state shall be bound by the supreme law, anything in the constitution or laws of any state to the contrary notwithstanding? Virginia turned this argument around and asserted that if state judges were required to take an oath to uphold the U.S. Constitution then there was nothing to fear from refusing to allow the Supreme Court to review final decisions of a state's courts. Otherwise, Virginia argued, federal courts were being disrespectful of state courts. Story's nationalistic leanings provided him a different perspective. He concluded that the Framers viewed the matter differently, too: "Judges of equal learning and integrity, in different states, might differently interpret a statute, or a treaty of the United States, or even the Constitution itself. If there were no revising authority to control these jarring and discordant judgments, and harmonize them into uniformity, the laws, the treaties, and the constitution of the United States would be different in different states...The public mischiefs that would attend such a state of things would be truly deplorable; and it cannot be believed that they could have escaped the enlightened convention which formed the Constitution."[21]

How important was Story's decision? As previously stated, some think the issue presented in the *Martin* case equaled, if it did not surpass, the *Marbury* decision, establishing the Court's authority to exercise judicial review.[22] Others have written that the decision "contributed as much as any the chief justice delivered to laying the jurisprudential foundation of a strong nation." Furthermore, the force of Story's argument, both in terms of logic and intellectual rigor, demolished any lingering doubts as to the Supreme Court's authority to rule on state court decisions. It had, according to some, "impact as great as any Marshall opinion."[23]

Marshall's turn would come. The incidents and legal actions leading up to Story's opinion in *Martin* occurred over a period of several decades. The Supreme Court's decision was rendered in 1816. In five years the Marshall Court would face a similar constitutional question, only this time the case would involve criminal rather than civil matters. Marshall would write this opinion, and his argument in *Cohens v. Virginia* was in large measure a reiteration of Story's opinion in *Martin*.

Many of the Supreme Court's decisions issued in the early years of the republic, at least those raising constitutional issues, were of extreme importance. *Marbury, Martin,* and *McCulloch* are considered by many to be the three most significant.[24] One twentieth-century justice, Oliver Wendell Holmes, who was not inclined to advocate judicial review of laws, could not deny the importance of the precedents established in *Martin* and *Cohen.* His assessment of the Court's role underscores the importance of these decisions: "I do not think the United States would come to an end if we lost our power to declare an Act of Congress void. I do think the Union would be impaired if we could not make the declaration as to the laws of the several states."[25] Just as Story's reasoning in *Martin* from the general language of the Constitution to specific means expressed by Congress predicted Marshall in *McCulloch,* Story's strong nationalist position seemed to come from the chief justice himself.[26] Not only were Story and Marshall good friends, but they also held similar beliefs on a number of fundamental legal issues. They agreed, for example, that the national government was not a compact of sovereign states, that logic and common sense were useful when interpreting the Constitution, and that both of these means of discernment could result in settling constitutional issues in a manner that increased the authority of the national government. Another important case demonstrating their similarity of thought as well as Story's unique approach to constitutional adjudication was the *Dartmouth College* case.

The *Dartmouth College* Case

Dartmouth College was created in New Hampshire under a charter from the British crown in 1769. That charter granted to twelve trustees "the usual corporate privileges and powers" to govern the college.[27] In 1816 the New Hampshire state legislature passed several measures modifying the provisions of that charter, basically placing the institution under the control of the state.

At issue in the case was whether the Dartmouth College charter was protected by the U.S. Constitution, or whether the New Hampshire legislature could modify the charter to serve the interests of its citizens. In addition to the direct effect the Court's ruling would have on the governance of the college, the decision would have important ramifications concerning the overall authority of all state legislatures. Both Marshall and Story must have been aware of these implications.

Marshall wrote the Court's opinion in the case; Story wrote a concurring opinion. The New Hampshire state legislature was of the opinion that what began as a private institution, partially due to its function of educating the young, should be made into a public institution; and thus, the legislature was within its authority in modifying the charter. One of Marshall's biographers describes the case as a "pivotal case in America's economic development."[28]

In his opinion, Marshall first established that the Dartmouth charter was in fact a contract. The Constitution contained a provision directly aimed at state legislatures concerning contracts. The first sentence of Article I, Section 10, stipulates, "No state...shall pass any law impairing the obligation of contracts...." But was a grant from a government (in this case the British government) a contract within the meaning of this constitutional clause? Since the Constitutional Convention had not stated precisely what the clause was intended to cover and the debate during ratification hadn't shed much light on the passage, Marshall had latitude to assert his opinion of the proper interpretation. He ruled that issuance of the grant by a government did not alter the fact that it created a private institution; thus it was a contract within the meaning of Article I, Section 10, and the New Hampshire legislature had impaired fulfillment of the contract. Then, Marshall described, in what has been called a "definition destined for constitutional immortality,"[29] a corporation: "A corporation is an artificial being, invisible, intangible, and existing only in contemplation of law.... it possesses those properties which the charter of its creation confers upon it. Among the most important are immortality, and if the expression may be allowed, individuality...."[30]

Marshall's opinion was grounded in logic. From that perspective it was a forceful decision. But anyone—such as states' rightists—operating from different premises or different definitions could argue that the opinion was merely Marshall's personal one. It was Story's concurrence that supplied the legal backbone of the decision. Story agreed with Marshall's conclusion that the college charter was, in fact, a contract and one which the Constitution included when forbidding states to impair contracts. But, unlike Marshall, Story did not rely merely on definitions and assertions. Marshall did not cite a single legal precedent in his opinion. Story cited over two dozen. Not content with citing precedent to buttress their arguments, Story also relied extensively on the common law, privileges and immunities, the notion of vested property rights, and due process of law.

The two latter references are of particular importance. Due process of law was not part of the Constitution of 1787. It first appeared in the Fifth Amendment, added in 1791, and again in the Fourteenth Amendment, ratified in 1868. Story's concurrence, longer than Marshall's majority opinion, supplied the legal basis lacking in Marshall's opinion. By buttressing Marshall's argument in this fashion, Story's concurrence conferred an authoritativeness without which the opinion would have been much more vulnerable to attack. But Story's concurring opinion did more than that.

In referring to "due process of law," Story anticipated how the "contract clause" would be used by the Court up to the Civil War and beyond, replaced only by a reliance on the actual "due process clause" itself. It was precisely the direction that Marshall, in earlier cases, had indicated he wanted to move in the regulation of state governments. A majority of the Court supported Marshall, but Story, by supplying legal precedents and legal rigor, made it harder for others to disagree. What was the impact? Most constitutional historians could agree with this assessment: "Marshall's efforts to transform the Contract Clause into a powerful guarantor of vested property rights profoundly affected constitutional law for the remainder of the nineteenth century." In fact, one study of the Court's use of the Contract Clause concluded that "up to 1889, it figured in about 40 percent of all Supreme Court cases involving the validity of state legislation (resulting in 75 invalidations of state laws on constitutional grounds)."[31] In practical terms, the impact can be seen by the rise of the corporation in the United States. By the end of the 1700s, American states had chartered 310 corporations—only eight to produce goods instead of provide a service. By 1830, there were more than 1,900 corporations in the New England area alone (over half of which were producing goods).[32] Eventually, Marshall and Story's application of the Contract Clause lost favor with the Court. One factor in the demise of the Court's reliance on the Contract Clause was the inclusion in the Constitution of an actual due process clause directed at the states. Another was Chief Justice Taney's decision in the *Charles River Bridge Company* case.[33] Story disagreed vigorously in that case, writing a dissent of 35,000 words, the likes of which, one of his biographers concluded, Marshall could never have produced.[34]

Swift v. Tyson

Marshall's death was difficult for Story. He commented, "I miss the Chief Justice at every turn."[35] Story, being a sociable individual, tried to fit in with Taney, Marshall's replacement, and other new justices on the Court. More and more, though, he found himself differing from the majority. His expert knowledge of the common law, and his desire to see it used generally, when necessary, in making judicial decisions, and specifically to interpret the U.S. Constitution, was something with which the majority became increasingly uncomfortable. A good example of this shift can be found in Swift v. Tyson, decided in 1842, only three years before Story's death. The case dealt with Article III of the Constitution and the Judiciary Act of 1789. One portion of Article III states in the appellate jurisdiction of federal courts, "the judicial power shall extend to...controversies between citizens of different states...." Early on, in these "diversity of citizenship" cases, the question arose as to which law should apply when the federal courts were deciding them. Congress declared in Section 34 of the Judiciary Act of 1789 that in deciding such cases, the courts should apply the laws of the several states. Swift was a diversity of citizenship case. At first glance it would appear that Story's decision in the case struck a blow to common law. That's because he ruled that in interpreting the "apply the laws of the several states" provision of the Judiciary Act, the decisions of the state courts were not to be treated as laws. Here is how he phrased it in the decision: "In the ordinary use of language it will hardly be contended that the decisions of courts constitute law. They are, at most, only evidence of what the laws are, and are not of themselves laws The laws of a state are more usually understood to mean the rules and enactments promulgated by the legislative authority thereof, or long established local customs having the force of laws."[36]

If state court decisions could not be used by federal courts when deciding diversity cases, then the courts must rely on state law. In that respect it seemed Story was denying the use of the common law. But, Story knew that often state laws would not cover issues involved in many cases being litigated in federal courts. This would mean the federal courts could turn to a national common law to decide such cases. After all, Article III of the Constitution itself stated that the judicial power of the federal courts would extend to all cases in laws and *equity* arising under the Constitution. Recent scholars have pointed out the predilection of the founding generation ,in general, and those of jurists, in particular, to rely on "fundamental principles." This was, of course, the very phrase Story used in some of his decisions. Reliance on the common law was another indication of this approach. Chief Justice Marshall indicated his endorsement of such reasoning in his *Fletcher v. Peck* decision, when he wrote that the Court could rely on "the reasoning spirit of the Constitution," not just the "words or letter" of that document.[37]

Story, who understood Blackstone perhaps better than anyone else in America at that time, sought to rely on a common law for civil cases that federal courts would pronounce and rely on when deciding disputes. Not only would this provide a "code for deciding disputes"; it would, in a more practical vein, promote uniformity in judicial decisions. That would be true since, if this reliance on common law caught on, states would emulate the federal courts. Story's expectation was never fulfilled. In fact, although it took the Supreme Court almost a century to do so, the Court explicitly overruled the *Swift* decision, with Justice Brandeis calling the Court's interpretation of federal law in *Swift* unconstitutional.[38]

Assessment

The *Swift* decision reveals another irony involving Justice Story. He was a man who was praised universally for his preparedness for a career as a jurist, when, in truth, he had no judicial experience prior to being appointed to the Supreme Court. The label "precocious" is accurate.[39] Bernard Schwartz, a professor who probably knew more about the Supreme Court than any other scholar and who listed Story fourth among the ten greatest justices ever to serve on that Court, described Story as supplying for Marshall "the one thing the great Chief Justice lacked—legal scholarship." Schwartz also lists Story's three-volume exposition of the Constitution, published in 1833, as ranking third among the greatest law books after *The Federalist Papers* and Kent's *Commentaries on American Law*.[40] Yet Story's opinion in *Swift* has the distinction of being the first and only time in its history that the Supreme Court later accused itself of having made an unconstitutional decision. [41]

In all, Story produced three edited works of law, nine major commentaries on the law, and thirteen volumes of judicial opinions, articles, statutes, law reports, and speeches.[42] Some of his published works were products of his lectures at Harvard, where he became the first Dane Professor of Law in 1829.

Sometimes Story "out-nationalized" the nationalist Marshall, leading one biographer to conclude that Story—not his more moderate chief—was the "leading defender of nationalism in the first fifty years of the nineteenth century."[43] His opinion in *Martin v. Hunter's Lessee* (1816) may have been his most important and "contributed as much as any [Chief Justice Marshall] delivered to the jurisprudential foundation of a strong nation; its impact was as great as any Marshall opinion."[44]

The "youngest justice" would build his career as a justice on upholding the "old law" notion of basing rulings on general principles of natural law, all as part of his desire to install a common law throughout the nation as a firm foundation for national government in general and the judicial branch in particular. Politics and a devotion by some to states' rights meant that Story's approach was not always followed nor his goals always achieved. However, this does not detract from the leading role Story played in the development in American constitutional law and his impact on American jurisprudence. Times have and will continue to change, politics and ideology will be in and out of fashion, precedents will come and go, but Justice Joseph Story's legacy as one of the greatest justices to ever serve on the Supreme Court will endure.

NOTES

1. James McClellan, *Joseph Story and the American Constitution* (Norman, OK: University of Oklahoma Press, 1971), 7.
2. Gerald T. Dunn, *Justice Joseph Story and the Rise of the Supreme Court* (New York: Simon and Schuster, 1970), 31–32.
3. McClellan, 8. See note 1.
4. Ibid., 12.
5. Ibid., 36–42 and Jean Edward Smith, *John Marshall: Definer of a Nation* (New York: Henry Holt, 1996), 399–405.
6. John E. Nowak, Ronald D. Rotunda, and J. Nelson Young, *Constitutional Law,* 3rd ed. (St. Paul, MN: West, 1986), 334.

7. McClellan, 306. See note 1.
8. Daniel A. Farber and Suzanna Sherry, *A History of the American Constitution* (St. Paul, MN: West, 1990), 248–251.
9. C. Herman Pritchett, *The American Constitution* (New York: McGraw-Hill, 1977), 52.
10. Smith, 1. See note 5.
11. Ibid., 428.
12. *Martin v. Hunter's Lessee,* 4 L.Ed. at 102 (1816).
13. A. Hamilton, J. Madison, and J. Jay, *The Federalist Papers* in Clinton Rossiter (New York: New American Library, 1961). See *Federalist* 39.
14. Idem.
15. Idem.
16. *Martin V. Hunter's Lessee,* 4 L.Ed. at 102 (1816).
17. Idem.
18. Ibid., 103.
19. Idem.
20. Ibid., 106.
21. Ibid., 108.
22. Smith, 428. See note 5.
23. Bernard Schwartz, *A History of the Supreme Court* (New York: Oxford University Press, 1993), 60.
24. Farber and Sherry, 248–251.
25. Nowak, Rotunda, and Young, 19. See note 6.
26. Schwartz, 60. See note 23.
27. *The Trustees of Dartmouth College v. Woodward,* 4 L.Ed. 656 (1819).
28. Smith, 434. See note 5.
29. Ibid., 436.
30. *The Trustees of Dartmouth College v. Woodward,* 4 L.Ed. 659.
31. Ralph A. Rossum and G. Alan Tarr, *American Constitutional Law,* 2nd ed. (New York: St. Martin's Press, 1987), 279–280.
32. Smith, see note on p. 438. See note 5.
33. Rossum and Tarr, 280.
34. McClellan, *Joseph Story and the American Constitution* (Norman, OK: University of Oklahoma Press, 1971), 302.
35. Ibid., 54.
36. *Swift v. Tyson,* 10 L.Ed. 871 (1842).
37. Hadley Arkes, *Beyond the Constitution* (Princeton: Princeton University Press, 1990), 10–24.
38. Pritchett, 114. See note 9.
39. G. Edward White, *The American Judicial Tradition* (New York: Oxford University Press, 1976), 42.
40. Bernard Schwartz, *A Book of Legal Lists* (New York: Oxford University Press, 1997), 190–199.
41. Pritchett, 114. See note 9.
42. McClellan, 42. See note 1.
43. Ibid., 296–297.
44. Schwartz, *History,* 60. See note 23.

FOR FURTHER READING

Dunn, Gerald T. "Joseph Story." In *The Justices of the United States Supreme Court (1789–1969),* vol. 1. Edited by Leon Friedman and Fred L. Israel. New York: Chelsea House, 1969.

McClellan, James. Joseph Story and the American Constitution. Norman, OK: University of Oklahoma Press, 1971.

Miller, F. Thornton, "Joseph Story's Uniform Rational Law." In *Great Justices of the U.S. Supreme Court.* Edited by William D. Pederson and Norman W. Provizer. New York: Peter Lang, 1993, 49–72.

Newmyer, R. Kent. *Supreme Court Justice Joseph Story: Statesman of the Old Republic.* Chapel Hill, NC: University of North Carolina Press, 1985.

Schwartz, Mortimer D. and Hogan, John C. *Joseph Story.* New York: Oceana, 1959.

Story, William Wetmore. *Life and Letters of Joseph Story.* 2 vols. Boston: Little, Brown, 1851.

CHAPTER FOUR

Roger B. Taney: A Jacksonian Chief Justice
Who Favored "Dixie" on the Bench

William D. Pederson
Frank J. Williams

A competent and energetic lawyer with a provincial perspective, Roger B. Taney was appointed the fifth chief justice of the United States Supreme Court (1836–1864) by President Andrew Jackson as a reward for his attorney general's loyalty. Appointed to succeed Chief Justice John Marshall, Taney never, however, came close to replacing his predecessor, the unanimous choice of scholars as the greatest justice. Taney's historical standing among justices is unique. Scholars in the past have rated him among the great justices, but he is universally associated first with the *Dred Scott* decision—the worst decision in U.S. Supreme Court history. Taney wrote that infamous decision for the Court. While some scholars credit Taney as a stabilizing force on the high court during his long tenure as chief justice, others dismiss him as racist. [1]

This chapter seeks to illuminate Taney's role in American judicial history by briefly contrasting him with his ultimate nemesis—Abraham Lincoln, who, coincidentally, is always ranked as the greatest president in polls of scholars. Like Lincoln, Taney was the product of a border state. Also examined will be Taney's two best-known cases, *Charles River Bridge* (1837), which reflects his innovative economic populism, and *Dred Scott* (1857), his atypical judicial activist decision that documents the racial views of the Jacksonians. In the final analysis, Taney became a judicial anachronism. He proved unable to adapt to the overall human rights legacy of American democracy because of provincial origins that were reinforced by Jacksonian jurisprudence, his legal Achilles' heel.

The Border State Lawyer

In contrast to the generation-younger Abraham Lincoln, who was born in the border state of Kentucky but relocated by his economically ambitious father to Indiana, then Illinois, Roger Brooke Taney lived out his privileged life in the same tidewater area of Maryland where his ancestors had settled in the 1660s. Born on St. Patrick's Day, 1777, in Calvert County, Taney was the second-born son, and third of seven children (three daughters and four sons) in a Roman Catholic family of a prominent aristocratic tobacco grower.

Like his father, Taney maintained his family's religious, social, and economic status quo in Maryland, even after Maryland became so pro-Confederate that President-elect Lincoln had to be spirited through Baltimore en route to his inauguration in Washington, DC. Taney's genteel society contrasted sharply with the frontier West that produced the rustic Lincoln, but of the pair, Lincoln was actually less provincial. Lincoln had traveled twice in his youth to New Orleans via the Mississippi; he rode circuit as a young lawyer; he lived in Washington, DC, while in Congress he saw Canada and the northeastern route to the nation's capital; and he campaigned for the presidency outside of Illinois. Taney's borders never broadened.

Taney was his father's son in more than provincial inclinations. Taney's father had inherited the family estate as the oldest son and continued to support the practice of primogeniture even after it was abolished in Maryland. As the second-born son, the future chief justice was slated by his father to become a lawyer. His father also selected his college, his training, and set the pattern of his early professional life.[2] Seeking his father's approval, Taney entered Dickinson College in Carlisle, Pennsylvania, at age fifteen. A diligent student, Taney graduated in 1795. His father next arranged for him to move to Annapolis to study law for three years with a prominent judge on Maryland's General Court. Dedicated to his studies, the young Taney spent twelve-hour days studying law rather than developing social relationships. He was admitted to the bar in 1799 and practiced briefly in Annapolis before he moved in 1800 to Frederick. In 1823 he relocated to Baltimore.

His father's very visible hand extended to arranging for his son to replace him in the Maryland legislature. The very year he was admitted to the bar, young Taney was elected to the Federalist seat formerly filled by his father, although he was only twenty-two years old and had been absent from home for six years while attending college and reading law. He misjudged the electorate, however, and was defeated for reelection during the Jeffersonian landslide the following year. Taney eventually made a local political comeback, but he was never a player in national politics, in part due to his poor eyesight and in part due to a certain amount of stage fright that he ultimately learned to conceal, but never truly overcame.

Nevertheless, Taney solidified his status in 1806 through marriage to the daughter of another wealthy plantation family. A Catholic priest married Taney and his wife, Anne, even though she was Episcopalian. His bride was the sister of his friend from youth, Francis Scott Key, later famous as the composer of "The Star-Spangled Banner." The couple had six daughters and a son who died in infancy.

Unlike many New England Federalists, Taney became the leader of the Federalist faction that supported the War of 1812, the same war that transformed Andrew Jackson into an American hero. The demise of the Federalist Party, his distrust in large commercial monopolies ingrained through his early life among small farmers, and the War of 1812 all influenced Taney toward Jacksonianism.

In 1816, Taney was elected to the Maryland Senate, but served only one five-year term. By 1826 he was a staunch Democrat, and in 1827 he was elected as Maryland's attorney general, achieving the one position that represented a personal goal. During the five years he held the post, he earned a reputation for competence.

While attorney general, Taney led Maryland's support for Jackson during the 1828 presidential campaign. This competent lawyer and the charismatic president complemented each other. Jackson gave the orders; Taney delivered the legal justifications for them. Both favored economic growth by entrepreneurs against monopolies; at the same time they both were sympathetic to the claims of slaveholders. Jackson kept his slaves and expressed no regret over the "peculiar institution," even though Taney had manumitted his slaves.

Jackson rewarded Taney for his support in the presidential campaign by appointing him attorney general of the United States. It was the first of several rewards that the populist president bestowed upon his loyal lawyer. Taney also served briefly as secretary of war and was one of the president's generals in the war against the Bank of the United States. Taney reversed his earlier support for the national bank to such a degree that he drafted Jackson's 1832 veto message that declared the bank unconstitutional, thus reversing John Marshall's landmark *McCulloch v. Maryland* (1819). After two of Jackson's secretaries of the treasury refused to withdraw federal deposits from the bank, Taney readily accepted Jackson's temporary appointment as treasury secretary to faithfully execute the president's directive. Congress retaliated and refused by a vote of 28–18 to confirm Taney in the position, making him the first cabinet nominee to be rejected by the United States Senate.

After thus serving Jackson in three cabinet posts, Taney returned to his private legal practice in Baltimore, where he remained for two years.

Taney always showed a preference for family life over political life. Both he and his wife suffered ill health, which led to his absence from the capital whenever possible, a circumstance that may have contributed further to his provincialism and isolation from the changes reshaping the nation.

In contrast to Taney, who was his father's son and the president's legal operative, Abraham Lincoln was always his own man. He had differed sharply with his father, who favored working with the back rather than the brain to earn a living. The political fortunes of the future president and chief justice differed, too. Lincoln's first love was elective politics, while Taney did not aspire to national office, although both had entered politics early. Taney easily won his first election, thanks to his father's intervention, but Lincoln's first election ended in defeat, as did many that followed. Lincoln, a persistent politician, entered politics while younger than any lawyer who later served as president. In fact, Lincoln ran for office even before he became a lawyer.[3] The self-taught frontier attorney bounced back in the next election, however, capturing the same seat he had failed to win earlier. Taney was a Federalist Party state leader; Lincoln became a leader of the Illinois Whigs. Unlike Anne Taney, Mary Todd Lincoln shared her husband's political ambitions and presence. Despite their Whig Whig connections, Lincoln's one term in Congress was a disappointment, but because the political arena energized both Abraham and Mary Lincoln, he did not retreat from public life like Taney.

Taney was pulled back into public life by President Jackson, a man who did not forget his loyal supporters and friends. Jackson had already appointed three jurists to the high court, and two more vacancies occurred. Jackson previously had nominated Taney as an associate justice, but the Senate rejected the nomination. After the death of Chief Justice John Marshall in 1835, Jackson resubmitted Taney's name as Marshall's replacement at the same time he proposed another nominee to fill the still-vacant associate justice seat. Taney became the first Catholic on the Supreme Court, appointed by Jackson, the son of immigrant Irish parents. It was a boost to the increasing importance of the Irish Catholic vote for the Democratic Party during a period when Catholics were immigrating to the United States. Three months after the nominations were submitted, on March 15, 1836, two days before his sixtieth birthday, the Senate confirmed Taney on a 29–15 vote. The Supreme Court was constituted now to support Jackson's philosophy of greater states' rights for western and southern entrepreneurs at the expense of entrenched eastern monopolies. Thus began the long Jacksonian revolution on the court.

Taney's Jurisprudence

Like Taney, Andrew Jackson had been a border state lawyer-politician. The energetic and ambitious Tennessee planter represented the third great shift of political power—from the Hamiltonians in the northeast to the Jeffersonians in the southeast to the Jacksonians on the frontier. Rather than eastern monopolists, Jacksonians favored smaller and newer entrepreneurs out West. Less federal government intrusion was desired to allow for economic competition, except for the protection of slaveholders. Indians were incidental in national development, slaves mere economic property among southern entrepreneurs under the Jacksonian philosophy. Jackson was a democrat, except when it came to racial minorities.

As chief justice, Taney had the power to overturn the Marshall legacy, but he merely modified it to allow greater leeway for entrepreneurs at the state and local level as the national expansion westward and concomitant economic development continued. Jackson's political philosophy of majority rule among whites was echoed in the legal positivism of Taney's jurisprudence on the Court. He rejected natural law as reflected in the Declaration of Independence and viewed the U.S. Constitution as a legal document existing apart from an American tradition. Taney could justify whatever white majorities wanted. This nondoctrinaire approach to the law worked relative to economic issues, but led to disastrous results in human rights when it created a set of blinders for Jacksonian jurists. This dichotomy is illustrated in the contrast between Taney's two most famous cases—*Charles River Bridge* (1837) and *Dred Scott* (1857).

Before examining those two cases, a brief look at Taney's actions on the bench in aspects other than his judicial cases will provide useful insights. He introduced several institutional changes to the Marshall Court traditions that might be construed as allowing for greater democracy on the bench. For example, he is credited with changing the attire worn by justices under their robes from the *de rigueur* formal knee breeches to ordinary trousers. More visible—and more substantive—was another change Taney instituted. He ended Marshall's tradition of the chief justice delivering majority opinions to give the appearance of unanimity among the justices and underscore the court's power. Andrew Jackson was even more suspicious than Thomas Jefferson had been of unelected judicial power, so Taney rejected Marshall's precedent of "imperial" presence on the bench and began assigning important decisions to others. This democratic innovation soon became institutionalized on the high court. Taney ended another custom: justices no longer had to live in the same boardinghouse.

Although Taney was personable and flexible overall with his fellow justices, these democratic changes were introduced by the chief justice among a group of like-minded men, many of them also Jacksonians. During forty-nine of the seventy-two years from 1789 to 1861 the presidents of the United States were Southerners—all of them slaveholders. The only presidents to be reelected were slaveholders. Two-thirds of the speakers of the house, chairmen of the House Ways and Means Committee and presidents pro tem of the Senate were Southerners. At all times before 1861, a majority of Supreme Court justices were Southerners...."[4]

Taney's democratic demeanor notwithstanding, it could not compare with the much more democratic John Marshall, who was so unassuming that he could pass as a grocery delivery boy or a head housecleaner.[5] In terms of behavior, Marshall was at least on the surface much more similar to Abraham Lincoln than to the more aristocratic Taney.

Taney's progressively Jacksonian jurisprudence on banking, commerce, and transportation matters effectively modified Marshall's decisions and allowed state legislatures greater latitude in setting economic policy. As always, the Jacksonians opposed economic monopolies and blocked their development, unless the monopoly was associated with the slavocracy.

It was in 1837, his first term on the Court, that Taney wrote what is often regarded as his finest opinion, the *Charles River Bridge Company v. Warren Bridge Company*. The 4–3 decision, the first in a series that allowed states greater flexibility in economic development, rejected the arguments of Daniel Webster. It held that legislative charters must be construed narrowly to protect the public under the Constitution's contract clause. As was typical in the vast majority of his decisions, Taney deferred to state legislatures. They were the elected branch and as such were free to make reasonable regulations and to authorize new projects for promoting economic development and the public good. Taney asserted in his majority opinion

> that the object and end of all government is to promote the happiness and prosperity of the community...and it can never be assumed, that the government intended to diminish its power of accomplishing the end for which it was created. And in a country like ours, free, active, and enterprising, continually advancing in numbers and wealth, new channels of communication are daily found necessary, both for travel and trade, and are essential to the comfort, convenience, and prosperity of the people. A state ought never to be presumed to surrender this power, because, like the taxing power, the whole community have an interest in preserving it undiminished.[6]

Whigs and Jacksonians both favored economic development, even though the Jacksonians opposed the American Plan of Henry Clay and the Whigs to permit federal funding of internal improvements. Abraham Lincoln, a Whig and railroad lawyer, favored a much greater role of government in the development of the West.[7] Jacksonian slaveholders saw further development of the West, with expansion of boundaries, as a means to increase the number of slave states and their resulting numbers in Congress.

Centralization of Political Power

The schizoid dimension of the Jacksonians and populists at the end of the nineteenth century is that both political movements called for a redress of their economic grievances while rejecting an expansion of human rights for others. Provincialism blinded them. Taney, having manumitted his inherited slaves, demonstrated paternal concern by giving a monthly allowance to the older ones unable to care for themselves. His ultimate solution to the problem of slavery was to allow for their colonization abroad.[8] Taney's support for the colonization movement was very similar to the position Abraham Lincoln held before—and some argue, early in—and, some argue, early in— his presidency. Colonization represented a convenient way to swiftly rid the Union of the contentious problem—until Lincoln learned firsthand from free blacks that they had no intention of leaving their homeland.[9] If one considers the outcome of *United States v. Amistad* (1841), which Steven Spielberg dramatized in a popular 1997 film, one might be more surprised by Taney's *Dred Scott* decision.

Amistad was the first *cause celebre* case to reach the Supreme Court. While the opinion was actually written by Joseph Story—portrayed by Justice Harry Blackmun in the film—Taney without comment joined the majority by ruling that the Sierra Leone slaves had been illegally taken by Spanish slave traders and had to be returned to Africa. Unfortunately, Taney's position was most likely inconsequential, as the *Amistad's* revolt leader, Cinque, later became a slave trader himself. By this time, the African slave trade was generally recognized as being illegal and immoral.[10]

Taney's fundamental hierarchical view of social life is probably reflected accurately in his *Dred Scott* decision, even though the decision was atypical for Taney in terms of its judicial activism. Like his father, who had supported primogeniture even after it was repealed by the state of Maryland, Taney supported the slavocracy despite rapidly changing conditions in the nation.

In nine separate decisions, the vote was 7–2, including a blistering dissent by Justice Custis, against Scott's plea for freedom. Taney, in an unpredictable way, went far beyond his customary judicial restraint. Rather than deciding the case on narrow grounds, his fifty-five page opinion focused on the property rights of the slave owner and asserted that Congress had abridged its rights when it refused the expansion of slavery into a territory of the United States. He also declared that the Missouri Compromise which prohibited slavery north of the Mason–Dixon line, had been an unconstitutional usurpation of the rights of individuals to exercise property rights. Although he accepted that Africans could be citizens of the states, he insisted that they would never become citizens of the United States with the right to sue in federal court.

After *Dred Scott,* critics heaped abuse on the chief justice, associating the opinion less with the Supreme Court than with its leader. For the eighty-year-old Taney, the personal attacks exacerbated his poor mental and physical health. It destroyed the reputation that he had worked so hard to build over two decades in order to overcome being compared unfavorably to John Marshall. While a highly respected chief justice, Taney was never beloved. As Kent Newmyer has pointed out, *Dred Scott* essentially "obliterated twenty-one years of effective judicial government and left the Court burdened with the moral obloquy of slavery."[11]

This decision, while not causing the Civil War, was a "self-inflicted wound," polarized the nation, and helped foster the emergence of the Republican Party to challenge it and set the stage for southern secession. The Republican Party's presidential candidate, Abraham Lincoln, emphasized the nonbinding character of judicial dicta. The 1860 Republican platform totally ignored the ruling. It took the Civil War amendments and the grim Civil War itself to resolve finally the issue of slavery and the right of secession. Attorney General Edwin Bates, in one of his opinions written on November 29, 1862, "overruled" the *Dred Scott* case by finding that a "free man of color...if born in the United States, is a citizen of the United States." *Dred Scott* was jurisdictionally limited to the citizenship of Scott in Missouri.[12] If that single decision had been an aberration in Taney's subsequent behavior on the Court, perhaps it could be explained as a lapse in balanced judgment attributable to a combination of his advanced age and the loss of his wife and youngest daughter two years earlier. He continued his obdurate behavior toward the Lincoln administration, however, until he died on October 12, 1864, seven years after *Dred Scott,* at age eighty-seven years. President Lincoln, along with Secretary of State William H. Seward, Attorney General Edward Bates, and Postmaster General William Denison, attended the funeral service at the Taney home on October 15. Only the attorney general attended the burial service in Frederick, Maryland.

While he administered the oath of office to Lincoln, whom he considered a despot, Taney then found opportunities to thwart him. Taney criticized Lincoln in the John Merryman case for suspending the writ of habeas corpus, although he had conveniently overlooked Andrew Jackson's even more egregious behavior after the Battle of New Orleans. Nor had Jefferson Davis been shy about liberally suspending the writ of habeas corpus in the Confederate States of America.[13] Taney repeatedly denounced Lincoln's blockade of southern cities and the suspension of the writ of habeas corpus, which had been approved retroactively by Congress. He leaked unsolicited opinions to the press including arguments against the constitutionality of the Emancipation Proclamation.

Ultimately, the North's "Battle Hymn of the Republic" drowned out the strains of "Dixie," even though the provincial Taney had used the Supreme Court to promote the inhumane institution of slavery in the South. Despite his rustic frontier upbringing, Lincoln had a broader perspective and understood, as well as appreciated, the nuances of music and the depth of human nature. His supporters may have been stunned that Lincoln even had "Dixie" played at the White House, but it was as if Lincoln used music to emphasize that life and relationships are more complex than either a simple hymn or tune during a Civil War.

Conclusions

Taney's ranking in the polls of judicial experts has slipped. When these polls, which are less knowledgeable than those on the rankings of presidents, become more ranked as a "great" president but more recently rated "near great." Both Taney and Jackson demonstrated many virtues in their national leadership roles, but, overall, each lags behind a half dozen others deemed as having performed better—whether it's John Marshall or Earl Warren among justices, or Abraham Lincoln and Franklin Roosevelt among presidents. That quartet of "great" leaders in particular shared Taney's energy and his competence, but they went far beyond him in their ability to view others very different from themselves as human beings. Their politics and "jurisprudence" grew out of this key ingredient in democratic leadership. Taney's aristocratic and provincial background diluted his Jacksonian ideology.

NOTES

1.   Peter Irons, *A People's History of the Supreme Court* (New York: Penguin, 2000), 183–184.
2.   Carl B. Swisher, *Roger B. Taney* (New York: Macmillan, 1935), 11–12, 30.
3.   Thomas M. Green and William D. Pederson, "The Behavior of Lawyer-Presidents: A 'Barberian' Link," in William D. Pederson (ed.), *The 'Barberian' Presidency* (New York: Peter Lang, 1989), 153–167.
4.   James M. McPherson, "Southern Comfort," *New York Review of Books,* vol. 48, no. 6 (April 12, 2001), 31.
5.   Jean E. Smith, *John Marshall: Definer of a Nation* (New York: Henry Holt, 1996), 288, 376.
6.   *Charles River Bridge Co. v. Warren Bridge Company* 11 Peters 420 (1837).
7.   William D. Pederson and Frank J. Williams, "The Abraham Lincoln Model of Modernization," *International Abraham Lincoln Journal,* vol. 2 (2001): 29–37.
8.   Swisher, 94–100.
9.   See Gabor Boritt, "Did He Dream of a Lily-White America?" in Gabor Boritt (ed.), *The Lincoln Enigma* (New York: Oxford, 2001), 1–9.
10. Walker Lewis, *Without Fear or Favor* (Boston: Houghton Mifflin, 1965), 337–346.
11. Kent Newmyer, *The Supreme Court Under Marshall and Taney* (Harlan Davidson, 1968), 9.
12. *Office Opinions of the Attorneys General of the United States*, vol. X, J. Hubley Ashton (ed.), (Washington, DC: W.H. and O.H. Morrison, 1869), 382–413.
13. Mark E. Neely, Jr., *Southern Rights: Political Prisoners and the Myth of Confederate Constitutionalism* (Charlottesville, VA: University Press of Virginia, 1999), 153–167.

FOR FURTHER READING

Fehrenbacher, Don E. *The Dread Scott Case: Its Significance in American Law and Politics.* New York: Oxford University Press, 2001.
Finkelman, Paul. Dred Scott v. Sanford: A Brief History with Documents. Boston: Bedford Books, 1997.

Holland, Kenneth M. "Chief Justice Roger B. Taney: Spokesperson for the South." *Quarterly Journal of Ideology,* vol. 15; 1–2 (1992); 7–43.

Jaffa, Harry V. *Storm over the Constitution. Lanham,* MD: Lexington Books, 1999.

Kutler, Stanley I. *Privilege and Creative Destruction: The Charles River Bridge Case.* Baltimore: Johns Hopkins University Press, 1971.

Smith, Charles W., Jr. *Roger B. Taney: Jacksonian Jurist.* New York: DeCapo Press, 1936, reprint, 1973.

Steiner, Bernard C. *The Life of Roger Brooke Taney, Chief Justice of the United States Supreme Court.* Williams and Wilkins, 1922

Stern, Robert L. "Chief Justice Taney and the Shadow of Dred Scott." *Journal of Supreme Court History* (1922), 39–52..

Swisher, Carl Brent. *Roger B. Taney.* New York: Macmillan, 1935.

Walker, Lewis. *Without Fear or Favor: A Biography of Chief Justice Roger Brooke Taney.* New York: Houghton Mifflin, 1965.

CHAPTER FIVE

John Marshall Harlan the Elder: Color-Blind Justice

Linda Przybyszewski

In July of 1871, a tall, broad-shouldered man faced a crowd of voters in the eastern Kentucky town of Livermore and tried to convince them to make him their state's first Republican governor. John Marshall Harlan was then a thirty-seven-year-old lawyer who had served as Kentucky' attorney general from 1863 to 1867 following his stint from 1861 to 1863 as head of the 10th Kentucky Infantry in the Union army. He had resigned from the army upon his father's death and returned to civilian life to salvage the family law firm. Now he was aiming for his state' top job.

Harlan's platform stressed the importance of economic development through government investment in education and infrastructure. He endorsed the Thirteenth, Fourteenth, and Fifteenth Amendments to the United States Constitution which had freed the slaves, guaranteed them civil rights, and allowed black men the possibility, but not the guarantee, of the vote. Harlan condemned "African slavery" as "the most perfect despotism that ever existed on this earth" and celebrated its end: "I rejoice that it is gone; I rejoice that the Sun of American Liberty does not this day shine, upon a single human slave upon this continent."[1]

But Harlan lost the governor's race in 1871 and again in 1875. His defeat is not surprising given that most white men in Kentucky did not approve of the changes wrought upon the Constitution by the Civil War, and the state remained solidly Democratic for decades. Although Kentucky remained part of the Union during the Civil War, its legislature refused to ratify the Thirteenth Amendment. Some joked that Kentucky had waited until after the war to secede.

John M. Harlan might have languished as head of a minority party had it not been for his role at the Republican National Convention of 1876. When the Kentucky delegation which Harlan headed abandoned hope for electing one of its favorite sons, it swung its votes to Rutherford B. Hayes. Once elected, President Hayes did not forget Harlan's support. As a southern Republican, Harlan represented an appealing combination for a Supreme Court justice. Hayes inquired of a friend in 1877, "Confidentially, and on the whole, is not Harlan the man? Of the right age—able—of noble character—industrious—fine manners, temper and appearance. Who beats him?"[2]

John M. Harlan was deeply honored to be appointed to the court that he once called "the most elevated place on the earth." He served there until his death in 1911.[3] During his twenty-four years on the high court, he participated in more than 14,000 decisions, wrote more than 700 opinions for the Court, and dissented from some 200 decisions. Harlan began his judicial career with men like Justice Stephen J. Field, an Abraham Lincoln appointee, and he ended amidst the likes of Willis Van Devanter, who would oppose Franklin Roosevelt's New Deal. His long tenure spanned a vast range of legal issues, but two areas are especially important for understanding Harlan: civil rights and property rights.

Although the Court had interpreted the Fourteenth Amendment for the first time in the *Slaughter-House Case* in 1873 before Harlan's arrival, it was in the 1880s and 1890s that the justices determined just what rights were guaranteed to blacks. The Spanish-American War in 1898 brought new groups—Puerto Ricans and Filipinos—under the broadening umbrella of American jurisdiction. Civil rights and the status of the races was just one issue before the Court, because the Civil War had caused economic as well as constitutional change. Congress and the states tried to control the effects of the industrial revolution during the late nineteenth century through laws on labor conditions, monopolies, shipping rates, and the income tax. The Court's reaction to those laws earned it an unwarranted reputation as a laissez-faire bench keen on striking down all corporate regulation. In truth, the court's record, as well as Harlan's record as a justice, was mixed. Still, it was Harlan's vigorous dissents in favor of economic regulation, more than his equally passionate dissents in favor of civil rights, that during his lifetime earned him the title, of "the Great Dissenter."

When he died, obituaries dubbed Harlan "the people's judge" for his stand against monopolies. He had often praised "the plain people" for their essential role in a republic. He spoke feelingly of how the jurors at a trial went "back to their farms in the country with a recognition of the fact that they are part and parcel of the Government under which they live."[4] Harlan would have enjoyed being praised for protecting the integrity of their Constitution.

The Origins of "The People's Judge"

Although Harlan thought of himself as ordinary, he actually came from a privileged background. His mother, Eliza Shannon Davenport (1805–1870), was from a family of Kentucky farmers. His father was James Harlan (1800–1863), a successful lawyer who had served as a U.S. Congressman and a district attorney, as well as a Kentucky representative, secretary of state, and attorney general. James was wealthy enough to offer his son John the then-rare opportunity of higher education, first at Centre College and then at the law department at Transylvania University, both in Danville, Kentucky, near Lexington.

James was also wealthy enough to own slaves. They worked in the household and kitchen gardens, typical forms of slave labor in a state with very few large plantations. James Harlan was a conservative on racial issues, as shown by a letter he wrote during his 1851 campaign for attorney general. An ally asked James Harlan to deny the charge that he was an abolitionist and he wrote back, "He who applies it to me lies in his throat."[5] Like most white Americans, John's father saw abolitionism as a threat to the Union. Indeed, William Lloyd Garrison had appalled many Americans when he condemned the Constitution as "a covenant with death and an agreement with hell" because it bound the free North to the slave South. James Harlan may have supported gradual emancipation—as did his friend and ally Henry Clay, a leader in the Whig party—but neither he nor his jurist son seems to have been particularly eager to end slavery.

John M. Harlan followed his father into the Whig Party, but the party shattered largely along sectional lines under the weight of the slavery issue during the 1850s. He turned briefly to the Know-Nothing or American, Party. Its anti-immigrant position may have seemed like a way to unite native-born whites, no matter what their attitude toward slavery. But the issue could not be denied, as the opponents of slavery demanded action and its supporters grew increasingly afraid. Faced with four choices in the presidential election of 1860, Harlan supported John Bell of the Constitutional Union Party who came in third. Bell won Kentucky and two other border states, while northern Democrat Stephen A. Douglas won only Missouri, southern Democrat John C. Breckinridge swept the South, and Republican Abraham Lincoln won the northern states and the election. Although the national Republican platform supported the authority of each state to control its domestic institutions (read: slavery), it opposed the spread of slavery to the western territories. This was enough to make some southern whites fear that they had lost more than the election. Lincoln's election provoked calls from South Carolina for an immediate dissolution of the Union on the grounds that a sectional party had taken control of the government and would soon target slavery and states' rights. By February of 1861, eleven southern states seceded from the Union and formed the Confederate States of America. In March of that year, Harlan advised Lincoln's secretary of war to remove federal troops from Fort Sumter and Fort Pickens or risk losing Kentucky to secessionist sentiment. He explained that "no earthly power will prevent the people" of the border states "from sympathizing and to a great extent taking part with 'their brethren of the South' against what is called an 'abolition' administration."[6] But Lincoln decided to provision Fort Sumter, and South Carolina's military forces responded by attacking in April. The Civil

War had begun. Kentucky's governor declared his state "neutral," but Union men gained power after Confederate forces invaded the state in August and were then forced to retreat. By September, Harlan had raised his own Union regiment of more than 800 infantrymen, and he led it for a year and a half.

Although Harlan's resignation from the army in 1863 coincided with Lincoln's Emancipation Proclamation, financial rather than political considerations prompted his return to civilian life and the family law office. Still, like many white Kentuckians, Harlan was furious that a war for the preservation of the Union had turned into a war for emancipation. He was still a part of the Conservative Union party and he made clear his opposition to emancipation. In June 1865, he declared that the Thirteenth Amendment "will destroy the peace and security of the white man in Kentucky." Immediate emancipation would be "a violent change in our social system" with "ruinous effects."[7] The next month, he opposed ratification of the Thirteenth Amendment as "a flagrant violation of the right of self-government."[8] Congress declared the amendment ratified in December of that year. "Neither slavery nor involuntary servitude, except as a punishment for crime" existed any longer as a legal institution in the United States.

In 1866 the Kentucky legislature rejected the Fourteenth Amendment, which declared that "all persons born or naturalized in the United States, and subject to the jurisdiction thereof, are citizens of the United States and of the State wherein they reside." The amendment further declared, "No State shall make or enforce any law which shall abridge the privileges and immunities of citizens of the United States, nor shall any State deprive any person of life, liberty, or property, without due process of law; nor deny to any person within its jurisdiction the equal protection of the law." The Fourteenth Amendment also contained provisions decreasing a state's representation in Congress in proportion to its refusal to enfranchise all men over twenty-one. (The Fifteenth Amendment, proposed in 1869 and ratified in 1870, would prohibit racial discrimination in voting entirely.)

Harlan complained in 1866 that if the radical Republicans had their way, they would "work a complete revolution in our Republican system of Government, and most probably the overthrow of constitutional Liberty."[9] The idea of former Confederates being disenfranchised while former slaves had the vote appalled him. As Kentucky's attorney general, Harlan prosecuted a Union general in 1866 for giving slaves passes to travel north to free states and for recruiting enslaved men into the army in order to automatically free them and their families. You may well be wondering how this man came to rejoice at the end of slavery by 1871 and how he then later voiced some of the most memorable words from the bench in defense of civil rights for blacks.

The answer lies in the interplay between his family's traditions and the ugly underbelly of political life in Kentucky in the late 1860s and 1870s, when roaming gangs of white men, encouraged by the Democratic Party, terrorized freed blacks and white Union supporters. So-called "Regulators," some of them former Confederate guerrillas, murdered, robbed, and assaulted those of whom they disapproved. Blacks from Frankfort, the state capital, petitioned Congress for help and described sixty-four attacks between 1867 and 1869. Some 30,000 blacks decided to flee Kentucky.[10]

If the situation had grown impossible for many black Kentuckians, it had also become intolerable to John M. Harlan. He was faced with a political choice, as the Democratic and Republican Parties became the only viable options. The Democrats upheld white supremacy and states' rights with violence. The Republicans stood for legal equality of the races and national power. As a Whig and the namesake of Justice John Marshall, Harlan had preferred an expansive view of national power under the Constitution. But as a slave owner, he had relied upon white supremacy to support his legal rights.

He had also apparently learned something from his father: his duty not to abuse the power that the law conferred. Although it was surely a simplified and blinkered view of the past, the Harlans remembered slavery as a benign and even affectionate institution as practiced in their household. They would retell well into the twentieth century a story about James Harlan that they believed summed up his righteousness as a slaveholder. It seems that one Sunday morning, James and John M. Harlan encountered a slave trader driving his human property down the streets of Frankfort. "His badge of office was a long snake-like whip made of black leather, every blow from which drew blood." Appalled at the man's business and brutality, James Harlan cursed the slave trader: "*You are a damned scoundrel. Good morning, sir.*" He did nothing more than that, but John's wife of fifty-five years, Malvina Shanklin Harlan, wrote of James in her memoirs in 1915, "Like some Old Testament prophet he seemed to be calling down Heaven's maledictions upon the whole institution of slavery."[11] John M. Harlan was supposed to never have forgotten the lesson he learned that morning: that honorable men did not engage in brutality. Other less benign racial lessons were also taught him, since the family conveniently forgot that James himself had bought and sold slaves and that one of his mixed-race slaves was rumored to be his son. But John M. Harlan chose to remember the lesson of paternalism above all. So when white supremacy became possible only through lawbreaking and violence against the powerless, Harlan turned to the Republican Party and abandoned his commitment to white supremacy. The party's support for a nationalist vision of the Constitution and for (the new) law and order made it easier for Harlan to embrace a radically new vision of racial equality.

On the Court

When Harlan rejoiced in the end of slavery before that crowd in Livermore, Kentucky in 1871, he admitted that he had once opposed freedom and citizenship for blacks. He acknowledged his checkered political past and answered his detractors with this: "Let it be said that I am right rather than consistent." This was an inadequate defense when President Hayes nominated Harlan to the Court. Some senators questioned whether his conversion to Republicanism was sincere. Harlan's advocates offered reports of his speeches from 1871 to 1875 to prove that he supported emancipation and black citizenship and condemned white terrorism. Harlan had also worked for the federal government in 1874 prosecuting white men accused of preventing black men from voting. In a letter to a friend from 1874, Harlan lamented that the rise of the Democratic Party "would make the condition of the Union men and the negroes of the South as intolerable as that of the children of Israel during their bondage in Egypt."[12] Northern Republicans had nothing to fear from this former slaveholder. Harlan would prove a staunch defender of the amended Constitution. His declaration in dissent from *Plessy v. Ferguson* in 1896 that "our Constitution is color-blind" would be hailed in the twentieth century as the words of a prophet of civil rights.

　　Harlan's jurisprudence is testimony to the clarity of his historical vision of the United States and its Constitution. Although he always expressed support for the structure of dual federalism, Harlan's first concern was preserving the power of the national government. The Civil War had proven to him how dangerous local feeling could become. He told an audience celebrating the opening of a new law building at the University of Pennsylvania in 1900 that Americans should never forget "that our all, and perhaps the hopes of freemen everywhere, depend upon the recognition of the right of the national government to exercise the powers belonging to it under the Constitution."[13] Harlan made sense out of the chaos of the Civil War and his own past by identifying the war as part of a divine plan whereby the country finally made good on the Declaration of Independence's self-evident belief that all men are created equal and endowed with certain inalienable rights. Harlan explained, "I believe that a destiny awaits America such as has never been vouchsafed to any people, and that in the working out of that destiny, under the leadings of Providence, humanity everywhere will be lifted up, and power and tyranny compelled to recognize the fact that 'God is no respecter of persons," and that "He hath made of one blood all nations of men."[14] These two passages from the Bible had been favorites of the abolitionists. Harlan had taken the constitutional tradition of legal nationalism supported by the Whigs and grafted onto it the branch of abolitionist thought much as early Republicans like Abraham Lincoln and Samuel P. Chase had done before the Civil War. As God had given the United States a mission,

Harlan felt he had a duty to see it accomplished, and much of the emotional power of his famous dissents expressed his devotion to that duty.

Views of Civil Rights

Harlan's first important dissent on black civil rights involved five separate suits brought against the owners of public accommodations—inns, theaters, and a railroad—for excluding or segregating blacks in violation of the Civil Rights Act of 1875. The Court declared that Congress had no power to pass the act. The Thirteenth Amendment prohibited slavery, not social segregation, the Court reasoned, and the Fourteenth Amendment targeted only state action and not the behavior of private citizens. Harlan had trouble writing his dissent from the *Civil Rights Cases,* according to his wife, who recalled in her memoirs that he was then the youngest member of the Court, "and standing alone, as he did in regard to a decision which the whole country was anxiously awaiting, he felt that, on a question of such far-reaching importance, he must speak, not only forcibly but wisely."[15] She decided to remind him of what the Civil War amendments had been meant to accomplish by placing on his desk a relic from antebellum days: the inkstand of Chief Justice Roger B. Taney, the man who had written in the *Dred Scott* decision of 1857 that blacks were not citizens from political equality, or a co-mingling of the two races upon terms unsatisfactory to either."[19] Brown argued that forced social mixing would violate "racial instincts," yet he insisted that no insult was intended by racial segregation (551). Still, the insult to blacks was obvious when he concluded that "if one race be inferior to the other socially, the Constitution of United States cannot put them upon the same plane" (552).

In his dissent, Harlan scolded the Court for invoking social equality in order to allow the states to deprive blacks of their civil rights. Social rights had nothing to do with the issue at hand, "for social equality no more exists between two races when traveling in a passenger coach or a public highway than when members of the same races sit by each other in a street car or in the jury box, or stand or sit with each other in a public assembly, or when they use in common the streets of a city or town."[20] Harlan had unwittingly described some of the forms of racial segregation that southern whites would actually enforce. But in his eyes, such practices were impossible because the inferiority that they imposed on blacks was contrary to the country's fundamental law. He wrote, "Our Constitution is color-blind, and neither knows nor tolerates classes among citizens. In respect of civil rights, all citizens are equal before the law. The humblest is the peer of the most powerful" (559). To allow segregation or other discriminatory laws to stand would be "to place in a condition of legal inferiority a large body of American citizens, now constituting a part of the political community called the People of the United States, for whom, and by whom through representatives, our government is administered" (563–564).

If Harlan's dissent from *Plessy* inspired many Americans who battled for civil equality, it also betrayed the persistence of his belief in racial identity that dated back to the prewar days. Paternalism not only required the slave owner to refrain from the abuse of power, it also assumed racial differences in order to justify the hierarchy that gave white men power in the first place. Harlan retained to some degree this belief in racial identity. For example, he did not reject the idea of social rights in *Plessy;* he simply called them irrelevant. Harlan acknowledged that "every true man has pride of race, and under appropriate circumstances when the rights of others, his equals before the law, are not to be affected, it is his privilege to express such pride and to take such action based upon it as to him seems proper."[21] Yet racial pride was relevant to the reasoning of Harlan's dissent. Just before he declared that the Constitution was colorblind, Harlan appealed to white racial pride: "The white race deems itself to be the dominant race in this country. And so it is, in prestige, in achievements, in education, in wealth and in power. So, I doubt not, it will continue to be for all time, if it remains true to its great heritage and holds fast to the principles of constitutional liberty."[22] If whites had any claim to superiority, it was that they obeyed their Constitution, which denied them civil superiority over blacks.

Harlan's persistent belief in racial identity may explain his complaint in *Plessy* that Chinese aliens could now ride alongside whites in Louisiana railroad cars while black Union veterans could not, and his dissent from *United States v. Wong Kim Ark* in 1898 when he refused to concede that the Fourteenth Amendment's citizenship clause applied to a Chinese-American. It may also explain his acquiescence in *Pace v. Alabama* in 1882 when the Court approved a law punishing interracial adultery more severely than same-race adultery, and his refusal to address the issue of segregation in public schools in *Cumming v. Richmond Board of Education* (1899) or *Berea College v. Kentucky* (1908). Because he continued to believe in racial identity, Harlan may have been uncomfortable with any social practices that might tend to offer opportunities for interracial intimacy and marriage. As a result, he did not always follow his own color-blind rule.

Yet even Harlan's appeal to white racial pride in *Plessy* acknowledged that behavior was more important than color. Whites had to remain true to their great heritage and hold fast to the principles of constitutional liberty if they were to remain dominant in prestige, achievements, education, wealth, and power. It was not enough to merely be white. Harlan attacked essentialist racial reasoning when Justice Brown argued in the Insular Cases in 1901 that the Court did not need to apply the Bill of Rights to the inhabitants of Puerto Rico because the administration could be trusted not to abuse them. Brown explained, "There are certain principles of natural justice inherent in the Anglo-

Saxon character which need no expression in constitutions or statutes to give them effect."[23] Harlan responded in his dissent that "the patriotic people who adopted [the Constitution], were unwilling to depend for their safety upon... 'certain principles of natural justice inherent in Anglo-Saxon character....'" The founding generation well remembered "that Anglo-Saxons across the ocean had attempted, in defiance of law and justice, to trample upon the rights of Anglo-Saxons on this continent" (381). Similarly, Harlan rejected an essentialist definition of race when he dissented from *Elk v. Wilkins* (1884) and insisted that an assimilated, taxpaying Indian had "become a part of the people of the United States" included in the Constitution's preamble, (112 US 94, 121 [1884]). If Elk acted like a citizen, then his race could not disqualify him from citizenship. But Harlan's dissents expressed what was only a minority opinion. White supremacy was supported by law, custom, and white public opinion.

View of Property Rights

Harlan had more success in arguing for the use of governmental power to regulate the economy, but still delivered several notable dissents. Here, too, he interpreted the Constitution in light of his understanding of the meaning of the Civil War. The Republican Party had inherited the Whig party's interest in promoting economic growth through national policies and had passed the Homestead Act of 1862, which opened the western territories to settlement, and the Pacific Railroad Act of 1862, which authorized a transcontinental railroad. Harlan saw the creation of a national economy as a way to bind together the different regions of the country. He supported a broad interpretation of Congress's power to regulate interstate commerce thus preventing the states from discriminating against each other's products. But the giant corporations that grew in this national marketplace frightened Harlan as well as many other Americans.

Although economists argued then—and still do that certain industries give rise to monopoly naturally, Harlan suspected that business tycoons amassed such great fortunes and economic power through shady means. He once remarked, "Half of the men in Wall Street should be in State's prison."[24] Muckraking journalists offered plenty of proof that businessmen bribed state legislators and rigged markets in the Gilded Age. Henry Demarest Lloyd investigated the Standard Oil Company in the 1880s and quipped that John D. Rockefeller had done everything to the Pennsylvania legislature except refine it. Agreeing that corporations had gotten too powerful, Congress passed the Sherman Antitrust Act of 1890, which prohibited business agreements that restrained trade. But when the federal government brought a suit against the American Sugar Refining Company, which was trying to buy enough companies to bring its share of the national market to 98 percent, the Court declared that the Sherman Act did not apply to manufacturing, but only to interstate commerce. Harlan protested that the individual states could not possibly control the rapacity of such an industrial giant. He asked rhetorically, "What power is competent to protect the people of the United States against such dangers except a national power?"[25]

By 1904, he had the satisfaction of delivering the Court's opinion in *Northern Securities Company v. United States,* which defined the exchange of stocks as commerce and thus subject to regulation by Congress. The public responded enthusiastically to the government's move against two great tycoons—J.P. Morgan and James J. Hill—for trying to combine their competing railroads. Experience showed that when a single firm monopolized the traffic for a town, rates went up. Malvina S. Harlan created a scrapbook to collect the laudatory letters that her husband received in response to this decision.

But the last antimonopoly decisions of Harlan's career, the *Great Trust Cases* of May, 1911, left him angry with the Court majority and worried over his country's future. The cases involved the prosecution of two enormous corporations, Standard Oil and American Tobacco, for antitrust violations. Chief Justice Edward D. White declared for the Court that the companies' business practices were indeed suspect and ordered them broken up. Harlan concurred and dissented in part. He approved of the results of the decisions, but he suspected that White's declaration that the companies had *unreasonably* restrained trade indicated that the majority intended to take upon itself the power to approve or disapprove of restraints of trade as it saw fit. The Sherman Act outlawed *all* restraints of trade, Harlan explained angrily, and he suggested that his fellow judges had decided to practice "judicial legislation, by inserting in the act the word 'unreasonable'" because they did not approve of this blanket rule.[26] According to Harlan, the Court's "rule of reason" left the country under the threat of "the slavery that would result from aggregations of capital in the hands of a few individuals and corporations controlling, for their own profit and advantage exclusively, the entire business of the country, including the production and sale of the necessaries of life."[27]

Several of Harlan's fellow justices were appalled at his opinions and called them bitter and demagogic, but many Americans greeted his words with praise. Harlan's youngest son, John Maynard Harlan, a lawyer, wrote from Chicago, "Many people from all walks of life have spoken to me about it, uniformly in praise of your position.... Many of those who have spoken to me have been lawyers, some of whom I haven't passed a word with in years, but they have spoken to me when they would have liked to speak to you yourself."[28] When Justice Harlan died on October 14 of that year, he was remembered for these attempts to protect the people from their would-be economic masters.

Harlan wrote many opinions for the Court even though he is remembered for his dissents. When he drew up a list of his opinions to be published, the largest category was majority opinions that upheld the police power of the states to protect the health, safety, and morals of their populations. Harlan and his brethren generally approved of such regulations despite several infamous decisions, such as *Lochner v. New York* (1905), where the Court struck down regulations designed to protect workers. Harlan dissented yet again in *Lochner* and in several decisions where he tried to apply all of the protections found in the Bill of Rights to those prosecuted by the states. Although Harlan was often part of a working majority that set up the rules for much of the functioning of the national marketplace and cities, he stood alone often enough for his fellow judges to make bad jokes about how he suffered from "dissentary." But many of the doctrines that Harlan championed in dissent were eventually adopted by the Supreme Court in the mid-twentieth century. Indeed, Harlan is called a great judge today because of the judicial revolution accomplished during the tenure of Chief Justice Earl Warren from 1953 to 1969.

Conclusion

Shakespeare wrote that some men are born great, some achieve greatness, and some have greatness thrust upon them. During Harlan's lifetime, he was called the Great Dissenter because of antitrust cases. Harlan's biographical entry in the 1953 edition of the *Encyclopedia of American History* dwells on his economic opinions. The *Insular Cases* were the only dissent mentioned concerning civil rights. Harlan's dissents favoring civil rights for blacks and applying the Bill of Rights to the states were ignored. In fact, such positions were considered eccentric by early scholars.

Then, in 1954, the Warren Court handed down *Brown v. Board of Education,* which overturned *Plessy* by declaring that segregated public schools were inherently unequal. Suddenly, Harlan became the center of scholarly attention. An authorized biographer was named and a flurry of articles were published. Harlan appeared on a list of great judges in 1958 on the strength of his dissents on civil rights. He has appeared on such lists ever since. Harlan became great for the very dissents that had made him an oddity in earlier decades.

Did Harlan have greatness thrust upon him by later generations? Obviously, as more whites came to condemn racial prejudice, Harlan's efforts to protect blacks in the exercise of their civil rights came to be admired. These dissents had long been admired by blacks. When he died in 1911, the Metropolitan African Methodist Episcopal Church in Washington, DC, held a memorial service for him. The program for the service displayed a photograph of Harlan with the caption "A True Friend of the People." The music began with Beethoven's "Upon the Death of a Hero."

More recently, historians have criticized Harlan for his failure to come out against segregated schools in *Cumming v. Richmond Board of Education.* As Asian-American history has gained attention, other scholars have noticed and disapproved of his remarks about the Chinese in his *Plessy* dissent. They have decided that he was a not-so-great justice. Clearly, the criteria for judicial greatness has changed over time, but few scholars seem conscious of it. My concern is that the effort to measure judges for greatness has hampered our understanding of the complicated biographical reasons for their judicial records. Paternalism is not an obvious source of support for racial equality, yet Harlan used it. By pursuing the question of greatness, scholars have sometimes ignored evidence that did not fit into the current definition of what makes a great judge. We may have confidence that our generation has finally grasped the true definition, yet the next generation may sneer at us and be equally smug over its definition. I tell Harlan's story not to argue for his greatness, but to show the importance of the choices made by individuals to the life of the Republic. As Harlan would put it, his story shows us that we are part and parcel of the government under which we live.

NOTES

1.   Quoted in editorial, "General Harlan's Republicanism," *Louisville Daily Commercial,* Nov. 1, 1877, typed copy, John Marshall Harlan Papers, Library of Congress, Manuscript Division, Washington, D.C. Abbreviated as JMH Papers and LC.
2.   Rutherford B. Hayes to William Henry Smith, Dec. 29, 1877, quoted in John Maynard Harlan to John Marshall Harlan, February 3, 1910, in the possession of Eve Dillingham.
3.   John Marshall Harlan to Melville Westin Fuller, May 3, 1888, Melville Westin Fuller Papers, LC.
4.   John Marshall Harlan, Constitutional Law Lectures, 1897–98, April 30, 1898, JMH Papers, LC.
5.   James Harlan to D. Howard Smith, Aug. 5, 1851, JMH Papers, LC.
6.   John Marshall Harlan to Joseph Holt, March 11, 1861, Joseph Holt Papers, LC.
7.   Quoted in Louis Hartz, AJohn M. Harlan in Kentucky, 1855–1877: The Story of His Pre-Court Political Career," *Filson Club Historical Quarterly* 14 (1940): 17–40. Hereafter referred to as Hartz.
8.   Quoted in E. Merton Coulter, *The Civil War and Readjustment in Kentucky,* (Gloucester, MA: Peter Smith, 1926, 1966), 270.
9.   Quoted in Hartz, 31. See note 7.
10. W.A. Lowe, "The Freedman's Bureau in the Border States," in Richard O. Curry (ed.), *Radicalism, Racism, and Party Realignment: The Border States during Reconstruction,* (Baltimore: Johns Hopkins University Press, 1969), 245–264.
11. Malvina Shanklin Harlan, "Some Memories of a Long Life, 1854–1911," 1915, microfilm, frame 119–120, JMH Papers, LC. Emphasis in the original. These memoirs are published in the *Journal of Supreme Court History* 26 (April 2001) with preface by Justice Ruth Bader Ginsburg and an introduction by Linda Przybyszewski.
12. John Marshall Harlan to Benjamin H. Bristow, Aug. 10, 1874, Benjamin H. Bristow Papers, LC.

13. John Marshall Harlan, "James Wilson and the Formation of the Constitution," *American Law Review* 34 (July-August 1900): 481–504.
14. Ibid., 503. Quotations are from Acts 10:34, 17:24.
15. Malvina Shanklin Harlan, ASome Memories of a Long Life, 1854–1911," 1915, microfilm, frame 188, JMH Papers, LC.
16. *Dred Scott v. Sanford,* 19 Howard 393, 407 (1857).
17. *Civil Rights Cases,* 109 US 3, 34 (1883).
18. *Civil Rights Cases,* 109 US 3, 62 (1883).
19. *Plessy v. Ferguson,* 163 US 537, 544 (1896).
20. *Plessy,* 561. When Harlan was still a Republican politician, he denounced attempts to practice so-called social equality.
21. *Plessy,* 554.
22. *Plessy,* 559.
23. *Downes v. Bidwell,* 182 US 244, 280 (1901).
24. Quoted in Linda Przybyszewski, *The Republic According to John Marshall Harlan* (Chapel Hill: University of North Carolina Press, 1999), 147.
25. *United States v. E.C. Knight Company,* 156 US 43, 45 (1895). E.E. Knight was one of the companies that American Sugar wanted to buy.
26. *Standard Oil v. US,* 221 US 1, 90 (1911).
27. *Standard Oil,* 83.
28. John Maynard Harlan to John Marshall Harlan, May 19, 1911, John Marshall Harlan Papers, University of Louisville School of Law, Law Library, Louisville, Kentucky.

FOR FURTHER READING

Chin, Gabriel J. "The Plessy Myth: Justice Harlan on the Chinese Cases," *Iowa Law Review* 82 (October 1996): 151–182.
Gordon, James W. Did the First Justice Harlan Have a Black Brother?," *Western New England* Law Review 15 (1993): 159–238.
Hartz, Louis. "John Marshall Harlan in Kentucky, 1855–1977: The Story of His Pre-Court Political Career," *Filson Club Historical Quarterly* 14 (January 1940): 17–40.
Kousser, J. Morgan, "Separate But Not Equal: The Supreme Court's First Decision on Racial Discrimination in Schools," *Journal of Southern History* 46 (1980): 17–44.
Maltz, Eric. "Only Partially Color-Blind: John Marshall Harlan's View of Race and the Constitution," *Georgia State Law Review* 12 (1996): 973–1016.
Przybyszewski, Linda. *The Republic According to John Marshall Harlan.* Chapel Hill: University of North Carolina Press,1999.
Westin, Alan F. "John Marshall Harlan and the Constitutional Rights of Negroes: The Transformation of a Southerner," *Yale Law Journal* 66 (April 1957): 637–710.

CHAPTER SIX

Oliver Wendell Holmes: The Evolution of a Great Justice

James Chowning Davies

Shakespeare wrote that some men are born to greatness, some achieve it, and some have it thrust upon them. This essay will try to show that Holmes, commonly acknowledged to be one of the greatest judges ever on the Supreme Court, was born to, achieved, and had greatness thrust upon him. Rather than try to rank him with John Marshall, Joseph Story, Roger Taney, Louis Brandeis, and Charles Evans Hughes, I will attend more to the background that produced this great jurist and note rather briefly what is very often the only aspect of a judge's life that is analyzed: his opinions. Holmes sometimes spoke for the entire court, sometimes for himself and one or two other justices, and sometimes he dissented alone. I will discuss the background that helps to explain the coherence of his judicial views; their surface inconsistency can be partially explained by their consistency with his fundamental orientation.

His Heritage and Family

The jurist's grandfather, Yale-educated Abiel Holmes, was chosen to head the prestigious First Church in Cambridge. The young, independent-minded, courageous Congregationalist minister was very well received—until the church elders booted him. In the Cambridge-Harvard community, Abiel Holmes was not liberal enough. They judged him to be inadequately receptive to non-Trinitarian—that is, to Unitarian—theology. Rather than recant his only somewhat strict Yale Calvinism, Abiel moved to a more orthodox Congregational church.

   The jurist's father, Oliver Wendell Holmes, Senior, was born in 1809 and started college at Harvard in 1825, at age sixteen. After graduation he decided on law as a profession but tired of it within a few months. He changed to medicine and studied in Paris, with the personal and financial support of his parents. This naturally very gifted person quickly became a protégé of a brilliant pioneer. After two years he returned to Boston to start his medical practice. He made a major contribution to American medicine in a journal article on childbirth fever. In 1846 he started teaching at the Harvard Medical School.

A very competent physician but not a profound philosopher (like his contemporary Ralph Waldo Emerson), he had a remarkable ability to write, with zest and wit. Holmes, Senior, who had been the official poet of his senior class at Harvard, continued to write and speak, and these activities gradually crowded out medical teaching and practice. In 1857 he helped to found *The Atlantic Monthly*. The aristocratic physician-writer, with son Wendell about to enter Harvard, almost immediately gained fame for his clear and pungent writing.

The Senior Holmes household and a downtown club became gathering places for many of the distinguished intellectuals of the time. Most guests, while not quite into politics, were highly moralist: Emerson, Longfellow, James Russell Lowell, and Harriet Beecher Stowe. Emerson, Stowe, and Wendell Phillips (Holmes's cousin) were staunch abolitionists. Mrs. Stowe was the very moral wife of a preacher named Calvin E. Stowe. Her intense indictment of slavery in the novel *Uncle Tom's Cabin* (1852) acutely raised the consciousness and conscience of people by presenting slaves as human beings.

Also among the household visitors was Charles Sumner. He had been a classmate of Holmes, Senior at Harvard and was both moral and very political. He was passionate as a senator in Washington in his opposition to slavery. For that reason, a southern Congressman honorably and savagely caned him on the Senate floor in 1856. Less noted but perhaps more noteworthy is the fact that the senator strengthened Mary Todd Lincoln's opposition to slavery. In turn, she strengthened her husband's opposition in 1862, the year before Lincoln proclaimed the emancipation of slaves.

Another close Holmes family friend was Benjamin Curtis, who became a justice on the Supreme Court. In 1857, Chief Justice Taney and the Court denied citizenship to Dred Scott, a slave, on grounds that moving from a slave to a free state was not reason enough for his emancipation; with this decision, they hoped that they had put to rest the slavery issue. Curtis wrote a dissent.

The young Wendell was casually and regularly meeting some of the nationally most influential citizens of his time, in self-satisfied, provincial Boston.

The father-son relationship was rather normal: not compliant or indulgent on either side, but ambivalent. Holmes, Junior was more influenced by and bonded to his famous father than he wanted to admit; Senior was perhaps less bonded to his son than he professed to be. The gifted, very energetic Senior did not look distinguished. And he was unusually short; in school he had been razzed for his size. The also gifted but not yet famous Junior was unusually tall—more than a head taller than his father—and very distinguished looking. Their ineluctable physical contrasts perhaps only aggravated their competitiveness for distinction.

Senior told Junior that law was not a great profession—so he could not achieve greatness as a lawyer—but he also opposed his son going into medicine. Wendell much later said his father pushed him into law. It is interesting to speculate whether Senior wanted Junior to go into a profession where he could not be great. If Wendell did not become great, then it would be the short son of Abiel Holmes, and not Abiel's tall grandson, who became a lauded war veteran, who could claim the greatest family distinction. Always self-centered, the most gifted son of Abiel may have hoped that the topmost Holmes family accomplishment would rest with the two-profession literary doctor, the Samuel Johnson or Will Rogers or Garrison Keillor of his time.

Endowed with his father's high intelligence and energy, Oliver Wendell Holmes, Junior also entered Harvard at the age of sixteen (in 1857) and was uncertain about what he wanted to do, just as his father had been. He began college just as his father's literary career was boldly blossoming—perhaps a blow to a young man who also had a way with words but wanted his own recognition. Though his family thought that cousin Wendell Phillips was too extreme a person and abolitionism was too extreme a cause, the tall Harvard senior was appalled by the institution of slavery. In 1861, before his graduation, he volunteered for duty in what was then expected to be a short, cousinly encounter but exploded into the most savage war in America's short history. And, like tens of thousands of his contemporaries, most of them not from Boston, Oliver Wendell Holmes, Jr. very bravely shouldered the burden of ending slavery and perpetuating the Union.

The Civil War

In October 1861—within months of enlisting—Holmes, Junior became immersed in armed conflict, at Ball's Bluff in Virginia near Maryland. It was an early and rather indecisive battle, but it was very notably portentous for its carnage. Half of the 1,700 men in his regiment were killed, wounded, or captured; for Holmes, it was particularly notable. A bullet entered his chest on the left side and came to rest just beneath the skin on the right side. The bullet was rather easily extracted but, like the one that felled Ronald Reagan in 1981, came close to changing history. He was furloughed home, where he spent several months recuperating.

In September, 1862 he was in battle again, about ten miles north of Harper's Ferry, West Virginia. This engagement, Antietam, was very notable; this time Holmes got a bullet through the neck. For the rest of his life he kept the two bullets that wounded him. After the battle, he was unsteadily walking through a nearby town when a young boy offered him lodging, and Holmes, Junior accepted. In a somewhat frantic search, Holmes, Senior left his busy Cambridge life to rescue the young hero. The famed writer recounted the story of his "Hunt after the Captain" for *The Atlantic Monthly,* perhaps suggesting to his readers that the caring father was suffering more than the little-known son.

The following spring, in May, 1863, Holmes was again in battle and was again wounded—in the heel. The metal was successfully removed, thereby removing the threat of amputation, commonly used in the nineteenth century as a crude means of avoiding infection. Two months later, one his first cousins was killed at Gettysburg. To my knowledge Holmes did not cite these events as reasons, but he decided he had had enough war. He wrote home that he planned to end his service when the current campaign was over. His father interpreted the letter to mean that he was quitting immediately. Holmes angrily wrote home to say that he planned to quit when his voluntary term of enlistment was over in the fall.

Even in such superficial detail as related above, we can perhaps understand the deep and lasting effect the war had on young Holmes, who was twenty-three when he left military service. He had shown enormous courage but was not foolhardy. On one occasion, in July 1864, when he was on a general's staff at a place where the city of Washington was close to being put under siege, Lincoln visited the front line of battle. One story, possibly legendary but apocryphal, is that Holmes said to the president: "Get down, you damn fool, before you get shot." Neither tall man was shot on that occasion, but the president was shot less than a year later, in a peaceful place where his height did not matter.

Holmes never abandoned his belief that the war was necessary, both to keep the Union intact and to end slavery, and he firmly concluded that the most elemental, at times the only, motivation for human behavior was survival. He was impressed by the random nature of casualties. Bullets and shrapnel were egalitarian: they did not single out victims on the basis of their family or military distinction. The intensity of his battle experience deeply and permanently affected Holmes, more deeply than the legal principles and cases that he learned in law school. Two elemental parts of his belief system—survival and democracy—were thus early and firmly established. They preceded his entry into law and remained basic to his orientation toward law for the rest of his life.

Holmes entered Harvard Law School when he left the army in the fall of 1864. His father, meanwhile, was becoming internationally famous, and went to Europe. In England, many men of great distinction welcomed him; he got lauded and degreed at Cambridge, Oxford, and Edinburgh. Before finishing law school, Junior followed Senior to Europe, and used the letter of introduction Senior gave him to visit with John Stuart Mill. He also established contact with several distinguished legal scholars, including Frederick Pollock and Frederick Maitland, and he met Lord Bryce and Joseph Chamberlain. It was all an easy extension of the distinguished company he had known before college.

The Law: Teaching, Writing, and Judging It

Holmes whizzed through law school and was admitted to the bar in 1867. He joined a firm, became attached to a warm father figure, George Shattuck, worked very hard, and advanced speedily. Three years later he was teaching constitutional law in Harvard College, and, a year after that, in its law school until 1882.

In 1872 he married Fanny Dixwell, and both before and after marriage he put first things first: his career. Like his father, she was short. Her father ran the private school that Holmes attended before college and before the war, so he had more than a decade to get to know her, and to appreciate her. She was also the object of attention of William James—as great a psychologist as Holmes was a jurist.

Like his parents' marriage, Junior's and Fanny's was an excellent Victorian one. It is evident that both Holmes and his father, and their respective wives, dutifully and happily accepted the model of wives who concentrated on their husbands' careers. Ambitious, high-energy husbands then enjoyed dutiful household companions who were dedicated to their husbands and accepted their husbands' priorities.[1] This career preoccupation was evident in the autobiographical sketch that Holmes wrote before the war, when he was a college senior: it did not mention his mother. His confidence in his mother's devotion was evident in letters he wrote home to her while he was away at war.

Excellent Victorian marriages would not be excellent a century later, but Fanny, four months older than her husband, remained devoted to him for the fifty-seven years they were married. Their solid, childless marriage was not without problems, including those related to a brilliant and exciting woman whom Holmes met and visited several times in England. Holmes's friend in England fulfilled some, but not necessarily all, the functions of an intellectually gifted mistress, a hetaira. Despite her weak eyes, Fanny would read to her husband when he came home exhausted from a day in court, and she lived until 1929, when she was eighty-eight.

Holmes's first independent intellectual acts were to edit Kent's *Commentaries on American Law* and a law journal. He then became intensely occupied with composing his passport to fame, *The Common Law*. It first appeared in the form of lectures in 1880–1881 and then as a book published shortly before his fortieth birthday in 1881. A year later he was appointed to the highest court of Massachusetts and served there for twenty years, the last three as chief justice.

He had found his place, where he could do what he most wanted: influence the development of law, following the British tradition of moving forward from precedent—actual litigated cases[2]—rather than outward from elemental principles expressed in a written code, which the Constitution became for many judges. Holmes's career progress was not supersonic, but it was steadily speedy. Being the son of a famous writer did not hinder his advancement, but he was determined to exceed his father's renown. He was once asked if he was the son of the famous writer, Oliver Wendell Holmes. The son replied that Senior was the father of the jurist.

Not quite twenty years after being appointed to the highest Massachusetts court, its chief justice welcomed a greater opportunity, to effect more than the development of both common and constitutional law in Massachusetts. With the intervention of Henry Cabot Lodge, another Brahmin and fellow Harvard man, Theodore Roosevelt—himself a Phi Beta Kappa graduate of Harvard—nominated Holmes in August 1902 to the United States Supreme Court. The Senate confirmed his nomination in December.

Holmes could no longer qualify as a young genius, but he enthusiastically set himself to his big challenge. He was close to sixty-one years old and proceeded to confirm at that age what *The Common Law* portended two decades earlier: he would influence the growth of law in the United States. I believe he succeeded, but more by what he usually refused to do—superimpose his preferences in lawmaking over those of elected lawmakers—than by his pronouncement of affirmative principles. His elemental posture—scoffing at certainty and rectitude—was a more significant contribution than the substance of his pronouncements. Most of the time.

What greatness is has never been precisely defined, not even by Shakespeare. Babe Ruth is considered by many to be the greatest baseball player ever. Was Henry Aaron greater? Was Mozart a greater composer than Beethoven? Holmes's record as a jurist is indeed awesome, admirable, and easily qualifies him as great. But it is perhaps better to leave open whether he ranks only after Marshall and above Joseph Story, Roger Taney, Louis Brandeis, and William Douglas; and it is premature to finally rank more recent great chief justices like Hughes and Earl Warren. In any case, it's too early to say that we don't get justices like we used to, or to say that recent chief justices like Harlan Fiske Stone and William Rehnquist need not be assessed. Holmes indeed deserved the greatness that he sought and that was easier for a Brahmin to attain, but he was nevertheless a mortal, with personal and professional flaws that were fateful but no more fatal than the three bullets that entered his body during the Civil War.

Some Cases in Which His Opinion Mattered

To assess Holmes's contribution, we need to look at several cases in which he was very critically involved. Perhaps the first was the *Northern Securities* case (1904), involving the issue of whether the effort of a small, powerful group of entrepreneurs to consolidate three major railroads was to be permitted. Liberals and President Roosevelt expected Holmes to side with those who wanted to bust the Northern Securities trust. Holmes wrote his first dissent, in which three of his fellow judges joined, depreciating the strenuous effort of Theodore Roosevelt to give teeth to the 1890 Sherman Antitrust Act. Holmes reasoned that bigness and indeed combinations in restraint of trade were not necessarily evil or even counterproductive. Theodore Roosevelt exploded, saying that he could have carved a justice with more backbone out of a banana.

Holmes went on the Court at a time when both Congress and state legislatures were beginning to establish limits to free enterprise. Responding to popular demand, legislatures were generating laws that directly or indirectly said entrepreneurs did not have a God-given right to get rich, regardless of what resources and what people they exploited. Holmes's dissent in the Northern Securities case not only infuriated Theodore Roosevelt; it also led conservatives to worry less about the political correctness of this new justices; and liberals to worry more. Both groups had reason to worry.

Holmes took positions that at times favored entrepreneurs and at times saw the effects of their actions as being constitutionally intolerable in a democratic society. That is, Holmes sometimes deferred to publicly mandated legislation, even though he disliked the legislation. In a 1922 case (*Pennsylvania Coal Co. v. Mahon*) he wrote the majority opinion, invalidating a Pennsylvania statute that prohibited coal mining that undermined urban land. He said the statute did not provide for compensating corporations that were stopped from mining when they already had mineral rights under the land that was subsiding. Chalk one up for entrepreneurs. But a year later Holmes dissented from a Court decision (*Pennsylvania and Ohio v. West Virginia*). He argued that the U. S. Constitution did not prohibit states (Pennsylvania and Ohio) from giving preference to their own citizens in allocating natural gas that flowed in interstate commerce.

In *Hammer v. Dagenhart,* a renowned case that is often regarded as an early (1918) hardening of the Court into a conservative stance, Holmes dissented from the Court's majority, which declared unconstitutional the regulation by Congress of the production of goods destined for interstate commerce. In a 1920 case—early among those involving protection of wildlife (*Missouri v. Holland*)—he spoke for the majority, supporting the power of the national government to protect migratory birds that otherwise might be depleted by citizens of a state who were shooting them down. However, he dissented in an earlier (1910) case (*Western Union v. Kansas*), arguing that the state of Kansas could charge an interstate carrier (Western Union) for business it conducted entirely within the state.

Conservatives and liberals are most likely to differ when economic factors are involved. Holmes sometimes took a position supporting private enterprise, sometimes opposing it. He tended to defer to the power of state governments to limit free enterprise. It is easier to understand his viewpoint on such cases as reflecting his deference to what the public in a democratic society wants, rather than what conservative interests want. But he also sometimes supported the conservative position, as in the Northern Securities case. Nonetheless, he did not regard the Constitution as the private property of wealthy conservatives.

When economic interests were less prominent, Holmes took a more liberal position. In the 1919 *Schenck* case, Holmes wrote for a unanimous Court, affirming the conviction of Schenck for distributing to draftees a pamphlet that urged (nonviolent) action against forcible service in the armed forces. In his opinion for the Court, Holmes coined the phrase "clear and present danger," and obviously decided that Schenck's pamphlets to draftees were a clear and present danger. In 1923, in *Moore v. Dempsey,* he spoke for the majority in insisting that a federal judge must examine the facts before affirming or denying a writ of habeas corpus.[3]

In 1925 in *Gitlow v. New York,* Holmes and Brandeis vigorously dissented from the majority. The decision denied to an anarchist the protection of free speech by the First Amendment and overlooked the clear and present danger argument. The majority said that even though there was no showing of any action following Gitlow's utterances, the free speech part of the First Amendment did not protect him. In the Gitlow case, in dissent, Holmes first declared what has become a cliché: "every idea is an incitement."

A later (1929) case (*United States v. Schwimmer)* involved a woman born in Hungary who applied for U.S. citizenship but said she would not serve in the armed forces. Holmes saw the absurdity, if not the humor, of expecting military service from a woman in her fifties, and dissented from the Court's solemn denial of citizenship to Rosika Schwimmer. Indeed, during the First World War, she did commit an act: she talked Henry Ford into sending a peace ship to Europe. Holmes said that the First Amendment was designed to protect "freedom for the thought we hate," but his main argument seemed to rest on the belief that Rosika Schwimmer was not really likely to overthrow, or even to really threaten the overthrow, of any government.

In the 1920s, along with strange hats, one of the major fads du temps was eugenics, and perhaps the fad's fanciest fondness was for sterilization of the unfit. In 1924, Virginia passed an act allowing sterilization of the insane, defining insanity as being "afflicted with hereditary forms of insanity that are recurrent—idiocy, imbecility, feeblemindedness or epilepsy." In 1927, Carrie Buck, a seventeen-year-old, was declared to be a feebleminded daughter of a feebleminded woman and an absent father and the mother of a feebleminded child and was later sterilized. Court-appointed attorneys appealed, ultimately to the Supreme Court.

Holmes wrote a stentorian opinion for all but one of the justices, including two liberal justices, Brandeis and Harlan Fiske Stone, vigorously supporting the popular effort against the unfit. He accepted the astonishing argument that the law mandating vaccination was "broad enough to cover cutting the Fallopian tubes." He made a general allusion to his own past by saying that nations are not prohibited from sending their finest youths into mortal combat ("we have seen more than once that the public welfare may call upon the best citizens for their lives.") He revealed indirectly his deference to eighteenth-century demographer Thomas Malthus, who feared the population explosion would make the nineteenth if not the eighteenth-century the final century. Holmes, in the twentieth century, was no more comforted in his worry about overpopulation than others who haven't bothered to note that the exploded population has been rather more prosperous than starved. Holmes was very emphatically a eugenicist—expunge the unfit and he ended with a characteristically clear and short judgment: "Three generations of imbeciles are enough." Sterilization thereby became constitutional and was adopted in thirty states.

Carrie Buck evidently had been raped by the nephew of her foster mother, and the daughter that was delivered in the asylum turned out to be at least normal: she was an honor student in the second grade in school but died of measles when she was eight. Her mother Carrie lived to the age of seventy-seven. Other members of the extended Buck family produced children whose intelligence quotient was well above the imbecilic. Justice Butler, the only Catholic on the Court, was the only dissenter (without opinion) from Holmes's rather rhetorical, supralegal opinion. The Virginia legislature, early in 2000, said it had made a mistake in its sterilization statute.

What *Were* Holmes's Legal Principles?

Several aspects of Holmes's judicial work merit emphasis. Let me mention first the ones that usually are the only ones considered. In his magnum opus, *The Common Law,* which led to his appointment to the highest Massachusetts court, he argued emphatically that logic, not experience was the life of the law. By this, as I see it, he meant that current law is not logically but experientially a product of prior law. This is a position decidedly opposed to the ancient Roman and modern Napoleonic codification of law that was operative in Europe when Holmes wrote *The Common Law.*

We can now see a reminder of the code orientation in present-day judicial invocation of what the Founding Fathers intended in the original Constitution. This is—unsurprisingly—just what the invoker believes, two centuries after the Constitution was established. One justice once put it this way: "When I decide whether or not an Act of Congress is constitutional, I put it beside a copy of the Constitution and observe whether the Act is in conflict." This is not to say that the judicial process in code-dominated jurisdictions is altogether inflexible, but, that the case method tends to allow for greater flexibility. Holmes's contribution was great in this emphasis.

He also gave great impetus to the judicial attitude that cases should be decided by prior cases rather than by ancient or even recent codes. Logically he did go to an ancient code, the code of survival. Holmes was not primarily concerned with federalism—for example, whether the interstate commerce clause mandated that states be allowed or denied particular regulations, or that the national government be allowed or denied particular regulations. But he came down hard when he thought that survival—particularly survival of a nation—was issue.

He would allow free speech, but he would not allow draftees opposed to military service to state their case, at least on a military base. He would allow free expression of opposition to established government, even advocacy of overthrow of established government—as long as the advocacy did not get too specific. It is by no means certain that if Holmes were judging the constitutionality of Thomas Paine's *Common Sense,* he would have allowed it. Published in January 1776, it had a lot to do with moving public opinion in the colonies toward the declaration, six months later, of independence. Paine came close to shouting "fire" in a crowded theater. And as we noted, Holmes was enthusiastic about Virginia's effort to purge the population of people who might be a drag on a nation's progress.

Critics of Holmes have landed hard on his enthusiasm for forced sterilization—but have not been so hard on the seven other justices who agreed with Holmes or with the popular consensus on eugenics. Holmes did not seem to see it as the fad du temps that his posthumous critics have. And it is as absurd to resort to logic rather than experience to say that he was a fascist and a racist. Dark hints at Nazism in Holmes are laughable: some of the best friends of the New England aristocrat were indeed Jews—notably Felix Frankfurter and Harold Laski—and the justice who may have influenced him most was Louis Brandeis.

If anything, such solemn criticisms of Holmes are as convincing as would be the late-twentieth-century observation that Orville and Wilbur Wright were so primitive at the start of the twentieth century, so uncivilized, so ignorant that they didn't produce even one jet aircraft. Or that Lindbergh in 1927 took almost thirty-three hours to cross the Atlantic, whereas any serious pilot can do it in six hours—and the Concorde can fly from Paris to New York in a little over three hours, ten times as fast as the laggard Lindbergh.

But there is a substantial downside to Holmes's jurisprudence. Like so many others who were influenced by the strange Social Darwinist spin-off of Charles Darwin's *Origin of Species* (1859), and so impressed by Herbert Spencer's *Social Statics* (1851), Holmes strongly believed that the strong will prevail, that the fittest will survive. But in *Lochner v. New York* (1905) he said the legislature, not the Supreme Court, must be allowed to decide how the fittest will survive.

He criticized those who believe that Herbert Spencer's *Social Statics* was part of the Constitution, but Holmes himself seemed to believe it. If he had not started with this premise and if he had troubled to define survival—as in the *Buck* case out of Virginia—to mean more than *physical* survival, possibly much of his judicial orientation would have been different. It involves no contortion of logic, no deliberately blind reading of either experience or the Constitution, to conclude that the survival of a civilization involves more than its physical survival.

Holmes was usually tolerant of doctrines he hated, but he did not live long enough to face the cultural and moral challenges that emerged shortly after his death. Two civilizations—Germany and Japan—shared his view of survival. But they twisted it with hypernationalist and parochial doctrine in the 1940s. Each of these nations really tried to dominate at least half the world. His logical critics might suppose that indeed he might have opposed these expansionist nations, but only because they threatened American expansionism. Such a view of Holmes would be preposterous.

And he did not face the complex challenges to free speech. To say that shouting fire in a theater is a no-no does not adjudicate the issue of racist utterances. These may not seriously threaten the life of the state but may merit limitation if they seriously injure the rights of people whose racial, sexual, or religious orientation differ from the majority. Racists in post-Hitler Germany may be puzzled: as everyone knows, majority rule is democratic and the majority of Germans are Nordic, so why may racist Nordics *not* brutalize Turks, Slavs, and Arabs? In the late twentieth century in Germany, after twelve years of Nazism and genocide, many such kinds of utterances—in addition to brutal actions—are forbidden. After Holmes's demise, many old issues in new form have boiled up: the regulation of interstate commerce, division of political power between the state and national governments, war as an instrument of national policy in the atomic age. Or what to do with ideological rigidity when it leads to the death of a few or a few hundred people inside a crowded building, on the sole grounds that the victims might not share the perpetrator's ideology. Or what can be done humanely to solve problems of mental acumen and social delinquency. In the United States and other advanced nations, these have become critical issues, both political and jurisprudential. They were not major issues until after the Civil War and two international wars had elementally assured national survival.

Perhaps Holmes's greatest contribution to jurisprudence was his reliance on national growth and confidence in the publics ability to decide what it wants and does not want. No more than any other judge or any philosopher could he foresee what would be the future of his beloved country or of the human race, but he was generally willing to let the democratic political system determine *how* progress was to be made. He did not embrace Mankind or People, but he was willing to tolerate them. He did not usually impose his own preferences or beliefs on his jurisprudence. An inescapable effect of certitude about basic principles is to aggravate the role that ideology plays in conflict, particularly in wars and revolution. Holmes was self-assured enough about his own intelligence to live and adjudicate without much ideology and without any omniscience.

The Unconscious and Preconscious Origins of Holmes's Jurisprudence

Holmes was both a product and an exemplar of the comfortable aristocracy, the benign Brahmin elitists of New England who so dominated American civilization from colonial times to perhaps the 1920s. But like his father, "the Autocrat of the Breakfast Table," who gave life to the Brahmin cliché while professing to ridicule it, Holmes did not reject democracy.

Holmes's family and Holmes himself were perhaps in the confident vanguard of a Protestantism that emancipated itself from dogma and emerged as a nonsectarian but moralistic orientation. It produced abolitionists in the nineteenth century—the liberals like Emerson—who became the vanguard of progressivism, and it nurtured the very moral Protestantism that produced moral Protestants in the New Deal at the middle of the twentieth century.

Holmes remained in many ways an aloof and rather self-centered Victorian Brahmin. Like his father, he regarded good women as very understanding helpmeets, and he had to go to England to meet a rather emancipated, very brilliant, and married woman. Holmes strongly, if quietly, admired Brandeis, who was launched onto the Court by Woodrow Wilson in 1916. But Holmes turned down Brandeis's proposal to take the proper Brahmin to see how poor people lived in the Boston slums. He may have thought he'd seen enough of the common people during the Civil War. In contrast, Franklin Roosevelt went with Eleanor to experience the miserable living conditions of poor immigrants in New York. Brandeis in 1922 wrote to Frankfurter, commenting that Holmes tended to lose contact with society in favor of intellectual abstraction. Brandeis, Theodore Roosevelt, and Franklin and Eleanor Roosevelt did not.

In one way Holmes was not at all aloof: he reveled in his close friendships with particularly congenial, highly competent colleagues. With one of these, Felix Frankfurter, the reveling was in part due to Frankfurter's deft obsequiousness. With another, Louis Brandeis, it was composed of great respect for the brilliant jurist that Brandeis was; also perhaps it included Holmes's vicarious involvement in not just humanity but human beings as well. Among the sensational critics who would make Holmes over into a racist, a fascist and a Nazi because of *Buck v. Bell,* there remains the problem of analyzing how this racist was at least not anti-Semitic. And the further problem of explaining why such a racist could be so opposed to slavery.

There was real continuity between Wendell Phillips, Charles Sumner, and Oliver Wendell Holmes in the Victorian era and Brandeis, Frankfurter, and Douglas in the mid-twentieth century. The last three of these were the bright, progressive, and mostly Harvard men who helped establish, administer, and then adjudicate reform in the 1930s. The institutionally religious and moralist reform of the nineteenth century broadened and became secular—even nonreligious—in an institutional sense. And in this Holmes was one of the earliest leaders. He was not simply or even always a liberal jurist, but he insisted on appraising what was lawful and constitutional on the basis of what the public wanted.

Holmes was also a product of his father, taller and much more single-minded than Senior, but not for sure brighter or more energetic. The ambivalence of their interactions proved to be enormously beneficial. Oliver Wendell Holmes, Senior achieved his life goals, fulfilled his potential, far more than all but a tiny fraction of his Brahmin peers. His medical contribution saved the lives of thousands of new mothers who might otherwise have died from postpartum infection. His literary contribution brought him more fame, which was what he seemed to want above everything else, including the welfare of his tall and outstanding son. If he perhaps used his son to confirm his own great patriotism, the senior did indeed search until he found his son, after Junior's second near-fatal wound. He provoked his son, perhaps mightily, as when he misread his son's intention to leave military service before the end of his contract period and before the Civil War ended. But he never really sought to destroy his son's life: his pressure on his son to stay in the army revealed at worst a lack of understanding of what it is like—not abstractly but really—to be close to death.

Holmes read widely among theorists and philosophers, from Hobbes, Malthus, Locke, and J. S. Mill. Perhaps he also read William James, his psychological and sometimes socially close friend at Harvard. But he did not judge human experience or development of the law *theoretically*. He believed slavery was wrong, but he evidently had no deeper understanding of the many profound causes of the deadly confrontation between Union and Confederate armies.

Holmes did not know what it was like to be humiliated as a black human being. He was closer to Stephen Douglas's popular sovereignty basis for accepting or rejecting slavery than to Abraham Lincoln's. Holmes did not see the *moral* basis for supporting the Union, even though he accepted the fact that the majority of people in the North were morally ambivalent about slavery. He seemed indifferent to the fact that he himself joined the fighting because he himself opposed slavery and favored the Union. If no moral principle was involved, only the accident of his cultural background in the North rather than in the South accounted for his repeated risking of his own life.

Who Was Holmes?

A major determinant of Holmes's predisposition toward the law, toward life, and generally toward his friends and associates was perhaps inborn. As a young man in the household of his parents people noticed that he was detached—he was often physically present among others but not mentally present. Perhaps the Civil War made him more detached than his father and less vulnerable to attempted intrusions. He absorbed being needled by his father about his physical appearance—an involved near-dwarf needling a detached near-giant. He tried to form his own life. He joined the army before graduating from Harvard. He withdrew from a medical career and turned to law, because of and perhaps despite the fact that his father turned to medicine after trying law. He stayed in combat contexts during the Civil War, when his wound at Ball's Bluff would probably have been accepted as adequate reason for resigning his commission.

These and other incidents manifesting his detached autonomy were precursors of his independence as a jurist. He did not bond his mind to a dogma, a doctrine, a belief system. He was intensely patriotic, from the time he left college during his senior year to the times he delivered patriotic addresses to colleges and other groups, to the end of his life when he left a portion of his estate to the United States of America. He did not bind himself to ideologies of capitalism or class conflict.

And in the 1920s, in *Buck v. Bell,* Holmes, like the Virginia legislature, could not empathize with the "female's desire to have children, again perhaps both because of and despite the fact that his marriage was childless. If he had lived a few more decades, after the Second World War and the Holocaust, he very likely, like the Virginia legislature, would have had a different view of eugenics.

Underneath his aloofness, his contented self-sufficiency, lay a layer of passion that perhaps he did not really want to recognize. He sought and treasured the friendship of gifted young men, even if they were neither natural-born Brahmins nor British. His opinion in the Buck case, fiery as it was, was not the only case in which he in effect let his deepest emotion govern his judicial judgment. He decried the intrusion of the personal and political values of judges on their opinions and decisions, and probably did not realize that these same values sometimes dominated his own judicial judgment. But Holmes, was in any event, not the only justice to be detached from unpleasant aspects of reality.

In one particular, Holmes differed from his writer-father. The jurist once remarked that his father tried to excel in too many fields, and had Senior concentrated on one proficiency, he might have made a great contribution. Quite aside from his fresh, clear, untangled writing, Holmes, Junior made a major contribution to American jurisprudence. He did not presume that writing was good law because it was entangled and muddled. It took both independence and strength of mind to scorn legal jungle-writing and thought. In effect he was saying—so clearly that only judges could fail to understand—to judges and professed worshipers of the law and the Constitution: "Back off! You—we judges—are not the sole or even the final arbiter of either virtue or of law: experience is. And the general public is experienced."

Trying to put all his complex personality together—in attempting to explain his juristic complexity—cannot produce a definitive appraisal. That he transcends popular labels that have been applied and misapplied to him may be a major reason for his greatness: liberals call him liberal and conservatives call him conservative. But it is quite clear that American constitutional law and the Constitution that is its basis have benefited greatly from Holmes's detached involvement in the nation and its institutions.

As we have noted, Holmes said that Senior was his father, rather than that Junior was his father's son. And he said that his father might have more completely fulfilled himself if he had not divided his gifts between medicine and writing. Holmes did indeed concentrate. Once he became a judge, at the age of forty-two, he stuck to relating human behavior and misbehavior to private and public law, in the courtroom. He broadened it and kept it open in four decades of judicial service. If sometimes he let his writing genius get separated from his judicial wisdom, he at least did better than virtually any other jurist. He remained on the United States Supreme Court from 1902, when Theodore Roosevelt appointed him, until 1932. Franklin Roosevelt came to visit him before his inauguration and asked him for his advice. Holmes told the president-elect: "Form your ranks and fight." After FDR left, Holmes commented to his secretary: "A second-class intellect. But a first-class temperament." Holmes died in March 1935, two days short of his ninety-fourth birthday.

The senior Holmes lived eighty-five years. Before the Civil War he wrote a long poem about a wonderful one-hoss shay. The poem fairly can be said to describe his son. It recounts the life of a carriage that was built in 1755, by a deacon determined to produce a perfect vehicle: each of its parts as strong as all the others. The shay did not fracture until 1855, when, after showing some general signs of decay, it suddenly collapsed.

> The poor old chaise in a heap or mound,
> As if it had been to the mill and ground!
> You see, of course, if you're not a dunce,
> How it went to pieces all at once,
> All at once and nothing first.
>   . . . . .
> End of the wonderful one-hoss shay,
> Logic is logic. That's all I say.

Holmes, Junior relied a lot on logic, but a lot more experience.

NOTES

1. Justice William O. Douglas had the same priorities as Holmes, with very different results. See chapter 11 on Douglas.
2. The case method of teaching was introduced not by Holmes but by Langdell about a decade before *The Common Law* was published.
3. Habeas corpus has often been a very contentious matter, very often involving the issue of whether a dissenter from predominant political or social views may be allowed to live undisturbed by a government that seeks to stop dissent. A most famous case was *Ex parte*

Milligan, in which the detention by the U.S. government of southern dissenters during the Civil War was declared unconstitutional, just one year after the war ended. The matter re-emerged glaringly during the Second World War, in which the Supreme Court—the Roosevelt Court declared that the president had legitimate authority to detain people of Japanese ancestry without infringing on their right to be freed under habeas corpus. (See discussion in chapter 11 on Justice William O. Douglas.)

FOR FURTHER READING

Alschuler, Albert W. *Law without Values: The Life, Work, and Legacy of Justice Holmes.* Chicago: University of Chicago Press, 2000. A well-documented lawyer's brief for indicting and convicting Holmes of a variety of judicial and political crimes, notably racism and eugenics. I haven't checked the references made by racial bigots to Holmes's opinions. Those inclined to check out such references are recommended to examine Hitler's *Mein Kampf* and perhaps the utterances of David Duke and some like-minded, self-styled Christians in Northern Idaho. One or another of Hitler's ghost writers would have had ample time to read and applaud *Buck v. Bell,* even though the first edition of *Mein Kampf* precedes the *Buck* case.

Baker, Liva. *The Justice from Beacon Hill: The Life and Times of Oliver Wendell Holmes.* New York: Harper Collins, 1991. A scholarly and fair-minded biography.

Bent, Silas, *Justice Oliver Wendell Holmes: A Biography.* New York: The Vanguard Press, 1932. A fair-minded biography published while Justice Holmes was still living.

Biddle, Francis. *Justice Holmes, Natural Law, and the Supreme Court.* New York: Macmillan 1961. An admiring but judicious memorial by one of Holmes's former law clerks and an attorney general in FDR's administration.

Burton, David H. *Political Ideas of Justice Holmes.* Cransbury, NJ: Associated University Presses, 1992.

Tilton, Eleanor M. (ed.) *Amiable Autocrat: A Biography of Dr. Oliver Wendell Holmes,* New York, Henry Schuman, 1947.

Tilton, Eleanor M., (ed.) *The Poetical Works of Oliver Wendell Holmes,* Rev. ed. Boston: Houghton Mifflin, 1975.

White, G. Edward. *Justice Oliver Wendell Holmes: Law and the Inner Self.* New York: Oxford University Press, 1993. A very thorough biography that frankly and with a little bias shows Holmes's juristic virtues and vices.

CHAPTER SEVEN

Louis D. Brandeis: The Justice as Prophet and Teacher

Stephen K. Shaw

Louis Dembitz Brandeis served on the United States Supreme Court from June 5, 1916, until his resignation on February 13, 1939. When the "people's Attorney" was nominated by President Woodrow Wilson on January 28, 1916, less than a month following the death of Associate Justice Joseph R. Lamar, to fill this vacancy on the High Court, "all hell broke loose in the financial, legal and political communities, where many powerful elements had long fought and feared him as 'radical.'"[1]

Nonetheless, on June 1, 1916, by a 47–22 affirmative vote, and following more than four months of delay and deliberation and over 1,000 pages of testimony before a Senate Judiciary Committee's subcommittee, the Brandeis confirmation battle, which "still ranks as one of the most bitter and most intensely fought in the history of the Court,"[2] was successfully concluded by the United States Senate.[3]

President Wilson later would confide to a reporter that he could never live up to his appointment of Brandeis; according to Wilson, "there is nobody else who represents the greatest technical ability and professional success with complete devotion to the people's interest."[4] With his appointment to the Court, Brandeis, the first Jewish member of that tribunal, "embarked on a new career; and a new era of jurisprudence had begun."[5]

His joining the Court was not just a turning point in his career or even in the history of the Court itself. Moving from lawyer Brandeis to Associate Justice Brandeis, he effectively and decisively altered the course of American jurisprudence, such that, as a result of his more than two decades-long tenure on the Supreme Court, it can be argued that without him, "there would have been no soaring early twentieth-century explication of the democratic value of free speech and an unrestrained press, nor any excoriation of a government that was threatening to corrupt the people by teaching that ends justified any means."[6] Given his vital contribution to First Amendment jurisprudence especially, as demonstrated by his eloquent concurring opinion in *Whitney v. California* (274 US 357 [1927]), it is plain to see and necessary to note that Brandeis "combined analytic brilliance with emotional power to create what is probably the most effective judicial interpretation of the First Amendment ever written."[7]

Justice Brandeis wrote 528 opinions in his twenty-three years on the Court. He developed and applied his "sociological jurisprudence" so carefully and keenly that it gradually became the jurisprudence of the Court and eventually of the entire federal system."[8] In addition to his alliance with the likes of Cardozo, Holmes, and Pound in the area of sociological jurisprudence, the other crucial contribution that Brandeis made to the growth of public law in the United States in the twentieth century concerned civil liberties. Of his over 500 opinions, 454 were written for or with the majority; only 74 were dissents. Among those opinions, two in particular merit close scrutiny: *Whitney v. California* (274 US 357 [1924]) and *Olmstead v. United States* (277 US 438 [1928]).

The Whitney Case

In 1927, at the age of seventy-one, Justice Brandeis wrote what is one of the most insightful and impassioned declarations of the First Amendment, freedom of speech and assembly, and the nature of the relationship between individual liberty and societal improvement. His concurring opinion in *Whitney* was a return to first principles, to fundamental values; in essence, his opinion was a blistering dissent from the Court's refusal to take seriously the relationship between the law and the Court's "clear and present danger" test, which was initially offered by Justice Holmes in 1919 in *Schenck v. United States* (249 US 47 [1919]). According to Brandeis, the Court needed desperately to examine the nature and extent of this test:[9] "This court has not yet fixed the standard by which to determine when a danger shall be deemed clear; how remote the danger may be and yet be deemed present; and what degree of evil shall be deemed sufficiently substantial to justify resort to abridgement of free speech and assembly as the means of protection. To reach sound conclusions on these matters, we must bear in mind why a state is, ordinarily, denied the power to prohibit dissemination of social, economic, and political doctrine which a vast majority of its citizens believes to be false and fraught with evil consequences."[10]

The case of *Whitney* centered on the action of Miss Charlotte Anita Whitney, a niece of former Associate Justice Stephen J. Field, who helped to organize the Communist Labor Party of America following its split from the American Socialist Party. In November 1919, Whitney attended a convention in Oakland for the purpose of organizing a California branch of the C.L.P.A.; she was elected to the credentials committee and was appointed to the resolution committee. After the convention adjourned, she was indicted and convicted for violating the 1919 Criminal Syndicalism Act of California, for she "did...unlawfully, willfully, wrongfully, deliberately and feloniously organize and assist in organizing, and was, is and knowingly became a member of an organization, group and assemblage of persons organized and assembled to advocate, teach, aid and abet criminal syndicalism.[11] The Supreme Court upheld her conviction, concluding that her actions were of the nature of a criminal conspiracy, and thus unprotected by the First Amendment. In the words of Justice Edward Sanford, "The statute must be presumed to be aimed at an evil where experience shows it to be most felt.... Every presumption is to be indulged in favor of the validity of the statute...."[12]

Justice Brandeis countered that "where a statute is valid only in case certain conditions exist, the enactment of the statute cannot alone establish the facts which are essential to its validity....The powers of the courts to strike down an offending law are no less when the interests involved are not property rights but the fundamental personal rights of free speech and assembly."[13] Brandeis was not nearly as eager as most of his colleagues to divest the Court of its power of judicial review, especially where fundamental rights such as speech and assembly were in question; neither was he so willing to label as criminal behavior that which very well might be, upon closer analysis, protected by the First Amendment. In what has been described as his "greatest free speech opinion,"[14] Brandeis eloquently protested the majority's apparent inability to take seriously the political and legal issues at stake in *Whitney*.

He sought to explain why and how the clear and present danger doctrine pointed the way to fundamental principles concerning free speech and democracy. In so doing, Brandeis "took the lead on the postwar Supreme Court in advocating expanded federal jurisdiction over free speech issues."[15] In *Whitney* (and in other cases)[16] he applied an "immediacy" criterion as an aid to the *Schenck* test: "Fear of serious injury cannot alone justify suppression of free speech and assembly. Men feared witches and burnt women. It is the function of speech to free men from the bondage of irrational fears. To justify suppression of free speech there must be reasonable ground to fear that serious evil will result if free speech is practiced. There must be reasonable ground to believe that the danger apprehended is imminent. There must be reasonable ground to believe that the evil to be presented is a serious one" (274 US 357, 376 [1927]).

As he had argued earlier in his dissent in *Schaefer v. United States* (251 US 466 [1920]), the clear and present danger test "is a rule of reason. Correctly applied, it will preserve the right of free speech both from suppression by tyrannous, well-meaning majorities, and from abuse by irresponsible, fanatical minorities" (482). Judgment was required of members of the judiciary. Fundamental rights such as those found in the First Amendment, while fundamental, were, of necessity, not absolute. Brandeis's strongest beliefs are reflected in opinions such as in *Whitney* and *Schaefer,* and he firmly believed that while judicial review was essential and should be used thoughtfully and with precision, it should be used nonetheless. No test nor formula was talismanic; reason and hard work (Brandeis excelled at each) were requisites for good judging.

"If," he wrote in *New State Ice Co. v. Liebman,* "we would guide by the light of reason, we must let our minds be bold" (285 US 262, 310–311 [1932]).

The exercise of reason on the part of Brandeis was fueled by both faith and reflection. He had faith in the promise of deliberative democracy and was aware of the "risks to which all human institutions are subject" (274 US 357, 375 [1927]). Liberty and authority had to be reconciled in our experiment in self-governance. "Those who won our independence by revolution were not cowards. They did not fear political change. They did not exalt order at the cost of liberty. To courageous self-reliant men, with confidence in the power of free and fearless reasoning applied through the processes of popular government, no danger flowing from speech can be deemed clear and present, unless the incidence of the evil apprehended is so imminent that it may befall before there is opportunity for full discussion" (377).

In *Whitney,* the majority disposed of the free speech issue in less than two pages. Under the majority's approach in *Whitney,* even the *tendency* toward incitement was sufficient to trigger regulation by the government. For Brandeis, "Prohibition of free speech and assembly is a measure so stringent that it would be inappropriate as the means for averting a relatively trivial harm to society" (377). Only an emergency, Brandeis contended, "can justify repression. Such must be the rule of authority if it is to be reconciled with freedom. Such, in my opinion, is the command of the Constitution" (377).

Brandeis's concurrence in *Whitney* includes a passage that is "quite wonderful,"[17] a passage that symbolizes his conviction that we have much to learn from the Framers' vision embedded in the Constitution, given that the Framers "believed that freedom to think as you will and to speak as you think are means indispensable to the discovery and spread of political truth" (274 US 357, 375 [1927]). He continues:

> They recognized the risks to which all human institutions are subject. But they knew that order cannot be secured merely through fear of punishment for its infraction; that it is hazardous to discourage thought, hope and imagination; that fear breeds repression; that repression breeds hate; that hate menaces stable government; that the path of safety lies in the opportunity to discuss freely supposed grievances and proposed remedies; and that the fitting remedy for evil counsels is good ones. Believing in the power of reason as applied through public discussion, they eschewed silence coerced by the law—the argument of force in its worst form. Recognizing the occasional tyrannies of governing majorities, they amended the Constitution so that free speech and assembly should be guaranteed. (375–76)

Underlying this constitutional commitment to individual freedom and social order, according to Brandeis, is a "fundamental principle" of politics: "that the greatest menace to freedom is an inert people; that public discussion is a political duty;..." (375). Deliberative democracy and individual freedom were inextricable for Brandeis, and his opinions, educational treatises as much as legal briefs, vividly illustrate the crucial function of free speech in democratic governance.

The Olmstead Case

Justice Brandeis possessed an "almost religious commitment to individual dignity,"[18] and that commitment clearly animated one of his greatest dissenting opinions, perhaps one of *the* greatest dissents in the annals of the Court. In *Olmstead v. United States* (277 US 438 [1928]), Brandeis directed his attention to the meaning of the Fourth Amendment, and, as he did in *Whitney,* explored the foundational principles entailed in the text of the Constitution, especially the rule of law in a constitutional democracy. The Supreme Court in *Olmstead* confronted electronic eavesdropping for the first time, forced, in the process, to interpret eighteenth century language in the context of technological change. The case arose as the federal government began to wiretap telephones to enforce Prohibition. Federal agents placed wiretaps on the phone lines at Roy Olmstead's home and office. These taps were in place for nearly five months, and, as Brandeis notes in his dissent, "The typewritten record of the notes of conversations overheard occupies 775 typewritten pages" (471). Olmstead and several associates were convicted of conspiracy to violate the National Prohibition Act, and the Court affirmed the convictions. Writing for the 5–4 majority, Chief Justice William Howard Taft, warning the Court not to adopt "an enlarged and unusual meaning" of the Fourth Amendment, concluded, "The amendment does not forbid what was done here. There was no searching. There was no seizure. The evidence was secured by the use of the sense of hearing and that only. There was no entry of the houses or offices of the defendants" (464, 466).

Brandeis objected strongly to the Court's wooden and literal interpretation of the Constitution. Echoing Chief Justice John Marshall's landmark opinion in *McCulloch v. Maryland* (17 US [4 Wheat], 315 [1819], he counseled that provisions protecting individual freedoms, as with provisions providing governmental powers, "must have a similar capacity of adaptation to a changing world" (277 US 438, 472 [1928]). Given scientific and technological novelties, "Discovery and invention," according to Brandeis, "have made it possible for the government, by means far more effective than stretching upon the rack, to obtain disclosure in court of what is whispered in the closet" (473). He continued:

> The progress of science in furnishing the government with means of espionage is not likely to stop with wiretapping. Ways may some day be developed by which the government, without removing papers from secret drawers, can reproduce them in court, and by which it will be enabled to expose to a jury the most intricate occurrences of the home. Advances in the psychic and related sciences may bring means of exploring unexpressed beliefs, thoughts and emotions (474).

Brandeis ended this prophetic passage with the plea, "Can it be that the Constitution affords no protection against such invasions of individual security?"(474). He essentially answered his own call to alarm, "As a means of espionage, writs of assistance and general warrants are but puny instruments of tyranny and oppression when compared with wiretapping" (476).

Essential to understanding and appreciating his dissent in *Olmstead* is recognizing the salient fact that Brandeis focused carefully on the underlying purposes of the Fourth Amendment rather than merely on the literal text alone.

> The makers of our Constitution undertook to secure conditions favorable to the pursuit of happiness. They recognized the significance of man's spiritual nature, of his feelings and of his intellect. They knew that only a part of the pain, pleasure and satisfaction of life are found in material things. They sought to protect Americans in their beliefs, their thoughts, their emotions and their sensations. They conferred, as against the government, the right to be left alone—the most comprehensive of rights and the right most valued by civilized men. To protect that right, every unjustifiable intrusion by the government upon the privacy of the individual, whatever the means employed, must be deemed a violation of the Fourth Amendment. (478)

Of particular significance for Brandeis was the fact that the eavesdropping was committed by the government rather than a private agent. Relying in part on what he described as the "maxim of unclean hands," Brandeis concluded his profoundly prescient opinion with this paragraph:

> Decency, security and liberty alike demand that government officials shall be subjected to the same rules of conduct that are commands to the citizen. In a government of laws, existence of the government will be imperiled if it fails to observe the law scrupulously. Our government is the potent, the omnipresent teacher. For good or for ill, it teaches the whole people by its example. Crime is contagious. If the government becomes a lawbreaker, it breeds contempt for the law; it invites every man to become a law unto himself; it invites anarchy. To declare that in the administration of the criminal law the end justifies the means...would bring terrible retribution. Against that pernicious doctrine this court should resolutely set its face. (485)

Brandeis failed in *Olmstead* in 1928 to dissuade the Court from accepting such a "pernicious doctrine." Yet, in his role as a prophet of change, his view did prevail four decades later when the Warren Court overruled *Olmstead* in *Katz v. United States* (389 US 347 [1967]). His majestic dissent in *Olmstead* virtually codifies the view once expressed by Chief Justice Charles Evans Hughes that a dissenting opinion is "an appeal to...the intelligence of a future day."[19]

The Brandeis Legacy

Louis Dembitz Brandeis often was described, from law clerks to presidents, as "Isaiah."[20] His prophetic insights drove his work long before he joined the Court. In 1890, writing in the law review that he helped create, Brandeis and his Boston law partner, Samuel D. Warren, Jr., published "The Right to Privacy,"[21] in the *Harvard Law Review,* and, in the words of Dean Roscoe Pound, "did nothing less than add a chapter to our law."[22] In what is arguably "the most famous essay on privacy ever written,"[23] Brandeis and Warren advanced a central Brandeisian perspective: that the law, of necessity, is dynamic and, while necessarily moored to its legitimate origins, must properly grow in the light of a changed and changing society.

In 1908, in the case of *Muller v. Oregon* (208 US 412 [1908]), representing the state of Oregon, Brandeis submitted a brief to the Supreme Court "that changed the course of American legal history."[24] The brief was 113 pages long; two pages were dedicated to traditional legal analysis and citations. The rest of the brief meticulously analyzed statistical data—hours of labor, health indices, factory legislation—relating to the special status of women in certain industries. The High Court, in one of its remarkably reactionary eras, nonetheless upheld Oregon's statute unanimously, and in the process cited Brandeis specifically for what is still known, almost a century later, as simply "the Brandeis brief" (208 US 412, 419–420 [1908]).

Brandeis was accepted into Harvard Law School without a college degree, and he graduated in 1877 as one of the youngest graduates in its history, with the highest academic marks of any graduate of the law school for over a century. By 1890, he was earning more than $50,000 a year, at a time when 75 percent of the country's attorneys were earning less than $5,000 annually. In 1882, he taught a course on evidence at Harvard Law School while the famed James Bradley Thayer was on leave. The course was so skillfully conducted by Brandeis that Oliver Wendell Holmes, Jr., his future colleague and ally on the Court, asked a student for his notes, and the faculty offered him a professorship at the age of twenty-five, which he declined in order to practice law full-time. Yet, at heart Brandeis remained an educator, as his later work on the Court bears witness.

Some justices of the Court acquire fame (perhaps infamy) after entering the marble palace; others are accompanied to the bench by the fame or reputation already in their possession. Still yet others, an elite of the elite, acquire and retain a standing of almost unparalleled heights. As his dissent in *Olmstead* attests, with his caveat about "an inert people," Brandeis clearly belongs in this latter category: "Experience should teach us to be most on our guard to protect liberty when the government's purposes are beneficent. Men born to freedom are naturally alert to repel invasion of their liberty by evil-minded rulers. The greatest dangers to liberty lurk in insidious encroachment by men of zeal, well-meaning but without understanding" (277 US 438, 479 [1928]).

NOTES

1. Henry J. Abraham, *Justices and Presidents: A Political History of Appointments to the Supreme Court,* 2nd ed., (New York: Oxford University Press, 1985), 179.
2. Ibid., 178.
3. See A. L. Todd, *Justice on Trial: The Case of Louis D. Brandeis* (New York: McGraw-Hill, 1964).
4. Quoted in Philippa Strum, *Louis D. Brandeis: Justice for the People* (New York: Schocken Books, 1984), 299.
5. Idem.
6. Ibid., 335.
7. David M. Rabban, *Free Speech in Its Forgotten Years* (Cambridge: Cambridge University Press, 1997), 369.
8. Quoted in Philippa Strum, *Louis D. Brandeis: Justice for the People* (New York: Schocken Books, 1984), 413.
9. "The question in every case," wrote Holmes, "is whether the words used are used in such circumstances and are of such a nature as to create a clear and present danger that they will bring about the substantive evils that Congress has a right to prevent. It is a question of proximity and degree." *Schneck v. United States*, 249 US 52 [1919]).
10. *Whitney v. California,* 274 US 357, 374 (Brandeis, J., concurring).
11. Ibid., 360. The law defined "criminal syndicalism" as "any doctrine or precept advocating, teaching or aiding and abetting the commission of crime, sabotage ... or unlawful methods of terrorism as a means of accomplishing a change in industrial ownership or control or effecting any political change." Ibid., 359–60.
12. Ibid., 370, 371.
13. Ibid., 374.
14. Cass Sunstein, *Republic.com* (Princeton, NJ: Princeton University Press, 2001), 47.
15. Rabban, 367. See note 7.
16. *Gilbert v. Minnesota*, 254 US 325 (1920); *Schaefer v. United States,* 251 US, 466 (1920); and, *Gitlow v. New York,* 268 US 652 (1925).
17. Quoted in Harry Kalven, Jr., *A Worthy Tradition: Freedom of Speech in America,* edited by Jamie Kalven (New York: Harper, 1988), 159.
18. Rabban, 358. See note 7.
19. Quoted in Bernard Schwartz, *A History of the Supreme Court* (New York: Oxford University Press, 1993), 223.
20. Strum, 339. See note 4.
21. Louis D. Brandeis and Samuel D. Warren, Jr., "The Right to Privacy," 4 *Harvard Law Review* (1890–91):193.
22. Strum, 38. See note 4.
23. Jeffrey Rosen, *The Unwanted Gaze* (New York: Vintage, 2001), 5.
24. Strum, 114. See note 4.

FOR FURTHER READING

Alexander Bickel. *The Unpublished Opinions of Mr. Justice Brandeis: The Supreme Court at Work.* Cambridge: Harvard University Press, 1957.
Louis D. Brandeis and Samuel D. Warren, Jr. "The Right to Privacy." 4 *Harvard Law Review:* 193 (1890–91).
Alpheus T. Mason. *Brandeis—A Free Man's Life.* New York: Viking, 1946.

Philippa Strum. *Louis D. Brandeis: Justice for the People*. Cambridge: Harvard University Press, 1984.
A. L. Todd. *Justice on Trial: The Case of Louis D. Brandeis*. New York: McGraw-Hill, 1964.
Melvin Urofsky. *Louis D. Brandeis and the Progressive Tradition*. Boston: Little, Brown, 1981.

CHAPTER EIGHT

Benjamin Nathan Cardozo: Striking a Balance
Between Stability and Progress

James B. Staab

> Law must be stable, and yet it cannot stand still... I can only warn you that those who
> heed the one without honoring the other, will be worshiping false gods and leading their
> followers astray. The victory is not for the partisans of an inflexible logic nor yet for the
> levelers of all rule and all precedent, but the victory is for those who shall know how to
> fuse these two tendencies together in adaptation to an end yet imperfectly discerned.
> *Benjamin Cardozo quoting Roscoe Pound* (1923)

Even though he served on the nation's high court a short five-and-a-half years, Benjamin Nathan Cardozo is almost always considered a "great" Supreme Court justice,[1] earning him a distinction not shared by the other justices receiving this accolade. Of all the Supreme Court justices who have been rated as "great," the average number of years that they served on the Court has been twenty-five. Cardozo's brief tenure pales in comparison, raising the question even more dramatically: What made him great—so great, indeed, that his stature can be commonly acknowledged after serving on the Supreme Court for such a brief period of time?[2]

Part of the explanation lies in the fact that, prior to his appointment to the Supreme Court, Cardozo served on the New York Court of Appeals for eighteen years, the last six of those as its chief judge. During his tenure on that court, which at that time was considered the second most influential court in the country, Cardozo earned a reputation as one of the nation's foremost common law judges. It was also during that time that Cardozo gave his most important lectures and addresses and wrote his four major books, including his critically acclaimed *The Nature of the Judicial Process*.[3] In fact, Cardozo's reputation as a state appellate judge was the primary reason why President Herbert Hoover felt compelled (other considerations notwithstanding) to appoint him to the Supreme Court in 1932. Thus, one intriguing aspect of the Cardozo legacy is that he is the only "great" Supreme Court justice whose rating rests as much on his pre-Court years as on his Supreme Court years.

More substantively, however, the question remains: What made Cardozo great? While this is a complex question, two explanations will be offered here, only the first of which will be examined closely. First and foremost, Cardozo's greatness can be based on his substantive contributions to the law, particularly his writings about the judicial process. Indeed, the latter were Cardozo's seminal contribution. While Oliver Wendell Holmes was regarded as the renowned legal philosopher (who Cardozo recognized as "the greatest judge that ever lived"[4]), Cardozo was the first person to describe how judges go about deciding cases. No one else had attempted to do this in such a systematic way, and the fact that Cardozo did so as a sitting member of the New York Court of Appeals made his observations seem all the more compelling. The second explanation of Cardozo's greatness, which will not be fully examined here, was the manner in which he wrote about the law. Cardozo was one of the Supreme Court's great stylists. It is often said that he wrote more like a poet than a legal theorist, and this is certainly the case. He wrote his judicial opinions and books about the law with unparalleled flair and elegance, and (like Holmes) will be remembered for the pithy and arresting epigram.[5] While some might question the significance of literary style as a measure of greatness, it cannot be denied that it has made some judges more memorable than others.[6] In fact, in an empirical study of Cardozo's reputation, federal court of appeals judge Richard Posner found that many of Cardozo's opinions are still cited with substantial frequency.[7] Thus, while style cannot be considered the sole (or even primary) factor in assessing a judge's greatness, Cardozo's literary genius certainly has contributed to his enduring legacy.

After providing a brief sketch of Cardozo's life and career, this chapter will examine his contributions to the law in two ways. First, it will outline Cardozo's understanding of the judicial process, the most fundamental and pervasive theme in all of his writings. Second, it will examine his jurisprudence by exploring the four major influences on his legal thought: legal realism, sociological jurisprudence, the common law, and morality. The biographical sketch is offered because it is suggestive of some of the things that influenced Cardozo's judicial behavior.

Biographical Sketch

Benjamin Cardozo was born in New York City on May 24, 1870, to Andrew Cardozo and Rebecca Nathan Cardozo, devout third-generation Sephardic Jews whose ancestors emigrated to the United States from Spain and Portugal in the mid-1700s.[8] The Sephardic Jews were considered the elite of American Jewry,[9] having already established themselves (economically, socially, and politically) in this country by the time the first waves of immigration from central and eastern Europe took place in the last third of the nineteenth century. While Benjamin was ambivalent about the precepts of Judaism and did not attend synagogue regularly after his bar mitzvah at the age of thirteen, his Jewish heritage was clearly important to him. For example, when some leaders of Shearith Israel, the congregation to which Benjamin's family belonged, wanted to discontinue the practice of segregated gender seating, the usually shy Cardozo gave an impassioned speech in opposition to the measure.[10] While there is no evidence that the tenets of the Sephardim influenced his voting behavior in particular cases, Cardozo's Jewish heritage, which placed great weight on tradition and custom, almost certainly influenced his general outlook about the law as well as his common law approach to deciding cases.

Cardozo's father was a prominent lawyer and judge whose early financial success allowed the family to live in spacious homes within affluent neighborhoods of downtown Manhattan, while his mother was the primary caregiver of the couple's six children.[11] Because both of his parents died when he was young,[12] much of the parental responsibilities for the family fell to Cardozo's oldest sister, Ellen. Benjamin and "Nell," as she was called, developed a very close relationship. She nurtured and looked after him when he was young, and he did the same for her when she became sick in the 1920s. The two were constant companions, intellectual peers, and soul mates. Since neither married, she was the person with whom Cardozo shared his life. Cardozo's affection for and loyalty toward Nell was so strong that he jokingly referred to himself as "Nellie's doggie," and once confided to a cousin that he would never marry because he could "never put Nell in second place."[13]

In early 1872 scandal rocked the Cardozo household when Benjamin's father, a judge on the New York Supreme Court since 1867, came under investigation by the Judicial Committee of the New York Assembly for malfeasance in office. Unlike his son, Andrew was politically ambitious and owed his judicial offices in large part to his political connections with Tammany Hall and, in particular, William Marcy ("Boss") Tweed. Although the committee was examining five separate charges (some of which alleged political favoritism in particular judicial rulings), the most serious allegation was a pattern of nepotism and kickbacks in the appointment of receivers in real estate transactions. In order to avoid probable impeachment, Cardozo's father resigned his position before the articles of impeachment could be issued against him. While he was able to resuscitate his legal career somewhat, and continued to provide financially for his family, Andrew Cardozo never regained the stature he once had. Many believe that the shadow of disgrace that fell over the Cardozo family had a profound influence on Benjamin, who likely chose the legal profession in order to redeem his family's name, and whose model of the ideal judge (impartial, dispassionate, and objective) was the opposite of his father's example. While Cardozo never denied that personal values sometimes influence judicial decision-making, he steadfastly eschewed a judicial philosophy that even faintly resembled political favoritism.

We do not know much about Cardozo's early education. Except for his twin sister Emily, none of the Cardozo children attended public school. Interestingly, in preparation for his college board examinations, Cardozo was privately tutored by the legendary (and now controversial[14]) rags-to-riches author, Horatio Alger, Jr. Under Alger's tutelage Cardozo studied such subjects as poetry, classical languages, history, literature, math, and geography—a training which ultimately proved successful. In the fall of 1885, Cardozo entered Columbia College at the young age of fifteen and finished at the top of his class four years later at nineteen. His area of concentration as an undergraduate was in the humanities, with a special emphasis on philosophy. Cardozo then simultaneously pursued a master's degree in political science and a law degree at Columbia, earning the former in only one year, but dropping out of Columbia Law School after his second year in order to help his brother run his father's law practice. Although he did not receive his law degree, Cardozo passed the New York bar exam in 1891.

Before embarking on his judicial career, Cardozo had a long and illustrious career as a trial and appellate attorney. Because he did not finish his legal education at Columbia, Cardozo had to learn some aspects of the law by doing it—what Roscoe Pound called "law in action" as opposed to "law in books."[15] By all indications, he was a very quick learner. His law practice consisted mainly of corporate, tort, and contract cases, and he became a specialist in appellate advocacy. After earning a reputation as an effective and able appellate litigator, other New York law firms hired Cardozo to argue their cases. His law practice, spanning twenty-three years, influenced Cardozo's functionalist views about the law and his conviction that the law should conform (albeit not perfectly) to the beliefs and mores of the people for whom it serves.

In November 1913, Cardozo was elected as a judge to New York's Supreme Court, a trial court of general jurisdiction. After serving only one month, he was appointed to the New York Court of Appeals, the highest appellate court in New York. During his eighteen-year tenure on that court, Cardozo wrote nearly 600 opinions, most of them majority opinions.[16] By closely examining the facts of cases and cautiously adapting legal principles to meet changing social conditions, Cardozo became a nationally recognized common law judge. His contract cases were marked by a willingness to instill fairness into ambiguous contracts and to broaden the concept of consideration.[17] Two of his most important tort opinions (which will be discussed later) were *MacPherson v. Buick Motor Co.* (271 NY 382 [1916]), and *Palsgraf v. The Long Island Railroad Co.* (248 NY 339 [1928]). These decisions, among others, can still be found in many casebooks today.

On January 12, 1932, Oliver Wendell Holmes announced his retirement from the Supreme Court, after twenty-nine years of distinguished service. Considerable pressure was placed on President Herbert Hoover to nominate someone with the stature and credentials to replace the legendary Holmes.[18] Cardozo was touted immediately as the one person in the country who could fill the vacancy. Cardozo did not want to campaign for the nomination himself, but an intense lobbying effort began on his behalf which included Associate Justice Harlan Fiske Stone, several U.S. senators, cabinet officials, interest groups, deans of leading law schools, and concerned citizens. Hoover, who had reservations about nominating Cardozo, eventually capitulated and formally announced his nominee on February 15, 1932. Cardozo was sixty-one years of age.

In making the Cardozo nomination, Hoover broke with traditional considerations: At sixty-one, Cardozo was older than the average age of previous Supreme Court nominees; Cardozo was a Democrat, while the appointing president was a Republican; the nominee was from New York, and there were already two New Yorkers—Charles Evans Hughes and Harlan Fiske Stone—on the Court; and Cardozo was Jewish,[19] and there was already one Jew—Louis D. Brandeis—on the nation's high court. But the support and praise for Cardozo was universal and, in the end, overwhelming. Rarely has there been such bipartisan support for a Supreme Court nominee. In Cardozo, Hoover had the equal of the venerable Holmes. Cardozo's impeccable credentials made him the quintessential merit-based appointment. Even so, Hoover was reluctant right to the end. In a last-minute meeting with Republican Senator William E. Borah of Idaho, Hoover presented his list of candidates for the Holmes vacancy and Cardozo's name was placed at the bottom. In response, Borah reportedly quipped: "Your list is all right, but you handed it to me upside down."[20] In finally appointing Cardozo, remarked Zechariah Chafee, Jr., "Hoover ignored geography and made history."[21] Even though he was not terribly enthusiastic about the nomination,[22] Cardozo accepted it immediately.

Cardozo's appointment to the Supreme Court was important for other reasons as well. His brief tenure (1932–1938) was among the most contentious in the Court's history, culminating in President Franklin Delano Roosevelt's proposal to reconstruct the Court—the so-called Court-packing plan of 1937. The central issue facing the Court at the time was the constitutionality of legislation enacted to meet the economic and social problems of the Great Depression. On this issue, the justices tended to divide along two lines. On one side was the conservative bloc of Willis Van Devanter, James C. McReynolds, George Sutherland, and Pierce Butler—"the Four Horsemen"—who staunchly opposed an expanded role for the federal government in regulating the economy. On the other side was the liberal faction of Louis D. Brandeis, Harlan Fiske Stone, and Cardozo, who had a more deferential view of federal regulation of the economy. The two swing votes on the Court belonged to Chief Justice Charles Evans Hughes and Justice Owen Roberts. For most of the 1930s, the conservative bloc was able to form a majority with either Hughes or Roberts (and often both) to invalidate many important state and federal laws regulating the economy, such as legislation governing the wages and hours of workers. Cardozo, joined by Brandeis and Stone, was often in dissent. Toward the end of his tenure, however, the Court made a radical about-face—"the switch in time that saved nine"—and adopted a more deferential approach toward state and federal regulation of the economy. This dramatic change, which took place during Cardozo's last full term on the Court, and only a few months before the president announced his Court-packing plan, is sometimes referred to as "the Constitutional Revolution of 1937."

What of Cardozo the man? It is difficult to describe Cardozo the man because his personal letters and papers were destroyed. Nevertheless, some general observations can be made. Cardozo was an exceedingly private person, and has been variously described as a "cloistered scholar"[23] who was "[m]onkish in his habits," and as "the bachelor judge" who lived "a hermitlike existence."[24] Cardozo never married,[25] had few close friends, and did not socialize much. As Judge Learned Hand put it, "Very few have ever known what went on behind those blue eyes." But this should not lead one to conclude that Cardozo lived an unhappy or unfulfilled life. While he probably suffered bouts of loneliness, Cardozo's life, as his superb biographer Andrew L. Kaufman has pointed out, "was neither a cold nor an empty one."[26] Cardozo's close friends were extremely important to him, and his sister Nell compensated for the companionship he may have lacked in not having a spouse. Moreover, Cardozo clearly placed a premium on his work and ideas, and likely understood the sacrifices that went along with that choice. As an intellectual, Cardozo probably preferred the confines of his study—surrounded by his large collection of books on history, politics, law, and literature—to gallivanting about town attending social events.

Cardozo was also a hard and indefatigable worker. In addition to his responsibilities as a New York Court of Appeals judge, he wrote four books and gave several major addresses. He was also not one to put things off. After being assigned an opinion on the eve of the Supreme Court's Saturday conference, Cardozo would have a draft (written in longhand) done by Monday morning. According to his law clerks, this made the second week of opinion writing rather slow and uneventful.[27] In order to protect the health of Cardozo, who suffered from coronary heart disease, Chief Justice Hughes would sometimes delay his assignments until Sunday evening. As with the other justices at that time, Cardozo was furnished with one law clerk, whom he chose from among the nation's elite law schools on a rotating basis. In general, Cardozo's law clerks were not extensively used. He would consult them about cases, and ask them to do cite checks and to research particular legal issues, but he wrote all of his own opinions.

Cardozo's "saintly" character also deserves mention. Learned Hand, his close friend from New York, described him in a touching eulogy as a man who "was wise because his spirit was uncontaminated, because he knew no violence, or hatred, or envy, or jealousy, or ill-will."[28] Chief Justice Charles Evans Hughes, at the exercises held in Cardozo's memory at the Supreme Court, described him as "a beautiful spirit, an extraordinary combination of grace and power."[29] Irving Lehman, who served with Cardozo on the New York Court of Appeals, and with whom Cardozo spent his last remaining days, referred to Cardozo's "vast and varied store of learning, his unflagging industry and his command of the gentle art of persuasion," but far above those he placed "the integrity of his mind."[30] While some of this saintly praise may be a bit exaggerated, and Cardozo himself recognized his own unsaintliness in the affectionate letter he wrote about his twin sister Emily upon her death,[31] by all accounts Cardozo was an exceptionally decent person. His demeanor was modest and unassuming; he was kind, considerate, and polite to his law clerks and staff; and he had good working relations with colleagues,[32] which was evidenced by his willingness to listen to their views and to withhold concurring or dissenting opinions unless deemed absolutely necessary. In short, Cardozo was a gentle and rare spirit.[33] Cardozo died at the age of sixty-eight on July 9, 1938, after having suffered a heart attack in December of the preceding year. He is buried in the Shearith Israel cemetery in Cypress Hills, Long Island.

The Nature of the Judicial Process

The common thread running through Cardozo's writings and speeches is the proper role of judges in a democratic system of government. In his first years on the bench Cardozo admitted that he was "troubled in spirit" by how "trackless was the ocean on which [he] had embarked." If you ask judges what it is that they do, they will often take refuge in the excuse that the subject is too difficult for the untutored. Cardozo, who had clearly been thinking about the subject for some time, did not want to avoid the question any longer. "What is it that I do when I decide a case? To what sources of information do I appeal for guidance? In what proportions do I permit them to contribute to the result?"[34] These are the questions he sought to address.

Of his four books, *The Nature of the Judicial Process* is the most systematic account of the judicial function. The book consists of four lectures delivered at and published by Yale University in 1921. Cardozo's method was not prescriptive, but rather descriptive. He discussed the various considerations that confront judges in making decisions, but he did not tell readers how judges should decide particular cases. His model for judging emphasized both its creative possibilities and its limits.

Cardozo began by stating that the problem confronting judges is twofold. First, they must "extract from the precedents the underlying principle, the ratio *decidendi.*" In other words, judges must separate the chaff, the nonessential dicta, from the wheat, the essential legal principles. This is probably what most people consider the heart of the judicial function to be. In order to determine whether the principles that govern earlier decisions should apply in the case before them, judges must determine what those principles are. And the task is not as simple as it sounds: "Cases do not unfold their principles for the asking," Cardozo wrote. "They yield up their kernel slowly and painfully."[35]

An oft-overlooked fact about Cardozo's theory of the judicial function is that he regarded the discovery function as the sum total of what judges do in most cases. In the majority of cases (in one instance he said nine out of ten![36]), the governing rules of prior decisions determine the result in the current case. As he put it, "[o]f the cases that come before the court in which I sit, a majority, I think, could not, with semblance of reason, be decided in any way but one."[37] In Cardozo's view, then, the creative opportunities for the judge were quite limited. We tend to concentrate on the innovative cases because they "have a maximum of interest,"[38] or it is in those cases where "the serious business of the judge begins,"[39] but they are the exception rather than the rule.

The next problem for the judge, provided an earlier decision does not govern the present case, is to "determine the path or direction along which the principle is to move and develop." It is here where Cardozo said "the creative element in the judicial process finds its opportunity and power."[40] In examining the path or direction of the law, Cardozo discussed four methods of decision-making available to judges: philosophy, evolution, tradition, and sociology. All four methods have their importance. The task of the judge is to determine which one is appropriate in a particular case.

The method of philosophy (or logic) is the approach of deciding cases by analogy from principles already established. While Cardozo did not believe that this method was the most important of the four approaches, he claimed that it had "a certain presumption in its favor." For one, it satisfies "a deep-seated and imperious sentiment" to find order and symmetry in the world. "Given a mass of particulars, a congeries of judgments on related topics, the principle that unifies and rationalizes them has a tendency, and a legitimate one, to protect and extend itself to new cases within the limits of its capacity to unify and rationalize. It has the primacy that comes from natural and orderly logical succession." What is more, the presumption in favor of logic was based on the equitable principle that like cases should be decided alike. "It would be a gross injustice," Cardozo wrote, "to decide alternate cases on opposite principles." In short, while Cardozo was critical of the "mechanical jurisprudence" of the late nineteenth and early twentieth centuries, he did not deny the importance of the rule of law. As he put it, "[l]ogical consistency does not cease to be a good because it is not the supreme good."[41] In fact, Cardozo gave logic a substantial place in the decisions he rendered.

The second and third methods—evolution and tradition—give rise to judicial decisions based on history and custom. According to Cardozo, some areas of the law—real property, contracts, and the powers and functions of executors, for example—can only be understood with a solid knowledge of history. In these areas, as Holmes famously said, "a page of history is worth a volume of logic."[42] By the same token, custom—for example, business, market, and professional practices—sometimes serves as a guide for the uncertain judge. It is clear, however, that —Cardozo regarded these two methods as being limited in scope and application. The method of history, for example, prevails over other methods only in those cases that turn on "conceptions of the law [that] owe their existing form almost exclusively to history." The two methods also often serve to *limit* (not expand) the creative role of judging. For example, judges "look to custom, not so much for the creation of new rules, but for the tests and standards that are to determine how established rules shall be applied.... When custom seeks to do more than this," Cardozo remarked, "there is a growing tendency in the law to leave development to legislation."[43]

Not so the fourth method—sociology—which decides on the basis of welfare, needs, and mores of the society, and provides for changing law to meet changing conditions. Unlike the other methods of decision-making, which find their proper direction of the law's growth by extension from earlier principles, the method of sociology focuses on social utility as a normative end. As Roscoe Pound put it, sociological jurists ask "not merely what law is and how it has come to be but what (in all of its senses) it does, how it does it, and how it may be made to do it better."[44] Interestingly, Cardozo defined the term "social welfare" quite broadly to include not only public policy, whose "demands are often those of mere expediency or prudence," but also adherence "to the standards of right conduct, which find expression in the mores of the community," and whose "demands are those of religion or of ethics or of the social sense of justice...."[45] Accordingly, Cardozo's creative judge, when given the opportunity, should make decisions that not only reflect current notions of good public policy, but that also take into account the community's sense of justice.

Of the four methods, Cardozo regarded sociology as the dominant method for two reasons.[46] First, it conformed with what he regarded the end of law to be. "The final cause of the law is the welfare of society," Cardozo concluded. "The rule that misses its aim cannot permanently justify its existence."[47] Second, the sociological method was the most comprehensive of the four methods. For example, a primary reason why judges follow prior decisions—the method of philosophy—is the utilitarian goal of maximizing reliance interests and stability in society. In this view, law is not followed simply because it is old, but because it serves society's needs to do so. Since social utility is the ultimate test of any law, the sociological method assumes the role of "arbiter between other methods, determining in the last analysis the choice of each, weighing their competing claims, setting bounds to their pretensions, balancing and moderating and harmonizing them all."[48]

In sum, Cardozo's approach to judging was eclectic and pragmatic. Most cases are predetermined by prior judicial rulings, which "make up in bulk what they lack in interest." The serious business of judging begins when prior case law is uncertain. In such cases, the judge must balance and weigh considerations of logic, history, custom, and sociology in order to determine which interest should prevail. Cardozo regarded sociology as the most important method, particularly in constitutional cases where the text tends to be ambiguous and public policy arguments are at their acme. When asked how he himself decides among the competing methods, Cardozo ambiguously stated: "I can only answer that he must get his knowledge just as the legislator gets it, from experience and study and reflection; in brief, from life itself." Interestingly, Cardozo did not regard his view of the judicial function as revolutionary; rather, "[i]t is the way that courts have gone about their business for centuries in the development of the common law."[49]

Cardozo's Jurisprudence. Cardozo the Legal Realist

Cardozo was a subtle and complex legal theorist, so in describing his jurisprudence, pat generalizations will not suffice. Nevertheless, his view of the judicial role can be said to have drawn from several sources. First, he was a legal realist. The realists were a diverse group of legal thinkers whose views came to dominate the legal academy in the 1930s. While they espoused many different theories about the law, the bond which held them together was a fundamental distrust of the conceptual jurisprudence that was popular during the *Lochner* era.[50] Conceptual jurisprudence regarded law as a closed, self-contained logical system whereby judges, trained in the science of the law, deduce legal conclusions from preexisting rules of law. On this view, judges never make law; they simply discover it. This view of judging finds support in the writings of the English common law judge William Blackstone, who described judges as "living oracles" of the law.

Cardozo rejected this model of judging. After describing conceptual jurisprudence as a process of "match[ing] the colors of the case at hand against the colors of many sample cases spread out upon their desk," Cardozo ridiculed it by saying that "no judge of a high court, worthy of his office, views the functions of his place so narrowly." For Cardozo, judging was a far more complex process than the mechanical (or slot machine) approach would suggest. While logic is an important ingredient of judging, Cardozo emphasized the nonlegal factors as well, including history, custom, and sociology. In each case that comes before the court, the judge must balance these various interests, "and adding a little here and taking out a little there, must determine, as wisely as he can, which weight shall tip the scales."[51] The skills required to perform this job competently approximate more those of an artist than of a scientist.

Cardozo also did not have any qualms about saying that judges make law. "I take judge-made law as one of the existing realities of life," he wrote in the opening pages of *The Nature of the Judicial Process*.[52] For Cardozo, judging was not simply a process of discovery; was also one of creation. As he saw it, the law was constantly being created and recreated in the courts of justice. One aspect of this creative process is what Holmes called the "inarticulate and unconscious judgment" of the judge.[53] A judge's decision requires the making of choices, which in turn reflect the judge's life experiences. As Cardozo candidly observed: "There is in each of us a stream of tendency... which gives coherence and direction to thought and action. Judges cannot escape that current any more than other mortals. All their lives, forces which they do not recognize and cannot name, have been tugging at them—inherited instincts, traditional beliefs, acquired convictions; the resultant is an outlook on life, a conception of social needs... which, when reasons are nicely balanced, must determine where choice shall fall."[54]

Cardozo also objected to the idea implicit in conceptual jurisprudence that law consists of fixed truths. Cardozo admitted that when he first became a judge he searched for certainty in the decisions he rendered, but he found the search ultimately futile. "Nothing is stable. Nothing absolute. All is fluid and changeable."[55] "The truth," he concluded, "is that every doubtful decision involves a choice between a nicely balanced alternative; no matter how long we debate or how carefully we ponder, we shall never arrive at certitude."[56] For this reason, Cardozo rejected the traditional understanding of natural law,[57] absolutist definitions of liberty[58] and property,[59] and formalistic interpretations of federalism[60] and separation of powers.[61] Like most realists, he defined law in a probabilistic manner: "When there is such a degree of probability as to lead to a reasonable assurance that a given conclusion ought to be and will be embodied in a judgment, we speak of the conclusion as law, though the judgment has not yet been rendered, and though, conceivably, when rendered, it may disappoint our expectation."[62]

An illustration of Cardozo's realist views can be found in *Hynes v. New York Central Railroad Co.* (231 NY 229 [1921]), an opinion he wrote as a member of the New York Court of Appeals. In that case, Harvey Hynes, a sixteen-year-old boy, was killed after being struck by an electric wire while diving off a springboard. At that time, the New York Central Railroad had a right of way on the Bronx side of the Harlem River and operated its trains by high-tension wires strung on poles and cross-arms. For approximately five years, a plank, which had been affixed by a heavy rock and nails to a bulkhead on the defendant's property, had been used by neighborhood swimmers as a diving board. On the day in question, Hynes was standing at the end of the board poised for a dive when he was hit by an electric wire that fell from a cross-arm maintained by the defendant, plunging him to his death in the water below. Hynes's mother, as administratrix, sued the railroad company for damages.

A central issue in the case was the spatial location of the teen when struck by the high-tension wire. The base of the springboard was affixed to the bulk-head located on the defendant's property, making that part of it private property. Under New York law at that time, landowners owed no duty to trespassers, except to abstain from intentional, reckless, and wanton injury—a situation which was not present here. On the other hand, approximately seven and one-half feet of the plank jutted out beyond the line of the railroad company's property over the public waterway, where it owed a duty of ordinary care to individuals swimming in the water. The courts below had refused recovery on the ground that Hynes was a trespasser, and therefore the defendant owed only a duty of abstaining from willful or wanton injury.

The Court of Appeals, in an opinion by Judge Cardozo, reversed the decision. Cardozo rejected what he regarded as the sterile logic of the lower courts' opinion. "Duties are [not] supposed to arise and to be extinguished in alternate zones or strata" (231 NY, 234 [1921]), he wrote. If the boy had been below or leaning against the board, the defendant would be liable; but because he was standing on top of it, the company is absolved from responsibility. "We may be permitted to distrust the logic that leads to such conclusions," wrote Cardozo (234). As Cardozo saw it, the use of the springboard was merely an extension, or "by-play," of the act of swimming, for which the defendant was responsible for any injuries resulting from the negligent condition of its electrical poles and cross-arms. "This case," Cardozo maintained, "is a striking instance of the dangers of 'a jurisprudence of conceptions'... the extension of a maxim or a definition with relentless disregard of consequences to 'a dryly logical extreme'"(235). In a revealing statement of his realist views, Cardozo summarized the case as follows: "In one sense, and that a highly technical and artificial one, the diver at the end of the springboard is an intruder on the adjoining lands. In another sense, and one that realists will accept more readily, he is still on public waters in the exercise of public rights. The law must say whether it will subject him to the rule of the one field or of the other, of this sphere or of that. We think that considerations of analogy, of convenience, of policy, and of justice, exclude him from the field of the defendant's immunity and exemption, and place him in the field of liability and duty" (236).Importantly, however, in debunking the conceptual jurisprudence of the *Lochner* era, Cardozo did not go as far as the "neorealists" (specifically, Karl Llwellyn[63] and Jerome Frank[64]) in casting doubt upon the rule of law. Frank, in particular, questioned the idea of an objective law existing independently of the individual decisions of judges. Using a psychological approach to study judicial behavior, Frank argued that the most important determinants in explaining what judges do are not preexisting rules and precedents (which he regarded as impermanent, artificial, malleable, and uncertain), but the idiosyncratic biases of the judge. As understood by him, the process of judging begins with a tentatively formed conclusion (or "hunch"[65]), which represents the biases and sympathies of the judge, then proceeds to the judge finding the law to back up that hunch, and then concludes with the written opinion, which represents the posthoc rationalization of the predetermined conclusion or hunch. According to Frank, until the judge actually makes a decision, the law does not exist. Frank attributed "the childish desire" for a certain and fixed law to a "father-controlled universe, free from chance and error due to human fallibility."[66]

In an important speech before the New York State Bar Association in January 1932, Cardozo criticized this view of the judicial process. Cardozo credited the neorealists for advancing our knowledge about the law, and "ridding *stare decisis* of something of its petrifying rigidity,"[67] but he claimed that they exaggerated the irrational and uncertain nature of law, as well as the amount of discretion involved in the judicial role. According to Cardozo, simply because law is tentative and not based on a deductive logic, does not mean that it does not exist. Cases are decided, in his view, by reference to underlying general rules and principles that are embedded in law. When a rule or principle emerges, it "becomes a datum, a point of departure, from which new lines will be run, from which new courses will be measured." These general principles, which are "at first tentative and groping, gain by reiteration a new permanence and certainty." On this view, there is an overall rationality to the law in that general rules and principles can (and often do) decide particular cases. The basis for certainty in the law, as Cardozo saw it, is that most people follow the rules and regulations found in statutes. "Statutes do not cease to be law," Cardozo reasoned, "because the power to fix their meaning in case of doubt or ambiguity has been confided to the courts."[68] On this basis, Cardozo rejected the neorealist view that law is "a doctrine of undisciplined surrender to the cardiac promptings of the moment, the visceral reactions of one judge or another."[69]

Cardozo also claimed that the neorealists exaggerated the amount of discretion in the judicial craft. While judges do make law, Cardozo did not believe that they exercise total free will. "Insignificant is the power of innovation of any judge," Cardozo maintained, "when compared with the bulk and practice of the rules that hedge him on every side."[70] In Cardozo's view, there are "jural principles" which limit the judge to stay within "the walls of the interstices, the bounds set to judicial innovation by precedent and custom."[71] The neorealists, according to Cardozo, mistake the distinction between right and power. Judges may have the power to go beyond their authority (i.e., ignore a statute or precedent), but they do not have the right to do so.[72] What Cardozo sought was a middle ground between what he regarded as a static understanding of law, on the one hand, and an "anarchical" view of law, on the other:

> We must get away at one extreme from the notion that law is fixed and immutable, that the conclusion which the judge declares, instead of being itself a more or less tentative hypothesis, an approximate formulation of a uniformity and an order inductively apprehended, has a genuine preexistence, that judgment is a process of discovery, and not in any degree a process of creation.... On the other hand, we must avoid another extreme...the conception of law as a series of isolated dooms, the general merged in the particular.... Each extreme has a tendency, though for a different reason, to stifle the creative element. Between these two extremes we have the conception of law as a body of rules and principles and standards which in their extension to new combinations of events are to be sorted, selected, moulded, and adapted in subordination to an end.[73]

Cardozo's speech before the New York Bar Association delineated the important differences between the neorealists, such as Frank and Llewellyn, and the traditional realists, such as Roscoe Pound and Cardozo himself. It was also a speech for which Frank never forgave him.[74] Nevertheless, like all other realists, Cardozo did recognize that there is considerable discretion involved in the judicial craft. Law is not stable or certain; rather, it can more accurately be described as provisional or tentative.

Cardozo the Sociological Jurist

Cardozo was also influenced by the sociological school of jurisprudence, a leading architect of which was Roscoe Pound. A guiding insight of this school is that law was not an exercise in pure logic, but rather a social phenomenon. As such, the sociological jurists embraced a purposeful attitude toward the law, and stressed the need for lawmakers (legislative, administrative, and judicial) to consider the social consequences of their decisions. In this view, law is not regarded as absolute or fixed, but rather it is pliant and functional; the lawmaker should consciously use the law to achieve desirable social goals. As Roscoe Pound described the school, "[t]he sociological movement in jurisprudence is a movement for pragmatism as a philosophy of law; for the adjustment of principles and doctrines to the human conditions they are to govern rather than to assumed first principles."[75]

The sociological jurists also placed great faith in progress and believed that the institution of law could be improved by intelligent design. For this reason, many of the sociological jurists, Cardozo included,[76] urged the creation of institutes which would bring the disciplines of law and sociology together. A classic example of the use of sociological evidence can be found in the famous "Brandeis Brief" filed in *Muller v. Oregon* (208 US 412 [1908]). In that case, the Court had before it a state law setting a maximum ten-hour workday for women employed in factories and laundries. In one of the few instances in which a labor law was sustained during the *Lochner* era, the Supreme Court relied upon a brief filed by then-attorney Louis Brandeis, which marshaled to gether 100 pages of labor statistics (and only two pages of legal precedents) showing the deleterious effects of excessive work hours for women.

The influence of sociological jurisprudence on Cardozo's thought is evident in many of his opinions. As a member of the New York Court of Appeals, Cardozo supported various economic and social measures that were challenged under the "liberty of contract" doctrine. For example, he voted to uphold New York's workers' compensation law,[77] a law prohibiting the night employment of women in factories,[78] and he wrote the majority opinions in two other cases, one upholding a bulk sales law,[79] and the other sustaining a health code for medicines.[80] Similarly, as a member of the Supreme Court, Cardozo rejected formalistic interpretations of the Constitution in favor of public policy arguments. In the area of state regulation of the economy, for example, Cardozo voted to uphold Minnesota's mortgage moratorium law,[81] New York's milk price control law,[82] and Washington state's minimum wage law.[83]

Cardozo's vote in *Home Building & Loan Association v. Blaisdell* (290 US 398 [1934]) deserves special mention. In that case, the Court upheld a state mortgage payment deferment policy, placing heavy reliance on the public policy arguments and rejecting a literal interpretation of the Contracts Clause. Cardozo originally wanted to file a concurring opinion in the case, but agreed to withhold it when Chief Justice Charles Evans Hughes, the author of the Court's opinion, agreed to incorporate his views. Nevertheless, Cardozo's unpublished opinion reveals his reliance upon sociological arguments:

> The economic and social changes wrought by the industrial revolution and by the growth of population have made it necessary for government at this day to do a thousand things that were beyond the experience or the thought of a century ago. With the growing recognition of this need, courts have awakened to the truth that the contract clause is perverted from its proper meaning when it throttles the capacity of the states to exert their governmental power to deal with matters which are basically the concern of government.... A gospel of laissez faire—of individual initiative—of thrift and industry and sacrifice—may be inadequate in the great society that we live in to point the way to salvation, at least for economic life. The state when it acts today by statutes like the one before us is not furthering the selfish good of individuals or classes as ends of ultimate validity. It is furthering its own good by maintaining the economic structure on which the good of all depends. Such at least is its endeavor, however much it may miss the mark.[84]

Cardozo's sociological jurisprudence was also evident in cases involving national regulation of the economy. In almost every federal regulatory case that came before the Supreme Court, Cardozo (often in dissent) sided with Franklin Roosevelt and the Congress. For example, he filed a sole dissent in *Panama Refining Co. v. Ryan* (293 US 388, 433), in which he supported the National Industrial Recovery Act's regulation of "Hot Oil"; he dissented in the two cases striking down the Agricultural Adjustment Act of 1933[85] and the Bituminous

Coal Conservation Act of 1935;[86] and he voted with the majority in upholding the National Labor Relations Act of 1935.[87]

Two of Cardozo's most important majority opinions came in disputes over the Social Security Act of 1935. In *Steward Machine v. Davis* (301 US 548 [1937], Cardozo wrote the 5–4 decision upholding the unemployment compensation provisions of the act. One of the principal arguments made by the petitioner in the case was that the federal grants given to the states to assist in administering their unemployment compensation laws violated the Tenth Amendment by coercing the states to pass laws that were within their reserved power. Cardozo rejected that argument, and the "dual federalism" theory on which it was based, relying instead on the federal government's argument that everyone benefits from this program of cooperative federalism. He also cited statistics showing the need for the unemployment compensation laws. On the same day, the Court handed down *Helvering v. Davis* (301 US 69 [1937]), where Cardozo (this time for six other justices) upheld the old-age benefits provisions of the act. Cardozo again rejected the argument that the provisions intruded on the sovereign interests of the states and cited statistical evidence demonstrating the necessity for the old-age benefits. The only instance where Cardozo did not side with the president and Congress came in *A.L.A. Schechter Poultry Corp. v. United States* (295 US 495 [1935]), the so-called "Sick Chicken" case. There the Court unanimously held that the "live poultry" provisions of the National Industrial Recovery Act violated principles of federalism and the non-delegation doctrine. Cardozo filed a concurring opinion, noting his basic agreement with the majority's analysis, but also distinguishing his earlier lone dissent in the "Hot Oil" case, *Panama Refining Co. v. Ryan* (293 US 388, 433 [1935]). While in *Panama Refining* Cardozo did not believe that the authority conferred on the president constituted an excessive delegation of power, in *Schechter* he determined that the authority granted to the president was not "canalized within banks that keep it from overflowing" and amounted to "delegation running riot."[88] As a general rule, however, Cardozo supported FDR and the New Deal programs, relying on arguments based on social utility and rejecting formalistic interpretations of separation of powers and federalism. In fact, more than any other Supreme Court justice during his tenure (Justices Louis D. Brandeis and Harlan Fiske Stone included), Cardozo voted to uphold federal regulation of the economy. According to constitutional historian Richard D. Friedman, "Cardozo was the prime bearer of the torch" during "the darkest time" of the New Deal.[89]

Cardozo the Common Law Judge

Cardozo is often recognized for his conscious efforts to adapt legal principles to modern needs, but he was also a judge who put great stock in tradition and the rule of law. In brokering a compromise between the twin goals of growth and stability, Cardozo utilized a common law methodology in both private and public law cases. Unlike the deductive approach of reasoning downward from preestablished rules, the common law method is an inductive approach where general principles are discerned from particular cases. Under such an approach, judges are regarded as important agents of change who, through their decisions, slowly evolve legal principles in the direction of greater social progress. But the common law approach also stresses the importance of *stare decisis*, where "adherence to precedent should be the rule and not the exception."[90] As seen in Cardozo's opinions, the common law method allowed him to relax the concept of precedent on occasion, but it was not the norm.

Cardozo and Growth of the Law

Cardozo's use of the common law as an instrument of growth is reflected in a number of his decisions. In *MacPherson v. Buick Motor Co.* (317 NY 382 [1916]), for example, one of Cardozo's most significant rulings as a member of the New York Court of Appeals, he wrote the 5–1 decision[91] extending the liability of automobile manufacturers beyond car dealers to consumers. In that case, the plaintiff, Donald C. MacPherson, traveling at a speed of about eight miles an hour, was injured when a wheel on his car made from defective wood suddenly collapsed. The defendant, Buick Motor Company, had manufactured the car but had purchased the wheel from another manufacturer and had been negligent in failing to ascertain the defect. Prior to that time, the general rule had been that automobile manufacturers were not responsible for injuries to consumers because the two did not enter into a contractual relationship. Cardozo, relying on a line of decisions involving inherently dangerous products, disregarded the earlier general rule and extended the scope of liability to automobile buyers. Privity of contract in the sale of automobiles might have been justifiable at one time, Cardozo reasoned, but it no longer was. Since automobile purchasers are the ones at risk if a car is defectively designed, it does not make any sense that manufacturers, who have a duty to inspect the cars that they sell, are liable only to the dealers and not to the actual users. "Precedents drawn from the days of travel by stage coach," Cardozo wrote, "do not fit the conditions of travel to-day" (317 NY at 391). Even though Cardozo glossed over contravening case law and fashioned a new rule out of an exceptional line of decisions, he regarded the extension of liability in this case as a reasonable adjustment of earlier principles to meet changing social circumstances.

Cardozo's evolutionary approach to the law is also evident in several constitutional cases. In the modern debate between the originalists and nonoriginalists, Cardozo clearly sided with the latter. In many of the constitutional decisions that came before the Court, Cardozo supported the idea of a "Living Constitution," as opposed to what some originalists call a "Dead Constitution." This is clear, for example, in his opinion for the Court in *Helvering v. Davis* (301 US 619 [1937]), where, in finding that Congress had the authority to pass old-age benefits under the Social Security Act of 1935, Cardozo rejected a "static"view of the General Welfare Clause: "Needs that were narrow or parochial a century ago may be interwoven in our day with the well-being of the Nation. What is critical or urgent changes with the times" (641). Moreover, in his unpublished concurring opinion in *Home Building & Loan Association v. Blaisdell* (290 US 398 [1934]), Cardozo emphasized a constitutional philosophy of growth. After acknowledging that his view of the Contracts Clause "may be inconsistent with things that men said in 1787," Cardozo went on to say that "They did not see the changes in the relation between the states and nation or in the play of social forces that lay hidden in the womb of time. It may be inconsistent with things that they believed or took for granted. Their beliefs to be significant must be adjusted to the world they knew. It is not in my judgment inconsistent with what they would say today, nor with what today they would believe, if they were called upon to interpret 'in the light of our whole experience' the Constitution that they framed for the needs of an expanding future."[92]

The Need for Stability

Cardozo was cautious in his advocacy of judge-made law, however. Even though he viewed judges as creative agents of change, he regarded their role as distinctly subordinate to the legislative and executive branches. In Cardozo's opinions, for example, one sees ample support for James Bradley Thayer's "reasonable doubt" test, pursuant to which the authority of judicial review should only be exercised when "the violation of the Constitution is so manifest as to leave no room for reasonable doubt."[93] "In this view, the test of a law's constitutionality is not its wisdom, but whether Congress had the legal authority to pass it. As Justice Holmes once said: "Young man [he was talking to the sixty-one-year-old Justice Stone!], about seventy-five years ago I learned that I was not God. And so, when the people... want to do something I can't find anything the Constitution expressly forbidding them to do, I say, whether I like it or not, 'Goddamit, let 'em do it.'"[94]

Moreover, Cardozo confined the legislative function of judges to that of filling gaps. When law is uncertain, judges "have the right to legislate within gaps," and "often there are no gaps."[95] Thus, Cardozo, the person who candidly reveals the dark secret that judges make law, qualifies this by saying that judges should not legislate at will: "The judge, even when he is free, is still not wholly free. He is not to innovate at pleasure. He is not a knight-errant roaming at will in the pursuit of his own ideal of beauty or of goodness. He is to draw his inspiration from consecrated principles. He is not to yield to spasmodic sentiment, to vague and unregulated benevolence. He is to exercise a discretion informed by tradition, methodized by analogy, disciplined by system, and subordinated to the 'primordial necessity of order in the social life.'"[96]

Cardozo's cautious spirit is also reflected in his understanding of change. While he was not an adherent of the historical school of jurisprudence (i.e., that the development of law is predestined in the fate of history), Cardozo's view of change was not unlike that of the British statesman Edmund Burke. According to Cardozo, the work of judicial modification in a common law system is gradual. "It goes on inch by inch. Its effects must be measured by decades and even centuries. Thus measured, they are seen to have behind them the power and pressure of the moving glacier."[97] In this view, a long train of injustices can presumably take place before a judge has the right to take action. Accordingly, Cardozo's view of change was not revolutionary but conservative. "Justice is not to be taken by storm," he once wrote. "She is to be wooed by slow advances."[98]

Palsgraf v. The Long Island Railroad Co. (248 NY 339 [1928]) is a case in which Cardozo's cautious nature is evident. In that case, a passenger, attempting to catch a moving train, was helped onto the train by two guards employed by the railroad. In the process the guards knocked loose a package the passenger was carrying which, unbeknownst to them, contained fireworks. The package fell to the ground and exploded, setting off vibrations which caused a penny-weighing machine on the station's platform to fall on Helen Palsgraf, who was sitting near the machine "many feet" from the train tracks. She sued the railroad company, seeking damages for the negligent actions of its two employees. A jury returned a verdict in Palsgraf's favor in the amount of $6,000.

In probably his most famous opinion while on the New York Court of Appeals, Cardozo authored the 4–3 decision reversing the trial court's judgment. In contrast to the dissent, which concentrated its analysis of negligence law on the element of causation—that is, whether the defendant's negligent act proximately caused Helen Palsgraf's injuries—Cardozo concentrated his analysis on the element of duty—that is, whether the defendant, through its two employees, owed a duty to Palsgraf. While Cardozo conceded that the defendant had a duty to the passenger trying to get on the train, as well as any innocent bystanders in the immediate area, he did not believe that the railroad company had a duty to Helen Palsgraf who, in his view, was "standing far away" from the tracks. For Cardozo, negligence was a term of relation: "The risk reasonably to be perceived defines the duty to be obeyed...it is risk to another or to others within the range of apprehension" (344). Since the guards did not know the package contained fireworks, and since Palsgraf was a considerable distance from the railroad tracks, Cardozo held that her injuries were not a foreseeable risk by the guards. Any other conclusion, Cardozo suggested, would have to be handled through the legislative process. "Life will have to be made over," Cardozo remarked, "and human nature transformed, before prevision so extravagant can be accepted as the norm of conduct, the customary standard to which behavior must conform" (343).

Cardozo's cautious spirit is also revealed in his interpretation of the "liberty" provision of the due process clauses of the Fifth and Fourteenth Amendments. While Cardozo recognized that liberty was an evolving concept, he restricted the judge's ability to interpret the liberty provision by couching it in the traditions and customs of the American people. This was most apparent in his opinion for the Court in *Palko v. Connecticut* (302 US 319 [1932]). Frank Jacob Palka (his name was misspelled in the case report) was convicted of second-degree murder for the death of two police officers in Bridgeport, Connecticut. The prosecutor appealed the verdict to the Supreme Court of Errors, which under Connecticut law was allowable "upon all questions of law arising on the trial of criminal cases" where the presiding judge grants permission. The prosecution claimed, in particular, that its case was prejudiced by the trial judge's ruling that Palka's confession was inadmissible, and by the judge's characterization of what constituted premeditated (first degree) murder in his instructions to the jury. The Supreme Court of Errors ordered a new trial, whereupon Palka was found guilty of first degree murder and sentenced to death. On appeal, Palka argued that the second trial violated the double jeopardy provision of the Fifth Amendment, which should be made applicable to the states under the Fourteenth Amendment's due process clause.

In his last opinion for the Supreme Court, Cardozo upheld Palka's conviction (8–1), and provided the rationalization for the selective incorporation approach to the Bill of Rights. According to Cardozo, there is no general rule that would make all of the provisions of the Bill of Rights applicable to the states. Instead, he advanced a selective incorporation approach in which some (but not all) of the Bill of Rights would be nationalized. The rights incorporated were those "implicit in the concept of ordered liberty," and those "so rooted in the tradition and conscience of our people as to be ranked as fundamental" (325), which included most of the provisions of the First Amendment, the right to counsel under certain circumstances, and the right to a trial. All other provisions of the Bill of Rights were, in Cardozo's view, merely formal rights, which the states were not required to provide, including the Fifth Amendment's double jeopardy provision.

Cardozo's selective incorporation approach is sometimes referred to as the "honor roll" of freedoms approach, but because of its inherently subjective nature it has been the subject of some controversy. Nevertheless, it was the method used by the Court to incorporate nearly every guarantee of the Bill of Rights to the states in the 1940s, 1950s, and 1960s, including the Fifth Amendment's double jeopardy provision.[99]

Cardozo's fundamental rights approach in *Palko* was not only significant in terms of the incorporation debate, but it still resonates today in substantive due process cases involving such "liberty" claims as abortion, homosexual rights, and the right to die. Cardozo's reliance on tradition and custom made his jurisprudence conservative in the area of criminal law and procedure, where he did not support much innovation by the courts.[100] His evolutionary approach to the Constitution, however, opened the door for other justices to read more rights into the liberty provision of the due process clauses. As a general matter, Cardozo's common law approach to deciding cases sought to balance the antinomies of change and stability in the law. As he put it, "[s]omewhere between the worship of the past and exaltation of the present the path of safety will be found."[101]

Cardozo the Moralist

A final theme in Cardozo's opinions and extrajudicial writings is justice; in fact, he often equated law with morality. As Judge Irving Lehman, his colleague on the New York Court of Appeals, put it: Cardozo "could not accept lightly a conclusion that the law ordains a result which conscience rejects...."[102] Recall that Cardozo's broad definition of the word "social welfare" included the mores of the community. "The judge," Cardozo reasoned, "is under a duty, within the limits of his power of innovation, to maintain a relation between law and morals...."[103] By this, Cardozo did not mean that every legal result had to satisfy some standard of justice. Rather, moral norms were a factor to be considered by the judge in making decisions.[104] Cardozo's attempt to connect law with morality marked another important distinction between him and the legal realists, who tended to regard morality as a purely relative concept.[105]

Riggs v. Palmer (115 NY 506 [1889]), a New York Court of Appeals case that predated Cardozo's service on that tribunal, illustrates the importance that Cardozo placed on law serving the ends of justice. The issue in that case was whether a grandson, Elmer E. Palmer, who was an heir named in the will of his grandfather, Francis E. Palmer, could inherit under that will, even though he had murdered his grandfather to do so. Because there were several directions in which the judges could go in the case, Cardozo referred to *Riggs* as "[t]he Judicial process...in microcosm." On the one hand, a judge who was a strict legalist could conclude that by the terms of the will the grandson should recover, which is what the two dissenters in the case decided. On the other hand, there are certain maxims of the common law—e.g., no one should profit from his own wrongdoing—which ran in the opposite direction. For Cardozo, as well as the *Riggs* majority, the equitable factors were ultimately decisive because they led to the more just result. "[T]he social interest served by refusing to permit the criminal to profit by his crime," Cardozo wrote, "is greater than that served by the preservation and enforcement of legal rights of ownership."[106] Importantly, however, morality for Cardozo was not the same thing as natural rights.[107] As a pragmatist, Cardozo rejected absolute or rigid definitions of justice. Natural law spoke of immutable principles that were anathema to his view that law was constantly developing, taking shape, and being created. Like Holmes, he did not believe that the law was "a brooding omnipresence in the sky."[108] Cardozo also warned that judges should not impose their own moral values into their decisions, but rather should search objectively for norms and standards of conduct in the mores of the community. For this reason, while on a personal level Cardozo opposed capital punishment, as a judge he felt duty-bound to enforce death sentences. In his search for moral principles that transcended particular cases, Cardozo was a forerunner of the legal process school and, in particular, the idea of "principled" decision-making through a process called "reasoned elaboration."[109]

The concern about law serving the ends of justice is seen in many of Cardozo's opinions. In *Wagner v. International Railway Co.* (232 NY 176 [1922]), for example, an opinion he wrote as a member of the New York Court of Appeals, Cardozo underscored the connection between law and morality in a case involving a rescue attempt. The plaintiff, Arthur Wagner, and his cousin, Herbert Wagner, were riding on an overcrowded train, with the doors wide open, when a violent lurch suddenly threw Herbert out of the train. At the next stop, and with darkness setting in, Arthur got off the train and walked back four hundred feet along a trestle to the spot where he thought he would find his cousin, who had died from the fall. While searching for his cousin, Arthur lost his footing, fell off the trestle, and injured himself. He sued International Railway Company, the owner of the train, claiming that the injuries he sustained were the direct result of the negligence of the company in causing Herbert to fall from the train. The trial judge instructed the jury that the defendant would be liable only if its conductor had invited Arthur to leave the train to search for his cousin and had followed Arthur with a light—neither of which happened. The jury therefore found for the defendant, and the Appellate Division affirmed.

The New York Court of Appeals reversed. In an opinion by Judge Cardozo, the court unanimously held that the trial judge's instructions were erroneous and ordered a new trial. In order to recover for his injuries, the court held that Arthur did not have to show that he was the defendant's invitee. "Danger invites rescue," Cardozo penned. "The cry of distress is the summons to relief. The law does not ignore these reactions of the mind in tracing conduct to its consequences. It recognizes them as normal" (180). Whether the plaintiff's injuries were the result of defendant's negligence in causing his cousin to fall from the train, and whether Arthur may have been contributorily negligent in conducting the search, were questions for the jury. The defendant also claimed that because plaintiff's actions were not "instinctive" (i.e., spontaneous and immediate), the rescue attempt was an intervening event that broke the chain of responsibility between any railroad negligence and Arthur's injury. Cardozo rejected that claim. Unlike in *Palsgraf*, Cardozo viewed the injuries suffered by Arthur as the direct result of a chain of events precipitated by the defendant's negligence. "The law does not discriminate between the rescuer oblivious of peril and the one who counts the cost. It is enough that the act, whether impulsive or deliberate, is the child of the occasion" (181). Accordingly, when a breach of duty could be established, Cardozo supported a broad notion of liability.

The moral aspect of the case should not be ignored either. In his extrajudicial writings, Cardozo argued that people have a moral responsibility to assist someone in distress, and he criticized the dearth of Good Samaritan laws that would make this a legal requirement.[110] When seen in this way, the trial judge's narrow instructions, which would have penalized Arthur's Good Samaritan act, did not likely sit well with Cardozo. Arthur Wagner, in Cardozo's view, should be able to recover for his injuries because he was performing a heroic act. The moral tone of Cardozo's opinion is indicated by his description of the rescue attempt: "The wrong that imperils life is a wrong to the imperilled victim; it is a wrong also to his rescuer.... The risk of the rescue, if only it be not wanton, is born of the occasion. The emergency begets the man. The wrongdoer may not have foreseen the coming of a deliverer. He is accountable as if he had" (232 NY 180 [1922]). Another illustration of the intersection between law and morality in Cardozo's jurisprudence came in *Graf v. Hope Building Corp* (254 NY 1 [1930]). There the court had before it an action in equity seeking enforcement of an acceleration clause under a mortgage agreement. The executors of Joseph L. Graf were the holders of a mortgage in the amount of $335,000 on a piece of real property owned by the Hope Building Corporation. Pursuant to the mortgage agreement, payments were to begin on April 1, 1925, and continue until January 1, 1935, when a payment in the amount of $276,500 would be due. The principal of the mortgage ($1,500) was to be paid on a quarterly basis together with a variable interest payment determined at a rate of 5 3/4 percent per annum. An acceleration clause was also included in the mortgage agreement, which stated that if a default in the payment of any installment of interest existed for twenty days the whole unpaid principal sum would be due.

On July 1, 1927, the quarterly installment of principal ($1,500), as well as an interest payment in the amount of $4,621.56, were due. When David Herstein, the president and treasurer of the Hope Building Corporation, who alone was authorized to sign its checks, prepared to go to Europe in early June 1927, he instructed his bookkeeper and the nominal secretary of the company to compute the interest which would be due for the next month and to draw a check for that sum and one for the principal amount. Checks were drawn and signed, but it was discovered after Herstein's departure that the check for the interest payment was underdrawn in the amount of $401.87. When the error was discovered, the mortgagee was notified and informed that the balance would be paid upon Mr. Herstein's return. Due to the secretary's oversight, however, Herstein was not notified about the underpayment and a foreclosure proceeding was commenced on July 22, 1927, one day after the grace period expired. Promptly that same day, the Hope Building Corporation tendered the interest sum due, but the mortgagee refused the tender and insisted upon its rights to claim the entire unpaid balance under the acceleration clause. The plaintiffs lost in both the trial court and Appellate Division, and appealed to the Court of Appeals.

In a 4–3 decision, the majority, with Judge John F. O'Brien authoring the opinion, reversed and ordered foreclosure of the mortgage in accordance with the acceleration clause. "Plaintiffs may be ungenerous," the majority reasoned, "but generosity is a voluntary attribute and cannot be enforced even by a chancellor" (4). While noting that the mortgagee could perhaps have made an exception under the circumstances of the case, the majority stressed that "[s]tability of contract obligations must not be undermined by judicial sympathy" (254 NY [1930]). Accordingly, the majority held the parties to the strict language of their agreement: "We feel that the interests of certainty and security in real estate transactions forbid us, in the absence of fraud, bad faith or unconscionable conduct, to recede from the doctrine that is so deeply embedded in equity"(6).

Cardozo, writing for two others in dissent, saw the case in a completely different light. While he conceded that enforcement of acceleration clauses is not as a general rule unconscionable, he believed it would be in the circumstances of this case. The deficiency in this case was the result of an accident or error; it was slight and unimportant when compared with the payment duly made" (14); and immediately upon discovery of the mistake Hope Building Corporation tendered the amount due. In Cardozo's view, the culpable party was not the defendant, but the holder of the mortgage, who "must have understood that he could have his money for the asking. His silence, followed, as it was, by immediate suit at the first available opportunity, brings conviction to the mind that he was avoiding any act that would spur the mortgagor to payment" (12). As Cardozo saw it, enforcement of the acceleration agreement in this case would make the court "an instrument of injustice," and "approach in hardship the oppression of a penalty...." (14–15). As he put it: "It is not unconscionable generally to insist that payment shall be made according to the letter of a contract. It may be unconscionable to insist upon adherence to the letter where the default is limited to a trifling balance, where the failure to pay the balance is the product of mistake, and where the mortgagee indicates by his conduct that he appreciates the mistake and has attempted by silence and inaction to turn it to his own advantage"(12).

Wagner and *Graf* illustrate that Cardozo was willing to invoke equitable principles in order to reach what he considered to be a just result. While Cardozo claimed that judges should not inject their own moral beliefs into their decisions, his reliance on communal moral values does raise an important question about the judicial role: How do we distinguish between the judge's personal values and those of the community?[111] While Cardozo's opinions in *Wagner* and *Graf* are perhaps agreeable from a moral point of view, not every case in which Cardozo invoked moral values can be assessed similarly. *People v. Carey* (223 NY 519 [1918]) serves as an example. In that case, Raymond Carey, a nineteen-year-old male, was convicted of raping Lillian Tate, a twenty-five-year-old female. The defense claimed that Tate consented to have sex, and sought to introduce the complainant's prior sexual behavior as proof of her willingness to have sex with Carey on the day in question. In ordering a new trial, the Court of Appeals, in a *per curiam* opinion, ruled that legal error was committed because the complaint was not corroborated "by other evidence" within the meaning of the statute, but also noted that a majority declined to support reversal on the additional ground "that error was committed in rejecting testimony tending to prove that the complainant was unchaste" (520). Cardozo, in an internal memorandum to his colleagues, argued that evidence of Tate's prior sexual conduct should have been allowed because, in his view, "[u]nchastity diminishes...the likelihood of resistance."[112] Not only does Cardozo's opinion not sit well from a moral point of view, but it raises the question of whether his own moral values about sexuality, which can be fairly described as Victorian, may have influenced his decision. In short, Cardozo's reliance on community mores is reminiscent of Justice Hugo Black's criticism of Justice Felix Frankfurter's use of moral standards, such as "shocks the conscience" and "fundamental fairness," in due process cases.

Conclusion

Cardozo's substantive contributions to the law were wide-ranging and tremendous. His opinions as a member of the New York Court of Appeals brought about significant doctrinal changes in the areas of torts and contracts, which can be substantiated by the high level of frequency with which they are still cited today. His most important opinions as a member of the U.S. Supreme Court came in the areas of federal regulation of the economy and the incorporation doctrine, where in *Palko v. Connecticut* he provided the rationalization of the selective approach to nationalizing the Bill of Rights. In the end, however, Cardozo's chief legacy will be his philosophical writings about the judicial process. For his generation, Cardozo was the great mediator between the inflexible deductive logic of the positivists and the excesses of the neorealists, some of whom denied the existence of an independent objective law.

Cardozo's approach to judging (both in a theoretical sense and as practiced) was eclectic and pragmatic. In rejecting a *mechanical* approach to judicial decision-making, as well as acknowledging that judges make law, he was a legal realist. In defining the ultimate end of law as social utility, he showed that he was influenced by the sociological school of jurisprudence. In attempting to broker a compromise between the competing goals of legal stability and progress, he used a common law approach in deciding cases. And in arguing for an intersection between law and morality, he was a forerunner of the legal process school.

This raises an important question: Was Cardozo an activist or restraintist? The answer to this question may depend on how one defines the terms. On the one hand, if the mark of judicial restraint is deference to the majoritarian process, then Cardozo could certainly be considered a restraintist. In the tradition of Holmes, Brandeis, and Frankfurter, he accepted James Bradley Thayer's reasonable doubt test. In terms of his judicial decisions, this was most pronounced in the areas of criminal law and procedure, and in cases involving state and federal regulation of the economy. On the other hand, if the mark of judicial restraint is strict obedience to text and adherence to precedent, then Cardozo was a cautious activist. Cardozo, for example, believed that the Constitution must be kept up with the times, and maintained that moral principles must occasionally trump positive law. Moreover, while he himself did not do so regularly, Cardozo called for the relaxation of the doctrine of *stare decisis*. Thus, Cardozo was both a restraintist and a cautious activist. To his right were the four horsemen. To his left were future Supreme Court justices William J. Brennan and Thurgood Marshall. Thus, both liberals and conservatives can find things to appreciate in Cardozo's approach to the judicial process. contract. It may be unconscionable to insist upon adherence to the letter where the default is limited to a trifling balance, where the failure to pay the balance is the product of mistake, and where the mortgagee indicates by his conduct that he appreciates the mistake and has attempted by silence and inaction to turn it to his own advantage"(12).

Wagner and *Graf* illustrate that Cardozo was willing to invoke equitable principles in order to reach what he considered to be a just result. While Cardozo claimed that judges should not inject their own moral beliefs into their decisions, his reliance on communal moral values does raise an important question about the judicial role: How do we distinguish between the judge's personal values and those of the community?[111] While Cardozo's opinions in *Wagner* and *Graff* are perhaps agreeable from a moral point of view, not every case in which Cardozo invoked moral values can be assessed similarly. *People v. Carey* (223 NY 519 [1918]) serves as an example. In that case, Raymond Carey, a nineteen-year-old male, was convicted of raping Lillian Tate, a twenty-five-year-old female. The defense claimed that Tate consented to have sex, and sought to introduce the complainant's prior sexual behavior as proof of her willingness to have sex with Carey on the day in question. In ordering a new trial, the Court of Appeals, in a *per curiam* opinion, ruled that legal error was committed because the complaint was not corroborated "by other evidence" within the meaning of the statute, but also noted that a majority declined to support reversal on the additional ground "that error was committed in rejecting testimony tending to prove that the complainant was unchaste" (520). Cardozo, in an internal memorandum to his colleagues, argued that evidence of Tate's prior sexual conduct should have been allowed because, in his view, "[u]nchastity diminishes...the likelihood of resistance."[112] Not only does Cardozo's opinion not sit well from a moral point of view, but it raises the question of whether his own moral values about sexuality, which can be fairly described as Victorian, may have influenced his decision. In short, Cardozo's reliance on Justice Felix Frankfurter's use of moral standards, such as "shocks the conscience" and "fundamental fairness," in due process cases.

NOTES

1.   See, for example, Albert P. Blaustein and Roy M. Mersky, Rating Supreme Court Justices," *American Bar Association Journal* 58 (1972): 1183–89.
2.   In other words, with the exception of Cardozo, a long tenure on the Supreme Court has been a necessary (albeit not sufficient) condition for the honor of "great."
3.   New Haven: Yale University Press (1921)
4.   Letter from Benjamin N. Cardozo to Oliver Wendell Holmes (Dec. 14, 1928), Holmes MSS, Harvard Law School, Reel 28 (quoted in Richard Polenberg, *The World of Benjamin Cardozo: Personal Values and the Judicial Process* (Cambridge: Harvard University Press, 1997), 173.
5.   See, for example, *The Nature of the Judicial Process*, note 4, 168 ("The great tides and currents which engulf the rest of men do not turn aside in their course and pass the judges by."); *Wood v. Lucy, Lady Duff-Gordon*, 22 NY 88, 91 (1917) ("The law has outgrown its primitive stage of formalism when the precise word was the sovereign talisman, and every slip was fatal."); *Wagner v. International Railway Co.*, 232 NY 176, 180 (1921) ("Danger invites rescue. The cry of distress is the summons to relief. The law does not ignore these reactions of the mind in tracing conduct to its consequences."); *People v. Defore*, 242 NY 13, 21 (1926) ("The criminal is to go free because the constable has blundered."); *Berkey v. Third Avenue Railway*, 244 NY 84, 94 (1926) ("Metaphors in law are to be narrowly watched, for starting as devices to liberate thought, they end often by enslaving it."); *Meinhard v. Salmon*, 249 NY 458, 464 (1928) ("A trustee is held to something stricter than the morals of the market place. Not honesty alone, but the punctilio of an honor the most sensitive, is then the standard of behavior."); *A.L.A. Schechter Poultry Corp v. United States*, 295 US 495, 551–553 (1935) (Cardozo, J., concurring) ("The delegated power of legislation which has found expression in this code in not canalized within banks that keep it from overflowing. It is unconfined and vagrant....This is delegation running riot."); *Carter v. Carter Coal Co.*, 298 US 238, 327 (1936) ("[A] great principle of constitutional law is not susceptible of comprehensive statement in an adjective.") ; *Palko v. Connecticut*, 302 US 319, 326–27 (1937) (The First Amendment's guarantee of freedom of thought and speech is "the matrix, the indispensable condition, of nearly every other form of freedom.").
6.   One should not underestimate the persuasive potential of the great legal craftsmen as well. Judge Irving Lehman, who served with Cardozo on the New York Court of Appeals, thought that Cardozo's graceful and eloquent style influenced the views of his colleagues on

a number of occasions. See *The Influence of Judge Cardozo on the Common Law* (New York: Doubleday, 1942), 11–13.

7.   Richard A. Posner, *Cardozo: A Study in Reputation* (University of Chicago Press, 1990), 74–91.

8.   For excellent biographical treatment of Cardozo, see Andrew L. Kaufman, *Cardozo* (Cambridge: Harvard University Press, 1998); and Richard Polenberg, see note 4.

9.   Stephen Birmingham, *The Grandees: America's Sephardic Elite* (New York: Harper, 1971).

10. Andrew L. Kaufman, "Benjamin N. Cardozo, Sephardic Jew," in *The Jewish Justices of the Supreme Court Revisited: Brandeis to Fortas* (Special Edition of The Journal of Supreme Court History, 1994), 42.

11. Cardozo had a twin sister, Emily, and four older siblings: Albert, Jr., Ellen, Grace, and Elizabeth.

12. Rebecca Nathan Cardozo died on October 28, 1879, when Benjamin was nine; and his father died on November 8, 1885, when Cardozo was fifteen.

13. Letter from Cardozo to Aline Goldstone (quoted in George S. Hellman, *Benjamin N. Cardozo: American Judge* (New York: Whittlesey House, 1940), 49. Although Benjamin and Nell had a unique and special relationship, and the letters between them have been described as "very, very intimate and personal," see Letter from Stephen Wise to George Hellman (Jan. 16. 1939), Cardozo MSS, Columbia Law School, there is no evidence that their relationship was anything more than platonic. Nellie's relationship to Cardozo can best be described as that of a mothersister.

14. As it turns out, Alger, the author of numerous best-selling children's stories allegedly had sexual relations with at least two boys who belonged to the Unitarian Church where he preached in the Village of Brewster, Massachusetts, during the period of December 1864 to March 1866. A church committee appointed to investigate the boys' allegations determined that Alger was guilty of the charges, which he never denied. At the request of Alger's father, Horatio Alger, Sr., who promised that his son would never again preach, the incidents were never disclosed. While Alger's past is shady (he immediately left town after he was notified about the charges), there is no evidence of an improper sexual relationship between Alger and Cardozo during their tutorial sessions in the mid-1880s. See Polenberg, note 4. See also Gary Scharnhort, *The Lost Life of Horatio Alger, Jr.* (Bloomington, IN: Indiana University Press, 1985).

15. "Law in Books and Law in Action," *American Law Review* 44 (1910): 12–36.

16. He wrote 551 opinions for the court, 446 of which were unanimous decisions. He also authored 15 concurring opinions and 17 dissenting opinions. See, unpublished dissertation, Janice B. Snook, *Judicial Philosophy and Judicial Behavior: The Case of Mr. Justice Cardozo* (University of Maryland, 1969), 27.

17. See, for example, *Wood v. Lucy, Lady Duff-Gordon*, 222 NY 88 (1917).

18. For superb accounts of the events surrounding Cardozo's appointment to the Supreme Court, see Ira H. Carmen, "The President, Politics and the Power of Appointment: Hoover's Nomination of Mr. Justice Cardozo," *Virginia Law Review* 55 (1969): 616–659; and Andrew L. Kaufman, "Cardozo's Appointment to the Supreme Court," *Cardozo Law Review* 1 (1979): 23–53.

19. Cardozo's ethnicity was certainly a factor in why he was not appointed to the Supreme Court earlier. In 1924, for example, President Calvin Coolidge passed over Cardozo after Justice Joseph McKenna announced his retirement, because, in his words, "we have one Hebrew on the Court now, Brandeis, and I don't want to be the one to add another." See Milton Handler and Michael Ruby, "Justice Cardozo: One-Ninth of the Supreme Court," *Yearbook 1988: Supreme Court Historical Society*, 51.

20. Quoted in Claudius O. Johnson, *Borah of Idaho* (New York: Longmans, Green, 1936), 452.

21. "Mr. Justice Cardozo," *Harper's Magazine*, June 1932, 34.

22.   Cardozo appears to have had sincere reservations about his appointment to the Supreme
       Court, which is probably the case for several reasons. First, New York was where his heart
       was. Cardozo grew up in New York and had lived there most of his adult life. It was there
       that most of his family and closest friends lived. By contrast, nothing was familiar to him in
       the nation's capital. After his appointment, Cardozo referred to himself as "the homesick
       exile" and called Washington, D.C. "my place of exile." See Letter from Cardozo to Louise
       Wise (April 28, 1932), Wise MSS, Stephen S. Wise Free Synagogue, and Letter from Car-
       dozo to Morris R. Cohen (Dec. 27, 2932), Cohen MSS, University of Chicago Library (both
       quoted in Polenberg, 170). Second, the kinds of cases that came before the New York Court
       of Appeals were probably more congenial to Cardozo's temperament than the "big" consti-
       tutional cases (with their attendant mix of law and politics) that he would see at the Su-
       preme Court. As Felix Frankfurter once remarked, with the exception of only Oliver
       Wendell Holmes, "no judge in his time was more deeply versed in the history of the com-
       mon law or more resourceful in applying the living principles by which is had unfolded
       [than Cardozo]; and his mastery of the common law was matched by his love of it." "Ben-
       jamin Nathan Cardozo," *Dictionary of American* Biography, IX, Supp. 2 (1958), 94. Third,
       in terms of career moves, an appointment to the Supreme Court might have not been seen
       by Cardozo as a promotion. At the time of his appointment, Cardozo was serving as the
       chief judge of the New York Court of Appeals, the second most distinguished court in the
       United States at the time, and had already earned the recognition as one of the nation's
       great common law judges. His appointment to the Supreme Court would mean in many
       ways, that he would have to start all over again, and some of the norms of the institution
       remind the justices of the pecking order. The junior-justice, for example, speaks last during
       conference and is often assigned the opinions that no one else wants. As fate would have it,
       Cardozo was the junior-justice for his entire term on the Court, and was not always as-
       signed the most interesting cases—a fact that he sometimes complained about. Finally, the
       New York Court of Appeals had a more collegial working environment than the United
       States Supreme Court. When the New York Court of Appeals was in session, the judges re-
       sided at the same hotel (Ten Eyck) in Albany. As a bachelor, the opportunities this pre-
       sented for getting together on an informal basis was probably socially and intellectually at-
       tractive to Cardozo. By contrast, when he started his appointment in Washington, the per-
       manent Supreme Court building had not yet been completed and the justices worked mostly
       out of their homes. Today the Supreme Court is sometimes described as "nine separate law
       firms," but its members were even more dispersed and isolated during Cardozo's tenure.
       The personal divisions among the justices at the time Cardozo sat did not help matters ei-
       ther. Justice James C. McReynolds, who was an unabashed anti-Semite, was particularly
       nasty. After Cardozo was appointed, he commented "that to become a justice one only had
       to be a Jew and have a father who was a crook, and at the swearing-in ceremony he con-
       spicuously buried himself in a newspaper." Polenberg, 171. See note 4.
23.   Felix Frankfurter, 94.
24.   Polenberg, 3.
25.   Much has been made of the fact that Cardozo never married, but there are a number of rea-
       sons of explanations for why this should not be seen as that surprising. First and foremost,
       marriages of the Sephardic community were not looked upon favorably, and the small na-
       ture of the community made it extremely difficult for its members to find suitable partners.
       In fact, of Cardozo's five siblings, only his twin sister Emily married, and she to a man who
       came from a Christian background. Second, Cardozo was a person who took moral obliga-
       tions very seriously and had probably never entertained any other thought than to care for
       his sister, Nell, during her illness in the mid to late 1920s. Third, Cardozo was completely
       dedicated to his work, and therefore by choice, did not allow for many opportunities to
       meet a woman with whom he could build a lasting relationship.

26. Kaufman, 483; 568. See note 8.
27. "A Personal View of Justice Benjamin N. Cardozo: Recollections of Four Cardozo Law Clerks," *Cardozo Law Review* 1 (1979): 5–22.
28. "A Tribute to Benjamin Nathan Cardozo," July 19, 1938, *Contemporary Jewish Record* 1 (1938): 29–31 at 31.
29. 305 US at xxviii (1938).
30. Lehman, see note 6, at 5 (quoting *Proceedings of U.S. Bar*, November 28, 1938).
31. Kaufman, 65–69. See note 8.
32. Cardozo, for example, was the only justice to pay a personal visit to Hugo Lafayette Black after his controversial appointment to the Supreme Court in 1936. See Roger K. Newman, *Hugo Black* (1994), 268.
33. Some of Cardozo's gentle and modest nature can be attributed to his common law under-standing of the law. According to this view, law develops in a piecemeal process (case by case) over the long centuries. While judges are important agents of change, their individual contributions to the law's development are, on the whole, insubstantial and unnoticeable. Generally speaking, individual judges do not lave lasting legacies on the law by bringing about far-reaching transformations. On this view, judges should have a humble attitude about their judicial role and not overestimate what it is that they do. The evidence of this common law perspective in Cardozo's thought is reflected in a comment he often made to his colleague Judge Irving Lehman of the New York Court of Appeals: "[T]he world would be little better or worse if every case that had come before our court during the last fifty years had been decided differently." Lehman, 22. See note 6, 178. ("The work of a judge is in one sense enduring and in another sense ephemeral.")
34. *The Nature of the Judicial Process,* 10, 166. See note 5.
35. Ibid., 28, 29.
36. See Benjamin Cardozo, *The Growth of the Law,* (New Haven: Yale University Press, 1924), 60 "Nine-tenths, perhaps more, of the cases that come before a court are predeter-mined—predetermined in a sense that they are predestined—their fate preestablished by in-evitable laws that follow them from birth to death".
37. *The Nature of the Judicial Process,* 164. See note 5.
38. Address before the New York State Bar Association Meeting at the Astor Hotel (January 22, 1932), *New York State Bar Association Report* 55 (1932): 262–307, 278.
39. *The Nature of the Judicial Process,* 21. See note 5.
40. Ibid., 28, 165.
41. Ibid., 31–35.
42. Ibid., 55 (quoting *N.Y. Trust Co. v. Eisner*, 256 US 345, 349 (1921).
43. Ibid., 52, 60.
44. *Jurisprudence* (St. Paul, MN: West, 1959), 349.
45. *Nature of the Judicial Process,* 71. See note 5.
46. Ibid., 66 ("Logic and history and custom have their place. We will shape the law to conform to them when we may; but only within bounds. The end which the law serves will dominate them all.")
47. Idem.
48. Ibid., 98.
49. Cardozo, see note 36, at 58, 113, 116.
50. The *Lochner* era, dating approximately from 1897 to 1937, was a period in which conserva-tive members of the Supreme Court read into the Fourteenth Amendment's due process clause a "liberty of contract" doctrine, striking down nearly 200 social and economic regu-lations in the process. The era is named after the most important case of the period, *Lochner v. New York*, 198 US 45 (1905), where the Supreme Court narrowly (5–4) struck down a New York law regulating the number of hours employees could work in bakeries.

51. *The Nature of the Judicial Process,* see note 3, at 20, 162.
52. Ibid., 10.
53. "The Path of the Law," *Harvard Law Review* 10 (1897): 457–478, 466.
54. *The Nature of the Judicial Process,* see note 3, at 12.
55. Ibid., 28.
56. Cardozo, 140. See note 36.
57. *The Nature of the Judicial Process,* note 3, at 132 ("The law of nature is not longer conceived of as something static and eternal. It does not override human or positive law. It is the stuff out of which human or positive law is to be woven, when other sources fail.")
58. See *Hartford Accident & Indemnity Co. v. N.O. Nelson Manufacturing Co.,* 291 US 352, 360 (1934) ("Liberty of contract is not an absolute concept....It is relative to many conditions of time and place and circumstance.")
59. See *The Nature of the Judicial Process,* 87 ("Property, like liberty, though immune under the Constitution from destruction, is not immune from regulation essential for the common good.").
60. See, for example, *Helvering v. Davis,* 301 US 619 (1937).
61. See, for example. *Panama Refining Co. v. Ryan,* 293 US 388, 440 (1935) (Cardozo, J., dissenting) ("The separation of powers between the Executive and Congress is not a doctrinaire concept to be made use of with pedantic rigor. There must be sensible approximation, there must be elasticity of adjustment, in response to the practical necessities of government, which cannot foresee today the developments of tomorrow in their nearly infinite variety.")
62. Cardozo, 33–34.See note 36. See also Oliver Wendell Holmes, "The Path of the Law," note 53, at 461 ("The prophecies of what the courts will do in fact, and nothing more pretentious, are what I mean by the law.")
63. "A Realist Jurisprudence—The Next Step," *Columbia Law Review* 30 (1930): 431–465.
64. Jerome Frank, *Law and the Modern Mind,* 6th printing (New York: Coward-McCann, 1949).
65. Joseph C. Hutcheson, Jr., "The Judgment Intuitive: The Function of the 'Hunch' in Judicial Decision," *Cornell Law Quarterly* 14 (1929): 274–288.
66. Jerome Frank, 34. See note 6.
67. Address before the New York State Bar Association Meeting, 270. See note 38.
68. *The Nature of the Judicial Process,* 48, 127. See note 5.
69. Address before the New York State Bar Association Meeting, 273. See note 38.
70. *The Nature of the Judicial Process,* 136–137. See note 5.
71. Ibid., 129–130. Cardozo described these limitations as follows: "Even within the gaps, restrictions not easy to define, but felt, however impalpable they may be, by every judge and lawyer, hedge and circumscribe his action. They are established by the traditions of the centuries, by the example of other judges, his predecessors and his colleagues, by the collective judgment of the profession, and by the duty of adherence to the pervading spirit of the law," (114).
72. Ibid., 129.
73. Cardozo, 53–55. See note 36.
74. Frank was one of Cardozo's few critics. *In Law and the Modern Mind* (1930) he lauded Cardozo as having "reached adult emotional stature" in terms of his understanding of the rule of law. Frank, 237. But in subsequent writings he became highly critical of Cardozo. See, for example, Anon Y. Mous, "The Speech of Judges—A Dissenting Opinion," *Virginia Law Review* 29 (1943): 625–641; and Frank, "Cardozo and the Upper-Court Myth," *Law and Contemporary Problems* 13 (1948): 369–390.
75. "Mechanical Jurisprudence," *Columbia Law Review* 8 (1908):605–623.
76. Cardozo was instrumental in the creation of the New York Law Revision Commission in 1934, and was a founding member of the American Law Institute in 1923, an agency whose

purpose was the codification of legal reforms. See his "A Ministry of Justice," *Harvard Law Review* 35 (1921): 113–126; and "American Law Institute, in *Selected Writings of Benjamin Nathan Cardozo*, Margaret E. Hall, ed. (New York: Fallon, 1947), 395–404.

77. *Matter of Jensen v. Southern Pacific Co.* 215 NY 514 (1915), overturning *Ives v. South Buffalo Railway Co.*, 201 NY 271 (1911).

78. *People v. Charles Schweinler*, 214 NY 395 (1915).

79. *Klein v. Marvelas*, 219 NY 383 (1916), overruling *Wright v. Hart*, 182 NY 330 (1905).

80. *Fougera & Co. v. City of New York*, 224 NY 269 (1918).

81. *Home Building & Loan Association v. Blaisdell*, 290 US 398 (1934).

82. *Nebbia v. New York*, 291 US 502 (1934).

83. *West Coast Hotel Co. v. Parrish*, 300 US 379 (1937).

84. Unpublished concurring opinion in *Home Building & Loan Association v. Blaisdell* (dated January 8, 1934), in *Harlan Fiske Stone Papers*, Library of Congress, Container 60, 3–4.

85. *United States v. Butler*, 297 US 1, 78 (1936) (Cardozo, J., dissenting).

86. *Carter v. Carter Co.*, 298 US 238, 324 (1936) (Cardozo, J., dissenting)

87. *National Labor Relations Board v. Jones & Laughlin Steel Corp.*, 301 US 1 (1937).

88. 295 US at 661, 663 (quoting *Panama Refining*, 293 US 388, 440).

89. "On Cardozo and Reputation: Legendary Judge, Underrated Justice?" *Cardozo Law Review* 12 (1991): 1923–1939, 1936.

90. *The Nature of the Judicial Process*, see note 3, at 149.

91. Judge Cuthbert W. Pound did not participate in the case.

92. Unpublished concurring opinion in *Home Building & Loan Association v. Blaisdell*, 6 (internal citation omitted).See note 84.

93. The Origin and Scope of the American Doctrine of Constitutional Law," *Harvard Law Review* 7 (1893): 129–156, 140 (quoting *Commonwealth v. Smith*, 4 Bin. 117 (1811); see, for example, *U.S. v. Constantine* 296 U.S. 287, 299 (1935) (Cardozo, J., dissenting) ("There is another wise and ancient doctrine that a court will not adjudge the invalidity of a statute except for manifest necessity. Every reasonable doubt must have been explored and extinguished before moving to the grave conclusion.")

94. Quoted in Charles P. Curtis, *Lions Under the Throne* (Boston: Houghton Mifflin, 1947), 281.

95. *The Nature of the Judicial Process*, 129; See note 5. See also *Southern Pacific Co. v. Jensen*, 244, U.S. 205, 221 (1917) (Holmes, J., dissenting) ("I recognize without hesitation that judges do and must legislate, but they can do so only interstitially; they are confined from molar to molecular motions.")

96. Ibid., 141 (internal citation omitted).

97. Ibid., 25.

98. Ibid., 343–344.

99. *Benton v. Maryland*, 395 US 784 (1969).

100. See, for example., *People of the State of New York v. Defore*, 242 NY 13 (1926) (rejecting application of exclusionary rule in the state of New York); *Snyder v. Commonwealth*, 291 US 97 (1934) (rejecting defendant's right to be present during the jury's visit of the crime scene).

101. *The Nature of the Judicial Process,*160. See note 5.

102. Lehman, 21. See note 6.

103. *The Nature of the Judicial Process,*133. See note 5.

104. As he put it: Justice or moral value is only one among many that must be appraised by the same method [of interpreting social *mores*]. Other values, not moral, values of expediency or of convenience or of economic or cultural advancement, a host of values that are not final, but merely means to others, are to be ascertained and assessed, and equilibrated, the less sacrificed to the greater, all in subjection to like tests, the thought and the will and the

desires of society as the judge perceives and interprets them supplying the measure and the scale. *The Paradoxes of Legal Science* (New York: Columbia University Press, 1928), 54–55.

105. See, for example, Holmes, "The Path of the Law," 462 See note 53. (In order to understand the law clearly we must "wash it with cynical acid and expel everything except the object of our study, the operations of the law.") While Cardozo agreed with the realists in their cynicism of traditional natural law, he did not agree with their efforts to strictly separate law from morality. Cardozo defended a moral concept or ideal of law that according to him, existed within the system of positive or customary law. See, e.g., *The Nature of the Judicial Process*, 134. See note 5; and *The Growth of the Law*, 52. See note 36.

106. *The Nature of the Judicial Process*, 43. See note. 5.

107. Ibid., 43.

108. See supra.

109. *Southern Pacific Co. v. Jensen*, 244 US 205, 222 (1917).

110. See, for example, Henry M. Hart, Jr. and Albert M. Sachs, *The Legal Process: Basic Problems in the Making and Application of Law*. Prepared for publication from the 1958 Tentative Edition, by William N. Eskridge, Jr. and Philip P. Frickey, eds. (New York: Foundation Press, 1994); Neil Duxbury, "Faith in Reason: The Process Tradition in American Jurisprudence," *Cardozo Law Review* 15 (1993): 601–705; and Herbert Wechsler, "Toward Neutral Principles of Constitutional Law," *Harvard Law Review* 73 (1959): 1–35.

111. *The Paradoxes of Legal Science*, 25–26.

112. This is a concern that Cardozo was very much sensitive to. In *The Nature of the Judicial Process*, he wrote: "We may try to see things as objectively as we please. None the less, we can never see them with any eyes except our own."

113. See Polenberg, 127. See note 4.

CHAPTER NINE

Hugo L. Black: Constitutional Literalist and Absolutist

Henry J. Abraham

The Blaustein/Mersky study results ably elucidated by Professor Bradley at the onset of this anthology had pointed to a compendium of qualities that characterized "greatness." All of the chosen twelve made significant, identifiable contributions to the development of law and its interpretation. Their agreed-upon success on the highest tribunal in the land was, in the observation of the two editors of this book, the product of the following several combined qualities: "scholarship; legal learning, craftsmanship and technique; wide general knowledge and learning; character, moral integrity and impartiality; diligence and industry; the ability to express oneself with clarity, logic, and compelling force; openness to change; courage to take unpopular positions; dedication to the Court as an institution and to the office of Supreme Court justice; ability to carry a proportionate share of the Court's responsibility in opinion writing; and, finally, the quality of statesmanship."[1]

Who comprised the twelve "greats" selected by the sixty-five experts? They included four chief and eight associate justices, bracketing a period from 1801 through 1969. In chronological order they were: John Marshall, Joseph Story, Roger B. Taney, John M. Harlan (I), Oliver Wendell Holmes, Jr., Charles Evan Hughes, Louis D. Brandeis, Harlan F. Stone, Benjamin N. Cardozo, Hugo L. Black, Felix Frankfurter, and Earl Warren. Their period of service ranged from Marshall, Harlan, and Black's astounding thirty-four years each (exceeded since then only by William O. Douglas's thirty-six years, and roughly equaled by Justices Stephen J. Field and William J. Brennan, Jr., all three of whom were ranked as "near great") to Cardozo's all-too-brief six years on the Court. Only one of the twelve received all sixty-five votes—not surprisingly it was John Marshall. In second place was Brandeis with sixty-two; Holmes was third with sixty-one, followed by Black with forty-two, and Frankfurter with forty-one. It is interesting to note that whereas the "greats" spanned all but the first decade of the Court's then 180 years existence, the eight rated as "failures" (Willis Van Devanter, James C. McReynolds, Pierce Butler, James F. Byrnes, Harold H. Burton, Fred M. Vinson, Sherman Minton, and Charles Whittaker) served in the fifty-year period of the twentieth century, from 1911 through 1962. There were fifteen "near greats," fifty-five "average," and six "below average."[2]

Because Hugo L. Black was the most recent among those named "great" to leave the Court (1971); because of his long tenure; and because he was such a fascinating, influential, towering figure, I have selected him as the example of a great justice I should now like to discuss in some detail.[3] It was my great privilege to know him at least somewhat personally: I had reviewed his magisterial *A Constitutional Faith*, which he acknowledged with a gracious note. He had dedicated his book, actually a revision of three lectures delivered at Columbia University in 1968, "to my Mother, my wife Josephine, my wife Elizabeth, and my daughter Josephine." When an opportunity to chat with him beckoned at Justice Brennan's daughter Nancy's 1969 engagement party, I asked him how he had managed "to get away" with such a charming multiple dedication. "I loved 'em all," he responded with the combination of warmth, pixiness, and confidence that characterized this remarkable human being who had surmounted such odds to become one of the twentieth century's towering influences.

FDR Selects an Autodidact

When Justice Van Devanter announced his retirement, the leading candidate for the vacancy was Joseph T. Robinson of Arkansas, the Democratic majority leader of the Senate from 1933 to 1937. A faithful New Dealer who had supported every New Deal measure that FDR had sent to Congress, the popular, hardworking Robinson had also been an early and key backer of the President's Court-reorganization bill. Everything pointed to his designation. FDR had evidently promised him a Supreme Court seat, although not necessarily the first available one. But according to the then still high-riding Postmaster General and Democratic National Committee Chairman James A. "Jim" Farley, Roosevelt had said that Robinson could count on being nominated.[4] And, in an unusual move, the Senate as a body endorsed the candidacy of its Democratic leader. Yet FDR had been forced to wait more than four years for that precious initial vacancy; now he would bide his time. He liked and was grateful to "Arkansas Joe," who had served in both branches of Congress since 1903. Still, there was just enough basic conservatism in Robinson's past to cast doubt on his jurisprudential "reliability." Then fate intervened: on July 14, 1937, while leading the floor fight for the Court-packing bill, Senator Robinson suffered a heart attack to which he later succumbed in his Methodist Building apartment, a copy of the *Congressional Record* in his hand. Roosevelt at once instructed Homer S. Cummings, his attorney general, to canvass the field of other "suitables," keeping in mind that the nominee had to be absolutely loyal to the New Deal program. By early August the search had narrowed to four such loyal New Deal Democrats: U.S. Solicitor General Stanley F. Reed of Kentucky, Senator Sherman Minton of Indiana, Senator Hugo L. Black of Alabama, and

Assistant Attorney General Robert H. Jackson of New York. All four would become Supreme Court Justices eventually; it was Black's turn now though there are sundry assertions on record—firmly denied by Justice Douglas, for one—that FDR offered Minton, who was closest of the four to Cummings and the president, first refusal. He did in fact offer it, but Minton actively promoted Black. "Jesus Christ!" exclaimed White House Press Secretary Stephen Early, when FDR disclosed his choice to him late at night on August 11. The president grinned—it had been a well-kept secret, indeed. Earlier that evening he had summoned Black to his White House study, showed him the nomination form he had filled out in longhand himself, and chuckled, "Hugo, I'd like to write your name here." A happy Black nodded assent. "I wish you were twins," FDR chuckled, "because Barkley says he needs you in the Senate; but I think you'll be more useful on the Court."[5]

Steven Early's reaction was understandable. At first glance there was precious little in the impoverished rural background of the then fifty-one-year-old senator from Ashland, Clay County, the eighth (and last) child of a small-town rural merchant, to qualify him for the Supreme Court. True, he had had considerable experience as a lawyer among country sharecroppers, as a county solicitor, and as a police court judge and prosecutor in Birmingham; moreover, he was a pillar of the church and had taught Sunday school at the Birmingham First Baptist Church for sixteen years; he had read widely; and he had a lucid, profound mind. But was he *really* the best FDR could do? The president of course knew precisely what he was doing: Black, now in his second term in the Senate, and facing a heavily contested battle, had not only demonstrated enthusiastic and outspoken support of the New Deal—confounding many predictions—but he had staunchly supported the Court-packing bill. Those two factors were decisive, but FDR also happily noted that Black had a long and effective record of siding with "little people" and "underdogs," and that he was from a part of the country that he, FDR, wanted to see represented on the Court. He was also aware of Black's principled discipline and his astounding educational achievements. His nominee never finished high school, moving straight into the Birmingham Medical School at age seventeen, finishing the four-year program in three. Black then switched to the law, studying for three years at the University of Alabama School of Law at Tuscaloosa—where he was so bored that he took an *entire* liberal arts curriculum concurrently(!), graduating with high honors in 1907.[6]

The nomination's announcement was met with approbation by most of Senator Black's colleagues and most New Deal spokesmen throughout the land. Yet it also evoked loud protests from both public and private sources. The intellectual and soft-spoken liberal was portrayed as being utterly unqualified by training, temperament, and constitutional dedication; as being blindly partisan; as being a radical rather than a liberal; as being, in fact, a phony liberal when it was revealed that he had been a member of the Ku Klux Klan (KKK) in the 1920s. Although FDR denied any knowledge of a Black-KKK link in a September 14, 1937, press conference, Black recalled a converse fact: He had discussed his erstwhile membership with the president at the time of his formal nomination and FDR had told Black not to worry about it, that "some of his best friends and supporters in the state of Georgia were strong members of that organization."[7] The press—no more a friend of the senator's than of his president—roasted Black for "combined lack of training on the one hand and extreme partisanship on the other,"[8] with the *Chicago Tribune* declaring that the president had picked "the worst he could find,"[9] and the *American Mercury* calling him a "vulgar dog." The Senate, however, although treated to the somewhat unaccustomed spectacle of a public debate on the merits of a sitting member, quickly confirmed its colleague (who had been backed 13–4 in the Judiciary Committee) by a vote of 63–16 on August 17th.[10] "My cup runneth over," a happy Sherman Minton wrote to FDR.[11]

When the verdict was in, Justice-designate and Mrs. Josephine Black sailed for a European vacation. In their absence, Ray Sprigle, a reporter on the *Pittsburgh Post-Gazette*, published a six-day series of articles repeating the known facts of Black's erstwhile KKK membership. Although acknowledging written proof of Black's resignation from the Klan in 1925, Sprigle alleged that, in fact, Black—notwithstanding on-the-floor denials by such powerful non-Democratic colleagues as Senator W.E. Borah (R.-Idaho), for example—was still a member of the hooded organization, having been secretly elected to life membership in 1926. Black was besieged abroad by reporters, but he characteristically disdained any comment until he stepped before radio microphones on October 1, 1937, to make the eleven-minute statement that was heard by the largest radio audience ever, save for those who listened to Britain's Edward VIII's abdication "for the woman I love": "My words and acts are a matter of public record. I believe that my record as a senator refutes every implication of racial or religious intolerance. It shows that I was of that group of liberal senators who have consistently fought for civil, economic and religious rights of all Americans, without regard to race or creed....I did join the Klan. I later resigned. I never rejoined. I have never considered and I do not now consider the unsolicited card given to me shortly after my nomination to the senate as a membership of any kind in the Ku Klux Klan. I never used it. I did not even keep it. Before becoming a senator I dropped the Klan. I have had nothing whatever to do with it since that time. I abandoned it...."[12]

The public was generally sympathetic and persuaded of his sincerity. Again characteristically, Justice Black—whose personality Gerald T. Dunne has aptly described as "steel wrapped in silk"[13]— said no more on the subject, refusing to discuss or reopen the matter during the remainder of his long life. "When this statement is ended," he had said, "my discussion of the question is closed." He meant it, and it was! Three days after the broadcast he donned the robes of associate justice. "He need not buy but merely dye his robes" was a favorite nasty contemporary quip.[14]

Thus began a remarkable Supreme court tenure of more than thirty-four years. It was one marked by a distinction and an influence rare in the annals of the Court. How right the *Montgomery Advertiser* had been when it observed: "What a joke it would be on Hugo's impassioned detractors if he should now turn out to be a very great justice of the Supreme Court. Brandeis did it when every Substantial Citizen of the Republic felt that Wilson should have been impeached for appointing him...."[15]

Democratic Populism and Strict Constructionism

Few jurists have had the impact that Justice Hugo Lafayette Black had. A constitutional literalist to whom every word in the document represented an absolutist command, he nonetheless used the language of the Constitution—"language plus history," he would avow—to propound a jurisprudence that has had a lasting effect on the development of American constitutional interpretation and law. It is one perhaps best characterizable as a blend of democratic populism and judicial strict constructionism. Black's contributions were seminal. They stand as jurisprudential and intellectual landmarks in the evolving history of the land for which he fought both literally and figuratively and loved so well—a devotion so touchingly and effectively manifested in his aforementioned *A Constitutional Faith.* In Harvard University's esteemed Paul Freund's view, Black was "without a doubt the most influential of the many strong figures" who sat on the Court during his thirty-four years of membership.[16] In the opinion of the University of Chicago's Philip Kurland, only one other member, John Marshall, "left such a deep imprint on our basic document."[17] He fully met FDR's expectations, of course. But that was in the short run; the New Deal as such had run its course by the end of the 1930s. In the long run Black's achievements encompass securing the central meaning of the Constitution and of the Bill of Rights. At the pinnacle of his legacy stands the now-all-but-complete nationalization of the latter, a doctrine known as "incorporation"—that is, its application to all of the states through the due process of law clause of the Fourteenth Amendment. In what was probably his most influential opinion on the issue, penned in dissent, *Adamson v. California* (332 US, 46 [1947]), Hugo Black called for such nationalization, dramatically expanding and elaborating Justice Cardozo's pioneering dichotomous classification in *Palko v. Connecticut* (US 319 [1937]), and Justice Stone's famed *United States v. Carolene Products,* (304 US 144 [1938]). He lost in *Adamson* by only one vote. But by constantly reiterating the theme of constitutional intent as he perceived it in the

Fourteenth Amendment—"I cannot consider the Bill of Rights to be an outworn eighteenth-century 'strait jacket,'" he had thundered in Adamson—and by his reading of the debates leading to the amendment's adoption, he coaxed the Court step by step to his side. By 1969 the Warren Court had, with but minor exceptions, in effect written its concurrence into constitutional law.[18]

It is generally agreed that the nationalization of the Bill of Rights was Black's most visible achievement, yet it is but one of the many that have rated him all but universal acclaim as one of the great justices. Among those accomplishments were his leadership in propounding an "absolutist" theory of the First Amendment's freedom of expression guarantees[19]—always provided that he viewed the issue at hand as one involving freedom of *expression* rather than one of proscribable conduct—a theory based upon the *specific verbiage* of the Constitution that contributed heavily to the Warren Court's broadly liberal definition of obscenity, to its tough standards on proof in alleged libel and slander cases, and to its striking down of much of the "subversive activities" legislation of the McCarthy era; his assertive majority opinions defining a "contra-establishment" line of separation between Church and State; his tenacious, literal interpretation of the protective guarantees of the Constitution in the administration of justice, including the specific provisions against coerced confessions, compulsory self-incrimination, double jeopardy, and those defining the conditions of trial by jury and the availability of counsel—while the presence of the qualifying adjective "unreasonable" in the Fourth Amendment's "searches and seizures" safeguard provisions would not infrequently find him on opposite sides of his customary liberal allies, such as William O. Douglas; his victory over Justice Frankfurter in the arena of "political questions" that legalized the egalitarian representation concept of "one person, one vote" now so broadly taken for granted, prompting the acerbic Frankfurter to pronounce Black a "rural country bumpkin in judicial robes," who "delivers flapdoodle in the name of democracy."[20]

One of Black's most touching victorious opinions was written for a unanimous Court in the celebrated case of *Gideon v. Wainwright* (372 US 335 [1963]), which overruled *Betts v. Brady*, (326 US 455 [1942]), decades earlier from which he had vigorously dissented. *Gideon* enshrined the principle that any criminal defendant in a state as well as in a federal proceeding who is too poor to pay for a lawyer has a constitutional right to be assigned one *gratis* by the government. For Black the opinion represented the affirmation of another touching plea written twenty-three years earlier in the famed case of *Chambers v. Florida* (309 US 227 [1940]). Still viewed as one of his most beautifully penned, and a moving signal of his commitment to constitutional civil liberties, it held for a unanimous Court that the confessions obtained by Florida authorities to condemn four black defendants to death were patently coerced after almost six days of continuous questioning and an all-night interrogation, and, therefore, a clear violation of due process of law. In the most celebrated passage, at the close of his opinion, Black wrote: "Under our constitutional system courts stand against any winds that blow as havens or refuge for those who might otherwise suffer because they are helpless, weak, outnumbered, or because they are nonconforming victims of prejudice and public excitement. Due process of law, preserved for all by our Constitution, commands that no such practice as that disclosed by [the *Chambers* case record] shall send any accused to his death. No higher duty, no more solemn responsibility, rests upon this Court, than that of translating into living law and maintaining this constitutional shield deliberately planned and inscribed for the benefit of every human being to our Constitution—of whatever race, creed, or persuasion" (241). "I think Chief Justice Hughes assigned *Chambers* to me because I was a Southerner," Black commented. "And there were these Negroes here who were so mistreated. He forced me to write the case. At first I didn't want to. He said, 'Don't worry, I'll get the Court for you.' [He did.]....There has been no case which I put more work in." On Lincoln's birthday the former senator from Alabama delivered his opinion, then styled by his future jurisprudential nemesis, Felix Frankfurter, as "one of the enduring utterances in the history of the Supreme Court and in the annals of human freedom."[21]

Hardly surprisingly, Black's evolving principled liberalism did not find ready favor in the Deep South, in general, and in his native Alabama, in particular, where for many years he would be regarded as a "traitor." As one Birmingham citizen put it bitterly: "Hugo Black used to go around in white robes, scaring black people. Now he goes around in black robes, scaring white people."[22] But by the end of the 1960s Hugo Black, a shining example of the triumph of a determined spirit and man's capacity for reflective change, returned to Birmingham to be honored by both the Alabama and Birmingham Bar Association, the latter declaring him "its most distinguished former member." On his death the Alabama House of Representatives passed a resolution honoring him. He would have been touched and pleased.

On-Bench Interactions

Black mounted the Supreme Court eager to learn. He came to respect and admire his colleagues and to be deferential. But he was also a strong-willed, principled, disciplined human being and an experienced public servant. Moreover, conscious of his being an obvious protagonist to cement the 1937 "switch in time that saved nine," it did not take long for him to apply his convictions. Thus, although highly respectful and fond of Chief Justice Hughes, it took him but a few months to write ringing dissents, often still alone until 1938, to opinions authored by the economic proprietarians on the bench. His early natural jurisprudential allies were Cardozo and Stone. They were followed by the string of pro-FDR pro-New Deal replacements Reed, Frankfurter, and Douglas by 1939, with Jackson, Murphy, and Byrnes to come in 1941, and Rutledge in 1943.

Black, "steel wrapped in silk," was a natural leader. Polite and kind, yet determined, energetic, and intellectually tough, he was not a natural jurisprudential compromiser. His agenda was an absolutist, literalist embrace of the Constitution, and his devotion to that commitment was paramount. There is little doubt that he and Felix Frankfurter possessed the finest minds on a Court blessed with a large number of splendid intellectuals. The two respected one another and became warm friends initially, but their evolving jurisprudential divergences were bound to result in friction. "F.F.," brilliant, supremely intellectual, proud, and professorial, sharp-tongued as well as sharp-minded, had clearly expected to become the leader of the post-1938 Court, certainly among the FDR appointees. But as the years progressed, he found himself losing steadily to Black's emerging leadership, especially in the judicial posture on civil rights and liberties, with particular relevance of the application of the Bill of Rights to the states, a goal for which Black fought with zeal for more than two decades until, besting Frankfurter's contrary position, he prevailed. Felix was not amused.

An arguably considerably nastier contretemps involved Robert Jackson. By 1945 it had become apparent that now-Chief Justice Stone's health was declining (and he would die in 1945). Jackson was eager to be a candidate for succession, and, knowing that Douglas was not interested, sensed Black as a potential chief rival for the post. He began to be vocally critical of Black, especially in his often diverse opinions. Matters came to a head in 1945 when Jackson excoriated Black for sitting in the *Jewell Ridge* case because a former Black partner had argued for the plaintiff in it. The gauntlet had been thrown! The now no longer even thinly disguised enmity was expanded when Jackson went to Nuremberg to become America's prosecutor at the War Crimes Tribunal, leaving the Court shorthanded and often facing 4–4 decisions. Like others, Black was critical of Jackson's absence. When Stone's death opened the chief justiceship, Jackson hoped to be nominated. Black did not desire the job for himself, but he certainly did not want Jackson. Truman solved the matter by choosing Fred Vinson from outside the judiciary. Sadly, Jackson went public with a venomous assault on Black, whom he clearly held responsible for his failure to attain the desired post. Robert Jackson died in 1954; Hugo Black continued to serve for another seventeen years, profoundly respected and admired.

My "Legal Bible"

One week after ill health compelled his retirement from his beloved Court on September 17, 1971, at age eighty-five, Justice Black died—but not until he had had one last good argument about the incorporation of the Bill of Rights with longtime colleague and good friend, John Marshall Harlan II, who also lay fatally ill in Walter Reed Hospital. Hugo Lafayette Black had written almost 1,000 opinions during his thirty-four years of exemplary service. His last opinion was truly appropriate: an eloquent, fitting lead concurrence in the Pentagon Papers case New York Times v. United States, (403 US 713 [1971]), a ringing defense and exhortation of freedom of the press under the First Amendment. "Honey," Elizabeth Black told her husband, "if this is your swan song, it's a good one."[23] It was, and it was. "The law," as one of those who knew him best wrote after his death, "has lost a kindly giant."[24] Friends who called at a funeral home in Washington before his burial in Arlington National Cemetery received a poignant parting gift—a copy of the Constitution. On a desk bearing a book for visitors' signatures was a pile of small paperbound copies of the document Black had so often referred to as "my legal bible"—a copy of which he always carried in his suit pocket. He would have approved. Laid to rest with him in the simple $165 pine casket with knotholes were several of them in his suit pocket. On a bench that she had placed adjacent to Justice Black's final resting place, his widow, Elizabeth Seay Black, had inscribed the words: "Here lies a good man." He was that, indeed—and a truly great justice of the Supreme Court.

NOTES

1. Albert S. Blaustein and Roy S. Mersky, *The First One Hundred Justices: Statistical Studies on the Supreme Court of the United States* (Hamden, CT: Shoe String Press, Archon Books, 1978), 50–51.
2. See my Justices, Presidents and Senators: *A History of the U.S. Supreme Court Appointments from Washington to Clinton* (Lanham, MD: Rowman and Littlefield, 1999), Appendix A, 412–14, for a convenient tabular account.
3. The remarks to follow borrow heavily from my *Justices, Presidents and Senators*, especially chapter 9, 160–165.
4. (New York: Alfred A. Knopf, 1968).
5. *Jim Farley's Story* (New York: McGraw Hill, 1948), 86.
6. Quoted by Virginia Van der Veer Hamilton, *Hugo Black: The Alabama Years* (Baton Rouge: Louisiana State University Press, 1972), 274–275. (Hamilton is also the source for the Minton claim) John B. Frank, "Hugo L. Black," *The Justices of the United States Supreme Court 1789–1978,* vol. III, in Leon Friedman and Fred L. Israel (eds.) (New York: Chelsea House, 1980), 2322.
7. Hugo L. Black, Jr., *My Father: A Remembrance* (New York: Random House, 1975), 16–17.
8. Van der Veer Hamilton communications, H.L.B. papers, Library of Congress, MSS Drive, Box 31.
9. *Washington Post,* editorial, August 13, 1937.

10. Quoted in 60 *Judicature* 7 (February 1977): 350.

11. Sixty Democrats and three Republicans—Robert La Follette (Wisconsin), Arthur Capper (Kansas), and Lynn J. Frazier (North Dakota)—voted aye, ten Republicans and six Democrats voted nay; and sixteen senators abstained from voting—an uncommonly high number.

12. Quoted in Charles Williams, *Hugo L. Black: A Study in Judicial Process* (Baltimore: Johns Hopkins University Press, 1950), 281.

13. Quoted in *New York Times* (October 2, 1937): 1.

14. Gerald T. Dunne, *Hugo L. Black and the Judicial Revolution* (New York: Simon & Schuster, 1977), 43.

15. Ibid., 274.

16. Quoted by John S. Frank, *Mr. Justice Black: The Man and His Opinions* (New York: Knopf, 1949), 102, fn. 12.

17. "Mr. Justice Black and the Judicial Function," 14 *UCLA Law Review* 467 (1967): 473.

18. "Hugo Lafayette Black: In Memoriam," 20 *Journal of Public Law* 359 (1971): 362.

19. For a detailed description see Henry J. Abraham and Barbara A. Perry, *Freedom and the Court: Civil Rights and Liberties in the United States,* 7th ed. (New York: Oxford University Press, 1998): 29–91.

20. See James J. Magee, *Mr. Justice Black: Absolutist on the Court* (Charlottesville: University of Virginia Press, 1980).

21. Quoted in John Noonan's book review of Gerald J. Dunne's *Hugo Black and the Judicial Revolution,* in 9 *Southwestern Law Review* (1977): 1131.

22. Quoted in Roger K. Newman's fine *Hugo Black: A Biography* (New York: Pantheon, 1994), 283–284.

23. Quoted by the *New York Times,* May 11 (1968) and Newman, 569. See note 22.

24. Quoted by Howard Ball in his *Hugo Black: Cold Steel Warrior* (New York: Oxford University Press, 1996), 200.

25. John P. Frank, "Hugo L. Black: He Has Joined the Giants," 58 *American Bar Association Journal* (January 1972): 25.

CHAPTER TEN

Felix Frankfurter: Constitutionalist Progressive

Dennis J. Coyle

Of the justices who are most deserving of being on a list of great justices, probably none is more likely to be left off the list than Felix Frankfurter. Perhaps no one else so combined the qualities of a judicial statesman with a propensity to reach conclusions in conflict with the preferences of many leading legal scholars. Consequently, scholars of the Court have been unsure of just what to make of Frankfurter, some hailing him as brilliant while many expressing their disappointment. Frankfurter had the misfortune of being one of the last great dissenters on an increasingly activist Court, a Court that captured the mood of the 1960s among the intelligentsia that fair results through strong leadership were what mattered. Institutions were reservoirs of reaction and resistance to be swept aside by moral certitude, and while some took their beliefs onto the streets, Earl Warren led a revolution from within the system, articulating a vision of law that emphasized a sense of justice and right results over precedent and legalistic reasoning, and that made the Supreme Court prominent in the lives and consciousness of everyday America. To the liberal scholars of the 1960s and the generations of law students in the decades since who have been drawn to the law in part by a romantic vision of judge-made law as a tool to transform society and do justice, Frankfurter has seemed a hopeless anachronism, unheeding the needs of the new juridical society.

Many of those students are the professors of today, and they and their predecessors have tended to lionize the leading figures of the Warren Court: the First Amendment absolutism of Hugo Black, the moral righteousness and informalism of William Douglas, the intellectual and political astuteness of William Brennan, the crusading sense of justice of Thurgood Marshall, the leadership and instrumentalism of Earl Warren. From 1953, when Warren ascended to the chief justiceship until 1962, when Frankfurter retired, the latter was, and still is, widely seen as an obstacle to the Warren Court, and his departure is even said to mark the beginning of the "real Warren Court."[1] In the eyes of the "adherents to The Liberal Creed,"[2] Frankfurter was a failure, even tragic. Fred Rodell of Yale Law School bemoaned Frankfurter as an "outstanding disappointment...the New Deal Court's...most tragically wasted brilliant mind."[3]

Similarly Melvin Urofsky has concluded that "Frankfurter ranks as one of the great disappointments in modern times,"[4] whose career, adds Bernard Schwartz, was "essentially a lost opportunity."[5] Frankfurter did not pursue an activist progressive agenda on the Court, and that remains a sore point for many liberal scholars. As Philip Kurland noted at a conference to commemorate the Warren Court, "Frankfurter adherents are at best, tolerated, at worst, disdained."[6]

Few would question Frankfurter's brilliance and eloquence. Said Franklin Roosevelt, "Felix has more ideas per minute than any man of my acquaintance. [His mind] clicks so fast it makes my head fairly spin."[7] And he was prolific, writing scores of books and articles as well as some 750 opinions as a Supreme Court justice. He was a fitting heir to the "scholar's seat," and to read Frankfurter"s opinions is to receive an education in the nature and function of law and courts, written with lyricism and clarity. Frankfurter once wrote that "every really good course in law is a course in jurisprudence,"[8] and for Frankfurter, so was every good legal opinion. He took seriously the educational role of the Court, and raised the level of constitutional dialogue on the Court and in the public through his opinion writing. His opinions were as much jurisprudence as doctrine, and his strength was his ability to blend the two. Frankfurter was intellectually rigorous, and contemptuous of slapdash, superficial work, often critical of the opinions of Earl Warren and William Douglas and others.[9] For the latter justices what mattered was the destination, not the artfulness of the path chosen, while for Frankfurter, consistency with the rule of law and basic constitutional principles took precedence.

Frankfurter has been not so much damned by praise as he has been elevated by condemnation. The criticisms that he was not active enough in promoting enlightened causes suggest that he was too judicial, not sufficiently political. But given that the Court *is* a judicial institution, not a political one, critics—sometimes consciously but often inadvertently—pay homage to Frankfurter's integrity and greatness. Max Lerner was more candid than most critics, pointing out that while he disagreed with Frankfurter, "I deeply respect Justice Frankfurter's concern with the legal fabric, and I have only scorn for those who, in their quick and shallow intolerance, attack him as some kind of antediluvian stick-in-the-mud."[10]

The time may be opportune to rethink the mantra of criticism of Felix Frankfurter. While ambitious architects of new worlds are hardly in short supply on the college campuses of America, by and large this is an era of chastened views about the capacity of governments, and of well-earned cynicism of the courts. In the wake of *Bush v. Gore,* even modern liberals are rediscovering the virtues of judicial restraint. And two decades of divided government, often with Republicans in the White House, has yielded a very different Supreme Court, one on which the ideas of Frankfurter would likely be seen as more mainstream. There is no longer such a strong sense in politics and society of the inevitability of progressivism. Frankfurter merits greatness because of the sum of the personal qualities he brought to the bench, and because of the kind of vision of the role of law and of courts that he articulated for over two decades. On the personal level his intellectualism has rarely if ever been matched on the court. Some may argue that this is not an essential or even a desirable trait, that law in a democracy should be "of the people," simple in principle and application and defended in clear and simple ways without obscure legalisms. But law is inescapably complex, and is most true to the rule of law and basic principles of the regime when careful minds can elucidate the connections between the particularities of the case and the broad abstractions of principle, and can comprehend the significance of conflicts between different principles inherent in any conflict and the complex institutional effects of any court action. This is not easy stuff, and complex relationships are more likely to be clarified by brilliance, not mediocrity. There is no pretense that the Court is representative or populist; leave that for the political branches. Of course, intellectuals are always tempted to mistake intelligence for wisdom, legal knowledge for political legitimacy. There is good reason why the Supreme Court has neither the purse nor the sword, lest we be ruled by self-congratulatory Platonic Guardians. Frankfurter understood better than most the importance of keeping the courts in their place, and not mistaking judicial review for political rule. That he was so brilliant, and such an activist liberal in politics, makes his understanding and accepting of his limited role as a jurist all the more remarkable.

Frankfurter was not without faults, of course. Much was made some years ago about his private arrangement, during the years before he joined the Court, with Justice Brandeis to do the justice's bidding in political circles.[11] And we now know that he worked behind the scenes with Philip Elman of the Justice Department while *Brown v. Board of Education* was before the Court, suggesting strategy for the government's argument.[12] But there has been no serious suggestion that he ever sold his vote or otherwise compromised the integrity of his opinions while on the Court.

Many persons on and off the Court found Frankfurter to be difficult and often condescending. A writer for the *Nation* observed pungently that when Frankfurter argued before the High Court two decades prior to taking his seat there, his attitude suggested that "he had merely exchanged one group of pupils for another."[13] One can only imagine what the august members of the Court thought of this display of intellectual confidence bordering on arrogance, and he did not change his stripes once he joined the Court. He likely would never have made a great *chief* justice, a role that demands as much social as legal skill, and his unwillingness to glad-hand and compromise may have hurt his potential to build court majorities even as an associate justice. Many who encountered Frankfurter were irked by "his irritating inner conviction of his own righteousness,"[14] and of his penchant for lecturing his peers Brennan once remarked that, "'We would have been inclined to agree with Felix more often in conference, if he quoted Holmes less frequently to us.'"[15] Today, Frankfurter could be a poster boy for the trendy emphasis in public schools on "self-esteem," as he apparently had a healthy regard for his own intellect.

Frankfurter was a legal scholar in the truest sense of the term, a student not just of particular doctrines or statutes, but of the nature of law itself. Through his opinions he sought to fulfill the Court's potential as a dispenser of knowledge and understanding of the rule of law, not just a producer of right outcomes. He was, above all else, a constitutionalist, cognizant of the place of law and courts in the larger scheme, and sensitive to the dangers of misusing both. He was able to move fluidly between the mundane particularities of a case and the great questions of liberal, democratic government, and see and express the relations between the two. As he said of Cardozo, "His conception of the Constitution cannot be severed from his conception of a judge's function in applying it....the clarity with which a specific controversy is seen in the context of the larger intellectual issues beneath the formal surface of litigation, and the courage with which such analysis infuses decision and opinion, are the ultimate determinants of American public law."[16] These "issues beneath the surface" are what kept his interest in the law and guided his analysis.

He was that most rare of species, a *progressive* constitutionalist, or perhaps more precisely, a constitutionalist progressive. That is, he did not seek to make the Constitution just another tool for progressives to promote their agenda on the judicial fast track, skirting the obstacles of democratic government. Liberal constitutionalism, with its emphasis on substantive and structural constraints on governmental power, has largely been anathema to self-styled progressives, from Woodrow Wilson to Herbert Croly and John Dewey and on to those today who continue to call for an end to separation of powers and other obstacles to centralized rule by the anointed.[17] For a constitutionalist, form and process are fundamental; to the progressive they are obstacles. Early progressives, exemplified by Holmes and Brandeis on the Supreme Court, sought to overcome this tension by emphasizing the democratic and positive government elements of liberal constitutionalism. Those "great dissenters" were gone from the Court before it began its postwar transformation from deference to activism, which strained the logic of their democratic vision. Frankfurter shared the progressive faith in an activist state to grapple with the problems of modern society, but for him the constitutional aspects were foremost. Constitutionalist arguments for a restrained Court were for him not merely a convenient bit of political rhetoric to be discarded once the righteous replaced the reactionary on the Court. He remained true to progressive causes in the political realm, and his capacity to distinguish the legal world from the political, even when that ran counter to his preferences, is testimony to his integrity and regard for constitutionalism. While egalitarian liberals sought to exploit their newfound influence on the courts to further their substantive agenda, Frankfurter held fast to his beliefs in democratic primacy, and thus came to be seen as a conservative obstacle, rather than a progressive leader. He essentially has been criticized for not being politically expedient. "He remained consistent, but consistency is not always a virtue," concludes Urofsky. "Felix Frankfurter did not make the transition [from the era of judicial deference to activism] and in that sense his story is a tragic one."[18] But this seems as much triumph as tragedy. It is hard to imagine one of the heroes of the intellectual left, such as William Brennan or Thurgood Marshall or Harry Blackmun, being criticized for not getting with the increasingly conservative program of the changing Court; rather they would be hailed as principled defenders of fundamental values.[19] It was Frankfurter's fate to be a defender of constitutional principles that were not in scholarly or legal fashion.

What was Frankfurter's constitutional vision? Stated most generally, it was that legal and especially constitutional questions are complex and defy easy, formulaic solutions, and that courts whenever possible should allow the balance of political forces to work out their differences. His emphasis on balancing and contextual analysis meant that Frankfurter rarely took ringing stands on behalf of particular "fundamental" rights or principles, often to the frustration of civil libertarians. I don't think it's quite fair to say, as some would, that Frankfurter dismissed the importance of constitutional rights. Rather, he saw rights as not so much natural in origin as evolutionary, developed largely out of the historical context of British society. As such they were always grounded in the realities of the day and never absolute. "The first ten amendments," Frankfurter wrote in *Dennis v. United States* (341 US 494, 524 [1951]), borrowing from a nineteenth-century case,[20] "were not intended to lay down any novel principles of government, but simply to embody certain guaranties and immunities which we had inherited from our English ancestors, and which had from time immemorial been subject to certain well-recognized exceptions arising from the necessity of the case." Thus he never accepted the view of Black and Douglas that when the First Amendment says "Congress shall make no law" abridging the freedom of speech, it means *no* law, period, because to Frankfurter the amendment was never conceived as creating an absolute barrier to legislation, but only to formally recognize the historically derived and limited expectations of free expression. Any simplistic formula or rule—such as preferred rights, the clear and present danger test, or the absolute and rote application of the first eight amendments to the states—was to be avoided as doing violence to the social complexity that these historically derived practices and principles were intended to address. Such phrases "tend to convey a delusion of certitude when what is most certain is the complexity of the strands in the web of freedoms which the judge must disentangle."[21] This put Frankfurter at odds with the modern trend to reduce law to a set of aphorisms, much like the slogans of a political campaign.

It was the democratic branches of the national government that could best balance the conflicting interests of modern society, and in recognition of this the judiciary should be restrained in the exercise of its authority, avoiding constitutional rulings when possible and keeping them narrow when unavoidable. It may seem peculiar to say that Frankfurter was a constitutionalist who ducked constitutional questions. But Frankfurter was exceptional in being a judge who did not see the courts as the center of the constitutional universe. Ultimately the interpreting of constitutional principles within a constitutional structure by the political branches was most essential to the system's viability. Yet he recognized that there was potential for exceeding constitutional authority in the political branches as well, as they too were inhabited by imperfect humans. His *Youngstown* concurrence expresses well his appreciation of the lessons of history and the need for institutional constraints:

> A constitutional democracy like ours is perhaps the most difficult of mans social arrangements to manage successfully.... The Founders of the Nation...acted on the conviction that the experience of man sheds a good deal of light on his nature. It sheds a good deal of light not merely on the need for effective power, if a society is to be at once cohesive and civilized, but also on the need for limitations on the power of governors over the governed.... For them the doctrine of separation of powers was not mere theory; it was a felt necessity. Not so long ago it was fashionable to find our system of checks and balances obstructive to effective government.... The experience through which the world has passed in our own day has made vivid the realization that the Framers of our Constitution were not inexperienced doctrinaires. [They] had no illusion that our people enjoyed biological or psychological or sociological immunities from the hazards of concentrated power.... The accretion of dangerous power [comes], however slowly, from the generative force of unchecked disregard of the restrictions that fence in even the most disinterested assertion of authority.

This might seem like an invitation for an aggressive Court to jump in and save the Republic in the name of the Constitution, but Frankfurter did not see it so simply. He goes on:

> The Framers, however, did not make the judiciary the overseer of our government.... Rigorous adherence to the narrow scope of the judicial function is especially demanded in controversies that arouse appeals to the Constitution ....Due regard for the implications of the distribution of powers in our Constitution and for the nature of the judicial process as the ultimate authority in interpreting the Constitution.... [requires] that clashes between different branches of the government should be avoided if a legal ground of less explosive potentialities is properly available. Constitutional adjudications are apt by exposing differences to exacerbate them.[22]

This shows several aspects of Frankfurter's reasoning: the grand sweep through fundamental concepts was prelude to handling specific disputes in a case, the emphasis on experience and human nature, and the avoidance of simple prescriptions. His understanding of politics and constitutionalism was in part a tragic one—unusual for a progressive—that saw some imperfections of politics as endemic to humanity. Contrast this with the optimism of Brennan, the intellect of the activist Court, whose "jurisprudence represents the side of the modern psyche that rejects as flawed, or at least as dated, the teaching about the tragic dimensions of the human condition and the limits of political life."[23]

As a jurist, Frankfurter could most directly seek to keep his own branch within its legitimate authority, and his vision left the judiciary with a restricted role. If the political branches were not to be intruded upon, it was essential that the justices distinguish constitutionality from morality and preference. Otherwise, "[i]f the function of this Court is to be essentially no different from that of a legislature, if the considerations governing constitutional construction are to be substantially those that underlie legislation, then indeed judges should not have life tenure and they should be made directly responsible to the electorate."[24] Surely an elected judiciary was not Frankfurter's aspiration, and he thought that guarding against an overreaching judiciary was the only way to legitimately preserve its privileged status. This would require that both judges and the public let go of notions that courts can provide the solutions for society, and that the Constitution is the cure-all. "So-called constitutional questions seem to exercise a mesmeric influence over the popular mind," he complained in *Youngstown*. "This eagerness to settle—preferably forever—a specific problem on the basis of the broadest possible constitutional pronouncements may not unfairly be called one of our minor national traits" (343 US 594 [1952]). This is a trait Frankfurter always sought to discourage, by turning beseeching eyes away from the courts and toward politics. As he stated so emphatically in *Baker,* "there is not under our Constitution a judicial remedy for every political mischief, for every undesirable exercise of legislative power.... Appeal must be to an informed, civically militant electorate. In a democratic society like ours, relief must come through an aroused popular conscience that sears the conscience of the people's representatives."[25]

In keeping with the limited role he saw for judge-made constitutional doctrine, Frankfurter recognized that a nation is bound, or constituted, by elements beyond the law, and thus to Frankfurter certain core institutions and practices, such as public schools and the flag, merited recognition for the function they serve in building and preserving a democratic political culture. Frankfurter came from a family whose fathers had been rabbis for centuries, and married the daughter of a Congregational minister, and one wonders if this perhaps inclined Frankfurter to attach a religious-like moral symbolism to elements of democratic society and take on the role of secular prophet of democratic constitutionalism, almost in the manner of the oral storytellers of Biblical days. In one of his most infamous opinions, *Minersville School District v. Gobitis,* the Court upheld a required pledge to the flag, and Frankfurter declared that "the ultimate foundation of a free society is the binding tie of cohesive sentiment. [Schools]... gather up the traditions of a people, transmit them from generation to generation, and thereby create that continuity...which constitutes a civilization. We live by symbols" (310 US 586, 596 [1940]). In a later case he applied religious metaphor to the social function of schools: "To regard teachers—in our entire educational system, from the primary grades to the university—as the priests of our democracy is...not to indulge in hyperbole. It is the special task of teachers to foster those habits of open-mindeness and critical inquiry which alone make for responsible citizens."[26] He even saw patents and trademarks as symbols: "The protection of trademarks is the law's recognition of the psychological function of symbols. If it is true that we live by symbols, it is no less true that we purchase goods by them."[27] In his emphasis on symbolism and institutions, Frankfurter can be seen as, fundamentally, more an institutionalist than a doctrinalist. Institutionalism is at the core of constitutionalism, and his perspective produces a fuller understanding of constitutional order than an emphasis on doctrine that can change with the shifting preferences of the members of the Court.

It is another of those interesting complexities of Frankfurter's character that he could be so intellectually arrogant at times, yet quick to recognize the delusions of grandeur to which members of such an elite and powerful body could be susceptible. The notion that the enlightened shall, or at least should, inherit the earth, and that the Supreme Court could be the means, is alluring to law scholars and students. Every major liberal activist justice of recent decades has been lauded for pushing the nation in a more progressive direction, regardless of their shortcomings in legal analysis or fidelity to the Constitution. Anthony Lewis vividly illustrated the adulation of the Warren Court when he wrote that the chief justice was the "closest thing the United States has had to a Platonic Guardian, dispensing law from a throne without any sensed limits of power except what was seen as the good of society. Fortunately, he was a decent, humane, honorable, democratic Guardian."[28]

Warren was lionized because he reached decisions that many commentators agreed with, although to call him "democratic" seems a bit stretched, as he achieved his following by leading the Court in *overturning* the democratically elected branches. Frankfurter would have none of this. He "though that the doctrine that the ends justified the means was pernicious. Having served with so many justices, he had doubts...that they fulfilled the qualifications for Platonic Guardians.... The history of the chosen did not dispel the doubt."[29]

Related to his wariness of judges imposing values through the overturning of political actions were his doubts about the legitimacy of a double standard of constitutional rights. For Frankfurter the historical and logical roots of a doctrine mattered greatly; it did not suffice merely to say it "worked." Under the double standard, which grew out of the famous footnote four of *United States v. Carolene Products,* the Court created a class of "preferred" or "fundamental" rights, such as expression, equal protection, and later privacy, that would merit strict protection, while other rights, usually pejoratively characterized as merely "economic," such as contract rights and protections against takings of property, were to be generally left to the discretion of the political branches. Probably no

other footnote or even doctrine captures so well the general pattern of the
Court's holdings in the decades following the New Deal. The double standard
allowed the Court to create a class of protected rights acceptable to the ruling
elite while denigrating those to which they objected, as Martin Shapiro has argued.[30] Politically, the double standard worked, but that troubled Frankfurter,
who could not see its historical and theoretical justification. "Please tell me," he
beseeched his colleague Justice Reed, "what kind of sense it makes that one
provision of the Constitution is to be 'preferred' over another.... The correlative
of 'preference' is 'subordination,' and I know of no calculus to determine when
one provision of the Constitution must yield to another, nor do I know of any
reason for doing so."[31]

In a book about Holmes, Frankfurter even questioned the lowly status of
property rights. "[C]ertainly in some of its aspects property is a function
to personality, and conversely the free range of the human spirit becomes shriv-
eled and constrained under economic dependence.... [A] sharp division between
property rights and human rights largely falsifies reality."[32] Despite Frankfurter's theoretical qualms with the double standard, however, in practice he
was not so far removed from his more activist colleagues. He shared their rejection of close scrutiny of economic regulation and, while not drawing as sharp a
line in the protection of other civil rights and liberties, he nonetheless was far
more likely to find expression and equality and the procedural rights of suspects
protected by either the specific language of the Constitution or the more general
implications of due process and equal protection.[33] He recognized this distinction in *Kovacs v. Cooper,* when he wrote, "Those liberties of the individual
which history has attested as the indispensable conditions of an open as against
a closed society come to this Court with a momentum for respect lacking when
appeal is made to the liberties which derive merely from shifting economic ar-
rangements" (336 US 77, 95 [1949]).

Frankfurter's skepticism about the courts stands in sharp contrast with the
faith he put in the political branches to promote the public interest and respect
rights. In one case he wrote, "Since these agencies deal largely with the vindi-
cation of public interest and not enforcement of private rights, this Court ought
not to imply hampering restrictions, not imposed by Congress, upon the effectiveness of the administrative process."[34] At times his constitutionalism becomes almost nonconstitutionalist, democcracy without limits. He seemed at
times to rationalize his deference by an almost romantic notion that people in
government could be counted on to do the right thing. "I am aware that men
who have power can exercise it—and too often do—to enforce their own will,"
he wrote in a letter to Justice Black. "But I am also aware of the forces of tradition and the habits of discipline whereby men entrusted with power remain
within the limited framework of their professed power."[35] Had he lived through
the experience of Watergate perhaps his views would have been less sanguine.

Of course, Frankfurter was in many respects a product of his time, and for the progressives of the early twentieth century the lesson of experience was that courts should not stand in the way of the democratic branches. Looking back on that century, it is easy to see that conflicting values, insufficient knowledge of how to accomplish public purposes, and the self-interest of elites bedevil attempts at centralized control,[36] and that people's rights and interests may get slighted in the process. But the Progressives had the optimism of moral certitude, and "like the Progressives," writes Jeffrey Hockett, Frankfurter "had enormous confidence in the capacity of administrative expertise and political leadership to articulate a unifying national purpose."[37] The tension between the Court and the political branches culminated in Franklin Roosevelt's infamous Court-Packing plan, and the capitulation of the Supreme Court on federal powers and economic rights in 1937. These experiences were fresh in Frankfurter's mind when he joined the bench in 1939, and shaped his philosophy of restraint.

What most recommends Frankfurter is not so much his specific constitutional views, although there is much to be said for them, but the consistency and eloquence with which he defended them. He saw no conflict in his constitutionalist vision of a restrained judiciary taking precedence over his progressive political ideology, while many of his political allies and friends and scholars were puzzled by this. And he always stated his views in intelligent and fluid prose, elevating the dialogue of the Court and educating his readers. Indeed, to read the opinions of Frankfurter is to get an education in civics, and the rigor and sophistication of his opinions set them apart from those of many of his colleagues. Indeed, that Frankfurter *had* a sophisticated constitutional vision is noteworthy in itself, as notions of constitutionalism have been criticized by legal and intellectual elites for over a century, and one would be hard-pressed to find anything in the curricula of most law schools on the rule of law, the structure and function of the constitutional system, the impact of the courts, and so on.

To get some perspective on Justice Frankfurter it may be helpful—or at least fun—to speculate as to where he would stand on the Court today. He would surely be a forceful and even entertaining justice, as he was in his day. He would give Justice Scalia a run for his money in his willingness to pester attorneys during oral argument and to engage in debate. Just to witness the interaction between Frankfurter and Scalia—the effective heir to the former's "scholar's seat," although technically Frankfurter's place has been filled by Blackmun and now Breyer—would be worth the wait to get in the courtroom. In conference Frankfurter likely would chafe under the businesslike leadership of Rehnquist, missing the chance for expansive lecture under Chief Justice Stone. Most importantly, he would raise the level of constitutional dialogue in the opinions of the Court, as much by inflaming his opponents as by inspiring his collegial allies. In this aspect his tenure might be welcomed by justices such as Thomas, who, although quiet in oral argument, tends to include in his opinions often striking reassessments of constitutional doctrine grounded in basic principles and to promote a certain vision of natural law. Frankfurter would likely take issue with the latter, and the result could be a stimulating and illuminating written exchange.

Substantive predictions are more hazardous, but I think he would be encouraged by many trends on the Court today. Urofsky would consign Frankfurter to irrelevance, even in his own time: "Time outran his vision; he would have been the perfect judge a generation earlier. Once on the bench he seemed ignorant of the tides of history.[38] But those tides have been receding of late, and his philosophy seems quite relevant today, when there is less enthusiasm for government by the judiciary. Frankfurter might often find himself in alliance with justices such as Kennedy and O'Connor, who are probably the two justices most uncomfortable with hard and fast rules, and most prone to finding small distinctions in cases on which to hang their opinions. But Frankfurter would likely spice his opinions with more vigorously defended connections to basic constitutional theory. He would almost surely not be as enthusiastic a defender of state powers against federal encroachment under the commerce clause,[39] given the nationalism that pervades both his political and judicial views, but the moderate way in which federalism has been restored would probably appeal to his sense of balance.

Frankfurter likely would applaud the retrenchment on some criminal rights precedents, as he had been wary of the Warren Court's sloganeering and sweeping revisions of constitutional law. Surely he would welcome the Court's tightening of the threshold rules that disputes must meet for court review.[40] He was a bitter dissenter to the landmark expansion of justiciability—the type of issues suitable for review—in *Baker,* and was retired from the Court when the "true" Warren Court essentially removed the standing requirement, at least for certain First Amendment cases, that a party show injury to gain a hearing in court.[41] This was doubly offensive to Frankfurter because it allowed the Court to reach disputes that would not satisfy traditional bounds of judicial cases and controversies" and because it created a privileged class of cases based in part on a hierarchy of constitutional rights, a notion that always troubled Frankfurter. The threshold requirements, rooted in prudence and the Article 3 requirements that the powers of the federal judiciary be limited to "cases and controversies" that are judicial in nature, are just the sort of dry, institutional rules that Frankfurter saw as vital to the proper functioning of the judiciary in the constitutional system.

Frankfurter was labeled with that most damning of terms, "conservative," because of his judicial conservatism during the activist Warren Court era. But he would surely part company on many occasions with the more substantively conservative members of the Court—Thomas foremost, secondly Scalia, who tends to fluctuate between activism and deference, and thirdly Rehnquist, the least committed to a particular constitutional philosophy of the three. Unless he became a devotee of public choice literature and changed his views on "economic" regulation, he would likely oppose the resurrection of property rights as a lamentable return to the era of *Lochner,* as Marshall warned in *Cleburne v Cleburne Living Center* (473 US 432, 460 [1985]). But I don't think he would be as troubled by this trend as many might expect, because the revival has been more modest and more explicitly rooted in constitutional text—the takings clause—than the pre-New Deal "liberty of contract" cases. Even Frankfurter said in dicta that "The right not to have property taken without just compensation has...the same constitutional dignity as the right to be protected against unreasonable searches and seizures."[42] Tests such as in *Nollan v. California Coastal Commission* (483 US 825 [1987])—that exactions imposed on property use must substantially further public interests that would justify denial of a permit—and in *Dolan v. Tigard* (512 US 374 [1994]) that there must be a "rough proportionality" between conditions imposed and the impact of the property use, would likely be appreciated by Frankfurter because they are essentially balancing tests, taking into account both the public and the personal interest. Even *Lucas,* with Scalia's grounding of takings doctrine in "background principles of the State's law of property and nuisance" (505 US 1003 [1992]), might find some favor, given Frankfurter's emphasis on the historical development and context of law.

In the areas, then, where he would most likely have substantive disagreements with the "conservative" majority—federalism and property rights—Frankfurter nonetheless might appreciate that the Court was moving away from the simplistic double standard that reduced much constitutional adjudication to ritual for several decades, and toward a more contextual and balanced jurisprudence. The takings and federalism cases have been criticized as being too ad hoc and not producing sufficiently predictable rules, but Frankfurter was always more comfortable with contextual interpretation. The midlevel standard of review—emphasizing qualitative criteria such as "substantial" relationships and "important" interests—that has become more common in recent decades yields less predictable results than do the more extreme standards of strict scrutiny or minimal rational basis, but also more nuanced and balanced holdings, a trend of which Frankfurter would likely approve. But, like Breyer and Ginsburg, he likely would have given greater weight to *legislative* rather than judicial judgments of what is "substantial" or "important."

The two central national political events that launched the twenty-first century—the extraordinary legal wrangling over the 2000 presidential election and the response to the terrorist attacks of 2001—have raised or may raise unique legal disputes in the courts. The latter crisis would likely provide a forum for Frankfurter to express his appreciation of the importance of national security and national symbols and deference to legislative judgments, and he might be more likely even than "conservatives" such as Scalia to reject constitutional challenges to measures that restrict privacy and civil liberties in the name of fighting terrorism. Along these lines it would have been interesting to see how Frankfurter would have voted in the flag-burning case.[43] Given his emphasis on the importance of the flag as a symbol of unity in *Gobitis* and his frustration at being repudiated three years later in *Barnette,* it seems probable that he would have sided with the dissenters in *Texas* and *Eichman* and supported the suppression of burning, possibly even providing the swing vote had he been on the Court instead of Scalia.

Bush v. Gore is not as easily assessed from Frankfurter's perspective. The most obvious conclusion, although not necessarily the most correct, is that he would bemoan the Court's involvement in an ostensibly political matter, and castigate his colleagues in the majority for following the tainted path of judicial intrusion into elections started in *Baker.* But how the dispute over the 2000 election unfolded in the courts was extraordinary. Had the matter come before the Court as a *threshold* question—whether courts had any jurisdiction to decide the matter and whether it was justiciable—Frankfurter might have argued that the outcome of the election must be decided by the political branches, however drawn out and painful that might be. He may have found some merit in the arguments of Chief Justice Rehnquist (with Scalia and Thomas concurring) that Article 2 placed extraordinary discretion with the legislature of the state, and that any post-election meddling by the courts with the legislative delegation of authority to certain executive officials would constitute a change of law in violation of federal statutory law and Article 2. But the case was *not* before the Court as a threshold matter, and so the Supreme Court could not avoid a ruling on the substantive merits of the case. And the dispute at the center of *Bush v. Gore* involved the orders of a *court,* not a legislature or executive. It was the extraordinary remedy ordered by the Florida Supreme Court—a complete recount of "undervotes" in the entire state under a tight deadline, without clear guidelines for judging votes or sufficient time to clarify the questions and allow for appeals and so forth—that doomed the state court decision. As distinct from the voting rights cases to which Frankfurter objected, the courts had already intruded, and thus there were not the same separation of powers concerns.

Similarly, the justices of the *Bush v. Gore* majority have been called hypocritical for abandoning their usual advocacy of federalism. But federalism was never as strong a concern for Frankfurter, who tended to see national government as the logical repository of authority to deal with the national problems of modern society. And the Article 2 interpretation means that presidential election disputes may be seen as uniquely federal issues, even when they involve the organs of state government. Thirdly, it could be argued, as Rehnquist did, that the majority in *Bush* was actually *defending* the federal role of the state legislature against encroachment by the Florida court. So it was not simply a matter of federal versus state, but one state entity versus another. Given Frankfurter's preference for legislative action, it is not clear that he would have supported the Florida Supreme Court. And he surely would have been appalled by the chaos that might surround the rushed recount. He passionately believed that courts must act deliberately and with decorum, giving due regard to all issues and positions and maintaining proper procedure. Slapdash work offended him, although perhaps he would have seen the Florida court as having little choice under the circumstances.

In any case he would surely have been frustrated with the time constraints placed on the U.S. Supreme Court to make a decision and issue opinions, and the media circus that surrounded its every move. He was a craftsman, and believed a long period of deliberation and writing before an opinion was published essential to proper judicial process. One could hear him complaining that this was no way to run a Court, and someone, perhaps Scalia, would lean across the table and say, "But Felix, we have no choice!" The current members of the Court may be glad the cantankerous scholar was *not* on the bench, as their relations were strained enough as it were. But there can be little doubt that, complaining as he might have been, he would work together with his clerks to produce the most thoughtful and stimulating of the opinions, regardless of the position he took.

An essential element of any stimulating of the opinions, regardless of the position he took great justice, I would argue, is to have an understanding of constitutionalism and a related theory of law, and Frankfurter exemplifies these qualities. Even if Frankfurter were around today, however, there is serious question as to whether anyone so thoughtful, let alone someone who expresses those thoughts forthrightly and eloquently, could survive the confirmation process. The heavy senatorial scrutiny and political demagoguery that has greeted some recent nominees for the Court has taught the lesson that nominees should be of modest intellect and disposition, devoid of provocative ideas or complex notions of constitutionalism that might ruffle someone's feathers and mobilize the network of naysaying interest groups. Frankfurter would be contemptuous of the attitude that sees virtue in mediocrity, either because the mediocre need representation on the court or because brilliance is too contentious for a confirmation process. "When 'elite' became a word of opprobrium, we entered a world totally foreign to Frankfurter's ethos."[44] For an intelligent and forceful candidate such as Frankfurter to be nominated and confirmed, he or she would likely have to have other redeeming political attributes that would provide insulation from the heat, or have someone deemed *more* controversial deflect the attention, as was the case when Scalia sailed through while the heavy artillery was aimed at the nomination of Rehnquist as chief justice.

The example of Frankfurter shows that you don't have to be compliant or even comprehensible to most people to raise the level of dialogue and quality of work on the court, and we might be well-advised to rethink our political criteria for acceptable nominees today. As Kurland says in tribute, "He was the latest of the great keepers of the legend: a legend of a nonpartisan Supreme Court dedicated to the maintenance of a government of law founded on reason and based on a faith in democracy. One hopes he was not the last."[45]

NOTES

1. David Currie, *The Constitution in the Supreme Court* (Chicago: University of Chicago Press, 1990), 415.
2. Philip B. Kurland, "Felix Frankfurter," in Bernard Schwartz, (ed.), *The Warren Court: A Retrospective* (New York: Oxford University Press, 1998), 229.
3. Fred Rodell, *Nine Men: A Political History of the Supreme Court from 1790–1955* (Random House, 1955), 269.
4. Melvin I. Urofsky, *Division and Discord: The Supreme Court Under Stone and Vincent 1941–1953* (Columbia: University of South Carolina, 1997), 20.
5. Bernard Schwartz, "Earl Warren," 258. See note 2.
6. Kurland, 225. See note 2.
7. Quoted in Arthur M. Schlesinger, Jr., *The Crisis of the Old Order* (Boston: Houghton Mifflin, 1957), 419.
8. Felix Frankfurter, "Joseph H. Beale," 56 *Harvard Law Review* (March, 1943): 701.
9. Melvin I. Urofsky, *Felix Frankfurter: Judicial Restraint and Individual Liberties* (Boston: Twayne, 1991), 173.
10. Max Lerner, "Felix Frankfurter and the Essential Tension," in *Nine Scorpions in a Bottle* (New York: Arcade Publishing, 1994), 164.
11. See Bruce Allen Murphy, *The Brandeis/Frankfurter Connection: The Secret Political Activities of Two Supreme Court Justices* (New York: Oxford University Press, 1982); and Melvin I. Urofsky and David W. Levy (eds.), *"Half Brother, Half Son"*: The Letters of Louis D. Brandeis to Felix Frankfurter (Norman, OK: University of Oklahoma Press, 1991), 7.
12. Lerner, 164. See note 10.
    Tattler, "Sketch," *Nation*, 104, March 15 (1917): 320.
14. Helen Shirley Thomas, *Felix Frankfurter: Scholar on the Bench* (Baltimore: Johns Hopkins University Press, 1960), 354.
15. Quoted in Dennis J. Hutchinson, "Felix Frankfurter and the Business of the Supreme Court, O.T. 1946–O.T. 1961," *1980 Supreme Court Review*, 143, 205.
16. Frankfurter, "Mr. Justice Cardozo and Public Law," 52 *Harvard Law Review* 440–1 (Jan. 1939): 440–441. Frankfurter observed that "every man who writes, in large measure writes autobiography," and often in his assessments of others we find a reflection of himself. Frankfurter, "Mr. Justice Brandeis," 55 *Harvard Law Review* (Dec. 1941): 181.
17. See, for example, Daniel Lazare, *The Frozen Republic: How the Constitution Is Paralyzing Democracy* (Harcourt Brace, 1996).
18. Urofsky, 178–9. See note 9.
19. See, for example, the substantial and largely congratulatory literature on Justice Brennan, including Roger Goldman and David Gallen, *Justice William J. Brennan, Jr.: Freedom First* (New York: Carrol & Graf, 1994); Frank I. Michelman, *Brennan and Democracy* (Princeton University Press, 1999); and E. Joshua Rosenkranz and Bernard Schwartz (eds.), *Reason and Passion: Justice Brennan's Enduring Influence* (New York: Norton, 1997).
20. *Robertson v. Baldwin*, 165 US 275, 281 (1897).
21. *Dennis v. United States*, 341 US 543 (1951).

22. *Youngstown Sheet & Tube v. Sawyer,* 343 US 579, 593B95 (1952).
23. David E. Marion, *The Jurisprudence of Justice Felix Frankfurter* (Lanham, MD: Rowman & Littlefield, 1997), 166.
24. *Board of Education v. Barnette,* 319 US 624, 652 (1943).
25. *Baker v. Carr,* 369 US 186, 270 (1962).
26. *Wieman v. Updegraff,* 344 US 183; 73 S. Ct. 215, 225 (1952). Frankfurter's concurring opinion was joined by Douglas, a rare alliance.
27. *Mishawaka R. & W. Manufacturing Co. v. S.S. Kresage,* 316 US 203, 205 (1942).
28. *The Justices of the United States Supreme Court, 1789–1969,* vol. 4 (New York: Chelsea House, 1969), 2726.
29. Kurland, 229. See note 2.
30. Martin Shapiro, "The Constitution and Economic Rights," in M. Judd Harmon (ed.), *Essays on the Constitution of the United States* (Port Washington, NY: Kennikat Press, 1978).
31. Letter of Frankfurter to Stanley Reed, Feb. 7, 1956, in Frankfurter Papers, Library of Congress; quoted in Urofsky, 37. See note 4.
32. Felix Frankfurter, *Mr. Justice Holmes* (Cambridge, MA.: Harvard University Press, 1938), 50.
33. Thomas, 354. See note 14.
34. *Ashbacker Radio Corp. v. FCC,* 326 US 327, 335 (1945).
35. Letter of Frankfurter to Hugo Black, Nov. 13, 1943, quoted in Kurland, 229–230. See note 2.
36. See James C. Scott, "State Simplifications: Nature, Space and People," in Ian Shapiro and Russell Hardin, (eds,.), *Political Order,* 65–77.
37. Jeffrey D. Hockett, *New Deal Justice: The Constitutional Jurisprudence of Hugo L. Black, Felix Frankfurter and Robert H. Jackson* (Lanham, MD: Rowman & Littlefield, 1996), 8. See also Sanford V. Levinson, "The Democratic Faith of Felix Frankfurter," 25 *Stanford Law Review* (1973): 430.
38. Urofsky, 178. See note 90.
39. On recent shifts in commerce clause jurisprudence, see *Lopez v. United States,* 514 US 549 (1995) and *Morrison v. United States* (2000).
40. See *Valley Forge Christian College v. Americans United* (1982) and *Lujan v. Defenders of Wildlife,* 504 US 555 (1992).
41. *Flast v. Cohen,* 392 US 83 (1964).
42. *West Virginia Board v. Barnette,* 319 US 648 (1943).
43. *Texas v. Johnson,* 491 US 398 (1989).
44. Philip B. Kurland, *Mr. Justice Frankfurter and the Constitution* (Chicago: University of Chicago Press, 1971), 1.
45. Ibid., xiii.

CHAPTER ELEVEN

William O. Douglas: A Judge for the 21st Century

James Chowning Davies

It is a large problem to judge whether particular jurists, notably those who have served on the Supreme Court, are great. Anyone can claim objectivity, but no one can gain everyone's agreement on what is truly objective. Let me state some yardsticks that may at least help to measure judges, including William Orville Douglas, for greatness.

Criteria for Greatness

A judge must have circumstances that allow him to exercise great influence. Judicial influence is limited by the degree of political consensus within a society. When there is deep social and political dissensus in a nation, judges cannot contribute much to improve matters. Judges in times of war and revolution must wait until instability is diminished before they can make much difference. Habeas corpus—the right of a detained person to be freed if a judge says government has no right to detain him or her—is one of the last judicial acts to be publicly accepted as times gradually stabilize. Milligan, detained during the American Civil War, was not released until it was over. Endo, a Japanese-American interned during the Second World War, got her release only when the war was approaching its end.

A judge must have the fortitude and tenacity to stick to and express basic principles. In nations corrupted by high degrees of greed for wealth and power, judges have much diminished influence. A judge must have the intelligence and empathy to understand the forces that will increase consensus and therefore stability and openness. This condition increases the ability of citizens to control themselves and their government. Early life experiences have more to do than training for law with establishing judges' elemental understanding and empathy, even though some judges may deny the effect of early experience on their judgments.

The United States has had a Supreme Court since its beginnings, but its powers were not established at the outset. Perhaps the greatest of the justices was John Marshall, a distant cousin of Thomas Jefferson. He was a midnight appointee of Jefferson's predecessor, John Adams, who wanted to save the republic from what to him was irresponsible popular rule.

Adams could not be sure what would come of Marshall, this shrewd and conservative opponent of Jefferson. But Marshall proved to be more than a conservative: he established not only respect for the Supreme Court but also fashioned several of the basic principles of federal government. Deciding how to divide power between the national and the state governments was no small task: the thirteen former colonies were hyperconscious of their sovereignty and determined to keep nearly all of it.

After Jefferson's election in 1800, liberals became less concerned about conservative tendencies to establish plutocracy and conservatives less concerned about populism. Political contests still occur about what governmental office has what power, but the elemental principal that no office, no official shall have preponderant power has been settled. Marshall (with later help from Justice Story), succeeded in the gigantic task of establishing a Constitution-abiding nation. He did that while delimiting the division of political power between the Congress, the president, and the courts. In England the Parliament is supreme and the prime minister is a member of Parliament. Marshall did not make either the Congress or the president supreme in the national government. And, in contrast to the English case, he established the Supreme Court as a power not subordinate or superior to but coordinate with the other two branches, and, in 1803 in *Marbury v. Madison,* as the final arbiter of constitutionality.

Douglas probably would not have been suited to Marshall's challenges, which have largely met and have become part of settled constitutional law. Douglas was less concerned, perhaps, than Marshall and two other chief justices—Charles Evans Hughes and Earl Warren—with establishing consensus among the Brethren. But Douglas was very concerned about the future of American society and government, and as he passed one decade after another as a justice, he became increasingly less concerned about convincing even a minority of his Brethren that he was right. But he was very involved in wakening his fellow citizens to the problems that an advanced democracy must face.

New Challenges

The issues that Douglas faced in the mature American polity, from his appointment to the Court in 1939 to his resignation in 1975, were indeed momentous. And I'll suggest that he did meet most, though not all, of them in a way that makes judges great.

Perhaps the most fundamental, dominant challenge during Douglas's public service was making the rulers responsible to the ruled—that is, responsible to the entire citizenry and not just to one regional, economic, religious, or eth-nic segment of it. Roosevelt played the principal part in meeting this challenge in the mid-twentieth century, as Lincoln had in the mid-nineteenth. In this po-litical process of making government responsible to its general public, Douglas played a major judicial role in the democratizing process, more perhaps than any of his contemporaries on the Court.

And he moved beyond the challenges of the New Deal era. One of the greatest of these challenges stemmed from the powerful innate desires of all human beings to achieve dignity, autonomy, and individual fulfillment. In highly integrated cultures, this involves helping individuals avoid being dimin-ished, manipulated, and standardized.

Another great challenge was, and is, the continuing process of establishing a world community in which America interacts equably with other nations and other cultures rather than attempting to dominate them. These challenges in-volve *collaborating* in the use of its power, in the service of interests that are worldwide rather than national and that are understood similarly—that is, equa-bly—by other nations.

Douglas's Origins

The origins of Douglas's enormous career are neither wholly innate nor wholly environmental. His hyperactivity had a large innate component, but the innate component never acted in a vacuum but always interacted with his physical and social environment. He was born in western Minnesota on October 16, 1898, and died on January 19, 1980. Into these eight decades he crowded an enor-mous amount of activity, both private and public.

His father had what Protestants call a mission church: the kind that national church organizations set up in areas that are too poor to self-sustain a local con-gregation. In Minnesota, a very young Douglas contracted polio and came close to death. His mother followed the doctor's recommendation of regular massage of his legs with warm salt water. His pipe-stem legs remained thin[1] for years but his mother's and his own determination not to be defeated by handicap be-came fundamental to his personality. His mother's stubborn refusal to be de-feated by adversity—including the death of her husband, a very sick son, and the poverty of the family—established a pattern in the son. Sensing sometimes that he was reared on the wrong side of the tracks, Douglas never felt that he was poor in the ability to overcome adversity.

The winters in Minnesota were more severe than the senior Douglas could stand, so the family moved from Minnesota to coastal California. The sun was too bright for his father's eyes, so they moved to Washington. They took a Presbyterian mission church in south central Washington, not far from Yakima. His father's failing eyesight caused him to dictate sermons for transcription by his wife. The father had not served long there before his stomach ulcerated. He went to Portland, Oregon for surgery, but it was not successful; he died in Portland in August 1904, when the future judge was two months short of his sixth birthday. There may have been more than climate to which the father was hypersensitive, but to my knowledge this is not known.

Douglas moved so far, so fast, from his origins that it is easy to overlook them as he strode rapidly into his future. After gaining elemental self-assurance by helping his childhood family survive and using the nurtured high velocity that he developed in college and law school, his career went up like a rocket. In less than a decade, in FDR's New Deal, he developed and stabilized a major new agency, the Securities Exchange Commission, and then went to the Supreme Court. The boy and young man who met the challenges of dangerous illness and hungry poverty almost achieved what his high school classmates nominated him for: the presidency of the United States. FDR and Truman both wanted him as a running mate, during and after World War II.

Douglas mentioned "the subconscious controls" that affect one's writing. This essay looks for the origins in the childhood and adolescence that shaped him: the mostly subconscious origins of his choice of the written word to make a difference in his world and to do it as both a judicial decision-maker and public advocate. Here I will suggest that, in the twentieth century, he saw elemental problems for the world's polities that are very crucial in the twenty-first century. His love of nature, his sheer activity, and his remarkable longevity are legendary. More legendary, I believe, are his foresight and his great courage.

Whatever the paternal health reasons, Douglas's mother was left with three small children to support. The insurance on her husband was enough for the purchase of a house in Yakima—with enough left over to be badly invested by a friend. The four-person family had much cooperative goodwill, but they lived on about fifty dollars per month, barely enough for them to maintain the genteel poverty that is the lot of the college-educated mission-church clergy.[2]

No later than in his early adolescence, Douglas discovered his strong affinity for mountains and for hiking and climbing them. He was comforted by the Biblical saying about strength coming from mountains. He watched Mt. Adams, which he saw from his father's grave in Yakima. His legs filled out. He vividly reports a two-person climb up the sheer side of a mountain not far from Yakima. The life-threatening task of rock climbing thrilled him and readers of his *Of Men and Mountains*. He got a scholarship at Whitman College and there became close to his English professor, William R. Davis, whom he later described as "indispensable to me" and "indeed, a second father." Years after his early mentorship with Davis, Douglas developed a "father-son relationship" at Columbia University in New York, where he bonded with George Draper, who taught clinical medicine and had tended FDR after his 1921 polio affliction. Draper was early in recognizing the close relationship between physical and mental health and helped Douglas probe his subconscious and get over his fear of fear.

Later, Douglas bonded closely to a succession of men, including Gifford Pinchot. Pinchot pioneered resource conservation, starting when he established the Forestry Service in the Department of Agriculture, implementing Theodore Roosevelt's interests in nature. Pinchot, Douglas said, "was the most enduring influence in my life." Another listing in *Go East, Young Man* of those most influential in Douglas' life included Robert Hutchins, Franklin Roosevelt, Benjamin Cohen, Jerome Frank, Louis Brandeis, and Hugo Black. Douglas was always ready to acknowledge his indebtedness to others who had given him help without which he might have failed.

His need for the companionship of women was also very strong. However, for most of his life it was of a different kind from his need for male mentors. Douglas said that his mother spoiled and pampered him as a small child, when she was helping him recover from his near-fatal bout with polio. And he expected that kind of help from all his wives. It was said that he so transferred his expectation of support from his mother to his wives that it became a major factor in destroying his first three marriages.

Until the 1960s his orientation toward women was evidently quite traditional, pre-women's lib. Wives were to be dutiful servants. His second wife, Mercedes Davidson, was at her best performing the role of hostess and party partner. He paid her for her secretarial work. His third wife, Joan Martin, was also paid to do research work that culminated in Douglas's book, *Mr. Lincoln and the Negroes,* in 1963. Douglas effectively expected the same clerical duty from his spouses as his father got from his mother. But he and his fourth wife, younger than his daughter, had a more equal relationship: she refused to wait on him and, with his encouragement, she got a law degree.

In October, 1949, a decade after being appointed to the Court, which may have already begun its annual session, Douglas was riding a favorite, spirited horse in the Washington mountains. The trail was difficult; the horse reared suddenly and threw Douglas about a hundred feet down a steep slope. The horse rolled down after his rider and fell on top of him. For fifteen minutes Douglas was quite alone, with twenty-three of his twenty-four ribs broken. It took him a half-year to recover from this trauma, but it only delayed rather than destroyed his determination and success to continue in activity to the very edge.

Only two years after the accident, in 1951, after getting advice from Nehru about routes that would avoid contact with Chinese troops, he crossed the Himalayas. For a week, his party hiked at 15,000 feet. His hiking in his final years diminished to walking, notably the water-level path of the Chesapeake and Ohio Canal near Washington. He reduced his physical challenges, but he always taxed his mental and physical strength to the extreme. In 1968 a pace-maker was installed to regulate his heart.

The grievous stroke that hit him on vacation in the Caribbean, in late De-cember, 1974, proved mentally to be both devastating and a struggle that brought out his elemental nature and nurture. He went to New York for special therapy, and there acted toward nurses the way he did with others whom he saw as failing to aid his return to hyperactivity. One side of his body lost most of its function. He came back to the Court in March, 1975, in a wheelchair and in almost continuous pain. Chief Justice Burger had a ramp built so he could come to sessions, even though he could no longer walk or even talk clearly. He re-signed from the Court in November, 1975.

A year later, one of his hips crumbled. Replacement surgery failed, and so did the second operation to correct the first one. From that time on, the judge, hiker, mountaineer, and world traveler moved in a wheelchair. The pain was excruciating. His kidneys had to be catheterized and finally failed. Having re-signed from the Court, he had to settle for writing the second volume of his memoirs, *The Court Years*. But only when he died four years later did his body have the last word.

When Douglas Wrote for the Court and When He Dissented

This northwestern product of a Presbyterian mission background and its genteel poverty went on the Court in April 1939. He had long been one of Roosevelt's favorites: the young man had taken brave, nonestablishment charge of the Secu-rities Exchange Commission and had lambasted the financial Establishment successfully. The head of the New York Stock Exchange, Richard Whitney, was found to have used others' funds without their knowledge. An idol of the rich had embezzled. If FDR had not weighed the courage of the young Douglas against financiers, and if the Senate had not appreciated what Whitney's em-bezzlement said about the Establishment, it seems doubtful that Douglas would have been so confidently nominated and confirmed. His courage and independ-ence persisted on the Court, most of the time: his high moral sense irritated perhaps most of his Brethren at least some of the time, and Frankfurter most of the time.

When Douglas entered the Court, the chief justice was Charles Evans Hughes. He talked amiably and privately with the forty-year-old neophyte, on one occasion saying: "Justice Douglas, you must remember one thing. At the constitutional level where we work, 90 percent of any decision is emotional. The rational part of us supplies the reasons for supporting our predilections." It is just possible that, hearing this from a chief justice whom he admired, Doug-las may have felt strengthened in relating his own emotional predilections to his legal judgments.

The most portentous of Douglas's judicial judgments seem to lie in three areas: racism, religious freedom, and privacy. A look at him in these areas from both his juristic and his emotional orientation can help explain him as a jurist. There is much more to the man that is politically relevant, but we will start with the judicial part of his influence, because that was his main professional work for most of his life.

Racism

Three of the racial cases that came up during Douglas's first decade on the Court are very relevant to judging his basic values. They involved the relationship of Japanese residents on the West Coast to the non-Japanese population, in a war that began at Pearl Harbor, Hawaii on December 7, 1941. The reaction against Japanese people, particularly on the West Coast, was intense, bitter, and very hateful. The bases of the reaction were economic (the Japanese were skilled and industrious farmers), but also racial: they were provident but clannish people with different customs and skin color, and their kinsmen across the Pacific had without warning attacked Pearl Harbor. FDR issued an order calling for removal of all Japanese people from the coast and their placement in detention camps away from the coast. About 120,000 Japanese, most of whom were native-born Americans, were detained in the camps. In Hawaii, not yet a state, a large majority of the population was Japanese, but no evacuation or detention of them took place there—despite the fact that U.S. armed forces virtually governed the territory during the war and had the physical but not the political power to detain them.

No Japanese people—whether born in Japan or the United States—were ever convicted of any crime, other than reluctance or refusal to abide by evacuation and curfew orders. An undergraduate student at the University of Washington violated the curfew and took his case to the Supreme Court. By a 6–3 vote, the Court in June, 1943 in *Hirabayashi v. the U.S.* upheld the power to enforce a curfew. Douglas was one of the six. Though anguished, he said in a court memorandum that the issue should not be whether Hirabayashi was Japanese but whether he was loyal.

A year and a half later, on December 18, 1944, the Court handed down two other related decisions. The date was about six weeks after the election that gave FDR his fourth term and the day after the Executive Order detaining and relocating Japanese was rescinded. FDR had decided that Japanese people were at least no longer a threat, and the Court waited till after the election, perhaps to avoid causing electoral peril for the president. The first of these cases, *Korematsu v. the U. S.,* was decided again by a 6–3 vote, the Court upholding the power of detention; again Douglas was in the majority. The second case, *Ex parte Endo,* involved a woman who sued for habeas corpus for being detained in a camp in Utah. The Court unanimously agreed that she could not be regarded as a military threat. The pair of decisions—*Korematsu* and *Endo*—reflected a political compromise of sorts. It is also possible that Douglas was being loyal to his beloved old boss, FDR.

A half-century after Pearl Harbor, it is hard to understand the racial tension in 1941–1945, particularly because of the goodwill that has replaced the hostility between the United States and Japan at the end of the twentieth century. But the American anger during the Second World War toward the Japanese, whether in Japan or the United States, was in some ways more intense than the feelings about Jews in Germany after the First World War. Japanese were visibly easier to distinguish from other Americans than were German Jews from other Germans. By late 1944, however, FDR, the Court, and perhaps the citizenry had lost at least their fear of a Japanese invasion, even though racial tension was still high.

Douglas repeatedly said in *The Court Years* that he deeply regretted his votes, and it seems evident that he truly did. In later years he consistently adopted a pro-minority, anti-ethnic orientation, but so by then had the rest of the Court. After Eisenhower appointed Earl Warren in 1953 to be chief justice, the entire Court (notably following its unanimous decision in the 1954 *Brown v. Board of Education* case) established an ethnically more liberal orientation. There is an evident diminution of ethnic bases for Court decisions, and Douglas experienced the diminution himself.

Religious Freedom

Before the New Deal, the Court had moved to a more liberal base on religious freedom. In 1925, in *Pierce v. the Society of Sisters* case, it decided that children did not have to be educated in public schools: private, church-based schools were inadmissible. The growing war clouds in the 1930s gave the Court pause. It decided in 1940, in *Minersville School District v. Gobitis,* that West Virginia was not denying freedom of religion to Jehovah's Witnesses when it insisted on compulsory saluting of the flag. Justices Black, Douglas, and Murphy—three liberals—were with the majority. But three years later, in *West Virginia Board of Education v. Barnette,* when the war was most intense and its outcome still uncertain, the Court reverted to a liberal position and supported Jehovah's Witnesses in their refusal to salute the flag, and three conservatives—Frankfurter, Roberts and Reed—were in the minority.

Freedom of political views has a cousinly if not brotherly kinship to religious views. In the loyalty cases that were a product partly of the Cold War and partly of the McCarthy-era hysteria about Communism, Douglas consistently opposed the suppression of political views that were casually called Communist and therefore deemed subversive by the hysterics. Sometimes the Court supported freedom of even radical political views, but it also at times invoked technicality to avoid discussing the principle at stake. Douglas usually favored freedom to express radical views, but where words and actions came close together, he was ready to face the issue of the degree of separation between words and deeds. He was uncomfortable with Holmes's precept—don't yell fire in a theater—but did not come up with a much different standard.

When the United States and the Union of Soviet Socialist Republics were no longer allies against Germany at the end of the Second War, Julius and Ethel Rosenberg were convicted of giving atomic energy secrets to the Soviet Union. Their execution was ordered, and the order was appealed. Douglas granted a stay of execution, which produced a telegram from Yakima that epitomized the public mood. It said: "If you grant the Rosenbergs a stay, there will be a lynching party for you here." He wired back: "If there is to be a Yakima lynching party, you'll have to furnish your own whiskey." The Court held a very heated, very intense session on the issue, and in *Rosenberg v. the United States* (1953) the Court overruled the stay by a 6–3 majority, with Douglas, Black, and Frankfurter in the minority.

Douglas said the public fascination with capital punishment was reminiscent of customs he had noted abroad: putting a murderer in a wire cage hung in a tree and letting him die; setting loose a town against a man accused of rape, and killing him by whatever savage means; allowing a brother to shoot a man convicted of raping his sister. Douglas wrote: "What I had seen in the Rosenberg case brought home to me vividly that capital punishment is barbaric, that its only value is in the orgasm of delight it produces in the public...." He quoted a 1913 statement of Oliver Wendell Holmes: "When twenty years ago a vague terror went over the earth and the word socialism began to be heard, I thought and still think that fear was translated into doctrines that had no proper place in the Constitution or the common Law. Judges are apt to be naïve, simple-minded men...."

Ending capital punishment remained a humane advance that took hold in Europe, possibly because Europe had been the bloody theater for two total wars. But at the end of the century, at least to several justices on the Supreme Court and to millions of citizens in the United States, capital punishment remained vaguely an expression of civic virtue and religious piety.

Privacy

The potentially most enduring contribution of Douglas was his elemental view that government should get off and stay off the backs of private individual citizens. This elemental view had long been voiced by conservatives, who restricted it to economic business, but also by liberals like Justice Brandeis, who applied it more widely. Douglas insisted on distinguishing—particularly in noneconomic matters—collective or individual activity that affected the public welfare from that which did not. He insisted on carefully distinguishing between public and private actions. He was willing to regulate activity of the financial community—which regarded itself as responsible to itself for its own regulation—but opposed interfering with action that did not affect the *general* welfare.

Privacy was the big issue on which Justices Black and Douglas—who agreed on nearly all issues—persistently disagreed. The reasons for this divergence are not wholly clear, but they did include Douglas's reaction to the criticism he got for his unconventional private life. Black was quite proper in his private life and was very upset that Douglas shunned both the public's and Black's view of propriety.

Douglas broadened his judicial views about privacy as his own personal life got more deviant. In a 1942 case (*Goldman v. United States*), Douglas did not object to the use of a concealed microphone in the gathering of evidence. Murphy was the judge who dissented, saying that the Fourth Amendment prohibited such a search because it violated "a right of personal privacy." But a decade later, in *Public Utilities Commission v. Pollak* (1952), Douglas dissented and vigorously objected to the very audible broadcast of radio programs on the public buses in the District of Columbia, saying that "the right to be let alone is the beginning of all freedom." Justice Black voted with the majority but wrote an amiable personal note to Douglas saying that his dissent was "one of the best pieces of writing you have ever done." In 1954, the year after divorcing his first wife, Douglas witnessed persistent observation of his rented apartment by police, who came into the apartment garage and made notes on private cars. He wrote a letter to the landlord protesting, and he soon moved out. In 1959, Douglas dissented from the Court when it upheld the power of a health inspector to enter a private home in search of rats. He said that not even such an unpolitical reason as public health could justify entering a home without the resident's permission.

Douglas played the crucial role in what is perhaps the most noteworthy privacy case, involving the right of women to get advice on the use of contraceptives. In this case, *Griswold v. Connecticut* (1965), Douglas wrote for the Court, saying that government may not interfere with communication between a planned-parenthood officer and a licensed physician. He mentioned both First Amendment grounds of free association and grounds of privacy "created by several fundamental constitutional guarantees." The right of privacy, he said, "is older than the Bill of Rights—older than our political parties, older than our school system. Marriage is a coming together for better or for worse, hopefully enduring, and intimate to the degree of being sacred. It is an association that promotes a way of life, not causes; a harmony in living, not political faiths; a bilateral loyalty, not commercial or social projects. Yet it is an association for as noble a purpose as any involved in our prior decisions." He noted that the

Ninth Amendment declared that the listing of several protected rights "shall not be construed to deny or disparage others." He talked about a "penumbra," a big umbrella that protected privacy, even though it was not specifically listed in the Constitution. Black was unconvinced, saying: "I like my privacy as well as the next one, but I am nevertheless compelled to admit that the government has a right to invade it unless prohibited by some specific constitutional provision."

In *Roe v. Wade* in 1973, the landmark case legalizing abortions, Douglas, unsurprisingly, was in the majority, though he wrote a concurring opinion emphasizing the right to privacy. *Roe v. Wade* was a landmark on more than women's rights. In arguing in favor of giving women the right to terminate pregnancy, Douglas was emphasizing his strong belief that government should stay out of people's private lives. This emphasis bothered some justices, who were willing to establish the right to abortion on other grounds, but not on grounds that had little precedent. Although Douglas did not casually flick precedents—*stare decisis*—aside, he didn't mind establishing new precedents. The Court majority accepted the right of privacy in doctor-patient relationships in *Griswold,* but Douglas extended it to abortion in *Roe v. Wade,* without getting Court consensus on his extension of privacy rights. He was willing to move where conservatives feared to tread, saying: "I'd rather create a precedent than find one," but the Court was slow to follow in his footsteps.

I don't know whether Douglas read George Orwell's *1984.* In that book the inquisitor O'Brien, using severe and prolonged torture in the government's Ministry of Love, finally gets his deviant victim, Winston Smith, to betray his beloved. Winston says: "Do it to Julia." The pain ceases and the government liberates itself from worries about even unorganized dissent. *1984* penetrates to the heart of the concern that Douglas had about privacy, and eventually the Court began to agree with his concern.

Oliver Wendell Holmes had a rather laissez-faire view of public policy, but Douglas did not. Even if Holmes did not agree with a policy, like antitrust legislation, which he thought senseless, he believed it should be allowed if the public demanded it. Douglas came to much the same populist conclusion for different reasons, but he also came to reject even a popular mood or policy— like McCarthyism—that he deemed dangerous to the sanctity of the individual.

He believed that the nation—the people, the Constitution, the culture— should head toward a gradual removal of government from controlling the lives of people. Far from having a laissez-faire attitude, he distinguished between laws and judgments that controlled economic and political activity and laws, and judgments that would control people's individual private actions.

Douglas said repeatedly that government should stay off people's backs and out of their lives. When individuals see more clearly, more truly, the relationship between individual and collective welfare, he believed, the distinction between economic and social and individual freedom diminishes, but that epoch is slow to generate. In the long interim, deciding just what is necessary interference remains a matter for broad political and judicial judgment.

In this process, neither the Court, nor Congress, nor the president, nor the general public has proven capable of always deciding rightly. The very definition of right and wrong remains political and indefinite. The claim of any congregation, any church, to final truth remains disproved by events as gross as the Protestant Reformation and the Civil War, which ended slavery, at least constitutionally. Great amounts of blood were shed in both these events, before the disputes became nonviolent and subject to adjudication. In sum, Douglas's elemental criteria seemed to derive from a strong belief that institutions—whether churches, legislatures, chief executives, courts, or semiprivate organizations (like the stock market and regulatory commissions)—must know their own limitations. When they move beyond influencing to controlling individuals, they move too far. To paraphrase Edmund Burke, when institutions control individuals too much, they endanger their own survival. While avoiding Holmes's laissez-faire view of both legislation and popular mood, Douglas moved the Court toward recognizing its own powers and the limits of not only legislative but also judicial power.

Domestic Matters of Other Nations

Much as Douglas enjoyed his judicial work, he worked with less assiduity than speed. And much as he enjoyed the electric atmosphere of the national center of political power, he had to get away from it—most frequently to his beloved Northwest, but increasingly abroad. There he used his ability to make friends with both powerful *and* ordinary people to gain a deeper understanding than the ordinary tourist gets of peoples, of nations.

In Iran in the early 1950s he befriended several prominents, including Mohammed Mossadegh. He was a reformist prime minister of Iran from 1951–1953 and he almost deposed the Shah. The domestically popular Mossadegh displeased not only the Iranian Shah but also the American CIA. Mossadegh also nationalized most of the British holdings in petroleum. Douglas not only spoke favorably to President Truman and the press about Mossadegh, he also wrote to the Shah. Douglas did not succeed in Iran. With CIA help, Mossadegh was deposed, and after intense domestic oppression by the Shah, the exiled Ayatollah returned triumphantly from banishment in France. With American help, the Shah at last achieved his own defeat and exile. The wretched, reactionary instability of Iran under righteous, orthodox-Muslim rule is something that probably neither the Shah nor the CIA expected, but their hostility to a popular leader was a factor contributing to empowerment of a theocracy in Iran. And their public nonresponse to Douglas could hardly be called either foresightful or prudent.

It is just possible that, if the United States government had taken the advice of its outspokenly liberal justice, crises in the Middle East and East Asia would have been diminished. But even generally liberal Presidents—from Truman to Kennedy and Johnson—relied more on the massive wisdom of the CIA. In 1951, Douglas advised Truman to deal with the Communist regime in China. Truman wrote him a steaming response, to which Douglas replied, "The day may not be far distant when we are left in all our loneliness and our atomic bombs." Truman, like other top officials, thought Douglas should stick to adjudication. After Truman's refusal to recognize Communist China and Johnson's colossal efforts to kill Communism in Vietnam, it was Nixon—"tricky Dick," as others and Douglas called him and who was never accused of being liberal—who recognized Communist China and helped end the Vietnam War.

Douglas made his opposition to the American war in Vietnam explicit and clear to Lyndon Johnson. Douglas at first was optimistic about the ability of Ngo Dinh Diem, a Christian, to govern Vietnam effectively and responsibly. He stretched reality a bit by writing Ngo in October 1954 to say that Ngo headed "a regime dedicated to the principle that all men are created equal, are endowed by their Creator with unalienable rights." And in 1966, Douglas proposed to President Johnson that he invite the North Vietnamese leader Ho Chih Minh to a conference of North and South Vietnamese, to be held in California at Robert Hutchins' Center for the Study of Democratic Institutions. Further negotiations broke down when it became impossible to get North and South government officials to agree to meet together. Douglas thought Johnson had sabotaged the conference, but it may have been the State Department. And Johnson, like Truman, ignored the advice of the meddlesome judge. In any event, it was not the Christian Diem but Ho Chih Minh, the incorrigible atheistic Communist, who actually held Jefferson's truths to be self-evident, when he published Vietnam's declaration of independence.

The most relevant factor in the international involvement of Douglas was his efforts against imperialism, masked as anticommunism. As a prestigious government official, Douglas was showing that many very powerful government officials and those citizens who support them may be suffering from a moral desire to control the rest of the world. He was arguing that the United States was beginning to face the problems of hubris. When a final break came between Johnson and Douglas, the President reportedly said, "Liberty and Justice, that's all you apparently think of. And when you pass over the last hill, I suppose you will be shouting 'Liberty and Justice!'" Douglas replied, "You're goddamn right, Mr. President." Douglas's widow Cathleen confirmed the story.

Douglas was good at pricking the conscience of kings, and he annoyed or angered many people in his own country. But he may have seen too far into the future to serve in a direct policy-making role. Harry Truman had wanted Douglas as his running mate in the 1948 presidential campaign, but not after the Iran matter boiled up. Lyndon Johnson admired Douglas, until he declared the disturbance in Vietnam a war and said only Congress could declare it.

But being prophetic is different from being politically effective. An active and occasionally violent minority (students) and a vocal justice of the Supreme Court meddled with the prevailing view about American action abroad during the Cold War. The minority view in America about both Iran and Vietnam was more farsighted than that of the Congress, the president, or even the information media and the general public.

Douglas and the Twentieth-First Century

A holistic picture of William Orville Douglas looks more like a scrapbook of photos and events than an integrated painting by, let us say, Rembrandt. He wrote as constantly as Rembrandt painted. In addition to hundreds of Court opinions, he wrote thirty-one books. He traveled all over our little planet, observing acutely and advising critically the governments of the places he visited. He did not hide but rather used his position as a judge on America's highest court to gain initially welcome entry into third-world nations.

Douglas avoided the often superficial view of some liberals of dividing the political scene between the American bad guys and the virtuous, exploited Third World. In 1963, in *Mr. Lincoln and the Negroes,* he emphasized the contradictions in third-world governments between the expression and the practice of egalitarian principles. Leaders of developing nations proceeded to establish *un*equal relations between Muslims and Hindus, Russians and Jews, white South Africans (after Boers wrested control of the government from British imperialism) and their apartheid stance toward black South Africans. It is as hard for those who practice democracy to say that the people can do *some* wrong as it is for true believers to say that their church and its doctrine are fallible. Douglas might have more explicitly pointed out that these leaders, with their democratic principles and racist practices, sometimes had a large following among their citizens. People of one tribe or religion regarded people of a different "race" or religion in their own countries as subhuman outsiders. Douglas needled, even harassed, successive presidents and other public officials about their contradictions—and, in the developing world, he at least needled dominant groups with their sense of ethnic or religious superiority. It was hard for such victims of Douglas's preaching to ignore a justice of the Supreme Court, but they mostly managed.

Billy Herndon, the law partner of Abraham Lincoln, said that Lincoln's ambition "was a little engine that knew no rest." Like Lincoln in politics, Douglas protested too much his lack of interest in the Supreme Court. He obviously wanted it and loved the job, but he put on the threadbare cloak of prudery about his ambition. In 1942 the young justice was invited to attend a big farewell banquet honoring one of Douglas's heroes: Senator George Norris, the New Dealer before the New Deal. A phone message came from the White House that the president wanted to play poker on that night. Douglas canceled his appearance at the Norris dinner for a poker session with FDR.

He was at least as restless about his domestic life as about his career. His first wife, with whom he had two children, very much disliked the politically electric social scene in Washington, and he never did have an easy, affectionate relationship with their children. His second wife sparkled in the electricity of Washington high society but didn't enjoy being his research assistant. His third wife didn't mind the research but failed to please her very intense husband. His fourth wife, Cathleen Heffernan, refused to let him dominate her and went to law school, and the forty-four years that separated them in age may have helped their very successful marriage.

Douglas said he had "a photographic mind, being able to take in a page at a glance, but it was not learning in depth." It seems to have been an accurate self-evaluation. Perhaps it is a common characteristic among lawyers, most of whom are not noted for their philosophical writing. Their judicial opinions do involve theory, of government and of law, however inarticulate. And it is ideological, being conservative or liberal regardless of whether they acknowledge a conservative or liberal orientation.

Douglas did indeed like to write. But the quality of his writing was not consistent. He always wrote clearly and without the cant of befuddled jurisprudence. But he wrote hurriedly,[3] and he quoted Charles Darwin as saying that a man who dares to waste one hour of time has not discovered the value of life. In *Go East, Young Man* he anticipated *The Court Years* by making many references to events after he went on the Court in 1939. Many of his non-Court writings were repetitive. He lacked Oliver Wendell Holmes's knack for the one-liner, the catch phrase, the epitome. On the Court, he continued his established habit of getting to the heart of issues and then speedily writing down his judgment. He said that the work at the Court was at most a four-day-a-week job; sometimes before the Court had wound up its business he would leave for his beloved mountains or for an overseas trip.

When it comes to the quality of his mind, it cannot surely be said what effects came from what causes. It was brilliantly, speedily capable of getting to the root of the matter, but it didn't have the depth of, let us say, either Justice Brandeis or Justice Cardozo or of John Dewey, the philosopher whom he knew at Columbia. He shared, perhaps more as a practice than a theoretical principle, the same view of law that Oliver Wendell Holmes had: the life of the law is experience, though at the Yale Law School it was called legal realism.

Holmes made sententious the phrase that the life of the law is experience, but it may not be of philosophy. At least his enormous experience did not make Douglas a philosopher. The experiences that so deeply affected him—like his polio, his parents, the hoboes with whom he dodged railroad policemen in the freight yards—were very different from Holmes's. Holmes was the fine-fashioned product of Boston's elite and of mortal combat in the Civil War. Douglas was a proper product of his religious, even evangelical background, and the hard-forged product of his early nurturance in genteel poverty. He cared palpably for people whom society and government shoved around. He wanted not so much to compromise differences as to make the world a better place, environmentally and socially. He strayed from his elemental concern, but it bothered his conscience when he did, notably in his frank autobiographical apologies for voting as he did in the Japanese cases. And the longer he stayed *on* the Court, the more emphasis he put on using his influence *off* the Court.

For Holmes the elemental experience, the basic reality was the sometimes deadly human pursuit of survival. For Douglas other needs included self-fulfillment, of whatever kind each individual found to fit him or her individually: the pursuit of happiness. It was on this elemental view that his concern for privacy was based. He wanted to live his own life as he saw fit; he did not want to fit a stereotype of public servants who acted as team players weighed down with a politically correct sense of responsibility to unexamined values. He thoroughly enjoyed the work of adjudication, but his energy, his intelligence, and his compassion demanded more. In his case, kinship with mountains and, later on, kinship with ordinary and extraordinary human beings around the world gave substance to his human interactions and his strongest values. Any appraisal of Douglas that is even penultimate cannot dwell simply on just his faults, or his successes, or his failures. But it is injudicious to judge him as if he were running for reelection to the ministry of the local Presbyterian church or as if he were competing for immortality with Plato and J. S. Mill. He was political though not presidential; Christian though not pontifical; and intuitively—though not theoretically—he was an intellectual. He outlasted Nixon—the president who wanted to remove him from the Court—but not Gerald Ford, the congressman who became vice president after trying to get Douglas impeached.[4]

By his life—though not by his lifestyle—Douglas does substantially and emphatically demonstrate that he is a natural product of his clerical and educational history. Like his parents, he was a protagonist of outsiders and underdogs. While in law school in New York, he worked in a settlement house for boys who were perhaps too poor to afford entrance to middle-class Boy Scout troops. There he organized the Yakima Club and took the boys on long hikes. When he got restless with the routines in the Supreme Court, he very much broadened the scope of his interactions with people whether high or low, but he saw them with the same presuppositions that he had as a child and young man. As his career on the Court came to an end, he said: "There will be no one on the Court who cares for blacks, Chicanos, defendants, and the environment.... If I'm only half alive, I can still cast a liberal vote."[5]

As a judge, he was bothered very little by swimming against the current: between 1960 and 1970 he wrote 171 dissents; from 1971 to 1975, he wrote 200. Even in *Roe v. Wade,* decided just two years before his retirement, as previously mentioned, he wrote a concurring opinion, emphasizing once more the right of privacy. Much of his jurisprudence was a resurrection of his father's values, a moralist who was not concerned about political correctness.

When Douglas sent his notice of retirement to the President on November 12, 1975, Gerald Ford responded promptly, in doubtless formally polite language. The man who had sought to get Douglas impeached, and who was now President, said: "Future generations of citizens will continue to benefit from your firm devotion to the fundamental rights of individual freedom and privacy under the Constitution." But Douglas, retired and frail, couldn't let go. After receiving the warm, appreciative, and well-wishing farewell from his Brethren, he said he wanted to continue participating in the conferences in which the justices orally discussed pending cases. He said his long experience with specific cases would be of real value. The Brethren politely refused his request. When Chief Justice Burger offered him the use of former Chief Justice Earl Warren's more spacious retirement office, Douglas politely declined—and asked for two secretaries and two clerks. He was told that for his personal staff he could have two secretaries or one secretary and one clerk, plus a driver, but not four people. He went back to writing his memoirs.

In 1976 he had two operations for a crumbled hip joint; the first was not successful and the second—involving removal of some muscles in his leg accentuated his immobility. He said the surgery "left him more of a cripple than ever." His young wife Cathy attended him well, and not only she but also his two children—both older than Cathy—were with him when he died on January 19, 1980. He had discussed where he should be buried, writing Cathy that he'd leave it up to her, and Yakima or Goose Prairie in his beloved state of Washington would be fine. His funeral was held in the denomination of his parents, in the National Presbyterian Church in the city of Washington, DC. He ended up buried twenty feet from Oliver Wendell Holmes in the Arlington National Cemetery.

A Great Justice?

To judge how great a *justice* Douglas was presupposes a rather narrow basis for evaluating his contributions. If there is any general basis, it is that he connected the process of adjudication with life and with human wants. He did this not only by his cogent opinions, whether with or against the Court majority, but also by his remarkable awareness of his own self. Holmes was profoundly affected by his near-death experiences in the Civil War, but seemed less aware of their influence on his adjudication than Douglas was of the effect of his experiences with both ordinary and extraordinary people. His autobiography demonstrates this, and his extralegal activities are an unavoidable part of a comprehensive evaluation.

Douglas often quoted a statement that Oliver Wendell Holmes had made, long before Holmes had gone onto the Supreme Court. He spoke to Harvard students about the secret isolated joy of the thinker, who knows that, a hundred years after he is dead and forgotten, men who never heard of him will be moving to the measure of his thought.

In the ever-increasingly integrated world, it is not only the natural environment that calls for the focused attention that Douglas advocated. Analysis of blood and even spit now can not only free people innocent of crime and establish parenthood, it can also give employers information used to deny health benefits to employees or even employment itself. It can be stored electronically, about millions of people, and is accessible to governments, corporations, and nosy individuals. Neither Douglas nor anyone else in his time could establish limits to invasion of privacy that the well-nigh universal accessibility of information now makes possible. The problem of realizing the Bill of Rights is not just one of recognizing these rights but of making them available to people regardless of their wealth—of making justice more truly equal.

If the United States continues as a very vital nation with a diverse, open, and integrated society and culture, Douglas's views as a judge and as a citizen are likely to gain increased respect and to have increased effect. If the United States is on a downward slide, Douglas may come to be viewed as a Cicero in a Rome that has lost its self-confidence, its optimism, and its sense of direction.

Douglas's long-term evaluation depends on circumstances that are not really yet predictable, for the Court and for the country. If new appointments to the Supreme Court are conservative ones, then his opinions—whether majority or dissenting—are less likely to be cited and valued. They are more likely to be valued if the Court takes a more liberal position in the collective process of making and affecting public policy in our complex nation. A myopic view would say that if the Court becomes more conservative, all is lost, forever. A presbyopic view would say that, even though in the long run we'll all be dead,

Douglas's opinions and his interactions with people all over the world will inevitably grow in their influence.

NOTES

1.   A picture of Douglas's son and daughter when they were very young shows the same pipe-stem legs, and the children never had polio.
2.   Douglas never really abandoned his Protestant Christian faith, the never articulated major premise of his values, and he had a Presbyterian funeral.
3.   In *Go East, Young Man* (1974), page 153, he directly and correctly quoted from FDR's 1933 Inaugural Address: "The only thing we have to fear is fear itself." In February, 1946 Truman offered Douglas the post of secretary of the interior. *In The Court Years* (the second volume of his autobiography), he says the offer was made in 1947. He wrote to his friend Fred Rodell in 1956 about Rodell's book, *Woe Unto You, Lawyers*, referring to his letter to *Woe Unto Ye Lawyer*.
4.   Curiously, Ford, acting evidently on the advice of his attorney general, Edward Levi, got John Paul Stevens appointed to succeed Douglas, and Stevens became a steadily liberal justice.
5.   Quoted in Artemus Ward, "The Tenth Justice: The Retirement of William O. Douglas," *Journal of Supreme Court History* 25 (3): 301.

FOR FURTHER READING

Ball, Howard, and Phillip J. Cooper. *Of Power and Right: Hugo Black, William O. Douglas and Americas Constitutional Revolution.* New York: Oxford University Press, 1992.

Douglas, William O. *Go East, Young Man: The Early Years.* New York: Random House, 1974.

——— *The Court Years: 1939–1975.* New York: Random House, 1980.

——— *Of Men and Mountains,* New York: Harper and Row Publishers, 1950.

Duram, James C. *Justice William O. Douglas.* Boston: G. K. Hall, 1981.

O'Fallon, James (ed.). *Nature's Justice: Writings of William O. Douglas.* Corvallis: Oregon State University Press, 2000.

Urofsky, Melvin I. (ed.). *The Douglas Letters: Selections from the Private Papers of Justice William O. Douglas.* Bethesda, MD: Adler and Adler, 1987.

Ward, Artemus. "The Tenth Justice: The Retirement of William O. Douglas." *Journal of Supreme Court History,* 25 (3) 296–312.

Wasby, Stephen L. (ed.). *'He Shall Not Pass This Way Again': The Legacy of Justice William O. Douglas.* Pittsburgh: University of Pittsburgh Press, 1990.

CHAPTER TWELVE

Charles Evans Hughes: An Eighteenth Century Statesman Redivivus

John R. Vile

Sometime before 1920, leaders of the liquor industry solicited Charles Evans Hughes's help in challenging the constitutionality of the Eighteenth Amendment. Although Hughes thought that prohibition was unwise and knew that the financial rewards for challenging the Amendment would be high (perhaps close to half a million dollars), he chose instead to file a brief on behalf of state attorneys general supporting the amendment. Though he could have pocketed lucrative fees, Hughes refused to compromise his belief in the power of the people to adopt broad constitutional amendments.[1]

In 1925, Hughes argued one of many cases that he brought before the U.S. Supreme Court between his service as an associate justice (to which former President, then Chief Justice William Howard Taft had appointed him) and chief justice. During a Court recess, Chief Justice Taft eagerly approached his friend Hughes and put his hand on his shoulder to welcome him. Hughes, who was quite affable with family and friends in private, coolly extended his hand and made a formal greeting. Hughes explained to his baffled client that he planned to win his cases "on their merits and not through friendship with the judges."[2]

As these two incidents reveal, Hughes was a man of great probity; he was dedicated to public service and motivated by a high sense of duty more frequently associated with the American Founding Fathers than with modern politicians. A longtime Republican, as an officeholder Hughes disdained the tools of patronage and cajolery wielded by many party leaders in favor of direct appeals to the people. Like many American Founders, however, Hughes deeply distrusted demagoguery, and his speeches appealed to reason rather than emotion. Rarely seeking public office on his own initiative and not serving in an elected position until he was forty-four, Hughes felt a duty to accept public offices when they were offered.

Judicial Helmsman in a Time of Crisis

Just as crises have provided opportunities for presidents like Washington, Lincoln, and Franklin D. Roosevelt to demonstrate extraordinary leadership, so too, crises have highlighted the skills of extraordinary justices. Although not all have been chief justices, they are undoubtedly in the best position to exercise leadership when such crises occur. As chief justice, John Marshall asserted the power of judicial review when there was danger that the strength of public opinion and the tool of impeachment would strip the Court of its power. Similarly, Chief Justice Earl Warren survived politically motivated attempts to construct judicial jurisdiction or impeach him after his Court inaugurated a near revolution in the field of civil liberties.

President Herbert Hoover appointed Charles Evans Hughes as chief justice during the Great Depression. Hoover responded weakly to this depression and was replaced by Franklin D. Roosevelt, who was an activist president. The only man ever elected to the presidency for four terms, Roosevelt radiated an optimism that raised the nation's spirits. He further launched an economic program that radically changed America's understanding of the role of the national government and prosecuted a war that saved the world from totalitarianism.

Likened both to a lion and a fox, Roosevelt had succeeded more than any previous president in getting an ambitious legislative agenda through Congress. Outwardly exuberant after his first presidential reelection in 1936, Roosevelt inwardly chafed at the numerous defeats that his legislative programs had suffered at the hands of the Supreme Court, to which he had yet to appoint a member. Shortly after his reelection, Roosevelt proposed what is generally called the court-packing plan. It provided for the appointment of one new justice (up to a total of fifteen) for every justice on the Supreme Court who was over seventy. Initially justifying his plan as a way of relieving aging justices of their heavy burdens, Roosevelt's real goal was to get the Court to approve his own programs. Had Roosevelt succeeded, his plan might have forever compromised the integrity of the Court.

Fortunately, the man who headed the Court, could look eye to eye at the president without blinking. Then seventy-four years of age, the bearded Hughes, who Justice Robert Jackson claimed "looks like God and talks like God,"[3] had established himself as a "lawyer's lawyer." Having successively served in a variety of appointed and elected positions, Hughes was widely respected as the personification of justice both on and off the Court. Without his prior knowledge, Hughes had been depicted in stone with Chief Justices Taft and John Marshall over the entrance to the New Supreme Court building.[4] Although his action evoked some controversy, Hughes's wrote a letter to Senators discounting Roosevelt's claims that the Court was behind in its business or that older justices were slowing the Court's work. Hughes's stance undoubtedly helped stop the court-packing plan dead in its tracts and preserve judicial independence.[5]

More controversial is the so-called "switch-in-time-that-saved-nine," in which the chief justice and Associate Justice Owen Roberts began more consistently voting in 1937 and thereafter with the Supreme Court's three most liberal justices (Louis Brandeis, Benjamin Cardozo, and Harlan Fiske Stone) to uphold the constitutionality of New Deal programs. Scholars still debate whether this switch was already in the works or was a conscious tactical response designed to safeguard the Supreme Court, but Hughes had certainly never joined the so-called "Four Horsemen" (Justices George Sutherland, Willis Van Devanter, Pierce Butler, and James McReynolds—the New Deal equivalent to the modern "Gang of Four") in unstinting opposition to either progressive legislation in general or the New Deal in particular. Moreover, a number of the programs that the Court struck down prior to 1937, some with the concurrence of the Court's liberals, resulted from hasty and shoddy legislation that, even in retrospect, deserved to be challenged.

Some scholars who accuse Hughes of essentially amending the Constitution to reconcile it to New Deal programs[6] recognize that the Four Horsemen and their Supreme Court predecessors had already ignored Justice Holmes's warning in *New York v. Lochner* (1905) against reading their personal ideological predispositions and economic theories into the document. Because Roosevelt proposed a court-packing plan rather than introducing one or more constitutional amendments either expanding and or clarifying national powers, one will never be able to say with certainty how an alternate course might have fared. However, absent the adoption of such a textual change, it seems unfair either to criticize the Court majority overly much for initially interpreting the Constitution as it had essentially done for the last thirty years or to complain that Hughes had other justices were unable to adjust their philosophy in 1937 and thereafter without exposing some contradictions. It is certainly possible to view Hughes as a "tragic figure, torn between the old and the new, seeking at first to stem the tide but then relentlessly caught up and moving with it."[7] It is, however, just as valid to join Hughes's award-winning biographer in praising him for saving the Court both "from executive domination" and "ossified thinking," maintaining a healthy balance between "sagacity and courage, determination and restraint," and protecting the Court while avoiding a personal "feud with the White House."[8]

Background of a Prodigy

Charles Evans Hughes was born in Glens Falls, New York, on April 11, 1862. His father, David Charles Hughes, was a Welch immigrant. Originally a Methodist minister, he became a Baptist in order to win the hand of Mary Connelly, the daughter of a Baptist pastor. Charles Evan Hughes was the only offspring of this couple who devoted their lives to ministering to various Baptist congregations. Although Charles abandoned the doctrinal orthodoxy of his parents while in college, he continued into adulthood to teach Sunday school classes (he was succeeded as a teacher at Fifth Avenue Baptist by John D. Rockefeller) and never lost respect for his parents' devotion to their beliefs or abandoned the ethical principles that they taught him.

Charles was a precocious child who learned to read at the age of three. He was introduced in his youth to Greek by his father and mathematics by his mother, and his parents allowed him at the age of six to establish his own "Charles E. Hughes' Plan of Study" rather than attending public schools; one scholar has commented that "the stories of Mr. Hughes' boyhood sound like a lost chapter from the autobiography of John Stuart Mill."[9] When he finally entered public schools, Hughes quickly graduated and enrolled in Madison College (now Colgate University). Excelling in his studies, Hughes moved to the more cosmopolitan, but still Baptist, Brown University, where he graduated third in his class at the age of 19. After a year's interlude as a school teacher, Charles enrolled in Columbia Law School, where he graduated first in his class, earned a 99.5 on the bar exam, and joined a law firm. He quickly became a partner and married Antoinette Carter, the daughter of a colleague, in a loving and devoted marriage producing four children and lasting fifty-seven years until her death.

Imbued by his parents with the virtues of thoroughness and commitment to duty, Hughes often exerted himself to a degree approaching exhaustion, periodically switching jobs or taking vacations—he particularly enjoyed climbing mountains in Europe. Early in his career, he left his practice for two years to serve successfully as a law professor at Cornell.

Importuned by his father-in-law, he subsequently returned to his firm (he would continue teaching some classes at Cornell and New York University over the next decade) and was asked in 1905 to direct a state investigation of gas and electric pricing within the state. Displaying his prodigious ability to work and a phenomenal memory for facts, in a series of public hearings Hughes exposed extensive corruption in the industry that saved New York City residents and the city government considerable money. Hughes followed this with another investigation of the insurance industry. Scrupulously fair to those he questioned, Hughes again uncovered considerable corruption within the industry and payments to politicians (many Republicans) that it supported; the investigation resulted in effective state legislation that was copied elsewhere. During his second investigation, Hughes was suggested as a candidate for mayor of New York City (perhaps in part as a way of deflecting him from his investigation), but, with a view to completing his investigations, he refused to run for the office.

A Good Government Governor

President Theodore Roosevelt and other Republican leaders, however, recognized that Hughes had a chance of winning the governorship. Hughes was the only Republican to win statewide office in 1906, defeating publisher William Randolph Hearst. Highlighting Hughes's signature beard, Hearst had disparagingly referred to him as an "animated feather duster."[10]

Hughes was a progressive governor who created independent regulatory commissions, instituted labor reforms, and sought political reforms—like a modified primary system—that furthered democracy. He opposed some popular reforms like a two-cent subway fare, which he did not think were properly justified by investigation, as well as a gambling measure that conflicted with the state's constitution. A scholar of this period of Hughes's life says that he "embodied the progressive independent spirit."

Although devoted to his party, Hughes justified party attachment as a way of transforming "the popular will" rather than reflecting "the interests of a particular group or region."[11] Thus, Hughes disappointed those in the party who wanted him to use behind-the-scene maneuvers or patronage for their benefit. Also independent of Roosevelt, who could have supported him for higher office, observers noted, "He would rather be Hughes than President."[12]

A Team Player Associate Justice

Hughes resigned as governor shortly before the end of his second term in 1910 to accept Taft's nomination, easily confirmed by a voice vote in the Senate, as an associate justice of the U.S. Supreme Court. Although Hughes did not lead the Court, he significantly contributed to its work during his nearly six-year tenure as an associate. He established himself as a "teamwork" judge[13] who worked well with Chief Justice Edward White and was particularly close to fellow Associate Justice Oliver Wendell Holmes, Jr.

Both Hughes and Holmes deferred to legislative prerogatives, but Hughes more frequently voided legislation that interfered with individual liberty. Thus, in *Bailey v. Alabama* (1911) Hughes struck down a state law, which Holmes voted in dissent to uphold, providing a criminal penalty for individuals who left a job without returning an advance payment; Hughes thought the law sanctioned a form of peonage contrary to the Thirteenth Amendment. In other notable cases, Hughes accepted broad federal power over state railroad rates that adversely impacted interstate commerce; joined the dissent in *Coppage v. Kansas* (1915), where the majority struck down a state law outlawing yellow-dog contracts; upheld a California law limiting the hours of women workers; wrote an opinion for the Court in *McCabe v. Atchison, Topeka & Santa Fe Railroad* (1914) striking down racial segregation on intrastate sleeping cars; dissented in *Frank v. Mangum* (1915) in a case where he believed mob violence had led to violations of due process in the trial of a Jew accused of killing a woman; and accepted fairly liberal restrictions of the contract clause. Hughes rarely authored solo dissents, and of the 150 decisions he wrote as an associate justice, dissents (most solitary) were filed in only nine.[14] An analyst of Hughes's tenure as an associate justice identified him "as one of the foremost, if not the foremost, liberal member of the Court during his initial period of service."[15]

This same analyst identified four principles that guided Hughes's jurisprudence. The first, consistent with Hughes's own rectitude, was his belief that democracy "was primarily safeguarded by the intelligence and public spirit of a free people, particularly as evinced in the selection of honest and competent public officers." A second was a belief in "progressive social legislation" balancing "personal freedom and public interest" after careful investigation of the facts. A third was concern for an "appropriate division of national and state power," and a fourth was an "unqualified acceptance of the authority of the Supreme Court as the final arbiter of all constitutional questions."[16]

This latter belief led to Hughes's most controversial and widely quoted statement. In a 1907 speech treating the relationship between courts and administrative agencies, Hughes noted that "We are under a Constitution, but the Constitution is what the judges say it is." Clearly understating the extent to which wise judicial interpretation is shaped by textual and historical meanings inherent within the document,[17] Hughes, who also said that he had "the highest regard for the courts" and considered the judiciary to be "the safeguard of our liberty and of our property under the Constitution," was not arguing for judicial willfulness but for a system that would protect judicial integrity.[18]

Writing about the United States Supreme Court in a book published before he became chief justice, Hughes later described such adventures into judicial activism as the *Dred Scott* decision, the *Legal Tender* cases, and the *Income Tax* case as "self-inflicted wounds." Noting that "the Supreme Court does not undertake to review questions of legislative policy," Hughes described the role that he thought was appropriate for a justice: "He recognizes that there is a wide domain of legislative discretion before constitutional boundaries are reached, and he holds himself to the duty of not allowing his views of the proper exercise of that discretion to control. He does his work in an objective spirit. If it be said that this is an impossible degree of self-control and that, even with the most conscientious judge, political and economic views will sway the judgment, albeit unconsciously, it may be answered that judges are constantly sustaining the validity of legislation which as legislators they would probably condemn."[19] Most of Hughes's decisions during his service on the Court can be squared with this philosophy.

Candidate, International Statesman, and Leader of the Bar

When queried in 1912, Hughes argued that it was improper for him to consider a bid for the presidency. He told an inquirer who appealed to his duty to run that "no man is as essential to his country's well being as is the unstained integrity of the courts."[20] The Republican Party subsequently split, resulting in the first election of a Democratic president in twenty years. Although he made no bid for the Republican nomination in 1916, Hughes, who thought that President Wilson had attempted to convey a promise to promote him to chief when White retired if he did not run,[21] did not reject the presidential nomination when his party offered it. As he explained: "I was torn between two profound desires, one to keep the judicial ermine unsullied, and the other not to fail in meeting what might be a duty to the country."[22]

The only such candidate ever nominated from the High Bench, Hughes promptly resigned from the Court to run a lackluster race against incumbent Woodrow Wilson, whose foreign policies Hughes especially criticized. Early returns pointed to a Hughes victory, but votes from the West, and especially from California, where Hughes's campaign had stumbled, reelected Wilson. Admitting that he "did not enjoy being beaten," he opined that "the fact that I did not have to assume the tasks of the Presidency in that critical time was an adequate consolation."[23] After this loss, Hughes returned to his successful private practice; he served during World War I as a member of the District Draft Appeals Board for New York City, and argued twenty-five cases before the U.S. Supreme Court in twenty-eight months.[24]

In 1921, President Harding appointed Hughes to be secretary of state, a post in which he continued into the Coolidge Administration until 1925. Hughes was clearly the most dominant member of Harding's cabinet, exercising almost complete discretion over foreign policy matters. Master of this domain, it is regrettable that Hughes did not see, and could not intervene to stop, the web of corruption and scandal that developed around Harding's domestic administration and ultimately disgraced his presidency.

Hughes favored the League of Nations but did not press support beyond what he thought public opinion would bear. Learning from Wilson's mistake with the League, Hughes included senators in diplomatic negotiations, and succeeded in obtaining approval of sixty-three of sixty-nine treaties that were negotiated during his tenure.[25] He successfully led the Washington Conference, which attempted to avoid an arms' race by freezing ship strengths among the great powers at existing levels. Working with Sumner Wells, Hughes advocated closer U.S. ties with, and less intervention in, Latin America. Hughes also negotiated agreements among the great powers regarding the Far East, promoted international law, and attempted to mediate disputes in Europe centering on German reparations. In retrospect, it is clear that Hughes's policies did not avert the Second World War, and an analyst of Hughes's tenure as secretary of state has claimed that he relied too heavily on reason and not enough on the role of power in international affairs.[26] However, Hughes represented a war-weary nation that was probably unwilling to make the investments necessary to maintain a more imposing presence.

In 1925, Hughes, who served as president of the American Bar Association (one of several such organizations, including the American Judicature Society and the New York City Bar Association, over which he presided) resigned to return to private practice. He was in great demand, particularly among corporate clients. Hughes could have made even more money, but believing that it was unethical to capitalize on his special knowledge of foreign affairs, he refused to represent foreign clients with claims against the United States. Similarly, he declined to appear in cases where his son, the solicitor general of the United States, was representing the government.[27]

Hughes was elected as a member of the Permanent Court of International Justice, where he served from 1928 to 1930. After consulting with the dying Taft, Hoover appointed Hughes (the oldest justice ever so appointed) to the Supreme Court. Hughes accepted in the unrealized hope that his confirmation as chief might be as uncontroversial as his earlier appointment as an associate. Eventually approved by a senate vote of 52 to 26, senators questioned Hughes's ties to the business interests he had represented and his decision to resign from the Court to run for president. After Hughes was confirmed, his son immediately resigned as U.S. solicitor general.

An Efficient Chief Administrator

Hughes headed a much more closely divided Court than the one he left in 1916, and he accepted his duties by recognizing that he could best lead by force of intellect and character. In writing about the Court, Hughes had earlier observed: "The Chief Justice as the head of the Court has an outstanding position, but in a small body of able men with equal authority in the making of decisions, it is evident that his actual influence will depend upon the strength of his character and the demonstration of his ability in the intimate relation of the judges. It is safe to say that no member of the Supreme Court is under any illusion as to the mental equipment of his brethren."[28] Citing the leadership that John Marshall had provided to the Court in an earlier age, Hughes properly concluded that "Marshall's preeminence was due to the fact that he was John Marshall, not simply that he was chief justice."[29]

Hughes was one of the most effective administrators ever to serve as a chief justice. He was a formidable presence to counsel before the bench, strictly enforcing time limits during oral arguments and reputedly once cutting a New York lawyer off in the middle of the word "if."[30] Like George Washington presiding over the U.S. Constitutional Convention, Hughes elevated the tone of the Court's private discussions of cases in conference, serving both as a consummate "social leader" and "task leader."[31] Like Washington, Hughes's integrity was unquestioned. A biographer noted that he "followed a strict rule of not sitting in cases involving former clients or in cases in which a former partner was counsel."[32] To his impeccable integrity and stately demeanor, Hughes added a near-photographic mind with an awesome grasp of facts, which he demonstrated in his opening summary of each case in conference. Hughes allowed everyone to participate in discussion while cutting off irrelevant digressions. Fellow Justice Owen Roberts observed that "in many cases his treatments [of cases] was so complete that little, if anything, further could be added by any of the Justices."[33] Responding to reports that talk in the conference room was unduly constricted under Hughes's leadership, Justice Felix Frankfurter observed: "Nothing could be further from the truth. There was less wasteful talk. There was less talk that was repetitious, or indeed foolish. You just didn't talk unless you were dead sure of your ground, because that gimlet mind of his was there ahead of you." Frankfurter further noted: "He never checked free debate, but the atmosphere which he created, the moral authority which he exerted, inhibited irrelevance, repetition, and fruitless discussion. He was a master of timing: he knew when discussion should be deferred and when brought to an issue." Frankfurter compared watching Hughes lead the Supreme Court deliberations to "witnessing Toscanini lead an orchestra." He further noted that "the same men were somehow or other better when he was chief judge than when they were the next day after he ceased to be chief judge."[34]

Consistent with Hughes's role in public life, Justice Roberts reported that Hughes eschewed private arm-twisting with the justices prior to a case: "What his conclusion was none of us knew until he announced it at conference. He neither leaned on any one else for advice nor did he proffer advice or assistance to any of us, but left us each to form his own conclusions to be laid on the table in free and open discussion. A nice sense of propriety undoubtedly brought about this practice." Roberts further testified to the power of Hughes's character in conference: "Strong views were often expressed around the conference table, but never in eleven years did I see the Chief Justice lose his temper. Never did I hear him pass a personal remark. Never did I know him to raise his voice. Never did I witness his interrupting a Justice or getting into a controversy with him, and practically never did any one of his associates overstep the bounds of courtesy and propriety in opposing the views advanced by the Chief."[35]

When voting with the majority, chief justices write or assign opinions. Hughes was a master of choosing the justice who could best rally the Court around his reasoning and keep dissents to a minimum. Specifically commenting on "the disinterestedness with which he made his assignments," Frankfurter compared Hughes's capacity in this regard to that of "a general deploying his army."[36]

As chief, Hughes pushed for reforms to further judicial efficiency. He successfully worked for the adoption of new Federal Rules of Procedure and oversaw the creation of the administrative office of the United States Courts and the Supreme Court's move from the Capitol Building to its own structure, commenced by William Howard Taft.

The Chief's Far-Ranging Opinions

As chief, Hughes penned 283 decisions and 23 dissents; the importance of the Hughes Court's decisions had been exceeded up to that time only by those of the Marshall Court.[37] Among the cases that civil libertarians cite favorably are *Stromberg v. California* (1931), in which Hughes struck down Stromberg's conviction for displaying a red flag; *Missouri ex rel. Gaines v. Canada* (1938), mandating that Missouri must provide in-state education for its African-American law students; *Near v. Minnesota* (1931), in which Hughes emphasized the role of the First Amendment in establishing a strong presumption against prior state restraint of even the most scurrilous publications; and *Lovell v. Griffin* (1938), where Hughes overturned an ordinance requiring Jehovah's Witnesses to get a permit before distributing literature. Hughes did not dissent, however, when the Court ruled in *Minersville School District v. Gobitis* (1940)—a decision overturned after Hughes left the Court—that Jehovah Witnesses who refused to salute the flag could be expelled from public schools.

The most critical cases during Hughes's tenure dealt with the exercise of state and federal powers to cope with the Great Depression. The fact that Roosevelt sought to pack the Court indicates that many of its early decisions during Hughes's tenure were unfavorable to New Deal programs. Thus, in the *Schechter Poultry Case* (1935), the Court struck down the provision of the National Recovery Act mandating industry-wide codes of fair competition as an improper delegation of power to the president. Similarly, in *United States v. Butler* (1936), the Court voided the Agricultural Adjustment Act as an invasion of state prerogatives. Still, under Hughes's leadership, the Court had upheld controversial federal fiscal policies in the *Gold Clause* cases (1935), accepted New York regulations of the dairy industry in *Nebbia v. New York* (1934), and upheld the Minnesota Mortgage Moratorium Act against charges that it violated the contracts clause in *Home Building & Loan Association v. Blaisdell* (1934).

Nonetheless, the Court made its greatest turnabouts in the economic field. Significantly, Hughes wrote both the 5–4 decision in *N.L.R. B. v. Jones & Laughlin Steel Corp.* (1937), upholding the National Labor Relations Act and a similarly divided decision that same year in *West Coast Hotel v. Parrish*, permitting state regulation of minimum wages. In both cases, Hughes knocked the constitutional props from under those who wished to use the doctrines of strict states' rights and of "freedom of contract" to kill New Deal programs. In *N.L.R.B.*, Hughes noted that it was unrealistic for industries like steel to operate on a national scale while seeking to avoid national regulation. In *West Coast Hotel*, Hughes further dismantled the distinction that conservative justices had drawn between hours and wages, which they had respectively designated as the "heart of the contract" and "mere incidents of employment." Known for writings that were generally more prosaic than his speeches, Hughes drew from an earlier dissent by William Howard Taft to observe that when it comes to hours and wages, "one is the multiplier and the other the multiplicand,"[38] and that the power to regulate one includes the power to regulate the other, earlier doctrines of "freedom of contract" to the contrary notwithstanding.

The switch in the dominant attitude of the Supreme Court to the New Deal was soon followed by resignations of superannuated colleagues and by Roosevelt's appointment of new justices who aligned the Court even closer to the president's policies. Only in recent years has the Supreme Court begun to reconsider whether Hughes's earlier concerns for maintenance of a federal system should sometimes temper judicial deference to congressional exercises of power under the commerce clause.

Hughes served on the Court until 1941, resigning before he lost the vigor that he believed was necessary to his job. His wife died in 1945, and the former chief, who spent part of his time writing autobiographical reflections for the benefit of his family, passed away in 1948.

Assessment

Hughes deserves credit for preserving the independence of the Supreme Court at a critical time and for his impressive example of personal integrity, public service, and judicial statesmanship. Observing that he combined "meekness with power," Hughes's foremost biographer opined that "Hughes's name is written beside [John] Marshall's in the same relationship that Lincoln holds to Washington."[39] Classifying Hughes as "a giant among men," who is "an overwhelming choice as one of the great members of the Court," Professor Henry Abraham has fittingly observed that "Hughes ranks at the pinnacle of achievement, perhaps second only to Marshall in administrative acumen and intellectual leadership and in a class with Taney, Stone, Warren, and Rehnquist in jurisprudential impact."[40]

NOTES

1.   Merlo J. Pusey, *Charles Evans Hughes* (New York: Columbia University Press, 1963), 1:386.
2.   Quoted in Pusey, vol. 2:635.
3..   Quoted in David J. Danelski and Joseph S. Tulchin, "Editor's Introduction," *The Autobiographical Notes of Charles Evan Hughes* (Cambridge: Harvard University Press, 1973), xxviii.
4.   Pusey, vol. 2:689. See note 1.
5.   Hughes's comments on the Court were not simply tailored to the situation at hand. Prior to being appointed as chief, Hughes had observed that "everyone who has worked in a group knows the necessity of limiting size to obtain efficiency." Refusing to say that the Court "could not do its work if two more members were added," he had noted that "I think the consensus of competent opinion is that it is now large enough." See Hughes, *The Supreme Court of the United States* (New York: Columbia University Press, 1928), 238.
6.   See especially Alpheus Thomas Mason, *The Supreme Court from Taft to Burger* (Baton Rouge: Louisiana University Press, 1979), 74–128.
7.   Samuel Hendel, "Charles Evans Hughes," *The Justices of the United States Supreme Court: Their Lives and Major Opinions* (New York: Chelsea House, 1997), 3: 966.
8.   Pusey, vol 2:791. See note 1.
9.   Kenneth B. Umbreit, *Our Eleven Chief Justices* (New York: Harper, 1938), 454.
10.   Quoted in Pusey, vol 1:176.
11.   Robert F. Wesser, *Charles Evans Hughes: Politics and Reform in New York, 1905–1910* (Ithaca, New York: Cornell University Press, 1967), 342.
12.   Quoted in Pusey, vol 1:234.
13.   Umbreit, *Our Eleven Chief Justices*, 474. See note 9.
14.   Pusey, vol 1:293.
15.   Samuel Hendel, *Charles Evans Hughes and the Supreme Court* (New York: King's Crown Press of Columbia University, 1951), 67.
16.   Ibid., 5-10.
17.   For a contemporary critique, see Ralph A. Rossum and G. Alan Tarr, *American Constitutional Law*, vol. I, *The Structure of Government* (New York: Worth, 1999), 1-4.
18.   Hughes, *The Autobiographical Notes*, 143–144. See note 3.
19.   Charles Evans Hughes, *The Supreme Court of the United States* (New York: Columbia University Press, 1928), 38.
20.   Quoted in Pusey, vol. 1:300. See note 1.
21.   Idem.
22.   Hughes, *Autobiographical Notes*, 180.
23.   Hughes, *Autobiographical Notes*, 185.
24.   Pusey, vol. 1:384.
25.   Pusey, vol. 2:611.
26.   Betty Glad, *Charles Evans Hughes and the Illusions of Innocence: A Study in American Diplomacy* (Urbana: University of Illinois Press, 1966), 324.

27. Dexter Perkins, *Charles Evans Hughes and the American Democratic Statesmanship* (Boston: Little, Brown, 1956), 144.
28. Ibid., 57.
29. Hughes, *Autobiographical Notes*, 58. See note 3.
30. Pusey, vol. 2:615. See note 1.
31. David J. Danelski, "The Influence of the Chief Justice in the Decisional Process," *Courts, Judges and Politics*, 4th ed., ed. Walter F. Murphy and C. Herman Pritchett (New York: Random House, 1986), 568–77.
32. Pusey, vol 2.:679.
33. Quoted in Pusey, vol. 2:675.
34. Felix Frankfurter, *Of Law and Men: Papers and Addresses of Felix Frankfurter, 1939–1956*, ed. Philip Elmon (Hamden, CT: Archon , 1956), 134–135, 141.
35. Quoted from Roberts's memorial address before the New York Bar Association, Dec. 12, 1948, in Pusey, vol. 2:676.
36. Frankfurter, 137, 142. See note 34.
37. Samuel Hendel, "Charles Evans Hughes," 956. See note 7.
38. 300 U.S. 377 at 396, quoting from Taft's dissent in *Adkins v. Children's Hospital*, 261 US 525 (1923). Hughes further observed: "The Constitution does not speak of freedom of contract. It speaks of liberty and prohibits the deprivation of liberty without due process of law. In prohibiting that deprivation the Constitution does not recognize an absolute an uncontrollable liberty. Liberty in each of its phases has a history and connotation. But the liberty safeguarded is liberty in a social organization which requires the protection of law against the evils which menace the health, safety, morals and welfare of the people."
39. Pusey, vol. 2:791. See note 1.
40. Henry J. Abraham, *Justices, Presidents, and Senators*, (Lanham: Roman & Littlefield, 1999), 151.

FOR FURTHER READING

Frankfurter, Felix. *Of Law and Men: Papers and Addresses of Felix Frankfurter, 1939–1956*, edited by Philip Elmon. Hamden, CT: Archon Books, 1956.
Glad, Betty. *Charles Evans Hughes and the Illusions of Innocence: A Study in American Diplomacy.* Urbana: University of Illinois Press, 1966.
Hendel, Samuel. *Charles Evans Hughes and the Supreme Court.* New York: King's Crown Press of Columbia University, 1951.
Hughes, Charles Evans. *The Autobiographical Notes of Charles Evans Hughes*, edited by David J. Danelski and Joseph S. Tulchin. Cambridge: Harvard University Press, 1973.
———. *The Supreme Court of the United States.* New York: Columbia University Press, 1928.Mason, Alpheus Thomas. *The Supreme Court from Taft to Burger.* Baton Rouge: Louisiana University Press, 1979.
Perkins, Dexter. *Charles Evans Hughes and American Democratic Statesmanship.* Boston: Little, Brown , 1956.
Pusey, Merlo J. *Charles Evans Hughes.* 2 vols. New York: Columbia University Press, 1963.
Umbreit, Kenneth B. *Our Eleven Chief Justices.* New York: Harper, 1938.
Wesser, Robert F. *Charles Evans Hughes: Politics and Reform in New York, 1905–1910.* Ithaca, NY: Cornell University Press, 1967.

CHAPTER THIRTEEN

Harlan Fiske Stone: New Deal Prudence

Theodore M. Vestal

In late April 1946, Washington, DC, was an upbeat, optimistic city. World War II was finally over, and the stresses of what would be called the Cold War were not yet at hand. The U.S. Supreme Court was nearing the end of its first postwar term in the always spectacular springtime of the federal district.

Monday, April 22, was a decision day at the Court, and the chief justice was in a good mood. He had spent Easter weekend with family and friends, and he had plans to host a dinner party that evening. After the customary call to order at twelve noon in the marble-colonnaded chamber, the justices took their seats at the long, elevated mahogany bench. In the center of the Roosevelt Court sat the imposing twelfth chief justice of the United States, Harlan Fiske Stone, looking every inch the New England patrician that he was. After some routine business was concluded, the justices read opinions of the Court or their dissenting opinions. Stone read his dissent from a case involving a conscientious objector's right to citizenship and concluded by saying, "It is not the function of this Court to disregard the will of Congress in the exercise of its constitutional power."[1]

A few minutes later, when it was time for the chief to deliver three opinions he had prepared for the Court, there was silence. Senior Associate Justice Hugo Black, sensing something was wrong, gaveled the session to adjournment, and he and justice Stanley Reed assisted the chief justice from the chamber. The unconscious chief was taken to a hospital where in the early evening he died, apparently without pain, of a massive cerebral hemorrhage.[2] Stone's final act literally had been on the bench and his last coherent words were a refrain of his often-voiced philosophy of judicial restraint. Thus ended the life of a justice whose service on the Court spanned the *Lochner* era to the age of the welfare state, whose opinions had a profound impact on the nation's struggle to meet the challenges of the Great Depression and a world war, and who guided the Court into the beginning of the judicial revolution in civil liberties and civil rights. For the Supreme Court in 1946, April was the cruelest month.

As chief justice, Harlan Fiske Stone was *sui generis*. He was the only university professor and law school dean to head the Court, and he was the only chief justice to serve under two predecessors. In the history of the Court, Stone alone sat in all the high-backed chairs of the Court, from the junior associate justice's place to the chief's center spot. He was the first Court nominee to submit to questions from the Senate Judiciary Committee during the confirmation process. Tragically, Stone had the briefest tenure as chief justice since 1801. He was one of only two chief justices appointed by a president of a different political party (the other was Democrat E. Douglas White appointed by Taft), and he was one of three chiefs who were "promoted" directly from the position of associate justice (the others were White and William H. Rehnquist; Charles Evans Hughes also had been an associate justice, but he resigned from the Court to run for the presidency several years before his appointment as chief justice).

Harlan Fiske Stone was born on October 11, 1872, at his family's farm in Chesterfield, New Hampshire. His parents were Frederick Lauson Stone and Anne Butler, a former schoolteacher. Two years after Harlan's birth, the Stones moved to Mill Valley, near Amherst, Massachusetts. In addition to farming, Fred Stone supported his family by a variety of small business ventures. Harlan's childhood was that of a typical, hardworking New England farm boy. In later years, Harlan attributed his independence, self-reliance, and sense of civic responsibility to his New England upbringing. He did not want to continue in his father's footsteps as a farmer, however, and after his sophomore year of high school, he attended the nearby Massachusetts Agricultural College (M.A.C., now the University of Massachusetts), intending to study science and possibly become a physician. In his second year, an untoward scuffle with an instructor in the college's compulsory chapel service led to Stone's expulsion.

M.A.C.'s loss was Amherst's gain. In 1890 Stone was accepted at Amherst College, where he excelled in academics (Phi Beta Kappa) and oratory, served as editor of the college newspaper, was three times elected class president, and played on the football team. "Doc," as Stone was known in college, graduated in 1894 and taught high school science for a year at Newburyport, Massachusetts. There he met district attorney William H. Moody, a future Supreme Court justice, who encouraged Stone to study law. In Newburyport, Stone frequently sat in on sessions of the state superior court and decided to pursue legal studies.

In 1895, he was admitted to Columbia Law School, where the case system of instruction had just been introduced. In New York City, Stone helped pay his way through law school by teaching history parttime at a Brooklyn high school. Stone received his L.L.B. degree in 1898 and was admitted to the New York Bar. He clerked one year for Sullivan and Cromwell, a Wall Street law firm.

In 1899, Stone married Agnes Harvey, a childhood sweetheart. He joined the firm of Wilmer and Canfield and began parttime teaching of equity and trusts at Columbia. In 1903 he was promoted to adjunct professor, with a seat in Columbia's Faculty of Law. Stone resigned his professorship in 1905, however, because of an inadequate salary and his disagreements with Columbia's president, Nicholas Murray Butler. He then became a full partner in the firm now called Wilmer, Canfield, and Stone.

Five years later, without relinquishing his work in the law firm, Stone was lured back to Columbia, where he was professor of law and dean of the law school. In 1915 he was named Kent Professor of Law, and his professorial accomplishments included writing several significant articles on trusts and equity rights for the *Columbia Law Review*. He was a gifted teacher reputed to be inspiring and effective in the classroom. One of his students was William O. Douglas, who later would serve on the Supreme Court with Stone. Under Stone's leadership, the law school upgraded its admission requirements and set high standards of scholarship for the faculty. During World War I, Stone served on a government board examining claims of conscientious objectors, and he subsequently wrote "The Conscientious Objector," a classic essay in defense of nonconformism.[3] During this time, he also defended free speech claims of professors and socialists and opposed the "red raids" of U.S. Attorney General A. Mitchell Palmer against suspected radicals. Columbia soon became a center of a new school of jurisprudence, legal realism. Legal realists rejected formalism and static legal rules; instead, they searched for the experiential and the role of human idiosyncrasy in the development of law. Although Dean Stone encouraged the realists, he was condemned by President Butler as an intellectual conservative who had let legal education at Columbia fall "into the ruts."[4]

In 1923, disgusted by his conflict with Butler and bored with "all the petty details of law school administration" that he dubbed "administrivia," Stone resigned the deanship and joined the prestigious Wall Street firm of Sullivan and Cromwell.[5] He received a much higher salary and headed the firm's litigation department that had a large corporation and estate practice (including J.P. Morgan's interests). In fulltime private practice for only a brief time, Stone was considered a "hard-working, solid sort of person, willing on occasion to champion the rights of mankind, but safe nevertheless."[6]

On 1 April 1924, Stone became attorney general of the United States, appointed by President Calvin Coolidge, who had been a contemporary of Stone's at Amherst. Coolidge needed someone who would be perceived by the public as beyond reproach to oversee investigations into various scandals arising under the Harding administration. These scandals had besmirched Harding's attorney general, Harry M. Dougherty, and forced his resignation. Stone immediately fired Dougherty's cronies in the Department of Justice and replaced them with men of integrity. He appointed a young lawyer, J. Edgar Hoover, as director of a reconstituted Federal Bureau of Investigation (FBI) and directed him to model the FBI on Scotland Yard and make it far more efficient than any other police organization in the country. A proactive attorney general, Stone argued many of his department's cases in the federal courts and launched an antitrust investigation of the Aluminum Company of America, controlled by the family of Andrew Mellon, who was Coolidge's secretary of the treasury.

In the 1924 presidential election, Stone campaigned for Coolidge's reelection. He especially opposed the Progressive Party's candidate, Robert M. LaFollette, who had proposed that Congress be empowered to reenact any law that the Supreme Court had declared unconstitutional. Stone found this idea threatening to the integrity of the judiciary as well as the separation of powers.

Shortly after the election, Justice Joseph McKenna resigned from the Supreme Court, and on January 5, 1925, Coolidge nominated Stone to replace him. His nomination was greeted with general approval, although there were rumors that Stone might have been kicked upstairs because of his antitrust activities. Some senators raised questions about Stone's connection to Wall Street making him a tool of corporate interests. To quiet those fears, Stone proposed that he answer questions of the Senate Judiciary Committee in person. Stone made such a favorable impression upon the senators that he was confirmed by a vote of 71 to 6. On March 2, 1925, Stone took the oath as associate justice administered by Chief Justice William Howard Taft.

The Supreme Court of the mid-1920s was primarily concerned with the relationships of business and government. A majority of the justices led by Taft were staunch defenders of business and capitalism from most government regulation. The Court utilized the doctrines of substantive due process and the new fundamental right of "liberty of contract" to oversee attempts at regulation by the national and state governments. Critics of the Court charged that the judiciary had usurped legislative authority and had embodied a particular economic theory, *laissez faire*, into its decisions. Despite the fears of progressives, Stone quickly joined the Court's "liberal faction," frequently dissenting with Justices Holmes and Brandeis, and Cardozo, after he took Holmes's seat, from the majority's narrow view of the police powers of the state. The "liberal" justices called for judicial restraint, deference to the legislative will.

In his jurisprudence, Stone searched not for a fixed point of law but for guiding principles. He was willing to look at nontraditional sources for information related to the legal rules the Court pronounced—a process advocated by legal realists. Stone wrote few opinions involving constitutional questions; instead he was assigned tort cases, admiralty causes, patent disputes, and income tax controversies. Because the Supreme Court did not have its own building at that time, Stone did much of his work at home or in a basement room of the Senate Office Building.

During the Hoover administration, Stone served as an informal advisor to the president and was a member of Hoover's pre-breakfast "Medicine-Ball Cabinet," a fitness group, at the White House. Hoover unsuccessfully tried to persuade Stone to become his secretary of state following the 1928 presidential election.

When Chief Justice Taft resigned because of failing health in 1930, however, Stone was rumored to be Hoover's choice to replace him. Hoover, perhaps to pay off a political debt for help in the 1928 election, instead appointed former Associate Justice Charles Evans Hughes, Stone's colleague in the Coolidge cabinet, to the post. Hughes, a judicial moderate, led the Court during the tumultuous times of the Great Depression and the Roosevelt administration's efforts to combat it.

A conservative bloc composed of Justices Butler, McReynolds, Sutherland, and Van Devanter, known as the "Four Horsemen," frequently joined by Owen Roberts and sometimes Hughes, dominated the Court and blocked government efforts to deal with the Depression. Stone continued in his role as a dissenter to the substantive due process activists who read their personal economic predilections into the Constitution. Feeling isolated on the Court, Stone considered returning to law practice in New York, a move encouraged by his Sullivan and Cromwell colleague, John Foster Dulles.[7] After Hoover's defeat in the 1932 elections, Stone's admirers urged him to enter politics and seek the GOP presidential nomination. Stone, however, heeded the advice of Judge Learned Hand and remained on the Court, emerging as the chief opponent of judicial conservatism.

During the 1930s the "Four Horsemen" and their sometime converts consistently attacked New Deal legislation because they disagreed with its wisdom. Using a catch-22 logic, the conservative bloc found states could not regulate much because of Congress's commerce power, and Congress could not regulate much because of the states' police power. In contrast, Stone upheld government regulations, voting for the abrogation of the gold clause contract in government bonds, the TVA, the National Labor Relations Act, and the Wage and Hour Law; and he dissented from decisions on the Guffey coal wage bill and on the New York minimum wage law for women. When the conservatives struck down FDR's Agricultural Administration Act in 1936 in *United States v. Butler,* Stone dissented, charging the majority with writing its own views into law, disregarding the wisdom of the legislature, and "torturing" the Constitution. Wrote Stone: "While unconstitutional exercise of power by the executive or legislative branches of the Government is subject to judicial restraint, the only check upon our own exercise of power is our own sense of restraint."[8]

Stone's constitutional interpretation respecting government regulation of the economy was based on the premise that the Constitution sanctioned government power to govern and that power changed to meet changing conditions. Further, it was not for the courts to determine what remedies were appropriate to meet economic problems that burdened the nation. The essential continuity, according to Stone, was not that of "rules" but of "aims and ideals," allowing government "to continue to function and to perform its appointed tasks within the bounds of reasonableness." Stone contended that judges must be alert to discover whether their decisions "will represent the sober second thought of the community, which is the firm base on which all law must ultimately rest."[9]

Stone opposed Roosevelt's Court-packing plan during the constitutional crisis of 1937, although he could well understand why the president suggested such a measure. Following the "switch in time," primarily by Justice Roberts, and retirements of other justices, Stone's views formerly raised in dissent became those of the Court's majority. New Deal regulatory measures were sustained and wide-ranging federal power over the economy was upheld. Stone wrote significant opinions about intergovernmental tax immunities, commerce clause restrictions on the states, equity, and patents.

One of Stone's greatest contributions to American jurisprudence came in his majority opinion in *United States v. Carolene Products* (1938), which included the most famous footnote in the Court's history.[10] In an otherwise insignificant case, Stone's footnote laid out a new direction for the Court's use of judicial review and the choice between activism and restraint. He suggested that although economic legislation might be assumed to be constitutional if it was rational, such a test might not apply to other types of legislation. There might be a narrower scope for the presumption of constitutionality if the legislation appeared to violate protections of the Bill of Rights. In addition, legislation restricting political processes should be subjected to more exacting judicial scrutiny, and the courts might have a special responsibility for protecting "discrete and insular minorities," such as religious, national, or racial minorities, particularly when political processes relied upon to protect minorities have been curtailed. After the *Carolene Products* footnote, a Court that had been primarily occupied with the business-government relationship became more concerned with the relationship between the individual and government. Much of the subsequent doctrinal and theoretical development of constitutional law in the United States was foreshadowed by footnote four, and the protection of civil liberties and civil rights became the main business of the Court.

Stone soon had the opportunity to apply his footnote-four theories in his opinions. In *Hague v. CIO* (1939), Stone made clear that the safeguards of the First Amendment applied to the states and were firmly anchored in the Fourteenth Amendment due process clause. Moreover, the Court would henceforth subject legislation restricting civil liberties to Amore exacting judicial scrutiny."[11] Stone echoed this sentiment as the sole dissenter in *Minersville School District v. Gobitis* (1940), where the majority had upheld a state law requiring public school children to salute the flag against a challenge from Jehovah's Witnesses that this violated their religious scruples. Stone found the law violative of the guarantee of "freedom of mind and spirit." For Stone it was incumbent upon the Court to extend freedom's benefits to the novel, the unpopular, the unorthodox—even "in times when the nation is subject to extraordinary stress."[12] Within a few years, Stone's ideas were endorsed by a majority of the

Court when it reversed the *Gobitis* decision in *West Virginia State Board of Education v. Barnette* (1943).

On June 2, 1941, Chief Justice Hughes retired, and President Roosevelt, in a gesture of national unity as war approached, nominated Stone, a staunch Republican, to fill the vacancy. His appointment was approved strongly by the public and the press, and the Senate unanimously confirmed Stone by a voice vote. The Court over which he presided, with the exception of Roberts, was composed of Roosevelt-appointed New Deal liberals who might have been expected to share Stone's views on judicial restraint.

As the Court moved away from issues of federalism and economic regulation and focused on civil liberties questions, however, the new men on the Court who called themselves "liberals" differed markedly over what that title meant. The justices increasingly divided into shifting majority and minority voting blocks. Internecine wrangling between strong-willed, prickly personalities—especially Black, Douglas, Frankfurter, and Jackson—as well as substantive disagreement on issues, characterized the Court's work. Quarrels that formerly had been kept secret in conference erupted into formal opinions. Even the writing of what should have been a routine retirement letter to Justice Roberts became a public squabble among the justices. The chief justice, who tended to minimize his role as leader, was criticized for failing to keep differences under control and to "mass the Court" as Hughes and Taft had done.

Stone's style of leadership doubtlessly contributed to the increase in strident dissents and public backbiting among the justices. Unlike Hughes, who dominated the Court's conferences with an iron will, Stone preferred to preside over a chief-moderated "university seminar" that emphasized deliberation and freewheeling discussion. Although Douglas wrote that "Stone's tolerance of full and free discussions produced a most healthy environment for judicial work," the justices' continuous disagreement on vital issues threatened the Court's authority and prestige.[13]

Despite the dissonance, the Roosevelt Court was productive and creative. In settling some of the most controversial issues facing the nation, the Court handed down a series of landmark cases expanding individual rights, recasting the role of the national government in the federal system, meeting the challenges of World War II, encouraging the rights of organized labor, and using the Equal Protection Clause to protect racial minorities. Stone shouldered his part of the work, and during his five years as chief he wrote 145 opinions (more per term than any of the other justices), 96 of which were for the Court. The chief frequently disagreed with his colleagues who were activists in using judicial power to protect individual liberties from legislative interference. Stone still believed in judicial restraint and objected to the justices trying to write their own liberal social views into law. Stone's insistence that the justices should be controlled by an informed sense of judicial self-restraint was just as applicable to the new liberal Court as it had been to the old conservative Court. He also protested against the justices' use of a "preferred freedoms" doctrine to invalidate any legislation affecting First Amendment rights.

The chief wrote for the Court in many of the most difficult and perplexing cases. In *United States v. Classic* (1941), he ruled that Congress could regulate a primary election if it constituted part of the overall machinery for choosing elected federal officials—a significant victory for African-American voters who had been disenfranchised in "white primaries" in the segregated South. When war powers of the executive and Congress clashed with civil liberties during World War II, however, Stone frequently upheld the government. His most controversial decisions involved constitutionally unprecedented cases involving German saboteurs, *Ex parte Quirin* (1942); the war crimes trial of Japanese General Yamashita, *In re Yamashita* (1946); and the imposition of a curfew on Japanese-Americans and their exclusion from the West Coast, *Hirabayashi v. United States* (1943). Stone reasoned that the Constitution committed war-making to Congress and the president, and that if that power was reasonably exercised, the justices should construe it with full cognizance of its special characteristics. In war, as in peace, according to the chief justice, the Constitution was a flexible instrument of government that both granted and limited power. It was the difficult task of the Court to balance power and individual liberties—to achieve a delicate equilibrium to preserve the related values of the public good and private rights.[14] The chief's coming down on the side of public good in the guise of military commanders disappointed his more libertarian admirers.

Stone's career on the Court extended over a transition from a time when judicial values emphasized property rights and dual federalism to the modern era that stresses what Felix Frankfurter called "the free play of the human spirit"[15] and an expanded national power. Cast as a liberal on the old Court, Stone truly was an independent-thinking pragmatist who sought balance in all aspects of life. As the justices of the new Court increasingly championed the judiciary's role as the palladium of the people's freedom, Stone's views became a restraining influence on their activism. His voice was one of prudence for the New Deal. He sought to temper predilection with restraint and carefully crafted opinions. For Stone, a personal preference for a particular policy was but one factor in his quest for judgment. He believed law was an evolutionary process, changing, as did the common law, in an orderly manner. Thus he preferred narrow holdings making incremental advances as the best way to accommodate change.[16] While the attitudes of the justices shifted around him, Stone's stayed in place, according to Wesley McCone, "like a block of New England granite."[17]

As an individual justice, Stone made dynamic contributions to American law, adapting the Court and Constitution to the problems of the twentieth century. Although critics found him disappointing as a chief justice, Stone, the "judge's judge," exerted a profound influence on the course of events. At its best, the legacy he left was the pillar of our constitutional law.

NOTES

1. *Girouard v. United States,* 328 U.S. 61 (1946) (H. Stone, dissenting) 70.
2. Alpheus Thomas Mason, *Harlan Fiske Stone: Pillar of the Law* (New York: Viking Press, 1956), 806.
3. Harlan Fiske Stone, "The Conscientious Objector," *Columbia University Quarterly,* October 1919.
4. Quoted in Melvin I. Urofsky, "Stone, Harlan Fiske," in *American National Biography,* volume 20, John A. Garraty and Mark C. Carnes (eds.) (New York: Oxford University Press, 1999), 850.
5. Melvin I. Urofsky, *Division and Discord: The Supreme Court under Stone and Vinson, 1941–1953* (Columbia, SC: University of South Carolina Press, 1997), 10.
6. "Stone, Harlan Fiske," *Current Biography: Who's News and Why, 1941,* Maxine Block (ed.) (New York: H.W. Wilson, 1941), 836.
7. Mason, 347. See note 2.
8 *United States v. Butler,* 297 U.S. 1 (1936); (H. Stone dissenting), 78.
9. Harlan Fiske Stone, "The Common Law in the United States," an address delivered at the Harvard tercentenary celebration, 1936. Quoted in Mason, 434. See note 20.
10. 304 US 144 (1938).
11. 307 US 496 (1939); (H. Stone concurring), 518.
12. 310 U.S. 586 (1940); (H. Stone dissenting), 601.
13. Robert J. Steamer, *Chief Justice: Leadership and the Supreme Court* (Columbia, SC: University of South Carolina Press, 1986), 265–266.
14. Mason, 683. See note 2.
15. Quoted in Robert G. McCloskey, *The American Supreme Court* (Chicago: University of Chicago Press, 1960), 181.
16. G. Edward White, *The American Judicial Tradition: Profiles of Leading American Judges* (New York: Oxford University Press, 1988), 218–219.
17. Quoted in Mason, 780. See note 2.

FOR FURTHER READING

Mason, Alpheus Thomas. *Harlan Fiske Stone: Pillar of the Law.* New York: Viking Press, 1956.
Pritchett, C. Herman. *The Roosevelt Court: A Study in Judicial Politics and Values.* New York: Macmillan, 1948.
Renstrom, Peter G. *The Stone Court: Justices, Rulings and Legacy.* Santa Barbara: ABC–CLIO, 2001.
Steamer, Robert J. *Chief Justice: Leadership and the Supreme Court.* Columbia, SC: University of South Carolina Press, 1986.
Urofsky, Melvin I. *Division and Discord: The Supreme Court under Stone and Vinson, 1941–1953.* Columbia, SC: University of South Carolina Press, 1997.

Wechsler, Herbert. "Mr. Justice Stone and the Constitution." *Columbia Law Review* 46 (1946): 764–800.
White, G. Edward. *The American Judicial Tradition: Profiles of Leading American Judges*. New York: Oxford University Press, 1988.

CHAPTER FOURTEEN

Earl Warren: Justice as Fairness

Norman W. Provizer
Joseph D. Vigil

In 1991, Clarence Thomas survived controversial confirmation hearings to become the sixth member of the Supreme Court nominated by the administrations of Ronald Reagan and George Bush. With Thomas on the Court, only Justice Byron White remained as a holdover from the days when Chief Justice Earl Warren presided over America's primary judicial institution.

Two years later, White left the Court. And then there were none. The two terms spent by Bill Clinton in the White House brought Ruth Bader Ginsburg and Steven Breyer to the bench of a deeply divided institution headed by Chief Justice William Rehnquist. In 2001, George W. Bush became the nation's forty-third president, and the speculation over the future direction the Court intensified. Exactly what would remain of the Warren legacy as the twenty-first century unfolded?

Of course, the constitutional paths cut by the Warren Court were not completely repaved by the Courts that followed in its wake (led, respectively, by Warren Burger and Rehnquist). Yet, those paths have and will continue to be altered by changing political realities. A cartoon that displayed an "Impeach Earl Warren" billboard sitting on top of the Supreme Court building may have been apocryphal but—by 1991 and, certainly, in 2001— it was not at all pure fantasy.

The irony was that 1991 also marked the centennial of Earl Warren's birth. And it is Warren's name that will forever be connected to the judicial revolution that shaped the face of constitutional law during the last half of the twentieth century—a revolution that is now in the midst of its own Thermidor.

The Man and the Question of Fairness

Earl Warren was born on March 19, 1891, in Los Angeles. Soon after, his family moved to Bakersfield, where his father was a repairman for the Southern Pacific Railroad. The son of immigrant parents from Scandinavia, Warren worked his way through an undergraduate and law degree at the University of California at Berkeley.

With the exception of a brief period of time right after law school, Warren spent his entire career in the public sector, moving from deputy city attorney of Oakland to deputy district attorney for that county. In 1938, the lawyer of lower-middle-class origins and no middle name won the nomination for state attorney general in the primaries of the Progressive and Democratic Parties, as well as that of his own Republican organization; in 1942, he continued his political rise by winning the California governor's race. He was twice reelected to that position, gaining the Democratic nomination on top of his Republican selection in 1946.

On the national scene, Warren was Thomas Dewey's vice presidential running mate in 1948 and supported Dwight Eisenhower at the 1952 Republican Convention after his own presidential aspirations stalled. That support provided the glue that would link Warren to the Supreme Court the following year.

Earl Warren possessed an enduring passion for justice. He believed in equal opportunity for the disadvantaged in society so they could become part of the expanding American economic scene. While Warren possessed great practical political skills, he could also appear as an Old Testament prophet, urging the nation to fulfill its promise (though doing so in a genial, deliberate, and decidedly nonprophetic fashion). In this regard, Warren demonstrated a clear belief that all Americans were entitled to search for justice under the broad umbrellas of equal protection and due process of the law, no matter what their social standing or color of their skin. And justice (what John Rawls would call "the first virtue of social institutions") required fair treatment.[1]

There is one story that well illustrates this crucial point. Not too long before the Court issued its opinion in *Brown v. Board of Education,* the chief justice toured Civil War battlefields in Virginia with his African-American chauffeur. During the tour, Warren emerged one morning from his hotel to discover that his driver had spent the night in the car because he couldn't find a place that accepted black guests. "I was embarrassed," Warren later recalled, "I was ashamed."[2] How could such a situation possibly be fair?

As chief justice (from October 5, 1953, until June 23, 1969), Warren was placed in a leadership role at a time when a wide range of controversial issues came before the Court. The Warren Court issued watershed opinions on questions of obscenity, school prayer, libel, and the criticism of public figures, criminal defendant rights, the desegregation of public facilities, gerrymandering, the right to privacy, equal protection doctrines, and the death penalty. And, in what the chief justice considered to be the most important decision affecting constitutional law issued during his tenure, the Warren Court shattered the political questions doctrine as a barrier for injured parties in voting rights cases.

The common sentiment espoused by detractors is that the Warren Court, especially after it coalesced in 1962 with the appointment of Arthur Goldberg to the bench, was an activist body that played the role of a "super legislature."

The critics charge that the Warren Court advocated positions on civil rights and guaranteed freedoms that were not part of the "original intent" of the framers of the Constitution. From the political world, one of the primary detractors of the Warren Court was Richard Nixon, an old rival from California. In the 1968 election, Nixon campaigned on a plank of remaking the Court with nominees who were "strict constructionists." Nixon harshly criticized the Warren Court's decisions on criminal defendant rights, civil liberties, and civil rights. His main attack concentrated on "activism" within the judicial branch of government. He argued that the role of the judiciary was strictly to interpret existing law, not to take any initiative in that field.[3]

Earl Warren began to have serious detractors during his first term on the Court. The John Birch Society focused its attention on the chief justice following his 1954 decision in *Brown,* mounting a billboard campaign to "Impeach Earl Warren." Warren was mildly amused by this and reasoned that it kept the members busy spending their time and money on something that was not going to happen. If Warren was not about to resign or be impeached and removed, however, there were still unsettling developments. Senator James O. Eastland (D-Mississippi), soon to become the powerful chairman of the Senate Judiciary Committee, declared that the Warren Court and the lower federal courts had destroyed the Constitution by disregarding the law. In a speech given to a Mississippi audience on August 12, 1955, Senator Eastland extolled the virtues of segregation and Southern life. Referring to the *Brown* decision, he told the audience, "You are not required to obey any court which passes out such a ruling. In fact you are obligated to defy it."[4]

Southern congressmen and other segregationists lined up in opposition to the *Brown* decision and to the Court in general. In 1957, for example, the House voted 241–155 to limit jurisdiction of the Supreme Court in matters of internal security. In the Senate, it was only the political maneuverings of Majority Leader Lyndon B. Johnson that provided the one-vote majority to procedurally defeat the initiative, 41–40. Southern state legislatures then began a series of legislative efforts designed to impede the desegregation edicts of the Warren Court using a loophole created by the Court's own "with all deliberate speed" language.[5] The Fifth Circuit Court of Appeals, however, still had the core of *Brown* available to overcome, over time, such legislative roadblocks.

Then, in 1962, the Warren Court announced another key decision that greatly affected discrimination and the question of fairness, but from a completely different angle. In *Baker v. Carr* (1962), the Court used the Fourteenth Amendment to rule that the issue of legislative reapportionment was indeed a justiciable matter, and that the Court would now allow claims based upon the equal protection clause to be heard. Though the far-reaching nature of the decision in *Baker v. Carr* (as well as its progeny) is often overlooked, that decision provided the opportunity for the redress of grievances that had previously been denied because of the political questions doctrine. An important door to the

Court had been pried open by Warren, and that opening created a second wave of blockbuster "fairness" cases. This time the focus was on voting—a focus, in Richard Cortner's words, that "involved the most remarkable and far-reaching exercise of judicial power in our history."[6]

The Backdrop of Race

For the majority of Court watchers and others, the Court's *Brown* decision is viewed as the most significant decision made during the tenure of Chief Justice Warren. Certainly, it was a decision that stands as a watershed in the history of American constitutional law.

The framers of the Constitution and the Bill of Rights addressed slavery and racial segregation within the framework of maintaining the nation's political and economic stability. But that approach would produce its own dire consequences. Slavery and racial discrimination continued to be divisive issues and, eventually, they provided the spark that ignited this nation's long and bloody Civil War. While the Thirteenth Amendment (1865) settled the issue of slavery, it, and the Fourteenth and Fifteenth Amendments that followed, did not end the debate over racial discrimination.

There are those who argue that positive law cannot end racism, just as Congress cannot legislate morality. Laws proscribe behavior that is considered criminally reprehensible. The act of legislating punishment for criminal conduct does not mean that all vices are outlawed, nor does it mean that all virtues are enhanced. The Court itself has said that a law need not be perfect to be constitutional. The Court requires only that there be a rational relationship between the classification created by the law and the means used to affect that group. This ends-means relationship is called the rational basis test. When using the rational basis test, the Court has decided that if the goal of the legislative enactment is constitutional, then the law is assumed to be constitutional as well. After all, it is within the proper power of legislatures to enact legislative measures.

Of course, when it comes to race and racial discrimination, America's history is, to say the least, compelling. At the Constitutional Convention it was declared that slaves were to be considered three-fifths of a person in matters of legislative apportionment and direct taxation. *Federalist 53* describes that compromise as an expedient to gain the adoption of the Constitution. In 1857, the Supreme Court decided the *Dred Scott Case*—a decision aptly described as one that "represents judicial review at its worst" and that "as much as any other single action...helped lead to the Civil War."[7] Led by Chief Justice Roger Taney, the Court ruled, 7–2, that blacks were not citizens, that Congress could not bar slavery from the new territories, and that slaves who were taken to free territories could not become free since they were property.

The Thirteenth and Fourteenth (1868) Amendments effectively overruled the *Dred Scott* doctrine. In the *Civil Rights Cases* of 1883, the Court ruled, 8–1, that the Fourteenth Amendment prohibited the states from discriminating against blacks because of their race, but did not restrict private organizations from such discriminatory actions. The decision meant that the Court would allow private discrimination to take place in theaters, restaurants, hotels, and transportation facilities. The Court felt that such private actions were not subject to the prohibitions set forth in the Fourteenth Amendment and the Civil Rights Act of 1875. While those laws did grant rights and privileges, they protected a group only from state laws and state procedures—and, even then, only when the action affected national rights and privileges.

In *Plessy v. Ferguson* (1896), the Court went further, establishing the doctrine of "separate but equal" that ruled America for the next fifty-eight years. The Court, by a vote of 7–1, allowed states to legislate racial segregation so long as the separate facilities provided were "equal." This case became the harbinger of a litany of laws and customs designed to discriminate against African Americans. In *Cumming v. Richmond County Board of Education* (1899), the Court went even further, not only approving the use of a white-only system, but also accepting the state's argument that the lack of money prevented it from providing for the high school education of blacks by building a separate facility. There was little that was equal under the rubric "separate but equal."

During the next half century, state and local governments generated Jim Crow laws, grandfather clauses, and poll taxes, as well as sponsoring or supporting violence against blacks. Property clauses were instituted to skirt the provisions of the Fifteenth Amendment (1870) and to disenfranchise African Americans, while grandfather clauses emerged to reincorporate poor whites who were related to voters in pre-Fifteenth Amendment elections. All of these actions were designed to intimidate racial minorities, prevent them from exercising their right to vote, and keep in place a state apparatus of discrimination. Racial and ethnic discrimination was not confined to the Deep South; Southwestern and Western states openly discriminated against peoples of Hispanic, Asian, and Native American ancestry.

In addition to efforts by states to disenfranchise and segregate minority groups, terrorism also occurred in the form of lynching and kangaroo courts that denied due process and equal protection of the law.

In only a few cases did the Court strike such provisions. In *Guinn v. United States* (1915), the Court voided an Oklahoma grandfather clause for violating the Fifteenth Amendment. That decision was then used as the basis to strike down the other grandfather clauses. In *Yick Wo v. Hopkins* (1886), the Court struck down a San Francisco ordinance that, in fact, discriminated against Chinese launderers. The ordinance, enacted under the cloak of public safety, called for a prohibition against the operation of wooden laundries unless there was a grant of waiver by the board of supervisors. Ninety-seven percent of the Chinese laundries were in wooden buildings. White laundry owners were routinely given the waiver but Chinese launderers were not, and the Court felt the ordinance was patently discriminatory.

Then, in 1896, came *Plessy*. While racism was well entrenched long before this decision, the ruling established the legal basis for official segregation in the post-Civil War world, reasoning that would shape American law for more than a half century, while turning the apparent words of the Constitution on their head. During the first half of the twentieth century (before *Brown*), the Court seemed satisfied to modify the *Plessy* doctrine rather than rule on its constitutionality. The Court conveniently sidestepped the doctrine's core issue by deciding equal protection cases on a case-by-case basis, and then issuing orders for remedial action in the particular case. In *McCabe v. Atchison, Topeka & Santa Fe Railroad Company* (1914), for example, the Court held that the practice of segregating dining cars might produce unequal service and that the solution would be to make the separate services more equitable. A quarter-century later, the Court refused to grant *certiorari* to a lower court case and thereby let stand a ruling that black teachers in Norfolk, Virginia, should be paid the same salaries as their white counterparts, even though the school system was segregated.

In the cases of *Sweatt v. Painter* (1950) and *McLaurin v. Oklahoma State Regents* (1950), the Court further reevaluated the definition of separate but equal. In *McLaurin,* the Court said that a young black man who had been admitted into a white graduate program must be accorded similar privileges as his white counterparts in the normal process of education. In this case, the student was placed in a room adjoining the lecture hall. The room was equipped with windows and air ducts so that he could hear the lecture and see the blackboard. The Court did not directly address the issue of separate but equal. Instead, the Court granted specific relief to the black plaintiff. Still, the opinion in *McLaurin* indicates growing dissatisfaction with the *Plessy* doctrine.

In *Sweatt,* the Court again skirted overruling the doctrine and relied on an order limited to the specific facts of the case. Homer Sweatt had been denied admission into the University of Texas Law School based upon his race. The state argued that a soon-to-be black law school would suffice to provide instruction on the fundamentals of law and provide the necessary resources for Sweatt to complete his studies. The trial court accepted that argument and gave the state of Texas six months to build the all-black law school. Mr. Sweatt refused to attend that school and pursued his case to gain admittance into the highly respected law school at the University of Texas. The appellate courts of Texas, however, upheld the lower court decision and the remedy of a separate law school for blacks. Sweatt appealed to the Supreme Court and won. The Court ordered his admittance into the University's law program. The Court stated that the all-black law school was inferior to one at the University of Texas. The all-black law school was not accredited, did not have its own faculty or library, and lacked items such as scholarship programs, alumni associations, and legal fraternities. Though the Court argued that the equal protection clause of the Fourteenth Amendment required the University of Texas to admit Mr. Sweatt, and ordered compliance, it did not go so far as to overrule the doctrine of separate but equal. Change, nevertheless, was in the air. The issue was ripe for fundamental reconsideration. What was needed was a new leader for a new day on the Court.

By 1952, a series of cases directly challenging segregated education were before the Supreme Court. The lead case was *Brown,* and it was argued in 1953. The Court, faced with internal divisions, asked that the case be reargued, but before that could take place, Chief Justice Fred Vinson died. Repaying a political debt, President Dwight Eisenhower named Warren as Vinson's successor. Thus during Warren's first term on the bench, the Court under his direction had the opportunity to override the *Plessy* doctrine and the accompanying Jim Crow laws that flowed from it. The new chief justice provided clear leadership in conference and together with his clerks wrote the opinion for the Court. On May 17, 1954, a unanimous Court announced that in the field of education separate but equal was no longer permissible. The chief justice described how *Plessy* had dealt with transportation and not education and reviewed the impact segregation had on education. Warren read aloud: "We come to the question presented: Does segregation of children in public schools solely on the basis of race, even though the physical facilities and other tangible factors may be equal, deprive the children of the minority group of equal educational opportunities? We unanimously believe that it does."[8]

The chief justice knew that the reference to unanimity carried with it the connotation that the Supreme Court was making an affirmative statement for the entire country to recognize.[9] The early Warren Court had different-minded justices who were strong-willed and had opposing ideologies. There was a staunch liberal wing that was juxtaposed with the more conservative members, Justice Frankfurter and Robert Jackson. There were distinct personality conflicts among the justices that, in earlier proceedings, had erupted into shouting matches. Under Chief Justice Warren's leadership this divided group agreed unanimously that the doctrine of separate but equal was inherently unequal and thus a violation of the equal protection clause of the Fourteenth Amendment. The strong leadership of Chief Justice Warren, in this important case, won the day. Justice Frankfurter, known for his personal dissatisfaction with Warren, wrote him on the day the decision was issued: "Dear Chief. This is a day that will live in glory. It's also a day in the history of the court, and not in the least for the course of deliberation which brought about the result. I congratulate you." From Justice Burton came this note: "To you goes the credit for the character of the opinion which produced the all-important unanimity. Congratulations."[10]

Under Warren, the Court directly overturned a public policy that it had created fifty-eight years earlier. Though World War II had highlighted the dangers of racist thinking, neither the executive nor the legislative branches had acted to end, in any clear manner, segregation policies. President Eisenhower never endorsed the *Brown* decision, he never advocated the correctness of it, and he warned that any concomitant violence would be in response to judicial activity for which the executive branch could not be held responsible. When the state of Arkansas directly confronted the president on the issue of school desegregation in Little Rock, he ordered action only as a last resort.

For Warren, however, the doctrine of separate but equal was inherently unfair. And the application of an unfair law could not possibly be just. The time for change had come.

Into the Political Thicket

While the Supreme Court's primary source of authority is found in the power of judicial review, a critical ancillary power rests in the Court's authority to determine what cases it hears. Before the Court can exercise its judicial power in a case, the litigant bringing the action must show damages or a threat to a legal right. Following that, the Court decides whether or not the party has standing to sue on a justiciable issue within the Court's jurisdiction.

Prior to *Baker v. Carr* (1962), the Court had imposed the barrier of the political questions doctrine against plaintiffs in reapportionment cases. Succinctly stated, the political questions doctrine denies standing to parties because the issue in question is political in nature and thereby not appropriate for judicial resolution. Chief Justice Warren felt that the application of the political questions doctrine to the issue of badly apportioned state legislatures was little more than Court "timidity."[11] Justice Frankfurter had written the opinion in the reapportionment case of *Colegrove v. Green* (1948), a 4–3 decision that less-than-decisively closed the judicial door to claims of voting fairness relative to malapportioned state legislatures. From Frankfurter's perspective, movement to decide such cases on their merit would lead the Court into a political thicket that would cause it much harm. For Warren, however, that thicket could not stand in the way of fundamental fairness, and, in pursuit of fairness, the Court created a new wave of blockbuster cases.[12]

The state of Tennessee had one of the most malapportioned legislatures in the nation. But Tennessee was not alone. Some forty states exhibited a similar situation. In Tennessee (and other locations), population had shifted from the rural areas to cities. The allocation of legislative seats did not, however, follow the population change, and instead adhered to the schematic drawn up at the beginning of the century. Despite a state constitution requirement to reapportion the legislature in line with census data, such efforts never gained legislative consent, as overrepresented rural districts clung to power. Even the districts, as they were drawn in 1901, were described as being contrary to the constitutional formula, in that the seats were allocated in an arbitrary and capricious manner. Yet, citizens, up to this point, had been told to seek relief in the legislature, not the federal courts. That relief, not surprisingly, never came, and the Warren Court decided to take up the issue.

The Tennessee case was argued and reargued in 1961. Archibald Cox, the solicitor general in the new Kennedy administration, presented the case against the state system in place, while Frankfurter was left to register a strong dissent over Justice William Brennan's majority opinion. The *Baker* opinion held that malapportionment legislature represented a denial of equal protection and was therefore justiciable. This legal reasoning clashed head-on with the ideals of Frankfurter, who lambasted the majority for overruling his plurality opinion in *Colegrove.* He noted that the Court was breaching the political questions doctrine and that the new ground it was embarking upon was tantamount to rewriting the Constitution. He further stated that the issue in the case involved the guaranty clause articulated in the Constitution, not equal protection.

Baker v. Carr represents a watershed in allowing equal protection claims to be heard by the Court when juxtaposed against the political questions doctrine. It shattered the barrier that the doctrine imposed for blacks and other urban dwellers who sought redress against state legislatures structured in a way that limited the political impact of their numbers. In the wake of *Baker,* the Court would decide *Gray v. Sanders* (1963), in which Justice William O. Douglas's opinion clearly stated the "one-person, one-vote" principle; *Wesberry v. Sanders* (1964) that extended the population equality idea to congressional districts (within, of course, the constitutional framework that provides for at least one member of Congress from each state regardless of its population size); *Reynolds v. Sims* (1964), where the Supreme Court challenged forty state legislatures to redraw boundaries for their upper, as well as their lower houses in compliance with the one-person, one-vote idea; and a host of other related cases, including *Lucas v. Colorado 44th General Assembly* (1964), that rejected the notion that a popular vote on the matter could negate the fundamental fairness issue involved.

The *Reynolds* decision was written by Warren and set to rest the various issues raised but not answered by *Baker*. The breakthrough in *Baker* was consolidated in full force in Warren's *Reynolds* opinion which, not surprisingly, fully extended his vision of fairness and justice to the mechanics of political representation.

Solicitor General Archibald Cox, Chief Justice Earl Warren, Justice William Brennan, Circuit Court of Appeals Judge David L. Bazelon, United States Attorney General Robert F. Kennedy, and a segment of constitutional scholars understood the far-reaching nature of the decision in *Baker v. Carr*. Without doubt, they understood that the decision provided for redress of grievances that had previously been denied. The door to the Court was being pried open by a new Court majority.

Cox was not a strong advocate of the one-person, one-vote principle, but he was deeply concerned with the application of equal protection of the law. Robert Kennedy was a strong advocate of the one-person, one-vote principle, in line with his insistence that the way to overcome racial strife was through the effective exercise of the franchise by blacks. Warren, Brennan, and Bazelon believed strongly in representative democracy and that the "right to vote freely for the candidate of one's choice is of the essence of a democratic society, and any restrictions on that right strike at the heart of representative government."[13]

Of course, one person's essence is another's overextension. In 2000, Warren's opinion in *Reynolds* was one of the cases cited by the Court in its *Bush v. Gore* decision to stop recounts in Florida and, thereby, hand the presidency to George W. Bush. Once opened, the doors of equal protection can accommodate a wide range of views. And Frankfurter's concern over the Court entering into the political thicket over the apportionment of state legislative seats would seem to pale in comparison to the concern voiced over the Court's leap into the bramble bush thirty-eight years later.[14] What would Warren think of this extension of his fairness doctrine?

When the Reynolds decision was handed down, writer Anthony Lewis was in the courtroom, and he passed a note to Archibald Cox asking "how it felt to be present at the second American Constitutional Convention." Cox replied, "It feels awful."[15] That might have been Warren's reply as well, if the had been asked the question on December 12, 2000.

Unlike *Brown, Baker* and its progeny played to a receptive White House administration in tune with its message. But, like *Brown*, it also produced reactions of outrage from within Congress. There were multiple efforts to overturn the decision through the constitutional amendment process, including both votes on a proposed amendment on Capitol Hill and the attempt to marshal two-thirds of the state legislatures to call for an amendment-proposing convention in line with Article V. If a very loose interpretation of what is needed to call for such a convention is followed, then this approach fell just short of the two-thirds participation required. Still, the political firestorm produced by reapportionment never generated the massive resistance that followed the Court's call to desegregate education. With reasonable speed, the states moved toward compliance with reapportionment mandates.

Despite the obvious importance of *Brown,* Warren argued that, in his view, the most important case decided by the Court during his tenure was *Baker.* Many would disagree with the chief, including Alexander Bickel, who said Warren was quite wrong in this judgment and, "His court's apportionment decisions are no significant achievement." In his review of the literature examining the actual impact of the reapportionment cases, Gerald Rosenberg follows a similar path, noting that, beyond obvious structural change produced, the reapportionment cases have had a very limited effect.[16] They provided what proved to be too little, too late. In fact, and most ironically, it is only with the Court's *per curiam* opinion in *Bush v. Gore* that new fuel can be added to support Warren's contention of the overriding importance of *Baker* and its progeny.

Conclusion

It is questionable whether Earl Warren was, in any meaningful sense, a prophet, a philosopher, or a historian—the three qualities Felix Frankfurter once listed for membership on the High Court. What Warren did possess was considerable moral character firmly rooted in the rectitude of his heritage and the ability to blend that moral sensibility with political skills and an engaging personality.

On the equality front Warren was "a dedicated leveller."[17] And it was the active pursuit of that goal which led President Eisenhower to proclaim that his selection of Warren was "the biggest damn fool mistake I ever made." Yet it was Warren's outrage at injustice and his commitment to the principle of fairness that provided the motivation for a legal revolution which was long overdue. That judge-led revolution was neither perfect nor problem-free, but it struck the chord of justice in compelling fashion, adding flesh to the outline of the Court's unique role in protecting freedom, as sketched in footnote four of the 1938 *Carolene Products* case.

Whether in matters of equal protection or reapportionment, Warren practiced the principle of justice as fairness long before John Rawls articulated the idea in philosophically sound fashion. Yet, by definition, judicial activism is a two-edged sword. In Warren's hands, the sword was used to cut away at inequity and inequality. Others would use the same sword to cut back on the advances made by the nation's fourteenth chief justice. Such is the non-Hegelian nature of constitutional law.

Through the impact produced by the Court that he led would be of great significance, the exact dimensions of that impact were not always what they first appeared to be. On the centennial of Warren's birth, seventeen years after his death from a heart attack on July 9, 1974, schools across the land continued to be marked by racial separation. The monster of *de jure* segregation had been slain in 1954, yet the courts could not effectively command *de facto* integration of public education. And on the reapportionment front, the continued population shift from central cities to the suburbs essentially negated that principle as a method of redressing the historical imbalances that had worked against urban America. These facts, however, do not erase the importance of Warren's fifteen-year stewardship of the nation's highest court and his willingness to err on the side of too much justice rather than too little.

As chief justice, he gave in to requests to head the commission investigating the assassination of President John F. Kennedy, which produced the still-debated report that carries Warren's name. While sitting members of the Supreme Court had established precedents for filling extrajudicial roles while on the bench, these activities, at best, represent a questionable practice. Warren's legacy would have been better served if he had refused the position. His legacy would also have been better served if he had kept politics out of his resignation as chief justice. In June, 1968 Warren announced his intention to resign, for reasons of health, to outgoing President Lyndon B. Johnson. The idea was that Johnson would appoint Warren's successor before leaving office. The president's nomination of Justice Abe Fortas, however, hit a snag in the Senate, where Republicans and Southern Democrats sensed that the upcoming election might send Richard Nixon to the White House. Under a cloud of controversy, the Fortas nomination for chief justice was withdrawn (and eventually he would leave his seat on the Court). Faced with the Fortas disaster, Warren withdrew his resignation and stayed on the Court until June, 1969.

Fortunately, greatness does not demand perfection. And Warren was not a perfect man. As attorney general of California he was a willing participant in the internment of Japanese-Americans during World War II—an act for which he would later express deep regret. Yet his commitment to justice was anything but shallow. While district attorney of Alameda County, Warren refused to sanction improper evidence-gathering techniques even when it came to his father's unsolved murder—to us a striking and personal example of his strong sense of propriety.

That commitment defined an era that has clearly etched its place in constitutional law. Changes in politics, policies, and personnel have occurred and that era has passed. Its import and impact, however, remain—living pieces of the fabric of the law and of the search for justice.

Just hours before he died, Warren was visited by Justices William Brennan and William O. Douglas, who informed him of the 8–0 conference vote in *United States v. Nixon* that would tell the president no man was above the law and compel him to comply with the subpoena to produce the "Watergate" tapes.[18] That must have provided a moment of joy before the final pain.

After Warren retired from the Court, at an unpublicized tribute to him at the Lincoln Memorial, newsman Eric Sevareid described the chief justice as possessing the quality that the Romans called *gravitas,* "patience, stability, weight of judgment, breadth of shoulders. It means that the strength of the few makes life possible for the many."[19] Yet, whatever the exact label selected to describe Warren, his record speaks for itself. In Henry Abraham's words, "he was the chief justice par excellence—second in institutional-leadership greatness only to John Marshall himself in the eyes of most impartial students of the Court as well as the Warren Court's legion of critics. Like Marshall he understood and utilized the tools of pervasive and persuasive leadership available to him; a genuine statesman, he knew how to bring men together, how to set a tone, and how to fashion a mood. He was a wise man and a warm, kind human being."[20] He was, after all is said and done, the chief. And while Oliver Wendell Holmes told us, "The life of the law has not been logic; it has been experience,"[21] it was Warren who continually reminded us that the experience that makes up the law must be informed by fairness to be just.

In many ways, Warren might well be seen as a "paradox," blending greatness with mediocrity.[22] Yet, there is little that is paradoxical about his vision. In his book, *A Republic, If You Can Keep It,* the chief justice writes: "Where there is injustice, we should correct it; where there is poverty, we should eliminate it; where there is corruption, we should stamp it out; where there is violence, we should punish it; where there is neglect, we should provide care; where there is war, we should restore peace; and wherever corrections are achieved we should add them permanently to our storehouse of treasures."[23] Today, the issue is not so much Warren's vision, but the nature of its permanence in the storehouse of constitutional law.

NOTES

1.   John Rawls, *A Theory of Justice* (Cambridge: Harvard University Press, 1971), 3. Also, see Rawls's *Justice as Fairness: A Restatement,* edited by Erin Kelly (Cambridge: Harvard University Press, 2001). In a 1955 essay, Warren notes that any child expresses a sense of justice "with his first judgment that this or that 'isn't fair.'" See the discussion in G. Edward White, *Earl Warren: A Public Life* (New York: Oxford University Press, 1982), 228.
2.   See Peter Irons, *A People's History of the Supreme Court* (New York: Viking, 1999), 417.
3.   For a brief discussion of this complex topic, see Norman Provizer, "Hegemony, Legitimacy and the Supreme Court," in Provizer and William Pederson (eds.), *Grassroots Constitutionalism* (Lanham, MD: University Press of America, 1988).
4.   Quoted in Jack Bass, *Unlikely Heroes* (New York: Simon and Schuster, 1981), 17.
5.   There is, of course, a vast literature on *Brown* and its companion cases from South Carolina, Virginia, and Delaware, as well as the case from the District of Columbia (decided separately, on due process grounds, as *Bolling v. Sharpe*). For the oral arguments on the case, see Leon Friedman, (ed.), *Argument, Volume One* (New York: Confucian Press, 1980). In *Alexander v. Holmes Country Board of Education* (1969), the Supreme Court finally stated that the time for "all deliberate speed" was over and ordered the desegregation of public schools.
6.   Richard Cortner, *The Apportionment Cases* (New York: Norton, 1972), 253. Also see Lucas Powe, Jr., *The Warren Court and American Politics* (Cambridge: Harvard University Press, 2000), 199–205.
7.   Malcolm Freeley and Samuel Krislov, *Constitutional Law* (Glenview, IL: Scott, Foresman, 1990), 34.
8.   *Brown v. Board of Education,* 347 US 483 (1954).
9.   Earl Warren, *The Memoirs of Chief Justice Earl Warren* (New York: Doubleday, 1977), 3.
10.   Ibid., 286.
11.   Ibid., 307–308.

12.   Bernard Swartz, *Super Chief: Earl Warren and His Supreme Court—A Judicial Biography* (New York: New York University Press, 1983), 410–430.

13.   From Warren's opinion in *Reynolds v. Sims,* 377 US 533 (1964).

14.   While the Court in *Bush v. Gore II* (December 12, 2000) used the equal protection clause as the basis for its decision, it included the rather astonishing statement that its ruling was "limited to the present circumstances, for the problem of equal protection in election processes generally presents many complexities." On the Bush-Carr connection, notes former Attorney General Griffin Bell's comment: "I do not deny that the federal courts have jurisdiction to vindicate rights under the United States Constitution in the context of elections for federal office—that has been settled since 1962 when the Supreme Court first adopted the principle of one person, one vote in *Baker v. Carr*" (from "Counting the Vote: Stop This Litigation," *Wall Street Journal,* Nov. 14, 2000 (A26). Also, see E.J. Dionne, Jr., and William Kristol, eds., *Bush v. Gore: The Court Cases and Commentary* (Washington, DC: Brookings Institution Press, 2001).

15.   Quoted in Powe, Jr., 252. See note 6. Also, see Archibald Cox's balanced comments on the appointment cases in his *The Warren Court: Constitutional Decision as an Instrument of Reform* (Cambridge: Harvard University Press, 1968), 114–134. Cox, who expresses confidence that the Warren Court will be judged overall as "in keeping with the mainstream of American history," also notes, "Only history will know whether the Warren Court has struck the balance right" (133).

16.   Gerald Rosenberg, *The Hollow Hope* (Chicago: University of Chicago Press, 1993), 196–302. Bickel's quote is from "The Supreme Court and Reapportionment" in Nelson Polsby, (ed.), *Reapportionment in the 1970s* (Berkeley: University of California Press), 58.

17.   E. Digby Baltzell and Howard Schneiderman, "From Rags to Robes," in *Social Science and Modern Society,* vol. 28, no. 4 (May/June 1991): 527.

18.   Ed Cray, *Chief Justice: A Biography of Earl Warren* (New York: Simon and Schuster, 1997), 526.

19.   Quoted in Cray, 515. See note 18. Warren, of course, had little regard for Nixon. And Nixon supported Warren's appointment to the Supreme Court as a way of eliminating him from California and national politics. That was not unlike Thomas Jefferson's view of John Marshall, relative to Virginia politics. In both cases, the results were not what had been anticipated.

20.   Henry Abraham, *Justices, Presidents, and Senators* (Lanham, MD: Rowman and Littlefield, 1999), 195.

21.   *The Common Law* (Boston: Little, Brown, 1881), 1.

22.   Jack Harrison Pollack uses the "paradox" idea in his book *Earl Warren: The Judge Who Changed America* (Englewood Cliffs, NJ: 1979), 3–14.

23.   Earl Warren, *A Republic, If You Can Keep It* (New York: Quadrangle Books, 1972) 6.

FOR FURTHER READING

Cox, Archibald. *The Warren Court: Constitutional Decision as an Instrument of Reform.* Cambridge: Harvard University Press, 1968.

Cray, Ed. *Chief Justice: A Biography of Earl Warren.* New York: Simon and Schuster, 1997.

Lewis, Anthony. "Earl Warren." Edited by Leon Friedman and Fred Israel. *The Justices of the United States Supreme Court 1789–1978,* vol. 4. New York: Chelsea House, 1980.

Pollack, Jack Harrison. *Earl Warren: The Judge Who Changed America.* Englewood Cliffs, NJ: Prentice-Hall, 1979.

Powe, Jr., Lucas. *The Warren Court and American Politics.* Cambridge: Harvard University Press, 2000.

Schwartz, Bernard. *Super Chief: Earl Warren and His Supreme Court—A Judicial Biography.* New York: New York University Pres, 1983.

Schwartz, Bernard, and Stephen Lesher. *Inside the Warren Court, 1953–1969.* New York: Doubleday, 1983.

Warren, Earl. *A Republic. If You Can Keep It.* New York: Quadrangle Books, 1972.

——— *The Memoirs of Chief Justice Earl Warren.* New York: Doubleday, 1977.

White, G. Edward. *Earl Warren: A Public Life.* New York: Oxford University Press, 1982.

CHAPTER FIFTEEN

William J. Brennan, Jr. and Human Dignity

Rodney A. Grunes

By any measure, whether length of service, institutional leadership, or the number and quality of significant opinions, Justice William J. Brennan, Jr. had an enormous impact on constitutional jurisprudence. For thirty-four terms, he was the Supreme Court's most articulate champion of freedom of expression, a strict separation of church and state, the rights of criminal defendants, and expanding equality for racial minorities, women, and the poor. Justice Brennan "so profoundly redefined the framework in which issues are discussed," explains Norman Dorsen, "that he may well be the most influential member of the Court in this century."[1]

Brennan, a Democrat, was appointed to the Supreme Court by Republican President Dwight Eisenhower in 1956. Spanning eight presidencies and three chief justices, Brennan served longer than any Brethren except colleagues William O. Douglas and Hugo Black and, from earlier years, Chief Justice John Marshall, and Justices Stephen J. Field, Joseph Story, and the first John Marshall Harlan. The most productive justice in the history of the United States apart from Douglas, Brennan wrote 425 opinions of the Court, 220 concurring opinions, 492 full or partial dissents, and 16 separate opinions prior to his retirement at the end of the 1989–90 term.

Although always the guardian of liberty, Brennan's leadership on the Court was especially apparent during the 1956–69 period when Earl Warren served as chief justice. Chief Justice Warren assigned so many significant opinions involving interpretation of the Bill of Rights to his junior colleague that many observers refer to the Warren Court as the Brennan Court.

Justice Brennan's role as the Supreme Court's leading spokesperson for the civil-libertarian creed changed after Warren's retirement. With the appointment of more conservative justices and the anti-Bill of Rights sentiments of Chief Justices Burger and Rehnquist, Brennan increasingly found himself as the leader of those justices who regularly dissented from the Court's judgment. Nevertheless, because of his exceptional coalition- building ability, Brennan continued, on occasion, to marshal majority support for his views in constitutionally significant cases. During his final term for example, Brennan spoke for the Court in upholding flag-burning and the use of minority preferences by the FCC in awarding broadcast licenses.

Regardless of political ideology, most evaluators have given Justice Brennan high marks for his accomplishments on the Supreme Court. In an assessment of all justices that served on the High Court from its creation to 1969, for example, Albert P. Blaustein and Roy M. Mersky report that a panel of sixty-five law school deans and professors of law, history, and political science ranked Brennan as a "near great" justice. More recently, commentators have called Brennan the person "who has had more profound and sustained impact upon public policy in the U.S." than any other individual, on or off the Court, over the last quarter century,[2] "the most skillful, most charming, and most intelligent advocate for his activist brand of jurisprudence,"[3] and "the most powerful and influential Supreme Court Justice in the history of the Nation."[4]

Are these evaluations accurate? Based on his record of almost thirty-four years of service, does William J. Brennan, Jr. now qualify as a "great" Supreme Court justice?

In evaluating "greatness," Blaustein and Mersky suggest that justices' majority and minority positions should be examined for "conspicuous attainments" or contributions to the development of constitutional law. Specifically, exceptional justices should possess the following qualities:

> Scholarship; legal learning analytical powers; craftsmanship and technique; wide general knowledge and learning; character, moral integrity and impartiality; diligence and industry; the ability to express oneself orally with clarity, logic and compelling force; openness to change; courage to take unpopular decisions; dedication to the Court as an institution and to the office of Supreme Court justice; ability to carry a proportionate share of the Courts' responsibility in opinion writing; and finally, the quality of statesmanship.[5]

We shall examine Justice Brennan's background, changing roles on the Supreme Court, major opinions, and impact on civil liberties and civil rights law. Finally, attention will be given to evaluations of Brennan's accomplishments by peers and scholars who have studied his contributions to the development of constitutional jurisprudence.

Background

William Joseph Brennan, Jr. was born in 1906 in Newark, New Jersey. The second of eight children of Irish-Catholic immigrant parents, Brennan was raised in a working-class neighborhood. His father, a former boiler stoker and coal heaver, became active in the labor union movement, eventually serving as a member of the Essex County Trades and Labor Council. Later, he served three terms as director of public safety and police commissioner.

As a youngster, Brennan attended a parochial grammar school and graduated from a public high school. He worked part-time making change for passengers waiting for trolley cars, delivering mail, and working in a filling station. Although not poor, Brennan was profoundly influenced by the hardships he saw. "What got me interested in people's rights and liberties," Brennan told Nat Hentoff, "was the kind of family and the kind of neighborhood I was brought up in. I saw all kinds of suffering—people had to struggle."[6]

After high school, Brennan earned a degree in economics with honors from the Wharton School of Finance and Commerce of the University of Pennsylvania. Following graduation, he married Marjorie Leonard of East Orange and entered Harvard Law School. A scholarship student, Brennan received his law degree in 1931, graduating in the top 10 percent of his class. While at Harvard, he nurtured his interest in the rights of the less fortunate by serving as president of the student legal-aid society.

But Brennan did not go into legal aid work. After graduating from Harvard, he joined and later became a partner in the large firm of Pitney, Hardin & Skinner, specializing in labor relations from a management perspective. During World War II, Brennan was an army officer assisting Secretary of War Robert B. Patterson in procurement and labor matters. He was discharged as a full colonel.

Following the war, Brennan returned to his law firm and actively participated in the movement to reform the New Jersey Constitution and its antiquated judicial article. Appearing before the judiciary committee of the constitutional convention of 1947, Brennan was instrumental in effectuating a completely reorganized court system in the state's new constitution. His work caught the attention of Republican Governor Alfred E. Driscoll, who, in 1949, appointed Brennan a judge of the superior court, a statewide tribunal of original jurisdiction. Upon the recommendation of Chief Justice Arthur T. Vanderbilt, who had been impressed by Brennan's proposals to relieve congestion and to facilitate speedier trials, Driscoll elevated Judge Brennan to the appellate division of the Superior Court in 1950 and, two years later, to the New Jersey Supreme Court.

Given his record as a moderately liberal jurist on an activist result-oriented state supreme court, Brennan must have been surprised when, on September 26, 1956, he was called to Washington, D.C. by Attorney General Brownell and informed that Republican President Dwight D. Eisenhower wanted to nominate him, a lifelong Democrat, to replace retiring Justice Sherman Minton on the U.S. Supreme Court. Yet his nomination made good political sense.

Brennan seemed to meet Eisenhower's three basic qualifications: relative youth (he was fifty at the time of selection), prior judicial experience (seven years on New Jersey courts), and strong endorsements by the American Bar Association and state bar. Equally important, Brennan's northeast

Irish background and Roman Catholicism were seen as political pluses in a presidential election year where Republican success required votes from "Eisenhower Democrats." And, he had the support of Attorney General Brownell and New Jersey Chief Justice Vanderbilt, who said that the nominee "possessed the finest 'judicial mind' that he had known."[7]

With the exception of Senator Joseph R. McCarthy, who accused the nominee of conducting "a guerilla warfare" against legislative committees investigating communism, Brennan's nomination was almost universally applauded. In addition to the New Jersey Bar Association and the A.B.A., which rated the nominee "eminently qualified," enthusiastic support came from the American Judicature Society, the Holy Name Society and other Roman Catholic organizations, the national media, and countless prominent individuals and private groups.

Brennan's response to the nomination was prompt and positive. A recess appointment, the new associate justice began his service on the Supreme Court on October 16, 1956. Confirmation hearings took place four months later, after Eisenhower's reelection and Congress's return. On March 19, 1957, the United States Senate confirmed Brennan's nomination. Only Senator Joseph McCarthy, the Republican Senator from Wisconsin, voted against confirmation.

Mr. Justice Brennan

Although President Eisenhower and other Republicans may have expected him to adopt a "middle-of-the-road" approach, Justice Brennan quickly became a reliable member of the Court's libertarian bloc. This was especially evident in cases involving First Amendment freedoms and procedural fairness. Nevertheless, he avoided the absolutism and doctrinaire liberalism of Justices Black and Douglas and sometimes, as evident in the obscenity area, was willing to limit individual freedom in search of pragmatic solutions to complex institutional problems.

He also established a special relationship with Chief Justice Earl Warren, who Brennan always called "The Chief." Reflecting their ideological and personal compatibility, Brennan began comparing notes on cases with Warren and, eventually, held weekly meetings with him, in chambers, prior to Court conferences. Not only did they agree in 89 percent of the 1400 cases they decided during their thirteen years together on the Court, but the Chief Justice often assigned Brennan the task of speaking for the Court in important cases. "In turning to Brennan," explains Owen Fiss, "Warren could be certain that the task of writing the opinion for the Court was in the hands of someone as thoroughly devoted as he was to the Court as an institution.[8]

Brennan's influence on the Court was greatest during the 1962–1969 period. Here, as the intellectual leader of a liberal activist majority, Brennan authored many of the landmark decisions associated with the Warren Court. He became the chief spokesperson for the values we associate with the Warren Court: freedom of expression, religious liberty, procedural fairness, and equality. "The overall design of the Court's position may have been the work of several minds," notes Fiss, "but it was Brennan who by and large formulated the principle, analyzed the precedents, and chose the words that transformed the ideal into law. Like many master craftsman, he left his distinctive imprint on the finished product."[9]

Justice Brennan's opinions often resulted from great behind-the-scenes skill in building and keeping majority support for his views. "On all the key issues," writes Mark Tushnet, it was Brennan who "put together the coalitions and persuaded the others."[10] A modest man, Brennan was always uneasy about accepting the title of master coalition builder. As he explained to one interviewer:

> I don't go around cajoling and importuning my colleagues to go along with my point of view. When I have been able to draw a consensus, I have done it by the drafts I circulated among my colleagues. Rather than try to talk something out with another Justice, I sit down and write concrete suggestions....I suggest changes in their drafts, and other Justices will suggest changes in what I've written.[11]

But, as former law clerk Jeffrey Leeds suggested, Justice Brennan leaves out a crucial detail. While it may be true that he didn't personally "buttonhole" his colleagues, Brennan monitored the pulse of the Court by having law clerks talk regularly with the law clerks of the other justices.

Perhaps this explains why Brennan's influence on the Supreme Court continued after the retirement of Chief Justice Earl Warren and the appointment of new and more conservative justices by Presidents Nixon and Reagan. Remarkably, few of his major Warren Court opinions were overturned by the Warren Burger– and William Rehnquist–led Supreme Courts and, at least during the 1970's, Brennan's result oriented "egalitarian activism" often prevailed in gender discrimination, reapportionment, and race-based affirmative action cases.

Increasingly, however, Brennan's views were expressed in dissenting opinions. While he averaged four dissents per term during the Warren Court period, his rate increased to more than twenty per term in cases decided during the Burger and Rehnquist Court periods. In addition to writing 433 full or partial dissenting opinions during the 1970s and 1980s, Brennan issued more than 1500 joint statements with Justice Marshall, dissenting from Court denials of *certiorari* in death penalty cases. This output has earned Brennan the distinction of being the Supreme Court's greatest dissenter.

In addition to his changing role on the Supreme Court, Brennan broke a long-standing policy and involved himself in three significant extrajudicial activities. First, in 1973, he publicly opposed the creation of a National Court of Appeals, which was proposed by the Freund Committee as a remedy to the

Supreme Court's heavy workload. Objecting to the establishment of new court which would screen cases for Supreme Court review, Brennan argued that this radical proposal would undermine the Supreme Court's "unique mission" of protective fundamental rights and assuring the uniformity of federal law.

Second, beginning with 1977 article in the *Harvard Law Review,* Brennan responded to the anti-civil-libertarian approach of the Burger Court by suggesting that Warren Court values might be maintained if state and federal courts relied more heavily on state constitutional provisions. In addition, he urged state courts to adopt higher standards than those required by the Constitution in civil liberties cases.

Finally, in what may be an unprecedented exchange, Justice Brennan publicly responded to an attack by Attorney General Edwin Meese on judicial activism and the liberalism of the Warren Court. In what became known as the "Meese-Brennan debate," though neither mentioned the other by name, Brennan denied that liberal activist justices wrote their own policy preferences into the Constitution and rejected the idea of a jurisprudence of "original intent." While conceding that the intent of the framers might be a useful starting point, Brennan emphasized that the Constitution's meaning changes over time and that judges are obligated to interpret the document in a manner that is consistent with the values of the contemporary community. As he explained to the New York City Bar Association in 1987, constitutional interpretation "demands of judges more than proficiency in logical analysis. It requires that we be sensitive to the balance of reason and passion that mark a given age, and the ways in which that balance leaves its mark on the everyday exchanges between government and citizen."[12]

Justice Brennan: Constitutional Rights and Liberties

For more than three decades, Justice Brennan remained faithful to the vision that an expansive interpretation of the Bill of Rights and Civil War amendments was necessary for the creation of a just and humane society. Underlying this vision was his core belief in the dignity of all human beings, including the powerless, and the idea that government cannot deny the fundamental rights of any individual.

Having written almost 1200 opinions during more than three decades on the Court, it is only possible to highlight Justice Brennan's most significant contributions to constitutional jurisprudence. Emphasis will be placed on a selection of noteworthy opinions in three areas: The First Amendment freedoms, the rights of the accused, and equality in American life.

The First Amendment Freedoms

Although never an absolutist, Justice Brennan consistently maintained that the power of government to restrict the exercise of First Amendment freedom is extremely narrow. Since freedom of expression is deemed necessary to the development of well-being of our democratic society, the "only considerations of the gravest urgency" can be deemed sufficient to justify federal or state intrusion. As Brennan explained in *Roth v. United States* (1957):

> The fundamental freedoms of speech and press have contributed greatly to the development and well-being of our free society and are indispensable to its continued growth....The door barring federal and state intrusion into this area cannot be left ajar; it must be kept tightly closed and opened only the lightest crack necessary to prevent encroachment upon more important interests.[13]

In addition, any governmental regulation touching on the area of freedom of expression must provide procedural safeguards against infringement of constitutionally protected rights.

From Brennan's perspective, his most important majority opinion was the one he wrote in *New York Times v. Sullivan,* the 1964 landmark decision establishing the Court's "actual malice" standard for resolving defamation claims brought by public officials concerning their official conduct. It remains good law today.

Here, L. B. Sullivan, the police commissioner of Montgomery, Alabama, had sued The *Times* for publishing an advertisement, "Heed Their Rising Voices," which contained several factually inaccurate statements. Designed to raise money for the civil rights movement, the advertisement was signed by prominent authors, actors, labor leaders, and black Southern preachers.

Although never directly mentioned by name, Sullivan contended that since he was in charge of the police at the time, the advertisement had falsely accused him of conducting "an unprecedented wave of terror" against black student demonstrators by "ringing" the Alabama State College campus with police and trying to starve the students into submission by padlocking their dining room. And it was he who was being charged with trying to intimidate Dr. Martin Luther King, Jr., by assaulting him, bombing his home, and arresting him on false charges. An Alabama jury agreed, awarding $500,000 in damages, the full amount claimed.

Writing for a unanimous Court, Justice Brennan broke new ground when, for the first time, he reversed Alabama's decision and declared that the freedom of speech and press guaranties of the First Amendment limit a state from awarding damages in libel actions brought by public officials against those who criticize their official conduct. Self-government, explained Brennan, required that "debate on public issues should be uninhibited, robust, and wide-open" and that this could not be assured by leaving libel controversies, as they had in the past, to the common law and procedures of each individual state.

Most important, Brennan articulated a constitutional standard which continues to be used in resolving defamation disputes. Suggesting the need to distinguish between unintentional and malicious misstatements, Brennan stated that a public official is prohibited "from recovering damages for a defamatory falsehood relating to his official conduct unless he proves that the statement was made with 'actual malice'—that is, with knowledge that it was false or with reckless disregard of whether it was false or not."[14]

The "actual malice" standard has become institutionalized. Brennan himself has suggested that it applied to criminal libel actions and to seditious libel, thus rendering unconstitutional the oppressive Alien and Sedition Acts of 1798. In later decisions, the Supreme Court extended the use of Brennan's standard to defamation cases involving public figures in general. And, as Chief Justice Rehnquist's majority opinion in *Flynt v. Falwell* (1988) demonstrates, even today's conservative Supreme Court continues to rely on the arguments and test set forth by Justice Brennan in the *New York Times v. Sullivan*.

Much less successful was Justice Brennan's attempt to find a constitutionally acceptable approach to the problem of obscenity. This was especially evident during the Warren Court period when Justice Brennan was the Court's chief spokesperson on this policy problem. Despite widespread agreement that most sexual expression was entitled to constitutional protection, Brennan was unable to maintain majority support for the approach he developed in his landmark 1957 opinion in *Roth v. United States* and the companion case of *Alberts v. California*.

Samuel Roth had been convicted for mailing obscene circulars and advertising, and an obscene book, in violation of the federal obscenity statute. David Alberts, on the other hand, was convicted for keeping obscene and indecent books for sale, and for writing, composing, and publishing an obscene advertisement of them in violation of California law.

Justice Brennan's *Roth–Alberts* opinion, the first major obscenity decision of the Supreme Court, was ambivalent and confusing, appearing to say one thing while doing another. Using very permissive and libertarian rhetoric, for example, Brennan wrote that "sex and obscenity are not synonymous," and that "all ideas having even the slightest redeeming social importance—unorthodox ideas, controversial ideas, even ideas hateful to prevailing climate of opinion" are protected under the First Amendment. Yet the Court affirmed the convictions of Roth and Alberts because obscene ideas are "utterly without redeeming social importance" and are not entitled to constitutional protection.

Having accepted a "two-tier" approach to sexual expression, Brennan proposed the following test for distinguishing between constitutionally protected artistic expression and obscenity: "whether to the average person applying contemporary standards, the dominant theme of the material taken as a whole appeals to prurient interest."[15]

Ironically, this test was intended by Brennan to be more permissive than the popularly used *Hicklin* test, which judged obscenity by the effect of isolated passages upon the minds and morals of young people. But the reliance on such vague and generally undefined terms as "average person" and "contemporary community standards" seemed to lack the precision necessary for the protection of non-obscene and "borderline" sexual expression.

Although Brennan attempted modifications of *Roth,* he never again achieved majority support for his reformulated test for determining obscenity. His only successes occurred when he accepted a "contextual" approach under which the obscenity of material was determined by the particular circumstances surrounding its dissemination or its effect upon children and other special audiences.

Demonstrating honesty and an "openness to change," Brennan abandoned his effort to define obscenity in 1973. While he continued to believe that obscenity was not entitled to constitutional protection, Brennan now conceded that obscenity could never be defined with enough clarity to provide fair notice to those who create and traffic sexual expression or to prevent the suppression of material that is entitled to First Amendment protection. As he explained in his dissent in *Paris Adult Theatre I v. Slaton*: "[A]t least in the absence of distribution to juveniles or obtrusive exposure to unconsenting adults, the First and Fourteenth Amendments prohibit the state and federal governments from attempting wholly to suppress sexually oriented materials on the basis of their allegedly 'obscene' contents.'"[16]

Although there was no single landmark decision, Justice Brennan was the Supreme Court's most consistent spokesperson for maintaining a high wall of separation between church and state, and during the Burger and Rehnquist Court periods, was its leading supporter of the *Lemon* test for resolving church-state disputes.

A devout Catholic, Brennan was the Court's chief antiestablishmentarian. Brennan's most systematic analysis on the history of the First Amendment's establishment clause and the practice of religion in American life came in what he has described as the "hardest decision" he had to make as a justice, a seventy-five page concurring opinion written in *School District of Abington Township v. Schempp* (1963) striking down state laws mandating the reading each day of at least ten verses from the Bible, without comment, and the recitation of the Lord's Prayer in the public schools.

In what may be his earliest discussion of the limitations of the "original intent" jurisprudence, Brennan argued that it was inappropriate to interpret the establishment clause solely on the basis of the eighteenth- century ideas. Given the "profound" changes that have taken place since then with respect to religious diversity and educational structure, explained Brennan, practices which might have been acceptable during the time of Madison and Jefferson might be highly offensive to both believers and nonbelievers today. Yet, even the Framers, continued Brennan, sincerely believed that "'members of the Church would be more patriotic, and the citizens of the State more religious, by keeping their respective functions entirely separate.'"

Yet Brennan was not willing, at least in 1963, to keep church and state entirely separate. By the 1980s, however, he had become a strict separationist. Showing rare judicial courage, Brennan admitted, dissenting in *Marsh v. Chambers* (1983), that he had been "wrong" in *Schempp* when he suggested that invocations before legislative bodies presented no establishment clause problems. Moreover, armed with the test established by the Court in *Lemon v. Kurtzman* (1971) to promote separation and neutrality, Brennan voted to strike down aid to parochial schools, the teaching of creationism in the schools, moment-of-silence legislation, and the placement of a nativity scene on public property.

Justice Brennan's contribution to First Amendment jurisprudence was also evident in his final years on the bench when, in *Texas v. Johnson* (1989), he spoke for a five-member majority in striking down Gregory Lee Johnson's conviction for burning an American flag while protesting outside the Republican National Convention in violation of Texas law.

Although Brennan acknowledged that the flag was a special symbol, he found Johnson's conviction inconsistent with the First Amendment. "If there is a bedrock principle underlying the First Amendment," explained Brennan, "it is that the Government may not prohibit the expression of an idea simply because society finds the idea itself offensive or disagreeable."[18]

The unpopularity of this decision led to Congress adopting the Flag Protection Act of 1989 which made it a federal crime for anyone to knowingly mutilate or deface an American flag. It was quickly challenged by Shawn Eichman, who burned an American flag to protest various aspects of American domestic and foreign policy, and by Mark Haggerty, who set fire to the flag to protest adoption of the act itself.

The following year, in *United States v. Eichman* (1990), Brennan again upheld flag burning as a constitutionally protected form of expressive conduct. In one of his last majority opinions, Justice Brennan argued that while flag burning offended many citizens, "[p]unishing desecration of the flag dilutes the very freedom that makes this emblem so revered, and worth revering."[19]

The Rights of the Accused

Although seldom the Court's major spokesperson, Justice Brennan was a loyal member of the liberal Warren Court majority which strengthened the rights of criminal defendants, brought about the *Miranda* revolution, and made virtually all of the provisions of the Bill of Rights pertaining to the criminal justice system applicable to the states through the due process clause of the Fourteenth Amendment. One example was *Malloy v. Hogan* (1964), where Brennan, writing for a five justice majority, held that the Fifth Amendment's privilege against self-incrimination was "fundamental" to the concept of ordered liberty and was therefore safeguarded against state action by the Fourteenth Amendment.

However, Justice Brennan's most significant contribution to procedural due process were his numerous dissents in death penalty cases. Believing that even the vilest criminal possessed common human dignity, Brennan spent his last fourteen years arguing that "the evolving standards of decency that mark the progress of a maturing society" would eventually result in the abolition of capital punishment.

According to Justice Thurgood Marshall, a fellow abolitionist, Justice Brennan's greatest contribution to death penalty jurisprudence was his success in imposing procedural limitations in capital punishment cases. His dissent in *McGautha v. California* (1979) is instructive, for there, Brennan disagreed with the Court's majority which had held that neither a bifurcated trial nor statutory guidelines were constitutionally required. Five years later, in *Gregg v. Georgia* (1976), Brennan's dissent became the majority view when five justices held that with proper procedural safeguards, the imposition of the death penalty did not violate the Eighth Amendment's prohibition against "cruel and unusual" punishment.

This offered little satisfaction to Brennan, who consistently held that the imposition of the death penalty, for whatever crime and under all circumstances, constituted cruel and unusual punishment. He articulated this view most systematically when concurring in *Furman v. Georgia* (1972), the short-lived Burger Court landmark decision striking down the death penalty as "cruel and unusual" punishment when procedural safeguards were absent.

William Henry Furman, a twenty-six-year-old African American with a sixth-grade education, killed a homeowner while breaking into the home at night. He shot the deceased through a closed door. Though not psychotic, Furman was diagnosed with "Mental Deficiency, Mild to Moderate."

For Brennan, the Eighth Amendment was designed to protect Furman, for it absolutely prohibited the infliction of "uncivilized and inhuman punishments." This conclusion is based on four principles: punishment by death is unusually severe and degrading; there is a strong probability that it is imposed arbitrarily, especially with respect to minorities; contemporary society has totally rejected death as a general punishment; and there is no evidence that the death penalty deters the commission other capital crimes more effectively than less severe punishment. "The function of these principles," explained Brennan, "is to enable a court to determine whether a punishment comports with human dignity. Death, quite simply, does not."[20]

Equality in American Life

While Justice Brennan was a champion of traditional civil liberties, he will also be remembered for his intellectual leadership and compassion in the area of equal protection analysis. Whether the issue was political, racial, gender, or economic equality, Brennan forcefully articulated the egalitarian ethic. On all of these issues, Justice Brennan's jurisprudence tended to favor the underdog and powerless in American society and promoted an expansive reading of the equal protection clause of the Fourteenth Amendment.

Apart from *New York Times Co. v. Sullivan,* perhaps Justice Brennan's most significant contribution to our democratic polity was his majority opinion in *Baker v. Carr* (1962). Not only did this decision provide the powerless access to federal courts, but it also led directly to the reapportionment revolution and the establishment of the "one person, one vote" principle.

At issue in *Baker* was the failure of the Tennessee legislature to reapportion its state legislative districts as required by the state's constitution since 1901. Because of urbanization, this meant that 37 percent of Tennessee voters elected over 60 percent of the state senate and 40 percent of the voters elected 64 percent of the house members. In short, rural voters exercised disproportionate voting power at the expense of city dwellers.

Overturning the 1946 Supreme Court decision in *Colegrove v. Green,* Justice Brennan declared that Baker and other urban voters had a constitutionally guaranteed right under the equal protection clause of the Fourteenth Amendment to have the federal courts decide whether they had suffered discrimination because of Tennessee's failure to reapportion its legislature. Legislative reapportionment was not, as the *Colegrove* Court had suggested, a "political question" outside the jurisdiction of federal courts.

In later cases, Brennan insisted on good faith efforts to achieve maximum population equality in legislative apportionment cases. Moreover, as his majority opinion in *Karcher v. Daggett* (1983) indicated, attainment of absolute equality was also required in congressional redistricting under the "equal representation" requirement of Article 1, of the Constitution.

Justice Brennan was also a powerful voice for racial equality, especially in school desegregation and affirmative action cases. Although he came to the Court after *Brown v. Board of Education I & II* (1954 and 1955), Justice Thurgood Marshall credits Brennan's majority opinion in *Green v. School Board of New Kent County* (1968) as doing the most to restore "Brownian" values to the Fourteenth Amendment following years of Southern resistance to integration.

In *Green,* the Warren Court unanimously struck down a court's "freedom of choice" plan because it did not lead to the dismantling of the dual school system. In Brennan's view, the *Brown* decisions imposed "an affirmative duty to take whatever steps were necessary to convert to a unitary [public school] system in which racial discrimination would be eliminated root and branch."[21] Noting that the school board had taken eleven years to begin its implementation of *Brown,* Brennan concluded that the burden was on the board to come up with a plan which would disestablish the dual school system "now."

For Brennan, school desegregation extended beyond the southern systems which had been segregated by state law. In *Keyes v. School District #1 Denver* (1973), for example, he argued that when one school board intentionally seeks to segregate students on the basis of race, it can have the effect of establishing a dual school system within an entire district and requiring remedies similar to those used in the South.

The need to eradicate the lingering effects of racial discrimination also marks Justice Brennan's approach to affirmative action cases. Beginning with *Regents of the University of California v. Bakke* (1978), Brennan not only was willing to use race as a "plus" in educational admissions, but sanctioned the use of racial quotas to ameliorate the effects of past societal discrimination.

Bakke, a middle-aged white male, twice applied for and was denied admission to the University of California Medical School at Davis, a state funded and federally supported institution. Applicants with significantly lower grade point averages and standardized test scores were admitted under a separate admissions program that set aside sixteen places exclusively for minority students.

Although he did not prevail on whether Bakke should be admitted or the legality of the 16-percent minority quota, Justice Brennan wrote the major defense of preferential admissions. Writing for Justices Marshall, White, and Blackmun, and joined by Justice Powell, Brennan argued that neither Title VI of the Civil Rights Act of 1964 nor the equal protection clause of the Fourteenth Amendment was intended "to bar all race conscious efforts to extend the benefits of federally financed programs to minorities who have been historically excluded from the full benefits of American life.[22]

For Brennan, even racial quotas were permissible as long as they furthered a "benign" or ameliorative purpose and, in addition, did not "stigmatize" the politically powerless in society. He used this reasoning to uphold voluntary employment quotas in *United Steelworkers v. Weber* (1979), and in *Metro Broadcasting, Inc. v. F.C.C.,* his last majority opinion, to sustain the minority preference policies of the Federal Communications Commission in the awarding of broadcast licenses.

Justice Brennan also sought to promote egalitarianism in another way: through expansion of "suspect" categories for resolution of equal protection claims. Under the Court's "two-tiered" approach, only suspect classifications such as race and alienage required the government to meet a "strict scrutiny" standard in which it had to demonstrate a "compelling" need for the dis-

crimination. Most other claims, especially those involving economic and social policy, were evaluated under the less demanding "ordinary scrutiny"
standard which required the state to demonstrate only a "rational" basis for a
chosen course of action.

In *Frontiero v. Richardson* (1973), Brennan sought, for the first time, to
extend "strict scrutiny" to gender discrimination. At issue here was a federal
law under which male members of the uniformed services automatically received extra housing and medical benefits if they had a wife, but married ser-
vicewomen had to prove that they paid more than half of their husband's
living costs to receive similar benefits.

Writing for a four justice plurality, Brennan criticized the attitude of "romantic paternalism" which placed women like Sharron Frontiero "not on a
pedestal but in a cage." In his view, classifications based on gender were
inherently suspect and the Air Force had violated equal protection by paying
lower benefits to spouses of female military officers than to those of male
officers. As Brennan explained:

> what differentiates sex from such nonsuspect statuses as intelligence or physical
> disability, and aligns with the recognized suspect criteria, that the sex characteris-
> tic frequently bears no relation to ability to perform or contribute to society. As a
> result, statutory distinctions between the sexes often have the effect of invidiously
> relegating the entire class of females to inferior legal status without regard to the
> actual capabilities of its individual members.[23]

Having failed by one vote to have gender discrimination be declared
"suspect," Brennan worked to win majority support for a standard that would
be more exacting than "ordinary scrutiny." He succeeded in *Craig v. Boren*
(1976) when six justices joined him supporting a "middle-level" approach in
which "classifications by gender must serve important governmental objectives and must be substantially related to achievement of those objectives."[24]

Finally, Justice Brennan's egalitarianism is evident in his support for the
economically disadvantaged. His majority opinion in *Goldberg v. Kelly*
(1970), one of the first cases to recognize the rights of welfare recipients, is
representative. Here, writing for a six-justice majority, Brennan found that
the due process clause of the Fourteenth Amendment required that welfare
recipients be afforded the right to an evidentiary hearing prior to the termina-
tion of benefits. "The opportunity to be heard," explained Brennan, "must be
tailored to the capacities and circumstances of those who are to be
heard...."[25] Since most welfare recipients lacked sufficient education to write
effectively or obtain professional assistance, only a personal appearance with
the opportunity to confront and cross-examine government witnesses would
protect the rights of poor people who might have no means of survival if
benefits were terminated.

Justice Brennan: An Assessment

By every standard of measurement, former Justice Byron R. White is certainly correct when he observes that William J. Brennan, Jr. "will surely be remembered as among the greatest Justices who have ever sat on the Supreme Court. And well he should be."[26] A prodigious and bright scholar, Brennan participated in more than one-quarter of the cases decided by the Supreme Court in this century and wrote more eloquent and significant opinions than anybody else. Many markedly changed the nation's constitutional and statutory landscape.

While many of Brennan's major contributions have been highlighted above, his overall impact on the law is truly extraordinary. As Nat Hentoff has written, he "greatly expanded and deepened First Amendment rights for the press, for teachers, for students, for book publishers, for moviemakers and for civil rights organizations."[27] In addition, he broadened the rights of the accused, helped assure equal protection for minorities, women, and the less fortunate, and consistently advanced the vision that law is an instrument of "civilizing change." As Court of Appeals Judge Abner J. Mikva has observed, Brennan's "greatest attribute of all was his unshakable belief that one could sit on the highest court, wrestle with the most complex and consequential issues, and still never forget that doing justice was the name of the game."[28]

In doing justice, Brennan wrote exceptionally well-crafted opinions. Whether for the Court, concurring, or dissenting, his opinions have been praised for their clear articulation, reason, logic, meticulous scholarship, choice of language, eloquence, dignity, civility, and passion. A master coalition builder, Justice Brennan was both a persuasive advocate and a careful listener. But he also was willing to admit mistakes and change his mind, as he did with obscenity and church-state cases. This took some courage since his views on these issues, as well as the death penalty and affirmative action were directly contrary to American public opinion. Also, Brennan, a devoutly religious Roman Catholic, was one of the Court's most vigorous supporters of a woman's right to reproductive freedom.

In advocating an expansive Constitution and unpopular opinions, Justice Brennan has been criticized for "over-reaching" and engaging in judicial policy-making. Colleague Byron White disagrees, arguing that Brennan "was absolutely dedicated to the Court as an institution and realized that the Court should not overstep its legitimate role...." But being an honest and caring statesman, suggests White, Brennan often thought, especially during his later years, that the Court's majority "had a far too narrow view of [its] function in this modern world."[29]

What distinguished Justice Brennan's statesmanship was his consistent vision of the proper judicial function. As Thurgood Marshall, another Brennan colleague has explained, "what so distinguished Justice Brennan was his faithfulness to a consistent legal vision of how the Constitution would be interpreted. That vision was based on an unwavering commitment to certain core principles, especially First Amendment freedoms and basic principles of civil rights and civil liberties."[30]

But greatness also involves moral integrity. Both supporters and critics of Brennan's jurisprudence acknowledge that he possessed unusual personal qualities. He has been described as loving, caring, warm, generous, good-hearted, honest, kind, and beloved. As Richard A. Posner, a former Brennan law clerk and current judge on the Court of Appeals for the Seventh Circuit, has observed, "[h]is career has been a triumph of character."[31]

Already assessed "near great" in 1969, it seems likely that history will confirm that Justice William J. Brennan, Jr. was one of the Supreme Court's most remarkable and influential justices and entitled to included among those classified as "great." As John J. Gibbons, the Seton Hall Law professor from Brennan's home state of New Jersey, has concluded: Justice Brennan "'appears far more humane than Holmes, broader in outlook than Brandeis, more practical and flexible than Black, a finer scholar than Warren, more eloquent than Hughes, more painstaking than any of them. He appears, in other words, as the most outstanding justice of the century....'"[32]

NOTES

1. Quoted in Nat Henthoff, "Profiles: The Constitutionalist," 66 *The New Yorker*: (March 12, 1990), 45.
2. Stephen J. Markham and Alfred S. Regnery, AThe Mind of Justice Brennan: A Two Year Tribute," 36 *National Review* (May 18, 1984): 30.
3. Norman Dorsen, "A Tribute to Justice William J. Brennan, Jr.," 104 *Harvard Law Review* 15 (1990): n. 1, quoting Bruce Fein and William Bradford Reynolds, described as "two Reagan Justice Department officials who had long disagreed with Justice Brennan."
4. Nat Hentoff, "The Justice Breaks His Silence," 38 *Playboy* (July 1991): 120.
5. Quoted in Henry J. Abraham, *Justices and Presidents*, 2nd edition, (New York: Oxford University Press, 1985), 10.
6. Hentoff, 46. See note 1.
7. Henry J. Abraham, 262. See note 5.
8. Owen Fiss, "A Life Lived Twice," 100 *The Yale Law Journal* (1991): 1117, 1119.
9. Ibid.
10. Linda Greenhouse, "An Activist's Legacy," *New York Times* (July 22, 1990): 1.
11. Hentoff, 59. See note 1.
12. Greenhouse, 16. See note 10.
13. 354 U.S. 476, 488 (1957).
14. *New York Times Co. v. Sullivan,* 376 U.S. 254, 279–280 (1964).
15. *Roth v. United States, supra,* at 489.
16. 413 U.S. 49, 112–113 (1973).

17. *School District of Abington Township v. Schempp,* 374 U.S. 203, 304 (1963).
18. *Texas v. Johnson,* 491 U.S. 397, 414 (1989).
19. *U.S. v. Eichman,* 496 U.S. 310, 319 (1990).
20. *Furman v. Georgia,* 408 U.S. 238, 305 (1972).
21. *Green v. School Board of New Kent County,* 391 U.S. 430, 438 (1968).
22. *Regents of the University of California v. Bakke,* 438 U.S. 265, 328 (1978).
23. *Frontiero v. Richardson,* 411 U.S. 677, 686–687 (1973).
24. 429 U.S. 190, 197 (1976).
25. *Goldberg v. Kelly,* 397 U.S. 254, 268–269 (1970)
26. White, *The Yale Law Review,* 1113.
27. Hentoff, 121. See note 4.
28. Abner J. Mikva, "A Tribute to Justice William J. Brennan, Jr.," 104 *Harvard Law Review* (1990): 9, 12.
29. White, *The Yale Law Journal,* 1116.
30. Thurgood Marshall, "A Tribute to Justice William J. Brennan, Jr.," 104 *Harvard Law Review* (1990): 1–2.
31. Richard A. Posner, "A Tribute to Justice William J. Brennan, Jr.," 104 *Harvard Law Review* (1990): 13–14.
32. John J. Gibbons, "Tribute to Justice Brennan," 74 *Judicature* (February–March 1991): 242.

FOR FURTHER READING

Grunes, Rodney and Jon Veen. "Justice Brennan, Catholicism, and the Establishment Clause." *University of San Francisco Law Review,* vol. 35 (Spring 2001): 527–563.
Hopkins, W. Wat. *Mr. Justice Brennan and Freedom of Expression.* New York: Praeger, 1991.
Marion, David E. *The Jurisprudence of Justice William J. Brennan, Jr.: The Law and Politics of "Libertarian Dignity."*

CHAPTER SIXTEEN

William H. Rehnquist and the Conservative Counterrevolution

Barbara A. Perry

When one of young William Rehnquist's elementary-school teachers asked him what he wanted to do when he grew up, he responded, "I'm going to change the government."[1] How prescient the future chief justice was! If the Supreme Court after 1937 presided over an accretion of power to the federal government, and if the Warren Court precipitated a revolution in civil rights and liberties in the 1950s and 1960s, William Rehnquist has steadfastly opposed both of those previous movements in constitutional jurisprudence and has led a counterrevolution against them. The Rehnquist revolution has played out slowly but steadily over his entire thirty-year career on the nation's highest tribunal. In his early years as an associate justice, appointed by Richard Nixon in 1972, Rehnquist was so often in solo dissent from more liberal Court opinions that he earned the moniker, "The Lone Ranger." His clerks presented him with a small figure of the erstwhile cowboy hero, which Rehnquist proudly displayed on the mantel of his chambers at the Court. Even after his promotion to chief justice by Ronald Reagan in 1986, Rehnquist had to bide his time while the superb marshaler of the Court, Justice William J. Brennan, often produced five-person liberal majorities. But with the liberal bloc on the Court decimated by the retirements of Brennan, Thurgood Marshall, and Harry Blackmun between 1990 and 1994, Rehnquist's opportunity to implement at least part of his conservative judicial philosophy finally presented itself.

Yet the Rehnquist Court has failed to roll back completely—indeed the Court has sometimes affirmed—the precedents of the Warren and Burger eras. Abortion is still legal, with some limits on access to the procedure; organized, state-sponsored prayer in public schools remains unlawful, but the wall between religion and public education is not unbreachable; free, exercise-of-religion claims have been upheld, but not if general secular laws impinge on those claims only incidentally; affirmative action programs can exist but now must meet the highest level of judicial scrutiny; majority-minority voting districts are also subject to such strict analysis; gender classifications trigger a slightly lower standard of scrutiny but generally have been nullified, except in the disparate treatment of males and females by the draft laws; gender preference has not been afforded protection under privacy rights or special status through the Fourteenth Amendment, but gays earned one victory even under the lowest level of Equal-Protection-Clause analysis; criminal rights have been diluted (except for the famed "Miranda rights"), especially in the search-and-seizure category, and death sentences are now more difficult to appeal from state to federal courts; indeed, national prerogatives, particularly when embodied in statutes passed under Congress's interstate commerce power, have generally been weakened to the benefit of state power (except in a few instances, such as term limits on members of Congress); and the office of the presidency has not fared well at the bar of the high court, with invalidation of the line-item veto, upholding of the independent counsel statute, and rejection of presidential immunity from civil suits.

Rehnquist's revolution has not come to complete fruition for a host of reasons related to the context in which the Supreme Court operates. The current ideological composition of the Court, for example, tends to produce highly nuanced opinions that avoid clear-cut extremes. Jurisprudential and ideological labels are imprecise at best, but most observers agree on general categories and descriptions of the current justices' voting postures. From right to left on the political spectrum, Justices Antonin Scalia and Clarence Thomas are considered the most conservative, with the former committed to a text-based, originalist understanding of the Constitution. Chief Justice Rehnquist is a lifelong conservative who pays considerable deference to federalism and the democratic legislative process. In the category of centrist-moderate-conservative "swing voters" are Justices Anthony Kennedy and Sandra Day O'Connor. Kennedy prides himself on his considered, sometimes agonizing, case-by-case approach to decisions. Although O'Connor struggles to find the middle ground on vexing issues of race and abortion, she sides with the more liberal position in gender discrimination cases, but will often switch to the conservative stance in her votes favoring state governments.

No liberals in the William Brennan or Thurgood Marshall image remain on the Court, but Justice David Souter has begun following in the footsteps of his late friend, Justice Brennan. Justices Souter, John Paul Stevens, Ruth Bader Ginsburg, and Stephen Breyer often side as a liberal bloc, and, if they can attract a fifth vote (usually O'Connor or Kennedy), will win the case. Justices Ginsburg and Breyer are usually deemed moderate liberals for their reluctance to impose broad standards even when they reach liberal decisions. With his unique vision of the law, Justice Stevens's maverick approach repeatedly obliges him to write solo dissents or concurrences.

Obviously, some of these justices, including Rehnquist, represent the ideological position that their nominating president expected. Still others, Souter and Stevens most obviously, have strayed from their appointing presidents' expectations. It is simply impossible to predict how justices will change (or be changed by) the Court's inner dynamics—jurisprudential and personal. As one astute Court observer has described the Court's current alignments: "What seems to be a 5–4 conservative majority is actually a complex pattern of shifting alliances with two centrists, O'Connor and Kennedy, usually casting the deciding votes."[2]

Perhaps William Rehnquist has stayed the ideological course throughout his professional life because his conservatism has deep roots in his upbringing. Rehnquist (the name means "mountain goat" in Swedish) is of Nordic stock. He was born on October 1, 1924, to William Benjamin and Margery Peck Rehnquist. His father, a first-generation Swedish American and paper salesman, did not attend college, but his mother was a graduate of the University of Wisconsin, where she majored in French. With her fluency in five languages, she worked as a translator for export companies in Milwaukee. Some say that the chief justice inherited his brilliance from his mother.

Young Bill and his sister, Jean, grew up in a wealthy suburb of Milwaukee, called Shorewood, in a home that their parents had bought new in 1923 shortly after their marriage. The community was unabashedly Republican in the midst of the Great Depression and FDR's New Deal. The latter was disparaged at every opportunity, and Republican leaders like Herbert Hoover, Alf Landon, and Wendell Wilkie (albeit losers in presidential politics) were lionized. Rehnquist's father was a conservative among conservatives and advocated his political views with vigor. In later years, he would rail against the welfare state. Ironically, the Rehnquists lost their house to foreclosure in 1939, and the family subsequently rented a series of houses.

The future chief justice attended public schools in Shorewood, where he was noted for his keen intellect, ability to quote Shakespeare and Winston Churchill, and encyclopedic knowledge of history. But he was not a grind; one of his close friends from his teen years recalls, "He was always phenomenal at school, and I can never remember him studying."[3]

Rehnquist graduated from high school in 1941, the summer before Pearl Harbor, and won a scholarship to Kenyon College, an all-male liberal arts institution in Gambier, Ohio. Although it had a fine reputation, it was small and isolated, and Rehnquist found the atmosphere not to his liking. He left after one quarter and joined the Army Air Corps as a weather observer. During his three-year service, he rose to the rank of sergeant and completed his tour of duty in North Africa. Photos of his last posting show him riding a camel.

Like numerous other veterans who had postponed higher education for service in World War II, Rehnquist enrolled in college on the G.I. Bill. This time he entered Stanford University and found the intellectual environment more suitable. He was elected to Phi Beta Kappa upon his graduation in 1948 with bachelor's and master's degrees in political science. During these years, Friedrick Hayek's book *The Road to Serfdom,* which argued against the welfare state, made a profound impression on the future justice. The study's thesis jibed perfectly with Rehnquist's early philosophy of government and economics. He decided to pursue another master's degree in political science, this time at Harvard. Not surprisingly, the left-leaning Ivy League campus galled him, and he escaped Harvard liberalism by returning to Stanford to pursue a law degree. He had earned a scholarship there with a score of 99.6 on the law school entrance exam.

Rehnquist's razor-sharp intellect was perfectly suited to the Socratic method. One of his fellow students recollects, "He obviously was a complete standout. When the professors got through abusing everybody and wanted the right answer, they would call on Bill."[4] His classmate, Sandra Day, who as Mrs. O'Connor would one day join him on the Supreme Court, attests to his intellectual superiority in law school. They both served as editors on the law review and graduated in 1952 with elections to the law honor society, the Order of the Coif. They even dated for a while before they each found different mates. Rehnquist married Natalie Cornell of San Diego in August, 1953.

Between graduation from law school and marriage, however, Rehnquist held the most prestigious postgraduate position a new lawyer can attain. While now virtually all Supreme Court law clerks serve one year on a lower federal court before assuming their jobs at the high tribunal, in the 1950s justices accepted newly minted law grads. While visiting Stanford to dedicate a building, Justice Robert H. Jackson interviewed Rehnquist, who had been recommended by one of his professors, an ex-Jackson clerk himself. The future justice tried to bone up on his constitutional law, but then decided that tactic was futile. He found Justice Jackson to be a very pleasant interviewer; they spent little time discussing substantive matters, however, so Rehnquist thought he had failed to secure the plum clerkship. To his surprise, he received an offer from Jackson in the fall of 1951 and was able to start in February, 1952 after his midyear graduation.

Rehnquist's own description of his first day on the job is vivid. He remembers his self-doubt over arriving halfway through the term, while all the other clerks had been on board since its beginning in October. He even despaired over his typing skills. Initially, he was fraught with concern over whether he had the expertise and wisdom to make the right recommendation to Justice Jackson regarding *certiorari* petitions. As a clerk, he was assigned to read a portion of the cases that had been appealed to the Supreme Court and make a determination on whether the case should be accepted. On his initial day, mulling over the first petition, he was tempted to put it aside until he felt more confident. Then he asked himself, "When will I know more than I do now?" As the chief justice notes, "Perhaps it is just my own way of working, but I have always preferred where possible to go through one thing from beginning to end, do what I had to do with it, and move on to the next thing."[5] To this day, that is how Rehnquist has approached his work on the Court. By his own account, his clerkship with Justice Jackson was a rewarding experience, but he later publicly criticized his fellow clerks for betraying an ideology that he described as "to the 'left' of either the nation or the Court." He also accused the majority of clerks of displaying "extreme solicitude for the claims of Communists and other criminal defendants, expansion of federal power at the expense of State power, [and] great sympathy toward any government regulation of business."[6]

Like all ex-Supreme Court clerks, Rehnquist could have had his pick of associate positions in top East or West Coast law firms, making what was then considered the princely sum of $700 a month. But quality of life has always been a chief priority for him, and he chose to go to a Phoenix law firm, Cunningham, Carson & Messinger, where the pressure would be less severe and the city a pleasant place to raise a family. Between 1955 and 1959, the Rehnquists had three children, James, Janet, and Nancy. He now enjoys telling the amusing story of how he attempted to persuade Cunningham, Carson to raise his starting salary of $300 per month by $50 in light of what he could have earned in New York or Los Angeles, but the Phoenix firm would not budge. He stayed with them for several years before hanging out a shingle with another attorney. Ultimately, Rehnquist practiced law for sixteen years in Phoenix, with a primary emphasis on civil litigation. He was also active in Arizona's Republican Party, including the presidential campaigns of Barry Goldwater and Richard Nixon. He met and impressed Richard Kleindienst, who would become attorney general in Nixon's cabinet. The contact paid off when Attorney General Kleindienst recommended Rehnquist for the position of assistant attorney general in the Department of Justice's Office of Legal Counsel. He began the job at the start of the first Nixon administration in January, 1969 and would henceforth make the Washington area his home.

At the Justice Department, Rehnquist established a visible role for himself defending the Nixon administration's legal policies before Congress. Not surprisingly, Rehnquist supported such conservative efforts as increased government wiretapping and surveillance of Americans (at the height of the anti-Vietnam War protests and the civil rights movement) and tightened limits on materials defined as obscene. Even members of Congress who disagreed with these measures found Rehnquist's defense of them to be cogent and articulate. He also argued a case before the U.S. Supreme Court in 1970, and continues to use the experience as a basis for offering advice to lawyers who might someday appear before the Court over which he now presides.

Another major duty of the assistant attorney general was the screening of possible nominees to the U.S. Supreme Court. Early on, the Nixon administration experienced a flurry of appointments to the high bench. Nixon had named Warren Burger to the chief justiceship in 1969 and Harry Blackmun to an associate's seat in 1970 (after the Senate rejected his first two nominees for the position, Clement F. Haynsworth, Jr. and G. Harold Carswell, Jr.). Within six days in September, 1971, two more justices (Hugo Black and John Marshall Harlan II) retired from the Court. Eventually, Rehnquist was told not to attend any more meetings of the screening committee at the Department of Justice—a sure sign that he was under consideration. Indeed he was, but apparently not as Nixon's first choice for the Harlan vacancy. Evidence obtained from taped Nixon conversations indicates that then-Senator Howard Baker, Jr. (R.-Tenn.) was the preferred nominee. Attorney General John Mitchell notified Baker, who had little interest in moving across the street from Congress to the third branch. While the senator from Tennessee mulled over the possible appointment at the Supreme Court with his friend, Justice Potter Stewart, the administration decided to move on to someone else—a man Nixon mistakenly called "Renchberg" and "Renchquist."

Many years later, Rehnquist chuckled over President Nixon's mangling of the Swedish surname. In retrospect, Rehnquist was not surprised that the president only knew that his name began with an R. After all, the assistant attorney general served in a subcabinet-level position in which he had met with Nixon only twice. As a law clerk, Rehnquist had briefly encountered Vice President Nixon. In the 1960 presidential campaign, Rehnquist secured hotel rooms for the Nixon campaign and met the entourage at the Phoenix airport. It was thus Rehnquist's loyal and competent service to the Nixon administration and his influential contacts in the Justice Department, rather than a close working relationship with the president, that led to Rehnquist's nomination to the high court. With just forty-eight-hours notice, the forty-seven-year-old Arizonan was nominated to the Supreme Court on October 21, 1971. In presenting Rehnquist to the national television audience, Nixon praised him as a "guardian of our Constitution...the president's lawyer's lawyer...[and] outstanding in every intellectual endeavor he has ever undertaken."[7]

Rehnquist has noted that his nomination was probably "sealed" by his Supreme Court clerkship with Justice Jackson.[8] It also precipitated a major controversy in the Senate's consideration of him. A memo, drafted by Rehnquist and discovered in Jackson's *Brown v. Board of Education* file, argued for maintenance of the "separate but equal" doctrine, the Supreme Court's 1896 creation validating racial segregation. The Rehnquist memo concluded that the Court should not void segregated public schools that were being challenged in the *Brown* litigation. When questioned about the memo in 1971, Rehnquist explained that he had merely outlined Jackson's own views on *Brown* when the justice requested such a précis for use in an upcoming conference with his colleagues. Although many senators were skeptical about Rehnquist's explanation of the memo, as well as his relative youth, lack of judicial experience, and consistent support of conservative causes, the Senate confirmed his nomination on December 10, 1971, by a vote of 68–26. He took the oath of office and joined the Supreme Court just after New Year's Day in 1972.

In a 1986 speech, Rehnquist explained that judges bring "to the bench a mind imprinted with previous experience, and that experience undoubtedly influences, to a certain extent, how we go about the process of deciding cases." Yet Rehnquist concluded that the traditional process of judging mitigates judges' "individual predilections in any given case. Judging has a large individual component in it, but the individual contribution of a good judge is filtered through the deliberative process of the court as a body...."[9]

Although Rehnquist's argument may have validity in any particular case, his own conservative views are readily apparent in the body of cases in which he has participated in more than a quarter-century on the Supreme Court. Whether writing for the majority or dissenting alone, Rehnquist has espoused widely recognized conservative viewpoints through his deference to government over individual rights, respect for legislative actions in contrast to judicial fiat, and faith in the constitutional drafters' intentions, especially regarding federalism. In his early years on the Court, for example, he publicly rejected the "living Constitution" jurisprudence advocated by his colleague Justice Brennan as a way of updating the U.S. Constitution, via judicial interpretation, to recognize modern views of human dignity. Instead, Rehnquist declared that representative government required constitutional revision through majoritarian movements that prevailed upon elected representatives (not appointed judges) to embody such changes in positive law. Article 5 in the Constitution provided for just such constitutional change through the amendment process.

In one of his most enduringly visible dissents, Justice Rehnquist was on the losing side with Justice Byron White in the 7–2 *Roe v. Wade* decision, handed down just one year after Rehnquist ascended the bench. His dissenting opinion reflects a deference to constitutional language by noting that the Court had invalidly discovered a right to abortion in the Fourteenth Amendment that was nowhere contemplated by the framers of that 1868 change in the Constitution.

Rehnquist was also in dissent in a 1979 statutory interpretation case in which Justice Brennan determined for the Court that, despite the letter of the law in the 1964 Civil Rights Act banning racial discrimination in employment, the "spirit" of the statute condoned affirmative action. Rehnquist's enraged dissent from Brennan's majority opinion in *United Steelworkers of America v. Weber,* in which the Court ruled against Weber's claim of reverse discrimination, excoriated the decision as analogous to the famous magician Harry Houdini's sleight of hand. Rehnquist, who had also voted against the University of California at Davis Medical School's affirmative-action plan in the 1978 landmark *Bakke* decision, concluded that the Court's ruling in *Weber* "introduce[d]... a tolerance for the very evil that the law was intended to eradicate, without offering even a clue as to what the limits on that tolerance may be. ...The Court has sown the wind. Later courts will face the impossible task of reaping the whirlwind" (443 US 193 [1979]).

In sex discrimination cases, Rehnquist has been reluctant to apply expanded equal-protection analysis under the Fourteenth Amendment to gender-based laws and public policy. He was once more in dissent in *Frontiero v. Richardson* (when the Court struck down in 1973 a federal law that automatically qualified male service personnel for spousal benefits but that required female personnel to show proof of dependency) and in *Craig v. Boren* (when three years later the Court invalidated an Oklahoma statute prohibiting sale of 3.2-percent beer to males under twenty-one but to females only under eighteen). Harvard Law Professor Laurence Tribe, a former Brennan clerk and advocate for liberal causes, conceded that "[e]ven in lone dissent, [Rehnquist] has helped define a new range of what is possible."[10]

In a 1980 lecture at the University of Arizona, Rehnquist defended the role of dissenting justices in the judicial process, arguing, "I simply do not think that one who reflects upon the wide range of issues which parties seek to litigate in courts today would conclude that unanimity of decision in every case is either a feasible or desirable goal."[11] Never permanently consigned to the minority, he wrote the majority opinion in the 1981 *Rostker v. Goldberg* case, in which he upheld for a 6–3 Court the Draft Registration Act of 1980 and its applicability only to males. As chief justice, though, Rehnquist departed from this consistent path in gender cases to join the Court's seven-person majority in the 1996 VMI Case, striking down the state-funded military academy's policy that banned females from enrolling. He contributed a concurrence that was narrower in its reasoning than Justice Ruth Bader Ginsburg's majority opinion.

Rehnquist's death-penalty jurisprudence exemplifies both his deference to government over individual rights and his confidence in legislative mandates, especially at the state level. In his first term on the Supreme Court, he dissented from the majority's view (albeit a splintered one expressed in an unusual *per curiam* judgment, with all nine justices filing separate opinions) that the death penalty as then carried out constituted cruel and unusual punishment in violation of the Eighth Amendment. Rehnquist urged in his dissent from the decision in *Furman v. Georgia* that democratic self-government, which had enacted death-penalty statutes in various states of the Union, was just as important as individual criminal rights. He was with the majority four years later when the Court reinstated the death penalty in *Gregg v. Georgia*. During his tenure as chief justice, Rehnquist has solidified and led a majority faction on the Court to limit state death penalty appeals in federal courts. In the 1993 case of *Herrera v. Collins,* he wrote for a six-person majority ruling that condemned prisoners who have exhausted their appeals and then produce new evidence that could prove their innocence have no right to be heard by a federal court. He also led the Court's sanctioning of the 1996 Antiterrorism and Effective Death Penalty Act, which imposed stringent limits on any federal court's consideration of a second or additional *habeas corpus* petition from a state convict. (The petition of habeas corpus, meaning literally "you have the body" in Latin, has become a procedural lifeline for death-row inmates, who use it to delay their executions.)[12]

Rehnquist's initial breakthrough victory in his crusade to right the balance between federal government and state and local governments came in the 1976 case of *National League of Cities v. Usery,* which struck down the Fair Labor Standards Act's application of federal wage and hour regulations to state employees. The Rehnquist-authored majority opinion for a narrowly split Court breathed life into the dormant Tenth Amendment, which reserves to the states powers not explicitly granted to the federal government or explicitly denied to the states. The *Usery* landmark was short-lived, however, as the Court overruled itself in 1985's *Garcia v. San Antonio Metropolitan Transit Authority.* Justice Blackmun facilitated the overturning of precedent by switching to the federal government's side, which he had eschewed in *Usery.* The Court vindicated Rehnquist's pro-federalism and pro-state posture in 1995 with its invalidation of the Gun-Free School Zones Act in *U.S. v. Lopez.* Chief Justice Rehnquist's majority opinion held that Congress had overstepped its interstate commerce power by enacting the anti-gun-possession law. He also happily joined the Scalia-led majority that struck down the "unfunded mandates" of the Brady Handgun Act, requiring states to monitor enforcement provisions of the congressional gun-control statute.

Although sitting Supreme Court justices are usually disinclined to comment publicly on laws that could come before them in the future, Rehnquist has challenged the wisdom of statutes such as the Violent Crime Control and Law Enforcement Act of 1994. The chief justice recognizes that Congress was responding to public outcries against violent criminal activity, but he is adamantly opposed to the "federalization" of criminal law, which creates federal offenses out of those acts that previously were addressed only by state criminal statutes. As Rehnquist concluded in an attack on the 1994 Crime Bill, "It remains for those of us who strongly believe in federalism—that the historic division between the proper business of the state courts and the proper business of the federal courts should be respected unless there is good reason to do otherwise—to work hard to see that the state courts do the best possible job of enforcing the laws presently on the books."[13]

Thus, in 2000, Chief Justice Rehnquist wrote the Court's opinion in *United States v. Morrison* for a 5–4 majority that invalidated a provision of the Violence Against Women Act (VAWA) that allowed victims of gender-motivated violence to sue their attackers for *civil* damages in *federal* courts. Rehnquist found no basis in either the Congress's interstate commerce or Fourteenth Amendment powers for passage of the VAWA.

Rehnquist has also crusaded on the Court for more government accommodation of religious claims in church-state cases. He was thus in dissent in *Stone v. Graham* (the 1981 decision banning a law that required the posting of the Ten Commandments in Kentucky public schools) and in *Wallace v. Jaffree* (the 1985 case invalidating a state-sponsored "moment of silence" for "meditation or voluntary prayer" in Alabama's school system). In the free-exercise-of-religion realm, Rehnquist authored a cogent analysis of the modern tension between the First Amendment's two religion clauses in his dissent from the 1981 ruling in *Thomas v. Review Board of the Indiana Employment Security Division*. He blamed the social-welfare state, application of the Bill of Rights to the states, and broad judicial interpretation of both religion clauses (none of which the framers of the First Amendment could have anticipated) for the clash between religion and government. As chief justice, Rehnquist led the 5–4 Court in *Zobrest v. Catalina School District,* a 1993 case allowing the use of public funds to pay for a sign-language interpreter to accompany a deaf child to a parochial school. The decision marked the first time a public employee was, in effect, allowed to be part of a religious school's instructional program.

Rehnquist has served as chief justice since President Reagan promoted him to the Court's center chair in 1986. (He is only the third justice to be elevated directly from associate to chief; Harlan Fiske Stone and Edward White were the other two.) To move from the title "Lone Ranger" "to chief justice" in a little over fourteen years represented a victory for both Rehnquist and the conservative movement led by the Reagan administration.

When Rehnquist's hearings began before the Republican-controlled Senate Judiciary Committee at the end of July, 1986, he made no apologies for his demonstrated conservative record on the bench and offered no hope to his critics that he would undergo an ideological conversion once installed in the Court's center chair. His most vociferous opponent, Senator Edward M. Kennedy (D.-Mass.), bolstered by support from Professor Laurence Tribe, assailed Rehnquist's "record of massive isolated dissent," concluding that he was "too extreme on race, too extreme on women's rights, too extreme on freedom of speech, too extreme on separation of church and state, too extreme to be chief justice."[14] Senator Kennedy's tirade was indicative of the bitterness that would mark the debate over Rehnquist's promotion. Critics scoured his personal and professional record for any shred of evidence that might derail the nomination. The memo supporting racial segregation which Rehnquist had written during his clerkship under Justice Jackson resurfaced; this time Rehnquist's allegedly racist views were buttressed by the revelation that the deeds to his homes in Phoenix and Vermont contained racially restrictive covenants. He was also accused of harassing black voters during the 1950s and 1960s while he was a Republican party official in Phoenix. Even his brother-in-law came forward to allege that Rehnquist had mishandled a family trust.

Nevertheless, the Judiciary Committee voted 13–5 on August 14 to recommend his nomination to the full Senate. The GOP majority in the upper house of Congress (ushered in on the coattails of Reagan's impressive win over Jimmy Carter in the 1980 presidential election) was decisive in Rehnquist's ultimate victory. After another month of bruising debate, on September 17 the Senate voted 65–33 to confirm William Hubbs Rehnquist as the sixteenth chief justice of the United States. The thirty-three negative votes represented the largest number of "nays" ever cast against a nominee who won confirmation. The day after his confirmation, Rehnquist made a rare appearance before journalists on the front plaza of the Supreme Court for a brief press conference. Described by the *Washington Post* as "characteristically amiable and acting for all the world as if nothing had happened," the newly confirmed chief justice predictably commented that he was glad the process had "run its course."[15] He was neither bitter nor smug in his reaction to the grueling battle that preceded his triumph.

On September 26, 1986, just a few days short of his sixty-second birthday, Rehnquist took two oaths of office (one at the White House and one at the Supreme Court), both administered by his immediate predecessor Chief Justice Warren Burger. The Burger era was now officially history, and the Rehnquist Court was in place, with its most junior justice, Antonin Scalia, also sworn in on the same day, in Rehnquist's vacated associate position.

As early as 1980, Rehnquist had made public some of his musings regarding the chief justice's role: "As long as the 220-odd million inhabitants of this country see fit to confide the 'judicial power of the United States' to 'one Supreme Court', it is surely best that it be a collegiate court which no Chief Justice needs to, or is capable of, 'dominating' or even of 'harmonizing' by virtue of his very limited special prerogatives as compared to those of his eight colleagues."[16] Even from ideological opponents on the Court, Rehnquist received high praise for his effective and affable leadership; the late Justice Brennan, before his 1990 retirement from the bench, categorized Rehnquist as "the most all-around successful" of the three chief justices under whom he had served.[17] (Earl Warren and Warren Burger were the other two.) Rehnquist runs a tight ship in private conferences with his colleagues, reportedly letting them speak their minds but keeping the discussion of cases on a narrow course. In public oral-argument sessions he is a dour presider, forcing counsel to stay directly on point and occasionally declaring, "The spectators are admonished to remain silent while the Court is in session!" He once vehemently chastised an attorney for giving opposite answers to the same question posed by two different justices. When the floundering lawyer apologetically said he did not mean "to confuse the Court," Rehnquist retorted, "You haven't so much confused us as just made us gravely wonder...how well-prepared you are for this argument." As the attorney sputtered, Rehnquist icily interrupted, "Your time has expired." The counsel, who not surprisingly went on to lose his case 9–0, later told a reporter, after Rehnquist's scathing treatment, "I felt like I dropped out of a tall cow's ass."[18]

Until his retirement in 1990, Justice Brennan used his formidable intellect and charm to marshal the five votes needed to achieve a victory for the liberal causes he championed during his thirty-four-year tenure on the high court. Chief Justice Rehnquist continued to play his previous role of dissenting when the case required a break from Brennan's expansive constitutional interpretation. In *Texas v. Johnson,* for example, Brennan wrote for the five-person majority (which he had persuaded Justices Scalia and Kennedy to join) that flag-burning as a form of political protest was protected expression under the First Amendment. The chief justice penned a bitter dissent, emphasizing the over 200-year history of the American flag's "unique position as the symbol of our Nation" and the fact that "millions of Americans regard it with an almost mystical reverence." Rehnquist argued that while "the Court's role as the final expositor of the Constitution is well established...its role as a platonic guardian...has no place in our system of government" (491 US 397 [1989]). He would have deferred to the Texas legislature's right to follow public opinion and protect the flag from desecration.

Occasionally, however, Rehnquist surprised longtime Court observers with an unpredictable vote or opinion authorship. He wrote the Court's decisions in *Meritor Savings Bank v. Vinson* (the 1986 sex discrimination claim resolved in the plaintiff's favor), *Hustler Magazine v. Falwell* (the Rev. Jerry Falwell's unsuccessful 1987 libel and emotional-distress suit against Larry Flynt's magazine for a crude ad parody of the Moral Majority's leader), *Morrison v. Olson* (the case rejecting the 1988 challenge to the independent counsel/special prosecutor law), and *Dickerson v. United States* (the 2000 decision that upheld the "Miranda rights").

Yet, in the 1990s, Rehnquist's leadership of a conservative faction on the Court helped to produce landmark rulings in cases challenging affirmative action (*Adarand v. Peña*), restricting Congress's commerce power (*United States v. Lopez*), limiting federal judicial power in school desegregation (*Missouri v. Jenkins II*), restraining death-penalty appeals from state to federal courts (*Felker v. Turpin* and *Herrera v. Collins*), reducing the number of "majority-minority" voting districts (*Shaw v. Hunt*), and elevating property rights to a higher plane of protection (*Dolan v. City of Tigard*). Neither Rehnquist nor his conservative colleagues on the Court, however, have succeeded in eliminating the right to abortion on demand or completely dismantling the wall of separation between church and state established by previous Courts.

In 1999–2000 the Supreme Court was split 5–4 in 20 cases out of the 73 signed rulings, which represented an increase in the rate (to 27.4 percent) of such closely decided cases. The most frequent winning alliance in these narrowly decided rulings was Rehnquist, O'Connor, Kennedy, Scalia, and Thomas, who voted together in 13 of those 20 cases decided by a one-vote margin.[19]

On a poignant note, the chief justice, who lost his wife in 1991 after a long battle with cancer, wrote for a unanimous Court in two 1997 cases (*Washington v. Glucksberg* and *Vacco v. Quill*) that there is no constitutional right to physician-assisted suicide. "The Chief," as Court employees refer to their boss, has remained a widower. For several years after his wife's death, and perhaps also because of his chronically painful back condition, he was far less animated in his public appearances. Yet since undergoing successful back surgery in 1995, his comedic timing and warm smile have returned to brighten his speeches. Some observers maintain that had his spouse survived, Rehnquist might have considered resigning from the Court to share retirement with her.

Instead, at seventy-six years of age in mid-2001, he was showing no signs of leaving the high bench. Remaining active through swimming, walking, and tennis, he seems to have overcome his back problem. He continues to play poker and bridge and enjoys listening to and attending operas. In 1995 he affixed a set of four metallic gold stripes to each arm of his black robe. Rehnquist confirmed that he patterned the decoration after the lord chancellor's costume in the Gilbert and Sullivan operetta *Iolanthe*.

In 2001 he appeared on televised interviews for PBS and C-SPAN to discuss his updated book, *The Supreme Court*. An amateur historian, the chief justice has written previous books on subjects ranging from impeachment to the Supreme Court during World War II. The former topic undoubtedly helped him to prepare for one of the sternest challenges of his long career—presiding over the 1999 impeachment trial of Bill Clinton in the United States Senate, as the Constitution requires the chief justice to do when the House impeaches the president.

Now in his twenty-ninth year on the Court, he had been (up to 1999) probably the least well-known, most powerful official in the federal government. The chief justice, who has so assiduously opposed cameras in his courtroom, then suddenly found himself on television daily during Clinton's Senate trial. Though he attained new celebrity as a result of that historic event, Rehnquist's influential conservative jurisprudence had already guaranteed his place in the history books as an agent of change in American government and society. Whether history will judge those changes, and their catalyst, as "great" remains to be seen. The label will, no doubt, depend on the ideological eye of the beholder. What is certain, however, is that young Bill Rehnquist's elementary school wish "to change the government" has indeed been fulfilled.

NOTES

1. Quoted in George Lardner, Jr., and Saundra Saperstein, "Chief Justice-Designate Sought to Redirect U.S.," *Washington Post* (July 6, 1986): A1.
2. Stuart Taylor, "The Supreme Question," *Newsweek* (10 July 2000): 21.
3. Quoted in Lardner and Saperstein, A12. See note 1.
4. Ibid., A12.
5. William H. Rehnquist, *The Supreme Court: How It Was, How It Is* (New York: Quill, 1987), 38.
6. William H. Rehnquist, "Who Writes Decisions of the Supreme Court?" *U.S. News & World Report* (December 13, 1957): 75.
7. Quoted in George Lardner, Jr., "Rehnquist Got Call That Baker Missed for Nixon Court Nomination," *Washington Post* (December 18, 1998): A6.
8. Personal interview, Washington, DC, September 24, 1985.
9. William H. Rehnquist, "Remarks on the Process of Judging," *Washington and Lee Law Review* 49 (Spring 1992): 264, 270.
10. Quoted in Craig M. Bradley, "William H. Rehnquist," in *The Supreme Court Justices' Illustrated Biographies, 1789–1995*, 2nd ed., Clare Cushman (ed.), (Washington, DC: *Congressional Quarterly*, 1995), 499.
11. William H. Rehnquist, "'All Discord, Harmony Not Understood': The Performance of the Supreme Court of the United States," *Arizona Law Review* 22 (1980): 977.
12. See David J. Garrow's "The Rehnquist Years," *New York Times Magazine* (October 6, 1996): 66.
13. William H. Rehnquist, "Convocation Address, Wake Forest University," *Wake Forest Law Review* 29 (1994): 1005–1006.
14. Quoted in Barbara A. Perry and Henry J. Abraham, "The Reagan Supreme Court Appointees," in William Pederson and Norman Provizer (eds.); *Great Justices of the Supreme Court* (New York: Peter Lang, 1992), 331.
15. Al Kamen, "For Rehnquist, Aftermath of Confirmation Is Routine," *Washington Post*, (September 19, 1986): A3.
16. Rehnquist, 985. See note 11.
17. Perry and Abraham, 332. See note 14.
18. Quoted in Tony Mauro, "Invoking the Wrath of Rehnquist,"*Legal Times,* March 1995.
19. Richard Carelli, "Ideologically, Court Was Hard to Pin Down," (Louisville) *Courier-Journal* (2 July 2000): A18.

FOR FURTHER READING

Boles, Donald Edward. *Mr. Justice Rehnquist, Judicial Activist: The Early Years*. Ames: Iowa State University Press, 1987.
Davis, Sue. *Justice Rehnquist and the Constitution*. Princeton, NJ: Princeton University Press, 1989.
Rehnquist, William H. *All the Laws But One: Civil Liberties in Wartime*. New York: Knopf, 1998.
———.*Grand Inquest: The Historic Impeachments of Justice Samuel Chase and President Andrew Johnson*. New York: Morrow, 1992.
———.*The Supreme Court,* new edition. New York: Knopf, 2001.
———.*The Supreme Court: How It Was, How It Is.* New York: Quill, 1987.
Yarbrough, Tinsley E. *The Rehnquist Court and the Constitution*. New York: Oxford University Press, 2000.

CHAPTER SEVENTEEN

Justice Sandra Day O'Connor: Tall in the Saddle

Neil T. Erwin

> *There is a tide in the affairs of men,*
> *Which, taken at the flood, leads on to fortune*
> > –William Shakespeare, *Julius Caesar*
> *On the ranch, there were no children, just me and the*
> *cowboys...I grew up that way and you just have to do*
> *your job. If you do your job, they will respect you.*
> > – Justice Sandra Day O'Connor

The 2000 presidential election was decided, in the end, in the surprisingly compact courtroom of One First Street, NE, in Washington, DC. This proved beyond doubt a basic but vital lesson in American civics—the U.S. Supreme Court sits atop a critically important third branch of government that can make or break the ascension and continued power of the president of the United States.

No one understands this role better than Justice Sandra Day O'Connor, appointed by President Ronald Reagan in 1981 as the first justice in forty-two years to have served in a state elective office.[1]

She sits tall in the saddle like a sheriff in her native West, reigning in the extremes of either wing of the Court by carefully considered 5–4 swing votes and separate opinions. Day in, day out, she fulfills two of the only things she is willing to analyze about herself—she is hardworking and does her job. She indeed has achieved respect, having been named by the *New York Times* "America's Most Powerful Jurist."[2]

In an era of political polarization and media overstatement, Justice O'Connor's strength is found in the middle ground and understatement, in her careful approach to deciding cases, narrowly tailored and based upon the particular facts in the record. She rejects bright line rules and what she calls "Grand Unifying Theories."[3] She is a pragmatic leader in a time requiring pragmatism, as will be explained in this chapter.

Justice O'Connor resists any temptation for being easily labeled. Her method of maintaining her independent stance on the Supreme Court while not alienating her conservative colleagues on the bench provides a new model for flexible judicial leadership. Her decisions appear from the record to be influenced more by her character, and experience that spans all three branches of government, than by her gender.

Her greatness arises from an unflinching work ethic, dedication, and perceptive understanding of the roles she has taken on—rancher's daughter, student, lawyer, wife, mother, civic leader, legislator, and judge. Each has helped prepare her for the coming of "the tide" spoken of by Shakespeare, ultimately finding her ready and able to be the right person, of the right gender, in the right place, at the right time, for her historic position on the nation's highest court.

Her roles have been unique, many lacking a script, and include several "firsts": first female leader of an American state senate,[4] first female named to the U. S. Supreme Court. Yet these do not seem surprising, even though she has risen without the aid of the conventional "old boy's network." Why this is so requires a look at her life, which reads like an epic Western saga, filled with distinct episodes that end on tense dilemmas awaiting a solution in the next chapter.

Life on the Frontier

As one is ushered into the immense quiet of her tastefully appointed chambers in the U.S. Supreme Court, Justice O'Connor, arguably the single most powerful woman in America, immediately charms and impresses a visitor with friendly grace, erect stance, and steady gaze. She makes one feel both like relaxing and standing straighter at the same time. The first thing the justice points out is a memento that opens a vista stretching far away from this center of government. It is a framed newspaper headline, from what passes for the closest thing to a hometown of the rancher's daughter, which reads, "El Pasoan Named to Supreme Court."

Justice O'Connor's story is one of the Western frontier, whose independence and limitless boundaries have held a place in the American myth from Daniel Boone and Abraham Lincoln to Walt Disney. Sandra Day O'Connor, so often referred to as the "first woman who...," is the genuine article. That American states*men* for generations have attempted to identify themselves with the West that was her own is one of the ironies of her rise to the pinnacle of the establishment.[5]

Sandra Day's childhood was spent in one of the most remote corners of America's "empty quarter" on the Arizona-New Mexico border. Home was her family's 200,000-acre Lazy B ranch, which sits on 640 acres of homestead land and the rest under perpetual lease from the U.S. government.[6] (The nearest town is Duncan, Arizona, 35 miles away, current population 662.) Started in

1880 with an investment in 5,000 head of cattle by Justice O'Connor's grandfather, the ranch was run by the justice's father, Harry Day, who had to abandon his plans for an education at Stanford University at eighteen when his father died unexpectedly.

Harry and Ada Mae Day, the justice's parents, were avid readers. Ada Mae, a graduate of the University of Arizona, brought the outside world to the ranch through subscriptions to publications like *National Geographic,* the *Los Angeles Times, The Saturday Evening Post,* and *Vogue,* which were read aloud to the innately curious Sandra.[7] Born in 1930 and an only child until she was eight, Sandra learned to shoot a gun and drive a truck by seven, doing chores alongside the ranch hands.

The experience of growing up on the ranch in a virtually all-male society molded the future justice's orientation toward hard work, and getting along by just getting the job done. Probably without realizing it, Sandra Day was incorporating key accepted traits of the American male establishment—common sense, practicality, congeniality, collegiality, and lack of introspection, that would carry her far in the male-dominated legal and political world of her time.[8] It would be uncharacteristic of her to see such things about herself since she admits, "I'm not good at self-analysis."[9]

Realizing that their daughter needed more than frontier life offered, the Western saga of Sandra's life turned to a new episode as her parents sent her at age five to El Paso (where she had been born) to stay with her grandmother, Mamie Wilkey, and attend the exclusive Radford School for Girls. Fighting homesickness, Sandra spent the remainder of her school years in El Paso. She gave in only during eagerly awaited summers on the ranch and by spending the eighth grade close to home in Lordsburg, New Mexico. (The justice and her brother, Alan Day, have written a memoir about their experiences on the ranch.)

Her grandmother's household included boarders of engineers and brakemen from the nearby train station. Justice O'Connor recalls that it never was quiet. "I always said that the reason I became a judge was that I learned as a child how to just listen and still get my work done," she remembers.[10] An admittedly shy child, Sandra had the benefit of the complete confidence of her grandmother, who told Sandra regularly that she "could just do anything." Sandra graduated from high school in El Paso at sixteen, having switched to public school, and started college at that young age. By then, she had spent the majority of her life away from her parents' home.

It was perhaps inevitable that Sandra Day would attend Stanford University, fulfilling her father's interrupted college dream. She made the most of it, finishing work on her major in economics in three years and using what would have been her senior year to start class work at Stanford Law School.[11] Her college mentor and inspiration for a legal education was Professor Harry J. Rathbun, who taught undergraduate business law.

Professor Rathbun's theme, which Sandra took to heart, was that "each of us as students could make a difference in the world. That we had that capacity. We could go out and help make the world a better place. And he wanted us all to do it. I'd never met anybody like him. I'd never heard anything like that." It was her mentor's legal background that Sandra found so effective. "He just seemed able to make sense out of everything."[12] Professor Rathbun also stressed the importance of family to the survival of society, and that the inequality of women was a great waste.[13]

Despite her early admission to law school, the future justice excelled there and she loved it. She was one of 5 women in her law school class of 150. It was a time when few women were admitted to any law school, and some, like Harvard Law School, accepted no female students. She was remembered by a classmate as someone who "use[d] time better than anyone else I know" and as having "remarkable powers of concentration."[14] She graduated third in her class, with her classmate and future Chief Justice William Rehnquist (whom she dated for a time) finishing first. She also began to date a fellow law student, John O'Connor, her future husband.

Upon law school graduation in 1952, her Western epic took another dramatic turn. Instead of breezing into a major law firm, or even a Supreme Court clerkship (as her classmate William Rehnquist did), as would have been expected with her stellar record, the future Justice O'Connor found no offers with any law firm to which she applied. The reason: none hired women attorneys. She did have one job offer from a law firm, as a legal secretary. (Another irony is the fact that a partner in that firm, William French Smith, as President Ronald Reagan's attorney general, later interviewed Sandra Day O'Connor for her Supreme Court appointment.)

The next episode is typical of Sandra Day O'Connor. Instead of giving up or leaving the law, she simply found a different solution, taking the first of her public sector jobs as deputy county attorney in San Mateo County, California. Recalling her application letter for the position, she candidly admitted, "If I received that letter from a young law clerk, I'd have thrown it out. I'd say she is obviously a nut. I poured out my whole life story. I really wanted that job."[15]

What had she learned from the experience? The "realization that opportunities [for women] were limited."[16] Not that she didn't make the most of it. Looking back she thought "it was a wonderful job. I think that in public employment one often gets more responsibility earlier than one does in the private sector. It influenced the balance of my life because it demonstrated how much I did enjoy public service."[17]

Sandra followed the advice of her college mentor, Professor Rathbun, to "make a difference." This career step into the public sector turned out to be only the first in a series of positions of increasing professional and civic responsibility. Eventually she served in all three branches of government (a point she was proud to point out in her Supreme Court confirmation hearings and important to her mainstay legal concept of federalism), had a private law practice, and held positions of active community leadership. True to the heritage of classical Western pioneer women, Sandra Day O'Connor wore many hats simultaneously, including wife to a fellow attorney and mother of three sons.

Wife, Mother, Legislator, Judge

Pick any role in her life, and Sandra Day O'Connor played each with consummate skill. She married John O'Connor, her law school classmate, the December following her graduation. What attracted her was the fact that "he made me laugh."[18] The wedding ceremony took place at the Lazy B ranch, with guests including the governor of New Mexico.

Sandra followed her husband to Frankfurt, Germany, during his army service, with Sandra working as a civilian lawyer for the Army's Quartermaster Corps. After a three-year stint, the O'Connors considered staying in Germany, but decided to move to Phoenix, where John had been offered a position with a law firm. The move to the small but prosperous and growing state capital was prompted by the recognition "that what we wanted was a life where we had a deep involvement with our community."[19]

Involved they both became, forming social and political networks that served them well. John became president of the Maricopa County Young Republicans Club. Sandra, the organizer, worked her way up local Republican Party channels to the vice chairmanship of her legislative district, meeting in the process Senator Barry Goldwater, who became her important political mentor.[20] Sandra opened a private law practice with another young attorney. She then took a five-year hiatus from life as a full-time professional to raise her three sons and contributed her leadership skills to volunteer activities. She served on the county planning and zoning commission and became president of the Phoenix Junior League. She kept her hand in the law by serving as a volunteer Juvenile Court referee, grading bar review exams, setting up a lawyer referral system for the county bar association, doing legal work for the Salvation Army, and taking on bankruptcy trustee work.[21]

Ultimately, she decided that "after five years of scrambling it made more sense to unload all this voluntary activity and to get a paid job to have a little peace and quiet in my life."[22] She again went to work in the public legal section, this time as assistant attorney general for the state of Arizona. She recalls this as "one of the most wonderful jobs I have ever had. I just loved it."[23]

In an interview, Justice O'Connor tells the story of her return to legal practice through her nomination to the Supreme Court. She remembers that the state attorney general's office "didn't know what to do with me," so they sent her to a job that "nobody wanted," which was representing the Arizona State Hospital for the Mentally Ill. With typical energy, she first met with doctors, staff, and patients to find out what their needs were, and wound up drafting an entirely new Mental Health Code, changing the standards for commitment. She also set up a lawyer referral service for the patients. She remembers the experience with clear relish as one that was "really interesting—to try to take a miserable situation and make something of it."

She was rewarded with "some very nice assignments" such as the state welfare department, all of the legal work for the state treasurer and state auditor, and legal representation of other state boards, agencies, and commissions. "I learned about state government," she recalls. "I really knew what was happening in the state of Arizona at every level, and I had a great time. I liked the people I worked with. It was just a marvelous experience."

Given her interest in state government, it was not surprising that she accepted the invitation of the county supervisors in 1969 to fill a vacancy in the state senate for her district. Once again, she was in the right place at the right time and ready. "I had learned so much about state government, and I thought I would try this legislative business to see what I could learn there."

She was a quick student of the legislative process. Three years following her arrival in the state senate (following her appointment, she won election three times to two-year terms), she was named senate majority leader. This made her, to her knowledge, the first female leader of a American state senate. She credits her selection to the fact that she was a lawyer in a legislative body having few lawyers."And lawyers have a certain knack for identifying issues, spelling out problems, seeing issues, and using language. And that is what legislators are doing." She knew Robert's Rules of Order, how things had to move on the floor, how to run a meeting, and the workings of Arizona state government from her years in the attorney general's office.

Her immediate challenge in the Arizona State Senate was governing with a Republican majority of one. The lessons she learned were in the area of federalism that she later was to champion on the Supreme Court. She found "the issues are the same all over the country in every state and at the national level. They are all considering the same things—welfare issues, tax issues. You name it, it's the same across the board, state and nationally."

She met the challenge of forming necessary political coalitions through her skills in building good personal relationships in groups. She condenses this trait into "liking people and getting along with people....To go along, you have to get along." Her trademarks included an annual party for the entire membership of the state senate and their spouses, always featuring Mexican food. (A routine she later would follow with her court colleagues and personnel.)

While the pressures were challenging ("My telephone started ringing by 5:00 AM and [was] still ringing at 11 PM"), her reward was being able to develop and put forward the changes that she most wanted to see Arizona make. These included, reflecting her service in the state executive branch, adoption of administrative procedures to insure public notice and input, and revised mental health laws. She acted to remove gender-based discrimination by going through "Every single law in the state of Arizona," including those giving the control of the community property regime in the state to the husband and those regulating the hours that women could work. She also worked to change Arizona's system of selecting judges from election to appointment.

Her interest in the state judiciary proved prophetic and began a new episode in her Western saga. In 1974, Sandra O'Connor decided to leave the state senate and "experience the third branch of government, because I thought I' like to work in all three branches of the government."She ran and won her robe as a trial court judge on the Maricopa County Superior Court.

The future justice's initial view from the bench was hardly Olympian. "I took the bench and was scared to death....It was like presiding over a soap opera all day, every day. I was so busy." In two well-reported criminal cases, she did not blink in sentencing a twenty-year-old man to death for committing murder in exchange for a $3,300 fee, and handed down a five-to-ten-year prison sentence to a middle-class mother of two young children who pleaded guilty to passing bad checks totaling $3,500. (Judge O'Connor reportedly wept in chambers afterwards over her concern for the children).[24] Typically, she became involved in programs to improve the court system. With the help of the National Center for State Courts (of which she became chairman of the Judicial Training and Education Committee), she succeeding in reducing trial delays from five to six years to less than two years.

By this point, Sandra O'Connor was a proven vote-getter, both as a legislator and judge. Her election campaigns had a common theme—someone who was "hard working" (combined with "effective" as a legislative candidate, and "fair" as a judicial one). Obviously, in the eyes of the voters, she got the job done.

Within a couple of years of her donning the robe of a trial judge, she was approached by leaders of the Arizona Republican Party to run for governor. The question (and a cliffhanger of her saga) was whether she would say yes. She said no, even though "I thought about it very seriously," she recalls. She has not elaborated on why, though she makes the point of saying that one of the reasons she chose to make the switch from the legislative to judicial branches was her growing discomfort with the flattery that came as a natural part of the political process. "I don't think that's a healthy thing. I really don't," she firmly declares.

Instead of running for governor, she was elevated in 1979 by the Democratic governor, Bruce Babbitt, to the Arizona Court of Appeals. It is surmised by many that her appointment was motivated, at least in part, by a desire on the part of the Democratic state administration to remove its most serious opponent.[25] Her reputation was as a tough but fair judge, handling a caseload made up chiefly of worker's compensation, divorces, bankruptcies, medical malpractice, disputes over wills and commercial contracts, and appeals from criminal convictions. O'Connor, for her part, simply recalls the experience on the Court of Appeals as one she "really enjoyed," particularly for its collegiality.

A fateful encounter, along with the O'Connors' social network, then played a major role in bringing the Western saga to its last chapter. When Chief Justice Warren Burger visited Flagstaff, Arizona, in the late 1970s, John O'Connor received an invitation for the couple to join a weekend houseboat cruise on Lake Powell. It introduced Sandra and the chief justice, who seemed to bond by sitting on deck and talking about law hour upon hour.[26] Chief Justice Burger subsequently raised Sandra Day O'Connor's profile among her state judiciary colleagues through an invitation the next summer to attend a month-long international judicial conference in England as representative of the state appellate courts.[27]

Getting the Call

Ronald Reagan, while campaigning for president in Los Angeles on October 14, 1980, made a pledge aimed at increasing his poll numbers among women voters: "I am announcing today that one of the first Supreme Court vacancies in my administration will be filled by the most qualified woman I can find."[28] This promise ultimately was fulfilled, and the epic tale dramatically concluded, by President Reagan's nomination of a fellow Westerner, Sandra Day O'Connor, following a lunch meeting on July 1, 1981, to fill the seat of retiring Justice Potter Stewart.

The factors that led to the match between O'Connor and Reagan have been termed "routine," including belonging to the same party in power, sharing a political ideology, O'Connor's impressive academic credentials, her proven judicial temperament, and her strong record of public service.[29] However, the impact of the call from the Hollywood actor and former governor of California to the horseback-riding daughter of the Arizona-New Mexico-West Texas borderlands, hardly has been routine. Instead, "everything changed."[30]

To put Ronald Reagan's pledge in perspective, women were a coming wave in the legal world, and Sandra Day O'Connor was placed in a position to ride the highest crest. For instance, during the 1970s, the number of women who enrolled in the nation's law schools increased by more than *300 percent*.[31]

Prior to her nomination, Justice O'Connor recalls, "There were very few women in high-level positions in this country at either the state or the national level. Very few. Never many in the Congress of the United States. Nor many in the legislatures. Very few women judges. Not many women in law schools or other professions. Not many in the medical profession or engineering." Her nomination, "had a ripple effect around the world. Women were taken on the highest courts around the world that hadn't been before....That appointment opened so many doors for women, it's unbelievable."[32]

To fully understand Sandra Day O'Connor, one must appreciate the fact that while she is a female whose leadership is important symbolically as a matter of gender, her position arguably transcends gender. Her particular gender is a factor, but not by any means *the* factor, in her public duties as Supreme Court Justice. She downplays any gender difference, and has criticized those who attempt to analyze her thinking through the lens of gender by saying, "Asking whether women attorneys speak with a 'different voice' than men do is a question that is both dangerous and unanswerable.[33]

The character of Sandra Day O'Connor was first displayed to a wide audience at her Senate confirmation hearings. There, while she paid homage to marriage as "the hope of the world and the strength of our country,"[34] she chose to stress her own appreciation of the proper role of the judicial branch, as being "one of interpreting and applying the law, not making it."[35]

Justice O'Connor's gender-aware, but not gender-defined, leadership style either is a great irony, or a mark of great achievement, given the far different path she took to the Supreme Court than her fellow male justices. Almost all of her colleagues on the bench came from the traditional background of federal judgeships. Consider, in probably the best contrast, that William H. Rehnquist, O'Connor's classmate at Stanford Law School, personally was recommended by one of the law professors as a clerk to Justice Robert H. Jackson (for whom the professor had himself clerked).[36] Justice O'Connor, on the other hand, while attaining comparable class ranking with the future chief justice, could not get a single offer as an attorney in private practice upon graduation, much less a coveted Supreme Court clerkship.

However, Sandra Day O'Connor took advantage of the public legal positions she was able to obtain to create a background for her legislative leadership, including first female leader of a state legislature. It was the way she was raised. As Justice O'Connor vividly recalls, "On the ranch, there were no children. There were just me and the cowboys....I grew up that way and you just have to do your job."[37]

A longtime tennis player, Justice O'Connor famously instituted a daily workout program in the Supreme Court gymnasium for female staffers of the Court. People with whom she has worked over the years often comment upon her no-nonsense dedication and hard work. This was best said by Burton Barr, Speaker of the Arizona House of Representatives, with whom then-State Senator Sandra Day O'Connor worked. He colorfully observed, upon his former colleague's nomination to the Supreme Court, "With Sandra Day O'Connor, there just ain't no 'Miller Time.'"[38]

Justice O'Connor's record on the U. S. Supreme Court has been as good as her word during her confirmation hearings, which resulted in a 99–0 Senate vote in her favor. She has been an interpreter of law, not a lawmaker from the bench. Her tenure has been defined largely by a careful, fact-based, approach, as a champion of President Reagan's basic governing philosophy of federalism and the rights of states against those of the federal government.[39] Given her unique firsthand knowledge of the three branches of government, Justice O'Connor has definite ideas about the proper role of the Supreme Court as leader of the judiciary. Moreover, she has staked out an independent position of leadership on the Court by being the key swing vote in crucial 5–4 decisions, and by making powerful use of separate concurring opinions.

Key Opinions

The strength of Justice O'Connor's independent yet collegial approach is seen in the fact that she has been in the middle, often literally as the key swing vote, in the most controversial issues coming before the Supreme Court during her tenure. These include: federalism (power of the states vs. those of the federal government), race, religion, and abortion.[40] Her impact has been through her carefully narrow, fact-driven, often separate opinions. One commentator has termed these "an inventive method of behaving institutionally across the horizontal dimension of judging."[41] In other words, she has found a new way of honoring precedent while staking out individualistic positions.

Federalism

If there is one motivating goal that has defined the conservative backlash of the "Reagan Revolution" to what its supporters considered the excesses of the Earl Warren-led Supreme Court, most would agree that it would be strenuous objection to "liberal judicial activism."[42]

Therefore, it comes as a bit of a shock to many that Justice O'Connor has been a leader in the conservative activism of the William Rehnquist Court (following his elevation to chief justice in 1986). This activism is aimed at revitalizing the strength of states vis-á-vis the expanded role of the federal government arising from national economic measures to combat the Great Depression of the 1930s. The continuing legal battleground is termed "federalism."

The vigor of this conservative counterrevolution is seen in the fact that in the 200 years following ratification of the Constitution, the Supreme Court struck down only 127 federal laws. However, from 1994–2000 alone, the

Rehnquist-led Court struck down 28 federal laws, with Justice O'Connor in agreement almost 80 percent of the time.[43]

This degree of activism, contrasted with Justice O'Connor's stated limitation of the courts as being law *interpreters*, not law *makers,* has confused some commentators. One the one hand, her jurisprudence is seen as defined, to a significant degree, by her deference to the interests of government through upholding a wide range of discretion for administrative agencies.[44] At the same time, she is seen by others as "refusing to defer to Congress and the president" and "eager to second-guess the judgments of state and federal lawmakers and executives."[45]

The resolution of this dilemma lies in the fact that Justice O'Connor has approached her duties on the Court as she said she would during her confirmation hearings. There she said, in elaboration on her belief in judicial restraint and the importance of precedent: "I believe that on occasion the Court has reached changed results [by] interpreting a given provision of the Constitution based on its research as to the true meaning of that provision—based on its research on the history of that provision."[46]

Therefore, Justice O'Connor honors both judicial restraint and conservative judicial activism by taking a new look at what might have been considered as acceptable congressional power, but often finding through her historical research evidence to support her belief that this is contrary to what was intended by the Framers of the Constitution.

In 1976, before Justice O'Connor's arrival, the Supreme Court in *National League of Cities v. Usery* (426 US 833 [1976]) struck down a congressional extension of federal "minimum wage and maximum hour" laws to employees of state and local governments. It was the first occasion since 1937, spanning a period of an expanded congressional role in the national economy under the Commerce Clause, in which the Court had used the Tenth Amendment for invalidating a federal act as an infringement on the states' fundamental sovereignty.[47]

Justice O'Connor lost no time joining the conservative-led fray. In 1982, in a partial concurrence, partial dissent in a case upholding federal exemptions of some energy-generating facilities from state regulation, she asserted her argument that looking to original intent bolstered states rights. "The Court's conclusion...rests upon a fundamental misunderstanding of the role that state governments play in our federalist system....State legislative and administrative bodies are not field offices of the national bureaucracy. Nor are they think tanks to which Congress may assign problems for extended study. Instead, each State is sovereign within its own domain...."[48]

After a series of dissents, Justice O'Connor finally was able to voice her defense of federalism in a majority opinion in which she recognized the rights of "joint sovereigns" against what the Court saw as unconstitutional federal interference with a state law establishing a mandatory retirement age of seventy for state judges.[49]

This trend by the Court to curb the power of the federal government over the states, with Justice O'Connor as a vocal leader of the majority, has only grown. For instance, in 1995, the Court, surely going against the grain of Justice O'Connor's law-and-order reputation as a state court judge, struck down the Gun Free School Zones Act, which barred firearms near schools, as outside congressional power under the commerce clause.[50] In 2001, the Court barred state workers from filing employment-discrimination claims against their employers under the Americans with Disabilities Act, with Justice O'Connor again as part of the majority.[51]

Civil Rights

Justice O'Connor's position in civil rights cases has been a conservative one, but measured and, as usual, carefully fact-based. One of her best-known civil rights opinions is in the area of affirmative action, which had an impact on public contracting nationwide. In *City of Richmond v. J.A. Croson Co.* (488 US 469 [1989]), Justice O'Connor wrote for the majority in invalidating a minority contractor set-aside program. Sounding like a former state legislator, she wrote: "Classifications based on race carry a danger of stigmatic harm. Unless they are strictly reserved for remedial settings, they may in fact promote notions of racial inferiority and lead to a politics of racial hostility."

However, in 2001, Justice O'Connor parted company both with her usual allies in voting rights cases, Chief Justice Rehnquist and Justices Clarence Thomas, Antonin Scalia, and Anthony Kennedy, and her own earlier ruling to uphold the constitutionality of a near-majority black voting district in North Carolina.[52] When the district, later redrawn, first had been challenged, Justice O'Connor had rejected it, saying such districts bear "an uncomfortable resemblance to political apartheid." The new ruling found that state legislatures act within the Constitution when such voting districts, despite their apparent racial imbalance, are drawn for reasons of politics, not race.

Religion

Justice O'Connor is credited with announcing a new governing standard in religion cases under the Establishment Clause.[53] The Court's previous "Lemon test" (from *Lemon v. Kurtzman,* 403 US 602 [1971]) had found statutes touching on religion to be permissible only if, among other things, they did not "foster an excessive government entanglement with religion."

Justice O'Connor contributed her "endorsement test" as a clarification of the "Lemon" standard. Her test evaluates a statute not on the basis of governmental "entanglement" with religion, which Justice O'Connor often sees as unavoidable. Instead, her test, which arose in a case approving a crèche in a public park, is whether a statute serves as a government "endorsement" of a particular religion, or disapproval of one. She wrote: "Endorsement sends a message to nonadherents that they are outsiders, not full members of the political community, and a...message to adherents that they are insiders, favored members of the political community."[54]

Abortion

Finally, confirming the concerns of her most conservative opponents at the time of her appointment, Justice O'Connor indeed has ruled in favor of limiting, but not abolishing, the right of women to choose abortion.

Justice O'Connor initially criticized the *Roe v. Wade* trimester framework as a judicial usurpation of what should be a matter for legislative crafting. Moreover, she announced that only regulations imposing an "undue burden" on the right to choose abortion should be subject to strict judicial scrutiny (*Akron v. Akron Center for Reproductive Health,* 462 US 416 [1983]).

However, in 1992, Justice O'Connor surprised some by joining with Justices Anthony Kennedy and David Souter in reaffirming the fundamental abortion rights of *Roe v. Wade.* This is where the law has remained, influenced, in her mind, by precedent and thus becoming new precedent. (*Planned Parenthood v. Casey,* 60 LW 4795 [1992]).

Conclusion—Sheriff of the High Court

Justice O'Connor deserves her status as a "great justice" for several reasons. Number one, by being the first woman appointed to the U.S. Supreme Court, and handling her duties with grace under the pressure of unusual scrutiny, she helped eliminate barriers that initially pushed her own career on a different path from her male colleagues. She is well aware it all might have turned out differently. As she has put it, "It is important to be first, but more important not to be last."[55] Justice Ruth Bader Ginsburg took her seat on the Supreme Court in August, 1993.

Second, as a former state legislative leader, her strong opinions on federalism have carried unusual credibility and have had a major impact on what has been perhaps the defining issue of the Rehnquist Court. Her viewpoint is not the result of an inward-looking philosophy. In fact, she has a keen interest in the need for international legal standards to facilitate a global economy.

Third, by carefully "picking her targets" through siding with the conservative majority but submitting separate opinions, Justice O'Connor has established a new model for judicial leadership. She reins in both the extremes on either wing of the Court and any overreaching she may find in the Court's opinion. Her method maintains her flexibility for future cases. By keeping litigants guessing as to whether their case's particular facts will fit her reasoning in prior cases, she has maintained maximum influence with them and her fellow justices. As Justice O'Connor herself wrote, "[f]lexibility is a virtue and not a vice."[56]

Justice O'Connor, a veteran of elected office, exemplifies regal charm and a rare ability to be both accessible and admired as a role model. She has "had it all," but in layers, built one upon the other. Even if the timing of each layer was not of her own choosing, all were mastered with dedication, hard work, and good humor. If fate had kept her in the political arena, it is not difficult to envision Sandra Day O'Connor as the first female U.S. president. However, it is doubtful that given her focus on solving each problem before her and an admitted lack of introspection, both remnants of her days on the ranch, Sandra Day O'Connor ever would feel she had the time to dwell on such a question. Besides, her Court decided who would be president.

NOTES

1. Robert W. Van Sickel, *Not a Particularly Different Voice* (New York: Peter Lang, 1998), 2, 21.
2. Jeffrey Rosen, "The O'Connor Court: America's Most Powerful Jurist." *New York Times Magazine* (June 3, 2001) cover story.
3. Nancy Maveety, *Justice Sandra Day O'Connor, Strategist on the Supreme Court* (Lanham, MD: Rowman & Littlefield, 1996), 20, 129.
4. Personal interview, Washington, DC, May 2, 2001. Also, Van Sickel, 26. See note 1.
5. See, for example, Michael Knox Beran, *The Last Patrician, Bobby Kennedy and the End of American Aristocracy* (New York: St. Martin's Press, 1998), 54–55.
6. Andrea Gabor, *Einstein's Wife: Work and Marriage in the Lives of the Five Great Twentieth-Century Women* (New York: Penguin Books, 1995), 236.
7. Ibid., 241.
8. Beran, 34 See note 5. Kai Bird, *The Chairman, John J. McCloy, The Making of the American Establishment* (New York: Simon & Schuster, 1992), 17–20; Walter Isaacson and Evan Thomas, *The Wise Men* (New York: Simon & Schuster, 1986), 194195.
9. Personal interview, Washington, DC, May 2, 2001.
10. Quoted in Gabor, 244. See note 6.
11. Personal interview, Washington, DC, May 2, 2001.
12. Ibid.
13. Gabor, 247. See note 6.
14. Ibid., 248.
15. Barbara Perry, *The Supremes* (New York: Peter Lang, 1999), 43, quoting Tony Mauro, "Hugs and Wine, Life Beyond the Court," *Texas Lawyer* (May 20, 1996).
16. Quoted in Perry. See note 15.

17. Van Sickel, 24, quoting from Joan S. Marie, "Her Honor: The Rancher's Daughter," *Saturday Evening Post* (September, 1985): 44. See note 1.
18. Quoted in Gabor, 250. See note 6.
19. Ibid., 253.
20. Ibid., 258. Also, personal interview, Washington, DC, May 2, 2001.
21. Ibid.
22. Ibid.
23. And following series of quotes. Personal interview, Washington, DC, May 2, 2001.
24. Van Sickel, 28. See note 1.
25. Gabor, 273. See note 6.
26. Ibid., 274.
27. Ibid.
28. Ibid., 275.
29. Van Sickel, 14. See note 1.
30. Personal interview, Washington, DC, May 2, 2001.
31. Van Sickel, 23, from Barbara A. Perry, "Gender: A Woman's Seat?" in David O'Brien (ed.), *A Representative Supreme Court?* (New York: Greenwood Press), 118.
32. Personal interview, Washington, DC, May 2, 2001.
33. Rosen, quoting a speech by Justice O'Connor at New York University in 1991. See note 2.
34. Quoted in Gabor, 278. See note 6.
35. Quoted in Van Sickel, 1.See note 1.
36. William H. Rehnquist, *The Supreme Court* (New York: Knopf, 2001), 4–5.
37. Personal interview, Washington, DC, May 2, 2001.
38. Ibid.
39. See, for the best analysis of this philosophy, Van Sickel, including 163–164. See note 1.
40. See, as a confirmation of these categories, Stuart Taylor, Jr., "The Supreme Question," *Newsweek* (July 10, 2000): 22.
41. Maveety, 234. See note 3.
42. See, e.g., Larry D. Kramer, "No Surprise. It's an Activist Court," *New York Times* December 12, 2000.
43. Rosen, *New York Times Magazine*. See note 2.
44. Van Sickel, 63. See note 1.
45. Rosen, *New York Times*. See note 2.
46. Van Sickel, 39. See note 1.
47. Van Sickel, 82. See note 1. The case later was reversed, 5–4, over Justice O'Connor's impassioned dissent, in Garcia v. San Antonio Metropolitan Transit Authority, 469 US 528 (1985). The Tenth Amendment to the U.S. Constitution reads: "The powers not delegated to the United States by the Constitution, nor prohibited by it to the States, are reserved by the States respectively, or to the people."
48. *F.E.R.C. v. Mississippi*, 456 US 742 (1982), quoted at Van Sickel, 85.
49. *Gregory v. Ashcroft*, 501 US 452 (1991).
50. 63 LW 4343 (1995).
51. *Board of Trustees of the University of Alabama v. Garrett*, 99B1240. See note 1.
52. *Easley v. Cromartie*, (2001).
53. The Establishment Clause of the First Amendment, which continues with the Free Exercise Clause, reads: "Congress shall make no law respecting an establishment of religion, or prohibiting the free exercise thereof ...."
54. *Lynch v. Donnelly*, 465 US 668 (1984), O'Connor concurring opinion at 687–688. Quoted in Van Sickel, 135. See note 1.
55. Personal interview, Washington, DC, May 2, 2001.

56. *Capitol Square Review and Advisory Board v. Pinette,* 63 LW 4684.

FOR FURTHER READING

Huber, Peter W. *Sandra Day O'Connor: Supreme Court Justice.* New York: Chelsea House, 1990.

Maveety, Nancy. *Sandra Day O'Connor: Strategist on the Supreme Court.* Lanham, MD: Rowman and Littlefield, 1996.

CHAPTER EIGHTEEN

Why No More Giants on the Supreme Court:
The Personalities and the Times

David Schultz

> *Even if he is mediocre, there are a lot of mediocre judges and people and*
> *lawyers. They are entitled to a little representation, aren't they? We can't*
> *have all Brandeises, Cardozos, and Frankfurters, and stuff like that there.*
> —Senator Roman Hruska
> (quoted by John Anthony Maltese)

Senator Hruska may have been right after all. He may also have been predicting
the future when, in 1970, he defended G. Harold Carswell, President Richard
Nixon's appointment to the Supreme Court, by stating that even average or me-
diocre judges deserve to sit on the bench of the highest court in the country.
Despite Hruska's impassioned plea, Carswell was not appointed to the Supreme
Court, but instead became in some circles a testament to the average. Yet
Carswell's nomination by Nixon demonstrated that not all presidential ap-
pointments to the federal judiciary are made with the aim of seeking to place
the best legal talent in the country on the United States Supreme Court. Here,
President Nixon was enraged that his previous nominee to the Supreme Court,
Clement F. Haynsworth, was not confirmed, and he nominated Carswell to
spite the Senate.

Similarly, when President George H. Bush nominated Clarence Thomas to
the Court, stating that he was the "best qualified" nominee to sit there, few took
that claim seriously. The president's aim was to replace retiring Justice Thurgood Marshall, the Court's first African-American justice, with a conservative
appointee that the Democratic-controlled Senate could not reject. He succeeded
in that aim with Thomas, an African-American who, while he may have been
the head of the Equal Employment Opportunity Commission and briefly a federal judge, was certainly not the best qualified person to be on the Supreme
Court. Yet, unlike Carswell, Thomas made it on to the bench, proving his critics
correct regarding his conservativism and deficient legal skills.[1] Mediocrity
might have finally been given its representation.

The Thomas and Carswell nominations demonstrate that the aim of presidents in making appointments to the Supreme Court is not always to place on it
the best legal talent in America. Instead, the aim, not just recently but through-

out history, is often to serve other political goals. President Eisenhower appointed Earl Warren because he owed him a political favor stemming from the latter's withdrawal of a challenge to Eisenhower for the 1952 Republican nomination for president. Similarly, William Brennan was selected for the Supreme Court by Eisenhower because the president felt he needed to appoint a northeastern Catholic judge to shore up political support. Yet, in the case of Warren and Brennan, some rankings list one or both among the greats to have been on the Supreme Court. One could go on, but the point has been made: the prospect of greatness, be it judicial or intellectual—is seldom the main reason why people are picked for the Supreme Court. To many, this is disturbing.

As one looks at recent appointments to the Supreme Court, no giants stand out. Some suggest that perhaps Chief Justice William Rehnquist, or Justices Sandra Day O'Connor or Antonin Scalia, might qualify for greatness, but it is unlikely. Similarly, the prospect that in the near future a John Marshall, or a Louis Brandeis, or a Benjamin Cardozo will make it to the Court is also dim. But why?

This chapter contends that there are several reasons why there are no more giants on the Supreme Court. To support that contention, a definition of greatness will be offered and then an explanation will be given as to why such greatness has not been present in the performance of recent nominees, and why the prospects for greatness are unlikely in the near future. Briefly stated, the argument will be that the main reason is that no one really wants them on the Court.

What Makes a Great Justice Great?

If beauty is in the eye of the beholder, might the same be said about greatness among justices? One person's definition of greatness might well be another's mediocrity. Proof of that might reside in the numerous studies or polls over time that have scaled, evaluated, or otherwise categorized members of the Supreme Court.

Robert Bradley's chapter in this book provides a wonderful review of efforts to distill who are the great justices. For example, in 1964, George Currie used overall ability, prophetic vision, and judicial statesmanship to produce his all-star nine-person Court. Bernard Schwartz's 1979 list ranked justices by their use of their judicial role, length of tenure on the Court, and the time period when they occupied the bench. Blaustein and Mersky's 1972 survey of law school deans and professors of law, history, and political science also produced a list of greats, although no criteria for the rankings was provided. Hambleton's list of greats is a compilation based upon other studies to rank justices, presumably making inclusion on one or more previous lists a criterion for selection. Finally, even Bradley himself ranks the great justices, with names suggested from previous surveys and criteria for inclusion ranging from writing ability and leadership, to another dozen factors. With all these surveys, polls, and selection criteria, one might conclude that determination of greatness is totally subjective and idiosyncratic.

Yet, despite the different scales, there is a convergence of opinion regarding who the greats are. John Marshall, Oliver Wendell Holmes, Jr., Benjamin Cardozo, Louis Brandeis, and Joseph Story, among a few others, repeatedly find their way onto everyone's list. What quality do they share? Essentially, two characteristics mark a justice as great. First, a great justice is one who creates a new paradigm for him or herself, the Court, or the law. Second, a great justice is one who is an entrepreneur, successfully seeking to persuade others on Court, in government, and in society to adopt a particular perspective on the law.

The idea of a justice creating a new paradigm can be traced back to Thomas Kuhn's 1962 book, *The Structure of Scientific Revolutions*. In that book, Kuhn sought to explain how scientific knowledge is acquired. The traditional view of science, according to Kuhn, is that knowledge is a cumulative and gradual process. New scientific knowledge or facts are built upon what is already known. Scientific knowledge is thus progressive, proceeding in a linear movement where new knowledge is based upon discoveries that build upon old facts about the world. Yet Kuhn argues that scientific knowledge does not really proceed that way. Instead, there are times when scientific knowledge confronts a crisis. These crises occur when a prevailing theory about the world, such as the belief in the sixteenth century that the earth was the center of the universe, have difficulty accounting for certain facts or observations. At this point, scientists are forced to abandon their old beliefs and adopt a new perspective on the world. Thus, when the astronomer Nicholas Copernicus had difficulty predicting the orbit of the other planets based on the assumption that the earth was at the center of the solar system, he proposed to explain their orbit by assuming that the sun was at the center and all the planets, including the earth, revolve around it.

This shift in perspective by Copernicus is what Kuhn calls the creation of a new scientific paradigm. A scientific paradigm has two qualities. First, it entails a scientific achievement sufficiently unprecedented to attract an enduring group of supporters from competing scientific activity. Second, a paradigm is open-ended, allowing for discovery and serving as a useful means for problem solving. A scientific paradigm is a way of seeing the world. It helps define what are relevant facts, how to structure and organize information, and how to solve present and future problems. In short, a new paradigm allows for new ways to understand and resolve old problems. In the case of Copernicus, his new model of the universe with the sun at the center made it easier to predict the movement of planets. Overall, according to Kuhn, scientific progress is not simply linear; it is occasionally marked by paradigm shifts, or bumps in the road, which force scientists to change their views on the world.

Kuhn's notion of a paradigm is also useful in explaining judicial behavior. A justice who creates a new paradigm seeks to define a new role for him or herself, the Court, or legal doctrine in a time of change and uncertainty or crisis. It is, for example, an effort to define what is the proper role for a justice— mere interpreter of the law, or creative definer of the law, as was John Marshall. It also includes redefinition of the role the Court in society, as exemplified by John Marshall in *Marbury v. Madison* (1803), which stated that the Court has the power and duty to declare void laws that are contrary to the Constitution. Or it includes justices such as Hugo Black, Louis Brandeis, or Oliver Wendell Holmes, Jr., redefining the relationship between the government and the individual, leading to the application of the Bill of Rights to state activity and the general expansion of individual rights and freedoms in society. It also includes Earl Warren's leadership in *Brown v. Board of Education* (1954) moving the Court to take a leadership role in society to end racial segregation and discrimination. Finally, the creation of a new paradigm occurs at a time of social or legal crisis, change, or uncertainty, necessitating a new legal doctrine or role for the Court to resolve that crisis. Hence, during the 1930s and in the height of the Depression, when President Roosevelt was experimenting with the New Deal programs as a way to resuscitate the economy, the Supreme Court struck down many of these efforts as unconstitutional. Yet new justices such as Felix Frankfurter, Hugo Black, and William Douglas offered a new way to rethink government power and at the same time preserve individual rights. Their solution, best captured in a case such as *United States v. Carolene Products* (1938), helped define the legal landscape for the next fifty or more years. Great justices are products of the times, and what separates them from the not-so-greats is their willingness and ability to use the Court and their role on it to define a new legal paradigm.

In addition to creating a new paradigm, a great justice also must be a successful judicial entrepreneur. According to Wayne McIntosh and Cynthia Cates, a judicial entrepreneur is one "who is alert to the opportunity for innovation, who is willing to invest the resources and assume the risks necessary to offer and develop a genuinely unique legal concept, and who must strategically employ the written word to undertake change."[2] Judicial entrepreneurs are justices who use their opinion writing, including major opinions, concurrences, and dissents, to articulate a legal vision. They may also, as in the case of Justice Brandeis, use their written word not simply to reach a holding or outcome in a case, but to seek to refashion existing legal theory so that it is acceptable to others on the Court, in government, and in society.

This means that a great justice is able to be a successful entrepreneur in the selling of a new legal paradigm. Great justices successfully sell their paradigm, or new vision of a judicial role or legal doctrine, to others on the Court, in the government, and in the nation. Thus a great justice is part legal scholar, part politician, part educator, and part public-relations person. He or she seeks to create a new way to look at the world and to fashion doctrine to adjust to that world. Blended together, what makes a justice great is creating a new legal paradigm and successfully selling it to others. That combination of skills contrasts with ordinary justices who view themselves as simple problem solvers, applying existing doctrine to the facts and seeking to obtain a total of five votes so that the outcome or holding of the case is what they want. All Justices, as Walter Murphy argued, act strategically in this way,[3] but what distinguishes strategic behavior or ordinary judicial behavior from that of great justices is that the latter not only seek to win the case, but successfully convince other members of the Court, those in government, and society in general to agree with the way they see the issue and how to resolve it.

Applying these two criteria, it is not difficult to see why some justices are great and, eventually see why many are not. For example, John Marshall deserves to be considered a great justice because he helped create the basic structure and power of the Court in *Marbury v. Madison* (1803), *Gibbons v. Ogden* (1824), *McCulloch v. Maryland* (1819), and a host of other cases that defined the general constitutional parameters of the federal government. At a time in the early republic when the status of the Supreme Court was unclear, he created the paradigm for how the Supreme Court should operate and what the Constitution means, and he was successful in convincing others on the Court, in government, and society to basically adopt his views to this day. The same is true of Joseph Story, a justice who served with Marshall for many years. Alone, Story's opinion in *Swift v. Tyson* (1842) created important law for almost one hundred years regarding when to apply state versus federal law. Similarly, his *Martin v. Hunter's Lessee* (1816) defined the scope of federal judicial review power over states. These decisions alone might make Story one of the great justices. But with Marshall, the two defined federal constitutional law in a way that all subsequent justices must address.

Oliver Wendell Holmes, Jr., and Louis Brandeis both served on the Court at a time of great social change. In the early part of the twentieth century the American economy was rapidly industrializing, and state legislatures attempted to pass legislation to regulate many of the evils associated with this change through workplace safety and minimum wage legislation. Unfortunately, in cases such as *Lochner v. New York* (1905) and *Hammer v. Dagenhart* (1918), a majority of the Court declared many of these laws unconstitutional. However, Holmes's dissent in *Lochner,* and Brandeis's opinion in *Muller v. Oregon* (1908), for example, eventually became the basis of later Court decisions upholding such legislation during the New Deal. Even to this day, the views of Holmes and Brandeis are good law.

Along with Holmes and Brandeis, Benjamin Cardozo and Hugo Black were important advocates of individual rights at a time when it was unclear what rights the Constitution really protected. Until the passage of the Fourteenth Amendment in 1896, the Bill of Rights did not apply to the individual states. This meant that states were free to pass laws limiting freedom of speech or religion, for example. In addition, not until the twentieth century did the Court really provide much guidance regarding the scope of rights that individuals had in this country. Beginning with Holmes's *Schenck v. United States* (1919) opinion and his and Brandeis dissents in *Abrams v. United States* (1919) and *Gitlow v. New York* (1925), the real incorporation or application of the Bill of Rights to the states first occurred. It was also in these cases that the modern definitions of what constitutional rights meant to individual freedom were first discussed. These opinions, along with those by Cardozo and Black, as in *Palko v. Connecticut* (1937) and the *Gideon v. Wainwright* (1963), were instrumental in providing important constitutional rights for all, including those accused of a crime.

Finally, under Earl Warren's leadership and through his opinion in *Brown v. the Board of Education* (1954) the road to dismantling segregation began. Warren took over the Court in the 1950s, a time when the issue of race and civil rights was becoming a major political debate in the country. Under his leadership the Court took an activist lead in pushing other judges, Congress, the president, and the American public to pass laws to remedy racial discrimination. Along with Justice William Brennan, the two defined the constitutional law on race that sets the paradigm for contemporary Court decisions. Finally, Brennan and Warren, in landmark decisions such as *Baker v. Carr* (1962), *Mapp v. Ohio* (1961), *Miranda v. Arizona* (1966), *New York Times v. Sullivan* (1964), and *Goldberg v. Kelley* (1970), launched legal revolutions in the areas of reapportionment, criminal due process, libel, and administrative due process, among other areas, and these decisions have similarly become the foundation for subsequent Court rulings in these areas.

All these justices wrote at a time of legal or social uncertainty, articulated a new legal paradigm, and were successful in convincing others to adopt that paradigm. This is what makes them great.

The Decline and End of Great Justices

Are there any great justices on the Court today, and what are the prospects for future great justices emerging in the near future?

Perhaps greatness is only recognized from a distance. Maybe one cannot tell who is great today by looking at present performance. One needs to see justices over their entire career and then see what happens once they leave the bench to determine if they were successful in selling a new legal paradigm. This means that evaluation of the status of current justices needs to stand the test of time before the next generation of legal scholars will perhaps be able to assess their greatness. Or perhaps the mantle of greatness is a form of myopia, and seeing greatness in justices is the wishful hoping and longing for some imaginary halcyon era that exists only in our minds. Either option is possible, but one can also apply the two criteria developed above to argue both that none of the current justices are likely to be ranked as great and that in the near future great justices will not be found on the Court.

There are several reasons why there are no more giants on the Court and why it is unlikely one will find any great justices in the near future. First, no one really wants them on the Court—at least, not the president and Congress, or the Senate.

In 1968, Richard Nixon ran for president by running against the Supreme Court. While this was not new for presidents and presidential candidates, Nixon said that if elected he would appoint justices who would use a "strict construc- tionist" reading of the Constitution. By that he might have meant several things, but among them was the argument that they would not read their own opinions into the law but instead read the Constitution according to what the Framers meant. In the case of Nixon, he sought "law and order" justices who would fa- vor limits on criminal rights as well as justices who would place limits on Court-ordered desegregation plans, including busing.

What Nixon launched was an effort to define narrowly what role justices and the Supreme Court could play in American society. He wanted to limit both the freedom of judges to interpret the law and the ability of the Court to play any role other than that of supporting the president's policy agenda. President Reagan continued that trend, again seeking to appoint, at least on the face of it, justices who would define for themselves a very narrow interpretive role and defer to Congress, the president, the bureaucracy, and the individual states. Cries of judicial activism were thrown at the Court, and individual justices such as William Brennan were attacked as engaging in legislating from the bench. Nixon, Reagan, and others were telling the Court and justices: "Scale back on what you do, especially if it runs counter to our policy preferences."

Robert Bork's 1987 failure to be confirmed as a justice by the Senate best represents this change in attitudes about the Court. Bork was described by lib- erals as so conservative that he was out of the mainstream of American law. Many Senators, liberals, and interest groups feared that he would become a conservative judicial activist and overturn many previous Court rulings. That fear was reinforced by Bork's own legal philosophy, which stated that the role of a justice and Court was to interpret the Constitution according to the intent of the Framers, and if the intent was unclear then the Court should not decide. His interpretive philosophy, along with his publicly stated opposition to civil rights laws and abortion rights, painted a picture of a justice hostile to rights.

In an effort to defend himself, Bork was unsuccessful in trying to convince the Senate that he saw a very small role for his own views to enter into interpre- tations of the Constitution and that, because of that, he did not envision that he or the Court would be activist. In effect, as a judge he would not have much impact on the law. Few believed this claim, leading even another conservative federal judge, Richard Posner, to argue that Bork was saying that justices were no more than "potted plants."

The point of all this is that starting with Nixon and Reagan, and clearly with the Bork nomination, the message has become clear—justices should not have grand visions of new paradigms about the law. It was no longer considered legitimate for members of the Court to have expansive views of the law, or to make policy, or to set policy in a way consistent with what a great justice does when creating a paradigm. Justices should simply be working as ordinary interpreters of the law, not seeking to influence Congress, the president, or the American public. In effect, the Court is asked to decide cases, not resolve causes or major issues. Given this more narrowly circumscribed role, any nominee to the high Court who looks like he or she might be seeking to develop a more paradigmatic vision would not be confirmed, let alone nominated. With that approach, the ideology of a constrained role for the Court also limits the ability of current justices to be great.

Along with the changed belief in the unacceptability of justices developing a paradigm and becoming entrepreneurs, increasingly the president is looking to Court appointees as delegates and not jurists. At a time when Congress and the president are deadlocked along partisan and ideological grounds—and this has been true for about the last twenty years—the federal courts are increasingly viewed as the place where major policy disputes such as abortion, gay rights, and criminal justice issues are resolved. In an era of divided government, presidents use the Court narrowly to fulfill a policy agenda. While presidents have done that in the past, what is new is how they use appointments and justices as political delegates placed on the Court simply to act out the president's agenda both while the president is in office and well after he has left. Presidents increasingly use "litmus tests" and issue screening to select justices. By more narrowly defining a role for justices and using them as policy proxies, the president and the Senate make it increasingly less likely that great minds and justices will reach the Court. Both of these issues significantly apply to the current Court, as well as to appointments through the Bush, and perhaps subsequent, presidential administrations.

Another reason why the future suggests no great justices can again be traced back to the failed Robert Bork nomination, which transformed the appointment and confirmation process by dramatically increasing the public scrutiny and the role of the media and interest groups in it. As a result, the appointment and confirmation process is more like an election or like a normal congressional policy-making process where there are many avenues for groups and the news industry to influence the issues debated and, more importantly, to use the threat of public exposure or conflict to defeat a nomination. Thus, candidates for the Supreme Court who have had significant visible "paper trails,"—

that is, a record that demonstrates any hint of a paradigm—are surely going to be tough to confirm. Mediocre candidates, those without either any real weaknesses or strengths, are easier to confirm. Perhaps even a Carswell could now make it on to the top Court! Justices are thus picked for popularity and acceptability, not brilliance.

Finally, justices to be confirmed in the future, are the products of a legal education that is vastly different from that provided for lawyers before World War II, when legal education was less technical than it is now. Legal education then included clerking with lawyers, more discussion of public policy issues, and, in general, an approach to the law that was more worldly and which saw the laws and lawyers as connected to the world beyond the courtroom. Legal education was, perhaps, more liberal arts-oriented, and that approach fostered a broader perspective of the law that kindled the conditions that make paradigmatic visions more likely.

Increasingly since World War II, legal education is confined to the law school. Law school has become more like a trade school, fostering a more narrow vision of what lawyers should do and what role they play in society. This narrow focus on the "black letter" of the law does not encourage a view that supports development of a larger and creative vision of law and society that is characteristic of great justices of the past. Educated in this environment, it is unlikely that future justices will come to the bench capable or, more importantly, willing to develop a paradigmatic vision required of great justices. They, too, will view themselves in a diminished role, seeking to simply resolve cases, not causes.

Evaluating the Rehnquist Court

Finally, are there any potential great justices on the Rehnquist Court? The simple answer is no, for several reasons.

First, all of the current justices on the Rehnquist Court from 1986 to 2001 were appointed since Nixon became president. This means all of them are operating under the constraint of being justices at a time when there is a diminished expectation or stated desire for them and the Court to engage in major jurisprudence or legal thinking. It is just not acceptable for them, at least on the face of it, to engage in broad policy pronouncements or to otherwise act in a way that it looks like they are challenging the new limited role for the judiciary. As a result, the opinions are less likely to make bold statements because such statements need to be draped in the language of restraint. Along with that, collectively the Court does not officially view itself as legitimately having an activist role in society, thereby also lessening any individual justice's reach towards greatness. In short, the current justices are not being permitted or greatness. In short, the current justices are not being permitted or encouraged to be great, even if they so desired.

Second, a majority of the justices were appointed after Bork and are a product of the new post-1987 confirmation process. They made it to the Court less because of their fine minds and more because they were simply confirmable. This is not to imply that these justices are idiots, but instead to suggest that an important reason for their being on the Court is that they were deemed acceptable and that they would be worthy delegates for the president who nominated them. Third, all of the current justices are products of a post-World War II legal education, developing their minds more in a technical and less in a liberal arts sense.

In addition to these three reasons, one can also cite a host of other factors as to why none of the current justices are great. For example, one can look to the issues that the Rehnquist Court is articulating or developing. Neither the Court nor any of the justices are developing a new legal paradigm but instead are operating out of old ones. Justice O'Connor's efforts to champion federalism are simply a rehashing of failed legal theories that have been around since the early days of the Republic. In the late nineteenth and early twentieth centuries, states' rights and federalism were important rallying cries for limiting federal power and racial intolerance. For the most part, her views and that of the Court are merely a rehashing of those old doctrines. Even in rehashing federalism, though, she is more of a technician or a tinkerer than one articulating a global vision.[4]

Efforts by Chief Justice Rehnquist and his Court to limit criminal rights, protect private property, or otherwise scale back individual rights are also not new. For one, Rehnquist Court opinions are forced to react to precedents set by the New Deal and the Warren Court and instead of rejecting them the Court has either trimmed the decisions at the edges or, as in the case of *Dickerson v. United States* (2000) (here reaffirming the constitutional requirement that defendants be read their *Miranda* warnings at the time of custodial arrest) or *Saenz v. Roe* (1999) (upholding the 1968 *Shapiro v. Thompson* decision that struck down a one-year residency requirement to qualify for welfare benefits), it has surprisingly reaffirmed older Warren Court precedents, although perhaps with new arguments. Moreover, the Rehnquist Court has not created a new paradigm to resolve old problems. One can still talk of the Court and its opinions as prochoice or prolife, pro or anti gay rights, and for or against criminal rights, affirmative action, civil rights, and so on. Instead of redefining these issues into a new legal paradigm that would perhaps resolve these conflicts, the Court remains bogged down in the same legal categories, concepts, and debates that they inherited.

Individually, there are reasons to think that some justices on the Rehnquist Court could have been great but will fail to be so. Antonin Scalia, often heralded for his intellect, will not be ranked as great for several reasons. First, his inability to work with other justices, specifically his capacity to alienate others, is a sure sign that he is unable to convince anyone besides Clarence Thomas to consistently agree with him. If a great justice is a successful legal entrepreneur, Scalia has failed on this score. Second, Scalia does not have a new and original vision of law and society that would suggest he is creating a new paradigm. He is operating out of concepts and theories inherited from the New Deal, with occasional appeals back to pre-New Deal theories regarding delegation and separation of powers.[5] His views, while interesting, are derivative.

Justice Ruth Bader Ginsburg was a pioneering litigator during the later 1960s and early 1970s in the areas of women's rights. She won five of six cases she argued before the Supreme Court, including *Reed v. Reed* (1971), and *Craig v. Boren* (1976). For that accomplishment alone she deserves some nod to greatness, since she was successful in extending the civil rights revolution to women and in convincing the Court to hold that distinctions based on sex or gender deserved heightened constitutional scrutiny. Yet as a Supreme Court member she has made no further innovations in this area and has not offered in her opinions a sense of a new paradigm to extend the women's rights revolution beyond where it is today. Morever, while she came to her Senate confirmation hearing with a significant paper trail, her record on the DC Court of Appeals was sufficiently moderate that it overcame her earlier role as a women's rights advocate.

Finally, Justices Kennedy, Breyer, Souter, and Stevens are all competent lawyers and jurists. But in their opinions one does not see efforts to build a paradigm. With Kennedy and Souter described as swing justices, they are looking to navigate compromises in the legal middle that, while acceptable to many, have not necessarily won over a majority of the Court. For example, their concurrence in *Planned Parenthood v. Casey* (1992) along with O'Connor was important in reaffirming *Roe v. Wade* (1973) and a woman's right to abortion, yet their reasons failed to win over the over six justices on the Court, and abortion rights remain contested on the highest Court, and in the nation. Furthermore, despite the occasional appearance at being moderate, O'Connor and Kennedy are clearly conservatives. Only Souter seems to be a surprise, gravitating towards a moderately liberal or left of center voting record. Yet with none of them is there a basic paradigm being articulated.

John Paul Stevens was appointed by President Ford to replace liberal Justice William O. Douglas. Stevens has surprised many by gravitating towards the liberal wing of the Court, but his liberalism is in comparison to a Court otherwise conservative and, except for a few decisions, his lasting fame will not be as a great justice who persuaded others to follow him but as either a semireliable liberal vote for Brennan or as a lone voice on the Rehnquist Court. Finally, Stephen Breyer came to the Court with an academic record that urged a rethinking of regulatory law, but so far there is no evidence that his views have effected a revolution in this or other areas of the law.

Conclusion

There are no giants on the Supreme Court today and the prospect is that for the foreseeable future that will remain true. Many structural and ideological forces are at work that make it difficult for a new giant to emerge, or for any of the current justices to rise to that level.

There is cause to be concerned by the absence of greatness on the Supreme Court. In part, the Court's legitimacy rests with the belief that those who sit on it are among the best legal minds in the nation. A Court that is merely competent, or even mediocre, promotes the belief that the decisions that it produces are the product not of genius but of petty partisan politics. In part, the criticism in December 2000 when the Supreme Court ruled 5–4 along ideological grounds that the Florida vote could not continue, stemmed from the fact that politics and not the law was the basis of its decision. Justice Scalia's concurrence in the initial decision to halt the recount, stating that he had five votes to prevail, simply heightened that suspicion.

A great justice—one seeking to articulate a new paradigm and convincing others to adopt it—provides leadership and direction on the Court that is not based (or does not look like it is based) simply upon raw ideology. Great justices provide ways out of difficult legal problems, they find new solutions to old problems, and they can guide the Court and the nation into a new direction. Lacking such a justice, the Court is rudderless.

Is it possible to change structural conditions such that great justices can yet again emerge? Maybe, but the prospects are daunting, and often not good. For example, some propose closing the confirmation process so that it is less political, but that solution would be undemocratic. The current format for considering nominations is not necessarily good, but it has opened up the process of government and changed the nature of the confirmation process, and that is good. Citizens have a right to know who sits on the bench. Closing the process would not encourage more support for the Court, but only undermine its legitimacy.

Perhaps the best way to again guarantee that great justices will sit on the Court is to make people want them to be there again. Until such time as the Supreme Court is again recognized as a third equal branch in the federal government and justices are agreed to have a legitimate role in interpreting the law, protecting individual rights, and influencing the policy process, it is unlikely that the conditions will be present for greatness to flourish.

Until such time, Senator Hruska may be correct about the Supreme Court: "We can't have all Brandeises, Cardozos and Frankfurters, and stuff like that there."

NOTES

Thanks go to Joyce A. Baugh at Eastern Michigan University who read an earlier version of this chapter and offered many thoughtful comments.

1. Christopher E. Smith and Joyce A. Baugh, *The Real Clarence Thomas: Confirmation Veracity Meets Performance Reality* (New York: Peter Lang, 2000), 19.
2. Wayne C. McIntosh and Cynthia L. Cates, *Judicial Entrepreneurship: The Role of the Judge in the Marketplace of Ideas* (Westport, CT: Greenwood Press, 1997), 5.
3. Walter F. Murphy, *Elements of Judicial Strategy* (Chicago: University of Chicago Press, 1964).
4. Robert W. Van Sickel, *Not a Particularly Different Voice: The Jurisprudence of Sandra Day O'Connor* (New York: Peter Lang, 1998), 175.
5. David A. Schultz and Christopher E. Smith, *The Jurisprudential Vision of Justice Antonin Scalia* (Lanham, MD: Rowman & Littlefield, 1996), 208.

FOR FURTHER READING

Abraham, Henry J. *Justices and Presidents: A Political History of Appointments to the Supreme Court.* New York: Oxford University Press, 1992.

Blaustein, Albert P., and Mersky, Roy M. "Rating Supreme Court Justices." *American Bar Association Journal* 58 (1972): 1183–89.

Gottlieb, Stephen E. *Morality Imposed: The Rehnquist Court and Liberty in America.* New York: New York University Press, 2000.

Hambleton, James E. "The All-Time All-Star All-Era Supreme Court." *American Bar Association Journal* 69 (1983): 462–64.

Maltese, John Anthony. *The Selling of Supreme Court Nominees.* Baltimore, MD: Johns Hopkins University Press, 1995.

McIntosh, Wayne C., and Cynthia L. Cates. *Judicial Entrepreneurship: The Role of the Judge in the Marketplace of Ideas.* Westport, CT: Greenwood Press, 1997.

Schultz, David A., and Christopher E. Smith. *The Jurisprudential Vision of Justice Antonin Scalia.* Lanham, MD: Rowman & Littlefield, 1996.

Schwartz, Bernard. *The New Right and the Constitution: Turning Back the Legal Clock.* Boston: Northeastern University Press, 1990.

Smith, Christopher E., and Joyce A. Baugh. *The Real Clarence Thomas: Confirmation Veracity Meets Performance Reality.* New York: Peter Lang, 2000.

CONTRIBUTORS

Henry J. Abraham is the James Hart Professor of Government and Foreign Affairs, Emeritus, at the University of Virginia.

Danny M. Adkison is an associate professor of political science at Oklahoma State University.

Robert C. Bradley is a professor of political science at Illinois State University.

Dennis J. Coyle is associate professor of political science at the Catholic University of America.

James Chowning Davies is professor emeritus of political science at the University of Oregon.

Neil T. Erwin is a lawyer in Shreveport, Louisiana and chair of the Louisiana Endowment for the Humanities.

Sherman G. Finesilver is a retired Federal District Court chief judge from Colorado.

Rodney A. Grunes is a professor and the chair of the history and political science department at Centenary College of Louisiana.

William D. Pederson is a professor of political science and the American Studies chair in Liberal Arts at Louisiana State University in Shreveport.

Barbara A. Perry is the Carter Glass professor of government at Sweet Briar College in Virginia.

Norman W. Provizer is a professor of political Science at Metropolitan State College of Denver.

Linda Przybyszewski is an associate professor of history at the University of Cincinnati.

David Schultz is a professor of political science in the Graduate School of Public Administration and Management at Hamline University.

Stephen K. Shaw is professor of political science and the dean of Arts, Humanities, and Social Sciences at Northwest Nazarene University.

James B. Staab is an associate professor of political science at Central Missouri State University.

Theodore M. Vestal is professor of political science at Oklahoma State University.

Joseph D. Vigil is an instructor of political science at Metropolitan State College of Denver.

John R. Vile is a professor and the political science department chair at Middle Tennessee State University.

Frank W. Williams is the Chief Justice of the Supreme Court of Rhode Island.

INDEX

A

A Republic, If You Can Keep It, 212
Aaron, Henry, 79
Abraham, Henry, ix, 132, 187, 211, 275
Abrams v. United States (1919), 3, 267
Adams, John, 23, 27, 30, 32, 158
Adams, John Quincy, 37
Adamson v. California (1947), 136–137
Adarand v. Peña, 240
Adkison, Danny, 35, 275
Agricultural Adjustment Act of 1933, 113, 186, 194
Akron v. Akron Center for Reproductive Health (1983), 258
A.L.A. Schechter Poultry Corp. v. United States (1935), 114, 186
Alabama State College, 221
Alberts, David, 222
Alberts v. California (1957), 222
Alien and Sedition Acts, 28, 222
Alger, Horatio, 102
Aluminum Company of America, 193
American Bar Association, 184
American Bar Association Journal, 5
American Colonization Society, 31
American Mercury, 135
American Socialist Party, 91
American Sugar Refining Company, 69
American Tobacco Company, 68
Americans with Disabilities Act, 257
Amherst, 191
Anabasis, 36
Annapolis, 50
Antietam, 83
Arlington National Cemetery, 140, 174
Armstrong, Louis, 23, 32
Articles of Confederation, 26, 40–42
Asch, 8 *Atlantic Monthly, (The),* 73, 75
Atlantic Monthly, (The), 75, 76
Aurora, 30

B

Babbit, Bruce, 252
Bach, 9
Bailey v. Alabama (1911), 180
Baker, Howard, 237
Baker v. Carr (1962), 148, 152, 154, 202–203, 208–210, 226, 267
Bakke, Alan, 227
Barr, Burton, 254
Barron v. Baltimore (1833), 29
Bates, Edwin, 58
"Battle Hymn of the Republic," 58
Battle of New Orleans, 58
Baum, Lawrence, 3
Bazelon, David L., 208–209
Beethoven, 10, 71, 79
Bell, John, 63
Berea College v. Kentucky, 68
Betts v. Brady (1934), 137
Beveridge, Albert, 32
Bickel, Alexander, 209
Bill of Rights, 68, 71, 118, 136–137, 140, 167, 174, 195, 203, 215, 220, 225, 241, 265, 267
Bituminous Coal Conservation Act of 1935, 113–114
Black, Elizabeth Seay, 133–134, 140
Black, Hugo L., 2, 4, 7, 10, 12, 13, 16, 123, 132–141, 142, 150, 161, 162, 166–167, 190, 196, 215, 218, 230, 234, 237, 262–266
Black, Josephine, 135
Blackstone, William, 108
Blackmun, Harry, 11, 57, 146, 224, 227, 232, 236
Blaustein and Mersky, 6–9, 18, 132, 213, 216, 263
Boone, Daniel, 247
Borah, William, 103, 135
Bork, Robert, 1, 15, 268–269, 271
Bradley, Joseph, 17–18
Bradley, Robert, 1, 132, 263, 275

Brandeis, Louis, 7, 12, 14, 16, 17, 47, 74,
　　79, 81, 83, 85, 90–98, 101–104,
　　110, 114, 124 132, 136, 144, 145,
　　162, 172, 193 227, 263–267, 274
"Brandeis Brief," 96, 112
Breckinridge, John, 63
Brennan, Marjorie Leonard, 217
Brennan, William, 9–11, 12–13, 15, 20, 124,
　　133, 144, 206–208, 215–231,
　　232–233, 238, 242–243, 263,
　　267–268, 272
Brewer, David J., 17
Breyer, Steven, 153, 200, 233, 272
Brown v. Board of Education (1954),
　　71, 144, 165, 201–202, 204, 207,
　　209, 226–227, 237, 264–265, 267
Brown University, 179
Buck, Carrie, 81–82
Buck v. Bell (1927), 83, 85, 86, 87
Buick Motor Co., 115
Bureau of National Affairs of Illinois, 8
Burger, Warren, 11, 116, 163, 174, 200,
　　215, 217, 219–220, 223, 232, 236,
　　242, 252
Burke, Edmund, 117, 169
Burr, Aaron, 30
Burton, Harold, 132, 204
Bush, George H., 200, 260, 262
Bush, George W., 200, 209, 269
Bush v. Gore (2000), 143, 153, 154, 209–
　　210
Butler, Nicholas Murray, 192
Butler, Pierce, 18, 83, 103, 132, 178, 194
Byrnes, James F., 132, 139

C

Cambridge, 77
Campbell, John, 17, 19
Cardozo, Andrew, 100–101
Cardozo, Benjamin, 2, 4–5, 10, 12, 14–15,
　　89, 99–131, 132, 137, 139, 145.
　　172, 178, 193, 263–264, 266, 274
Cardozo, Ellen ("Nell"), 100
Cardozo, Emily, 105
Cardozo, Rebecca Nathan, 101
Carey, Raymond, 123–124
Carswell, G. Harold, Jr., 222, 236, 262, 270
Carter, Jimmy, 239
Cates, Cynthia, 265

Centre College, 63
Chafee, Zechariah, 101
Chamberlain, Joseph, 77
Chambers v. Florida (1940), 137–138
Charles River Bridge (1837), 46, 51,
　　55–56
Chase, Samuel, 30, 37, 64, 66
Chicago Tribune, 135
Churchill, Winston, 234
Cinque, 57
City of Richmond v. J.A. Croson Co.
　　(1989), 257
Civil Rights Act of 1875, 67, 204
Civil Rights Act of 1964, 227
Civil Rights Cases (1883), 67, 204
Clay, Henry, 56, 63
"clear and present danger," 3, 81, 91,
　　146
Cleburne v. Cleburne Living Center
　　(1985), 153
Clinton, Bill, 200, 244
Cohen, Benjamin, 162
Cohens v. Virginia (1821), 29, 43
Colegrove v. Green (1948), 207–208,
　　226
Columbia Law Review, 192
Columbia Law School, 110, 179, 191
Columbia University (New York),
　　102, 133, 161
Commentaries on American Law, 48,
　　78
Common Law (The), 78–79, 83
Common Sense, 83
Communist Labor Party, 91
Confederate States of America, 61
Congressional Quarterly, 20
Congressional Record, 133, 144
Constitution (U.S.), 24, 26, 28, 37, 39,
　　41–44, 46–48, 56, 61, 62,
　　65, 69, 80, 82, 83, 87, 92–
　　93, 114, 124, 136, 140, 147,
　　149, 162–163, 168, 189,
　　194, 198, 202–203, 212,
　　216, 220–221, 226, 229,
　　230, 233, 238, 255, 265–
　　266, 268
Constitutional Faith, 133, 136
Cooley, Thomas McIntyre, 17
Coolidge, Calvin, 183, 192–194
Copernicus, Nicholas, 264
Coppage v. Kansas (1915), 180

Cortner, Richard, 203
"Court-packing plan," 103–104, 133, 186, 195
Court Years, The, 163–165, 172
Cox, Archibald, 208–209
Coyle, Dennis, 142, 275
Craig v. Boren (1976), 228, 239, 272
Croly, Herbert, 145
Crosby, Bing, 23
Cummings, Homer S., 133–134
Cummings v. Richmond Board of Education (1899), 68, 72, 204
Currie, George, 263
Curtis, Benjamin, 17–19, 75
Curtis, Charles, 30

D

Dartmouth College, 44–45
Dartmouth College v. Woodward (1819), 29, 44
Darwin, Charles, 83, 172
Davies, James C., 74, 158, 275
Davis, David, 19
Davis, Jefferson, 58
Davis, William R., 161
Day, Ada Mae, 248
Day, Alan, 248
Day, Harry, 248
Declaration of Independence, 55, 66
Denison, William, 58
Dennis v. United States (1951), 146
Dershowitz, Alan, ix, x
Dewey, John, 145. 172
Dewey, Thomas, 201
Dickerson v. United States (2000), 243, 271
Dickinson College, 52
Disney, Walt, 247
Doe, Charles, 17
Dolan v. Tigard (1994), 153, 243
Dorsen, Norman, 215
Dougherty, Harry M., 192
Douglas, Cathleen Heffernan, 170, 172, 174
Douglas, Joan Martin, 162
Douglas, Mercedes Davidson, 162
Douglas, Stephen A., 63, 86
Douglas, William O., 9–10, 13, 16, 19, 79, 85, 132, 131, 134, 137, 139, 142, 143, 167, 158–176, 192, 196, 215, 218, 237, 262, 269, 272

Draft Registration Act (1980), 239
Draper, George, 161–162
Dred Scott decision (1857), 51, 55, 57–58, 67, 73, 203–204
Driscoll, Alfred E., 217
Dulles, John Foster, 194
Dunne, Gerald T., 135

E

Early, Stephen, 134
Eastland, James O., 202
Edward VIII, 135
Eighteenth Amendment, 176
Eighth Amendment, 225, 239
Einstein, Albert, ix, x, 9
Eisenhower, Dwight D., 5, 165, 200, 206–207, 210, 217–218, 263
Election 2000, ix, 3, 246
Elk v. Wilkins, 69
Ellsworth, Oliver, 23
Elman, Philip, 144
Emancipation Proclamation, 64
Emerson, Ralph Waldo, 75, 85
Encyclopedia of American History, 71
Equal Employment Opportunity Commission, 262
Equal Protection Clause, 196
Erwin, Neil T., 246, 275
Ex parte Quirin (1942), 197

F

Fair Labor Standards Act, 240
Fairfax's Devise v. Hunter's Lessee (1813), 40
Falwell, Jerry, 243
Farley, James A., 133
Fauquier County, Virginia, 25
Federal Bureau of Investigation, 192
Federalist 39, 41
Federalist 51, 37
Federalist 53, 203
Federalist 78, 38
Federalist Papers, 48
Felker v. Turpin, 240
Field, Stephen J., 17–18, 62, 89, 132, 215

Fifteenth Amendment, 61, 64, 202–204
Fifth Amendment, 45, 118, 129
Finesilver, Sherman G., ix, 275
First Amendment, 8, 81, 90–92, 118, 140,
        146, 152, 167, 195, 197, 218,
        221–222, 229–230, 241, 243
Fiss, Owen, 218–219
Flag Protection Act of 1989, 224
Fletcher v. Peck (1810), 29, 37–39, 47
Flynt, Larry, 243
Flynt v. Falwell (1988), 222
Ford, Gerald, 173–174, 272
Ford, Henry, 81
Fortas, Abe, 211
Fourteenth Amendment, 43, 61–62, 64, 67–
        68, 118, 136, 195, 203–206, 223,
        225–227, 232, 238–239, 266
Fourth Amendment, 94–95, 127, 137, 202–
        203, 225
Frank v. Mangum (1915), 198
Frank, Jerome, 110–111, 162
Frank, John, 4–6, 19
Frankfurter, Felix, 2, 4–6, 10–13, 15, 18, 19,
        81, 83, 124, 125, 132, 137–139,
        154, 142–157, 166, 184, 196–197,
        206–210, 262, 265, 272
Freud, Sigmund, 9
Freund Committee, 219
Freund, Paul, 136
Friedman, Richard, 114
Frontiero, Sharron, 228
Frontiero v. Richardson (1973), 228, 239
Furman, William Henry, 225
Furman v. Georgia (1972), 225, 236. 239

G

*Garcia v. San Antonio Metropolitan Transit
        Authority* (1985), 240, 263
Gardner, Howard, ix, x
Garrison, William Lloyd, 63
Gerry, Elbridge, 27
Gettysburg, 77
Gibbons, John J., 230
Gibbons v. Ogden (1824), 29, 266
Gibson, John Bannister, 17
Gideon v. Wainwright (1963), 137, 267
Ginsburg, Ruth Bader, 153, 200, 233, 239,
        258, 272
Gitlow v. New York (1925), 81, 267

Go East, Young Man, 162, 172
Gold Clause cases (1935), 186
Goldberg, Arthur, 201
Goldberg v. Kelly (1970), 228, 267
Goldman v. United States (1942), 167
Goldwater, Barry, 236, 250
Graf v. Hope Building Corp. (1930),
        121–123–124
Graf, Joseph, 122
Gray, Horace, 17
Gray v. Sanders (1963), 208
Great Trust Cases (1911), 70
Greeley, Horace, 31
*Green v. School Board of New Kent
        County* (1968), 226
Gregg v. Georgia (1976), 225, 236,
        239
Griswold v. Connecticut (1965), 167–
        168
Grunes, Rodney A., 215, 275
Guinn v. United States (1915), 204
Gun Free School Zones Act, 240, 257
Gunther, Gerald, 30–31

H

Haggerty, Mark, 221
Hague v. CIO (1939), 195
Hambleton, James, 6, 19, 263
Hammer v. Dagenhart, (1918), 80,
        266
Hand, Learned, 104, 194
Harding, Warren G., 183, 192
Harlan, Elizabeth Shannon Davenport,
        62
Harlan, James, 62–63, 65
Harlan, John I, 10, 11, 13, 16, 19–20,
        61–73, 132, 215
Harlan, John II, 12, 140, 237
Harlan, John Maynard, 70
Harlan, Malvina Shanklin, 70
Harper's Ferry, 76
Harvard, 36, 48, 74–76, 78,–79, 83,
        85, 87, 105, 136, 217, 235
Harvard Law Review, 96, 220
Harvard Law School, 77, 96, 236, 249
Harvard Medical School, 74
Haskins, George, 30
Hayek, Friedrick, 234
Hayes, Benjamin, 61, 66

Haynesworth, Clement, Jr., 236, 262
Hearst, William Randolph, 180
Helvering v. Davis (1937), 114–116
Henry, Patrick, 26
Hentoff, Nat, 216, 229
Herndon, Billy, 172
Herrera v. Collins (1993), 2339
Herstein, David, 121–122
Hill, James J., 70
Hirabayashi v. the U.S. (1943), 164, 197
Hobbes, Thomas, 86
Hockett, Jeffrey, 151
Holmes, Abiel, 74, 76
Holmes, Fanny Dixwell, 78–79
Holmes, Oliver Wendell, 3, 4, 5, 7, 10–11,
   13–15, 16, 17–19, 32, 44, 74–89,
   90, 96, 102–103, 107, 116, 120,
   124, 132, 145, 150, 166–168,
   172–174, 190, 193, 198, 212, 227,
   264–266
Holmes, Oliver Wendell, Sr., 74–76, 79, 88
*Home Building & Loan Association v. Blais-
   dell* (1934), 113, 116, 186
Homer, 36
Homestead Act of 1862, 69
Hoover, Herbert, 99–103, 111, 193–194,
   234
Hoover, J. Edgar, 192
Hope Building Corporation, 121–122
Houdini, Harry, 238
Hruska, Roman, 262, 274
Hughes, Antoinette Carter, 196
Hughes, Charles Evans, 4–6, 9–10, 15, 17–
   19, 74, 79, 95, 101–105, 113, 132,
   136–138, 158, 163, 176–188, 191,
   194, 196, 230
Hughes, David Charles, 178
Hunter, David, 40
Hustler Magazine v. Falwell (1987), 243
Hutchins, Robert, 162
Hynes, Harvey, 109–110
Hynes v. New York Central Railroad Co.
   (1921), 109

I

In re Yamashita (1946), 197
Insular Cases, 71
International Railway Co., 120
Iolanthe, 244

J

Jackson, Andrew, 31, 49, 51, 52–54,
   58–59
Jackson, Robert H., 18, 134, 139, 177,
   196, 206, 235–237, 254
James, William, 78, 84
Jay, John, 23
Jay Treaty, 27, 40
Jefferson, Thomas, 23–26, 30, 35–36,
   55, 158–159, 173, 224
John Birch Society (The), 202
Johnson, Gregory, 221
Johnson, Herbert, 30
Johnson, Lyndon, 170–171, 185–186,
   202, 211
Johnson, Samuel, 76
Johnson, William, 17–19, 29
Judiciary Act (1789), 38, 44–47
Judiciary Act (1801), 30

K

Karcher v. Daggett (1983), 223, 226
Katz v. United States (1967), 95
Kaufman, Andrew, 104
Keillor, Garrison, 76
Kennedy, Anthony, 152, 229, 233,
   241, 243–244, 255–257, 272
Kennedy, Edward M., 241
Kennedy, John, 170, 210
Kennedy, Robert F., 208–209
Kent, James, 17, 19
Kenyon College, 234
Key, Francis Scott, 52
Keyes v. School District #1 Denver
   (1973), 227
King, Dr. Martin Luther, Jr., 221
King, Rufus, 32
Kleindienst, Richard, 236
Korematsu v. the U.S. (1944), 164–
   165
Kovacs v. Cooper (1949), 150
Ku Klux Klan, 135–136
Kuhn, Thomas, 264–265
Kurland, Philip, 136, 143, 155

L

La Follette, Robert M., 193
Lamar, Joseph, 90
Landon, Alf, 234
La Rochefoucald-Liancourt, 26
Laski, Harold, 83
League of Nations, 183
Leeds, Jeffrey, 219
Lehman, Irving, 105, 119
Lemon v. Kurtzman (1971), 224, 257
Lerner, Max, 143
Lewis, Anthony, 161, 209
Lincoln, Abraham, 23, 51–54, 56–59, 62, 63, 66, 77, 86, 149, 160, 172, 176, 204, 246
Lincoln, Levi, 36
Lincoln, Mary Todd, 54, 73, 75
Lindbergh, Charles, 83
Livy, 36
Lloyd, Henry Demarest, 69
Llwellyn, Karl, 110
Lloyd, Henry D., 67
Lochner v. New York (1905), 71, 90, 106, 112, 153, 190, 266
Locke, John, 86
Lodge, Henry Cabot, 79
Longfellow, Henry Wadsworth, 75
Los Angeles Times (The), 248
Lovell v. Griffin (1938), 186
Lowell, James Russell, 75
Lucas v. Colorado 44th General Assembly (1964), 208

M

MacPherson v. Buick Motor Co. (1916), 102, 111, 115
MacPherson, Donald, 115
Madison, James, 35–40, 41, 224
Maitland, Frederick, 77
Malloy v. Hogan (1964), 225
Maltese, John Anthony, 262
Malthus, Thomas, 82, 84, 86
Mapp v. Ohio (1961), 267
Marble Palace, 4–5
Marblehead Academy, 36
Marbury v. Madison (1803), 29–32, 36–37, 39, 43, 158, 262–263, 265–266
Marsh v. Chambers (1983), 224

Marshall, John, ix, x, 3, 10, 11, 14, 16, 17–19, 23–34, 33, 35–38, 40, 42–44, 49, 53, 54, 57, 59, 65, 70, 74, 79, 86, 94, 132, 136, 153, 158, 176, 184–185, 187, 211, 215, 219, 263–264–266
Marshall, Mary, 24
Marshall, Polly Ambler, 25
Marshall, Thomas, 24
Marshall, Thurgood, 11, 19, 124, 142, 158, 167, 222, 225–227, 229, 232–233, 262
Martin, Denny, 40
Martin v. Hunter's Lessee (1816), 39–43, 46, 48, 266
Massachusetts Agricultural College, 191
Massachusetts Supreme Court, 17
Matthews, Stanley, 18
McCabe v. Atchison, Topeka & Santa Fe Railroad (1914), 198, 205
McCarthy, Joseph, 135, 165, 218
McCone, Wesley, 197
McCulloch v. Maryland (1819), 29, 32, 40, 42, 53, 94, 266
McGautha v. California (1991), 225
McIntosh, Wayne, 265
McKenna, Joseph, 193
McLaurin v. Oklahoma State Regents (1950), 205–206
McLean, John, 19
McReynolds, James C., 103, 132, 194, 212
Meese, Edwin, 220
Mellon, Andrew, 211
Meritor Savings Bank v. Vinson (1986), 243
Merryman, John, 58
Metro Broadcasting, Inc. v. F.C.C. (1979), 227
Mikva, Abner J., 229
Mill, John Stuart, 77, 86, 173, 179
Miller, Samuel F., 17–19
Minersville School District v. Gobitis (1940), 148, 161, 164–165, 180, 186, 195
Minnesota Mortgage Moratorium Act, 186
Minton, Sherman, 132, 133, 217

Miranda v. Arizona (1966), 267
Missouri Compromise, 57
Missouri ex rel. Gaines v. Canada (1938), 186
Missouri v. Holland (1920), 80
Missouri v. Jenkins II , 243
Mitchell, John, 237
Montgomery Advertiser, 136
Moody, William, 17–18, 191
Moore v. Dempsey, (1923), 81
Morgan, J.P., 70, 192
Morrison v. Olson (1988), 243
Mossadegh, Mohammed, 169
Mr. Lincoln and the Negroes, 162, 171
Muller v. Oregon (1908), 96, 112, 266
Murphy, Walter, 139, 164

N

Nation (The), 143
National Geographic (The), 248
National Industrial Recovery Act, 114–115, 186
National Labor Relations Act of 1935, 114, 187, 194
National League of Cities v. Usery (1976), 240, 256
National Prohibition Act, 94
National Recovery Act, 203
Nature of the Judicial Process (The), 99, 105, 109, 118
Near v. Minnesota (1931), 186
Nebbia v. New York (1934), 186
New State Ice Co. v. Liebman, 93
New York Central Railroad, 109
New York Court of Appeals, 17, 99–105, 109, 113, 116–120, 123
New York State Bar Association, 109–112
New York Supreme Court, 99
New York Times (The), 246
New York Times v. Sullivan (1964), 221–222, 226, 267
New York Times v. United States, (1971), 140
New York v. Lochner (1905), 178
New York University, 196
Newmyer, Kent, 57
Ninth Amendment, 168

Nixon, Richard, 170, 172–173, 202, 220, 211, 219, 232, 236–237, 262, 268, 270
N.L.R.B. v. Jones & Laughlin Steel Corp. (1937), 187
Nollan v. California Coastal Commission (1987), 153
Norris, George, 172
Northern Securities Company v. United States (1904), 70, 79, 81

O

O'Brien, David, 2
O'Brien, John F., 122
O'Connor, John, 250–251
O'Connor, Sandra Day, 11, 152, 233–235, 244, 246–261, 263, 271–272
Odes of Horace, 36
Of Men and Mountains, 161
Olmstead v. United States (1928), 90, 92–94
Origin of Species, 83
Orwell, George, 168
Oxford, 77

P

Pace v. Alabama, 68
Pacific Railroad Act of 1862, 69
Paine, Thomas, 83
Palka, Frank Jacob, 118
Palko v. Connecticut (1932), 118–119, 123, 136, 267
Palmer, A. Mitchell, 192
Palmer, Elmer, 119
Palmer, Francis, 119
Palsgraf v. The Long Island Railroad Co. (1928), 102, 117, 119–121
Palsgraf, Helen, 117
Panama Refining Co. v. Ryan (1935), 113–114
Paris Adult Theatre I v. Slaton (1973), 223
Patterson, Robert B., 217
Peck, John, 38–39

Pederson, William D., 51, 275
Pennsylvania Coal Co. v. Mahon
　　(1922), 80
Pennsylvania and Ohio v. West Virginia
　　(1923), 80
People v. Carey (1918), 123–124
Perry, Barbara A., 232, 275
Phi Beta Kappa Society, 25, 79, 191, 234
Phillips, Wendell, 75–76, 85
Phoenix Junior League, 274
Picasso, Pablo, 9
Pierce v. the Society of Sisters (1925), 165
Pinchot, Gifford, 162
Pinckney, Charles, 27
Pittsburgh Post-Gazette, 135
Planned Parenthood v. Casey (1992), 258,
　　272
Plato, 173
Plessy v. Ferguson (1896), 66–68, 71–72,
　　204–205
Pollock, Frederick, 77
Posner, Richard A., 98, 229, 269
Pound, Roscoe, 6, 17, 96, 102, 107, 112,
　　121–122
Powell, Lewis, 227
Power of Solitude (The), 35
Provizer, Norman W., ix, 23, 200, 275
Przybyszewski, Linda, 61, 276
Public Utilities Commission v. Pollak
　　(1952), 167
Publius, 37–38, 39, 41

R

Randolph, John, 32
Rathbun, Harry J., 248–249
Rawls, John, 210, 229
Reagan, Ronald, 76, 82, 200, 218, 219, 232,
　　241–242, 249, 253, 255, 268
Reed, Stanley F., 133, 139, 150, 165, 190
Reed v. Reed (1971), 272
Regents of the University of California v.
　　Bakke (1978), 227, 235
Rehnquist, Marjorie Peck, 234
Rehnquist, Natalie Cornell, 235
Rehnquist, William, 2, 10–13, 16, 79, 151–
　　152, 154, 166–168, 187, 191, 200,
　　215. 219, 222, 232–245, 249,
　　254–255, 257, 263, 270–271
Rehnquist, William Benjamin, 234

Reynolds v. Sims (1964), 208–209,
Riggs v. Palmer (1889), 119
Road to Serfdom (The), 234
Roberts, Owen, 103, 165, 177, 184,
　　195–196
Robinson, Joseph, 133
Rockefeller, John D., 69, 178
Rodell, Fred, 23, 142
Roe v. Wade (1973), 168, 173–174,
　　238, 258, 272
Rogers, Will, 76
Roosevelt, Eleanor, 85
Roosevelt, Franklin, 59, 65, 83, 85,
　　88, 103, 113–114, 131, 135,
　　139, 143, 151, 160, 162–
　　163, 186–187, 190, 194,
　　196, 265
Roosevelt, Theodore, 79–80, 88, 95,
　　162, 197
Rosenberg, Ethel, 166
Rosenberg, Gerald, 209
Rosenberg, Julius, 166
Rosenberg v. the United States (1953),
　　166
Rostker v. Goldberg (1981), 239
Roth, Samuel, 222
Roth v. United States (1957), 221–223
Ruffin, Thomas, 17
Ruth, Babe, 79

S

Saenz v. Roe (1999), 271
Sanford, Edward, 92
Saturday Evening Post (The), 248
Scalia, Antonin, 152–155, 164, 166–
　　168, 233, 242–244, 257,
　　263, 271–273
Schaefer v. United States (1920), 92
Schechter Poultry Case (1935), 203
Schenck v. United States (1919), 81,
　　91–92, 267
School District of Abington Township
　　v. Schempp (1963), 223
Schultz, David, 262. 276
Schwartz, Bernard, 6, 20, 47–48, 263
Schwimmer, Rosika, 81–82
Securities and Exchange Commission,
　　163
Sedition Act, 27

Selection of Pleadings in Civil Actions, 36
Sevareid, Eric, 211
Seward, William H., 58
Shakespeare, William, 69, 74, 79, 234, 246–247
Shapiro, Martin, 150
Shapiro v. Thompson (1968), 271
Shattuck, George, 78
Shaw, Lemuel, 17, 19
Shaw, Stephen K., 90, 276
Shaw v. Hunt, 243
Sherman Antitrust Act of 1890, 69–70, 80
Slaughter-House Case, 62
Smith, Jean Edward, 23
Smith, William French, 249
Social Security Act of 1935, 116
Social Statics, 83
Souter, David, 8, 233, 254, 258, 272
Spanish American War, 62
Spencer, Herbert, 83
Sprigle, Ray, 135
Staab, James, 99, 276
Standard Oil Company, 69–70
Stanford Law School, 235, 248, 254
Stanford University, 234, 272
Stevens, John Paul, 233, 254, 255, 269, 272
Steward Machine v. Davis (1937), 114
Stewart, Potter, 237
Stone, Agnes Harvey, 191
Stone, Anne Butler, 191
Stone, Frederick Lauson, 191
Stone, Harlan Fiske, 9, 10, 19, 81, 103–104, 116, 124, 132, 136, 139, 151, 187, 190–199, 241
Stone v. Graham (1981), 241
Story, Elisha, 35
Story, Joseph, 2, 9, 10, 12, 15, 17–19, 25, 35–50, 57, 74, 79, 132, 158, 215, 234, 261, 263–264, 266
Story, Mary Lynde Fitch, 35
Story, Mehitable Pedrick, 35
Stowe, Calvin E., 75
Stowe, Harriet Beecher, 75
Stromberg v. California (1931), 186
Structure of Scientific Revolutions (The), 264
Sullivan, L. B., 221
Sumner, Charles, 75, 85, 92
Supreme Court (The), 244
Sutherland, George, 18, 103, 178, 194

Sweatt, Homer, 206
Sweatt v. Painter (1950), 205
Swift & Co. v. United States (1905), 3, 48, 49, 50,
Swift v. Tyson (1842), 46–47, 266

T

Taft, William, 10, 11, 18, 94, 176–177, 184–185, 187, 193–194
Talleyrand, 27
Taney, Anne, 52, 54
Taney, Roger, 9, 10, 12, 15, 18, 19, 20, 46, 51–60, 67, 75, 79, 132, 188, 203
Tate, Lillian, 123–125
Tenth Amendment, 240, 256
Texas v. Johnson (1989), 153, 224, 240, 243
Thayer, James Bradley, 30, 105, 116, 124
Thirteenth Amendment, 61, 64, 65, 67, 180, 203–204
Thomas, Clarence, 1, 8, 152, 154, 166, 167, 200, 233, 257, 262, 272
Thomas v. Review Board of the Indiana Employment Security Decision (1981), 241
Translvania University, 66
Traynor, Roger John, 19
Tribe, Laurence, 241, 263
Truman, Harry S, 139, 161, 169–171, 184, 185
Tushnet, Mark, 219
Tweed, William Marcy ("Boss"), 101

U

Uncle Tom's Cabin, 75
United States v. Amistad (1841), 57
United States v. Burr (1806), 3
United States v. Butler (1936), 186, 194
United States v. Burr (1806), 2
United States v. Carolene Products (1938), 136, 149, 195–196, 210, 262, 265
United States v. Classic (1941), 197
United States v. Eichman (1990), 224

United States v. Lopez (1995), 240, 243, 262, 265
United States v. Morrison (2000), 240, 262
United States v. Nixon (1974), 211
United States v. Schwimmer (1929), 81
United States v. Wong Kim Ark (1898), 68
United Steelworkers v. Weber (1979), 238–239
University of California at Berkeley, 200
University of Massachusetts, 191
University of Pennsylvania, 216
University of Pennsylvania Law School, 4
University of Texas Law School, 224
University of Wisconsin, 255
Urofsky, Melvin, 143, 146, 152

V

Vacco v. Quill (1997), 244
Valley Forge, 29
Van Devanter, Willis, 60, 103, 132, 178, 194
Vanderbilt, Arthur T., 19, 20, 217–218
Vestal, Theodore M., 190, 276
Vigil, Joseph D., 200, 276
Vile, John R., 176, 276
Vinson, Fred M., 132, 151, 196
Violence Against Women Act, 240
Violent Crime Control and Law Enforcement Act of 1994, 240
Vogue, 248

W

Wage and Hour Law, 194
Wagner v. International Railway Co. (1922), 120–124
Wagner, Arthur, 120–121
Wagner, Herbert, 118
Waite, Morrison, 19
Walker and Hulbary, 5
Wallace v. Jaffree (1985), 241
Walter Reed Hospital, 140
War of 1812, 53
Ware v. Hylton (1796), 32
Warren, Earl, 9, 10, 11, 13, 14, 15, 19, 20, 58, 71, 79, 93–95, 132, 134, 137,
141, 143, 149, 152, 158, 165, 174. 187, 200–214, 215, 218–219, 222–223, 230, 232, 242, 255, 263, 265, 267, 271
Warren, Samuel D., 96
Washington, DC., 36, 52, 71, 77, 81, 83, 174, 190, 217, 246
Washington, George, 23–27, 28, 29, 31, 176, 184, 204
Washington Post, 241
Washington v. Glucksberg (1997), 244
Watergate, 150, 211
Webster, Daniel, 56
Wells, Sumner, 183
Wesberry v. Sanders (1964), 208
West Coast Hotel v. Parrish (1937), 187
West Virginia Board of Education v. Barnette (1943), 165, 196
Western Union v. Kansas (1910), 78
Wharton School of Finance and Commerce, 216
White, Byron, 200, 218, 227, 229, 238
White, Douglas, 191
White, G. Edward, 17, 24, 68, 180, 225, 241
Whitman College, 161
Whitney, Charlotte A., 91
Whitney, Richard, 163–164
Whitney v. California (1927), 90–03, 102
Whittaker, Charles, 132
Wilkey, Mamie, 248
Wilkie, Wendell, 234
William and Mary College, 25
Williams, Frank J., 51, 276
Wilson, Woodrow, 85, 89, 90, 145, 183, 200
Wolcott, Alexander, 36
Worcester v. Georgia (1832), 31
Wright, Orville, 83
Wright, Wilbur, 83
Wythe, George, 25

X

XYZ Affair, 27

Yale, 105
Yale Law School, 173
Yazoo Land Companies, 38
Yick Wo v. Hopkins (1886), 204

Z

Zobell, Karl, 19
Zobrest v. Catalina School District
    (1993), 241

TEACHING TEXTS IN LAW AND POLITICS ⚖

David Schultz, *General Editor*

The new series Teaching Texts in Law and Politics is devoted to textbooks that explore the multidimensional and multidisciplinary areas of law and politics. Special emphasis will be given to textbooks written for the undergraduate classroom. Subject matters to be addressed in this series include, but will not be limited to: constitutional law; civil rights and liberties issues; law, race, gender, and gender orientation studies; law and ethics; women and the law; judicial behavior and decision-making; legal theory; comparative legal systems; criminal justice; courts and the political process; and other topics on the law and the political process that would be of interest to undergraduate curriculum and education. Submission of single-author and collaborative studies, as well as collections of essays are invited.

Authors wishing to have works considered for this series should contact:

> Peter Lang Publishing
> Acquisitions Department
> 275 Seventh Avenue, 28th floor
> New York, New York 10001

To order other books in this series, please contact our Customer Service Department at:

> 800-770-LANG (within the U.S.)
> (212) 647-7706 (outside the U.S.)
> (212) 647-7707 FAX

or browse online by series at:

> WWW.PETERLANGUSA.COM